GOD'S SACRIFICE

The Epic Saga of Hussein And His Legendary Martyrdom

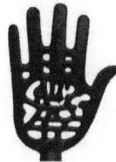

Sayed Hadi al-Modarresi

First English Edition, January 2016
Published in the United States by Enlight Press
twitter.com/enlightpress
An imprint of *Enlight Foundation*

MODARRESI, SAYED HADI
Twitter.com/HadiAlModarresi
God's Sacrifice — al-Modarresi, Sayed Hadi

ISLAM; GOD; HUSSEIN; SHIA; RELIGION; FAITH; HISTORY; KARBALA; ASHURA; IRAQ

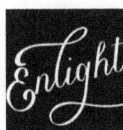

بسم الله الرحمن الرحيم

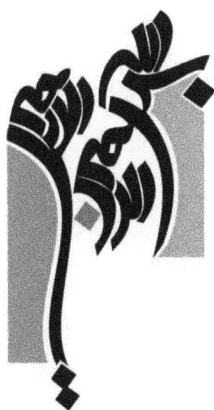

TIMES OF UNREST

674 C.E., Kufa, Iraq

Abdullah Ibn Muslim, a small, wizened man with skin browned and wrinkled from years spent shepherding in the sun, welcomed his guest into his home. He received the young carpenter with many salutations and led him to sit cross-legged on a roughly woven rug made of dyed sheep's wool.

After the customary exchange of pleasantries, Abdullah fell silent. Rahman was accustomed to the ways of his host, so he watched him pour coffee from the charred dellah, an Arabian coffee pot, and patiently waited for the tumultuous thoughts in Abdullah's mind to untangle themselves into speech. Abdullah harrumphed and mumbled to himself unintelligibly, swilling the aromatic coffee around in the cup before handing it to his guest. At last he looked up and said, "If we were to measure things as they are now against the standards brought by the Prophet, then we are in one valley and Islam is in another!"

Rahman looked over the rim of his brass coffee cup. He was a much younger man in his mid-thirties with dark, wiry hair that poked out from beneath his turban. His thick eyebrows knitted together in a frown. "What do you mean, brother?"

Abdullah pushed his turban back off his sweaty forehead. It was an unmercifully warm summer that year in Kufa, and this day was one of the hottest. "Have you forgotten that Ali was slain here, Rahman? The one who was the right hand of the Prophet — the first person to accept the Prophet's message and the one who supported him against the persecution of Quraysh?"

He took a sip of coffee and stared into the dregs that remained in the cup. He could almost make out the shape of a sword in the damp coffee grains. He continued in a lower voice, subdued by pensiveness, "Since Ali was ten years old, he accompanied the Prophet and chased away the children who would throw stones at him in the street. When the Prophet emigrated from Mecca to Medina, it was Ali who took his place, spending the night in his bed so that the tribesmen of Quraysh would think that the Prophet was still home. The moment the intended assassins saw Ali, they scattered as if they had found a fierce lion in the room!"

Abdullah's voice grew stronger with enthusiasm as he recounted his hero's life. "He fought in all the battles that were waged against the Prophet and all hopes of victory were pinned on him. Ali could face the warriors of Quraysh with nothing but his sword, Dhul Fiqar: the forked sword like no other, and triumph. The Prophet depended on Ali for his courage and valor, his loyalty and integrity. Even Omar said 'We looked to Ali in the time of the Prophet as we would look to a star!' This was the man to whom almost all Muslims pledged allegiance. Only a few people revolted against him and one of them was Muawiya."

Rahman interrupted. "Muawiya was the rightful caliph, akhi!"

"Please do not cut me off, my brother. History speaks for itself and the evidence of treachery is there and open for all to see." He rubbed his white beard. "Muawiya was a known tyrant who sought to preserve his own authority over Syria. But since Imam Ali refused to grant him that, war broke out between them. Do you remember how Ali was slain? It was through a sword blow to the back of the head while he was in prostration. He was in prayer! It is shameful to think that Ali was not slain by the disbelievers in the battles of Badr, Uhud, Ahzab, or Khaybar, but in the end, it was the hands of the so-called Muslims that killed him during Muawiya's rebellion."

Abdullah sighed, his breath ruffling his mustache. Rahman finished his coffee, said a small prayer of thanks for the provision, then spoke to his friend. "Please continue, brother. There are gaps in the history I've been taught that cannot be accounted for, and you're the most knowledgable of recent history than anyone I know."

"Very well, I will tell you the true account of things, but be warned - these events are not as simple as you've been told they are.

After Ali's martyrdom, Muawiya began to rule the Muslim world, not according to the teachings of the Prophet, but according to his own whims. He cut off the stipend of anyone who dared to quote Ali and ordered his governors to arrest the supporters of the Prophet's Household on the grounds of accusation and execute them on the basis of mere suspicion."

He looked at his younger friend. "Rahman, tell me, did you know that God's Messenger used to say 'Loving Ali is faith and hating him is infidelity?'"

"Of course, it's a well-known Prophetic quote," Rahman responded.

"Tell me, did you know that he would also say to Ali, 'Only a true believer would love you, and only a hypocrite would hate you'?"

"My respected brother, Ali — though undeniably a great man — has passed now. He has moved on from this world. The prophets and saints do not come back to life! To act like they are still alive is blasphemy. We must come to terms with the present. Muawiya now holds power, and as you well know, power urges its possessor to resort to force and whatever else is necessary to maintain it."

"I am well aware of the situation at hand, but ignoring the past will lead to our demise, mark my words. The ideals that our Prophet struggled to teach us will surely be lost if we let rulers like Muawiya do as they please."

Rahman picked at the loose threads from the woolen rug thoughtfully. "Yes. He's no saint, that is certain. In any case, he has grown old and rumors are widespread that he wants his son to inherit the Caliphate."

Abdullah watched him fray the distressed threads, his mind agitated. "This, too, is something that makes me think that they are in one valley and Islam in another. According to the settlement agreed upon by Muawiya with Hassan, the eldest son of Ali, the Caliph after Muawiya belongs to him. And yet this man looks to entrust the Caliphate to his son, Yazid, despite his pledge not to. There's not a person in all of Arabia who doesn't know the kind of person Yazid is!'

"You are right. Anyone who knows Yazid does well to be afraid. It would be a disaster if this man becomes the Caliph of the Muslims."

"That is what distresses me, my brother. I think it is a little late for that. The disaster has already happened.'

"When?"

"For a long time now," Abdullah sighed again. "Do you not see that the dominion of the Muslims today is the product of the struggles of the Prophet and his Household – that they are the ones who made it? Where were the Arabs before the Prophet came, and where are they today? In those days, even the Umayyad clan's only claim to authority depended upon their monopoly on trade in Mecca, which was then nothing more than an oversized village! The most they did was to organize the summer and winter caravans to Syria. As for today, Muawiya rules most of the civilized world. But where is the Prophet's Household? What happened to them? Where is the reward of the Prophet who faced great aggression and lived under the threat of death from the moment he was sent with his message? The one who fought battle after battle, such that in twenty three years of preaching he faced more than seventy such battles?"

"But the Prophet lived a life of asceticism," remarked Rahman.

"He did, but that does not mean people should neglect their duties towards him. It's not power and wealth that his family seeks. This is their legacy, their ideals. What have we done about the Prophet's Household? Lady Fatima, his dearest daughter and only surviving offspring, saw not a day of comfort in this world after his death. She spent her days weeping and died distressed. She joined her father in the afterlife only a few months after he himself had passed away!

"May God bless their legacy."

"Ali was then denied any position of importance for twenty four years," Abdullah's voice rose, "He was not even offered the position of a court clerk!

"He did not seek it."

"Was he offered any position or post so he could share his wisdom and help guide the nation?"

Rahman remained silent.

"Was not Ali the most knowledgeable and virtuous companion of the Prophet, his most trusted advisor, and his right hand in every battle? Did not the Prophet himself praise him as he praised no one else and entrusted him with responsibilities he entrusted to none but him? Was he not the first to believe in the Prophet and offer prayers with him, when doing so was nothing short of a death wish? Did he not deserve at least to be offered a position whereby his knowledge and his skills would be put to use, and was it not the duty of everyone to refer to him after the people pledged their allegiance to him? Why did one group renounce their pledge, another rebel, while the rest remained indifferent? Why were Ali's companions assassinated one after another and wars waged against him just as they were waged against his cousin, the Prophet? Why was he struck atop his head by the sword of injustice as he prostrated in prayer?"

Abdullah held his head between his hands. "What happened to his son, Hasan, about whom his grandfather said 'Hasan is from me and I am from Hasan' and 'Hasan and Hussein are the leaders of the youth of Paradise?' Right now Hussein is in Medina, cut off from everything and everyone, surrounded by the regime's agents, and prevented from meeting his followers.

Whatever happened to acting on God's words: 'I do not ask you any reward for it except love of [my] near family..?' Whatever happened to following the instructions of the Prophet who said: 'My household amongst you are like stars, whichever of them you follow you will be guided' and 'Verily I am leaving amongst you two weighty things; the Book of God and my Household?'"

There was a long silence interrupted only by distant braying of goats and the clatter of wagons. After several moments, Rahman spoke at last. "Tell me about this rumor, Abdullah. Is it true that Muawiya intends for his son to inherit the Caliphate, and is this part of the Prophetic tradition or even the previous Caliphs? From where did this idea originate?"

"I will give you the full story. It all started with Mughira son of Shuba, the governor of Kufa. He sensed that Muawiya wanted to remove him from his post and appoint Saeed son of al-As in his place. To discover whether or not this was the case, Mughira wrote a letter to Muawiya in which he said: 'I have become enfeebled with old age and the Meccan tribe of Quraish are hostile towards me, so if you see fit to remove me from my post, I resign.'

Muawiya replied with 'You wrote to me that you are elderly. By my life, your age wears on no one save you. You said that the Quraish are hostile towards you. By my life, I have found nothing good save from them. You asked me to remove you from your post and I have done so. So if you are truthful, I have interceded on your behalf. But if you are deceitful, I have outfoxed you.'

When this letter reached Mughira, he said to those around him: 'I think I shall go to Muawiya and tender my resignation so that people see my disdain for the governorship.'

When he arrived, he told his companions: 'If I do not secure you a governorship and position of authority now, then I never will.'"

Rahman cut in, "Mughirah had no intention of resigning at all then?"

"Precisely. He wanted to be confirmed in his position, not removed from it! So he thought about this matter a great deal, until he settled upon a plan that would force Muawiya to reaffirm his position. This plan was to suggest to Muawiya that he should be succeeded by Yazid. he knew that Muawiya wanted this to happen despite the stigma that surrounded his son. No one, not even Muawiya's own courtiers, believed that Yazid was fit to rule. It was true that the Muslims had remained largely silent during Muawiya's reign because of his atrocious cruelty, deceit, and wealth, but Yazid's ascension to the throne was inconceivable. He was known to be a promiscuous drunkard and a profligate sinner of the most vile caliber."

Rahman leant closer, his eyebrows raised in interest. "What happened between Muawiya and Mughira? Did he get what he wanted?"

"Let us go to the market, my son. There are some things I need to get for the preparation," said Abdullah mysteriously. He leant his hands on his knees as he stood up creakily.

"For what?" Rahman asked, standing with much more limber.

"I'll tell you soon enough."

They made their way out of the tent and past Abdullah's flock of goats, which stood tethered to a date palm. They treaded the dirt road leading to the marketplace, their robes and cloaks bringing up clouds of dust from the loose sand. Abdullah spoke again, "Mughira first visited Yazid and said 'Indeed the leading companions and family members of the Prophet have gone, as have the greatest of the Quraish. All that remains now are their sons, of whom you are the best, the most sound in opinion, and the most learned in the practice of the Arabs and in politics. I do not know what prevents your father from taking the pledge of allegiance to you!'

Yazid was taken aback and said 'Could such a thing be accomplished?'

Mughira then replied 'With the right people on your side, I don't see why not.' Once Mughira had left him, Yazid went to see his father and informed him of what he had said. So Muawiya summoned Mughira and asked, 'What is it that Yazid says of you?' Mughira replied: 'O Commander of the Faithful! I saw the bloodshed and infighting after Othman, but in Yazid you have the most suitable successor. Take the pledge of allegiance for him so that if anything happens to you, he will be a shelter for your people and a successor. This will spare us the evils of bloodshed and dissension.'

'And who do I have to accomplish such a thing?' said Muawiya.

Mughira replied 'I will suffice you for the allegiance of the people of Kufa. Ziad will do the same for the people of Basra. With these two cities on your side, no one will oppose you.'"

The two men reached the village and Abdullah's narration began to get frequently interrupted by responding to and offering salaam, the traditional Muslim greeting. The villagers hailed the two men as they passed, and stopped them on their path to inquire about their families.

"They call upon me like a sultan, though I am merely a goatherd," Abdullah murmured.

"You are a good man, and it is your righteousness that elevates your status," Rahman said smilingly.

They passed the pottery maker's house and reached a field of date palms. They walked through the shady trail and Abdullah continued, "Muawiya was undoubtedly ecstatic to find support in the unlikeliest allies. He asked Mughira to return to his post and consult those whom he trusted about Yazdi's ascension to the throne.

Mughira left and returned to his companions who were eager to hear his outcome. He said 'I have placed Muawiya's foot in a stirrup far indeed from the traditions of Muhammad and opened up a tear which they shall never be able to mend!' He was so jovial, he couldn't stop singing these lines:

'With the likes of me a witness to secret colloquy

All manner of vicious enemies do highly esteem me.'

He returned with his companions to Kufa and began to consult people whom he trusted and whom he knew to be supporters of the Umayyad clan. He spoke with them about Yazid and they agreed to pledge their allegiance to him, so he sent a delegation of forty men from them, which was led by his son Musa, giving them thirty thousand dirhams as a reward. They went to Muawiya and promoted the idea of taking the pledge of allegiance for Yazid as his successor and called on him to do so without hesitation."

The pair had reached the marketplace and began to talk of other things as they made their way around the street vendors selling bolts of differently colored fabric, weaved wicker baskets, brass pots and kettles, and a diverse array of other handmade utensils. The hubbub of buyers and sellers bargaining over prices made further conversation impossible, so Abdullah and Rahman watched the the scene around them in silence. Just as the heat from the direct sunlight that was hitting their turbaned heads was becoming unbearable, Abdullah stopped walking and turned to face an old building the same color as the pale dirt on the road. Rahman knew this building. It was the ironmonger's store where weapons and armory were sold. He turned to Abdullah questioningly.

"I need a new sword," Abdullah said, in reply to his friend's unspoken inquiry.

SUCCESSION

The next day Rahman saw Abdullah speaking to a wealthy merchant in the marketplace. The man gave Abdullah a pouch that sagged with the weight of whatever it carried and raised his hand in farewell. After the man left, Rahman approached Abdullah who turned and hailed him with salaam.

"Ah, Rahman! I was going to send for you," he said, pocketing the pouch.

Rahman eyed Abdullah's cloak pocket. "Have you sold something, my brother?"

"I have."

"May I ask what?"

"My goats."

"Your goats? Why? They are your livelihood - your hard work and sweat! They are all that you have in this world!"

"My dear brother, you are far too attached to this material world and its fallacies. To God we belong and to Him will we return."

"What will you do now? Will you take up another profession in your home?"

"I have sold my house as well."

"You have? Why? Are you going somewhere?"

"I am. I am going to Medina."

"May I ask why?"

Abdullah didn't answer.

Rahman sighed with frustration. He knew his friend very well and knew that he was not going to answer a question until he felt that it was the right moment. He spoke again in a more polite tone. "May you at least continue your narrative? We did not get to finish it yesterday."

At this, Abdullah brightened. Storytelling was every Arab's favorite pastime, and they did it exquisitely. He took a seat on a worn-out camel saddle that lay on the ground and Rahman leant on a palm tree."Very well... We left off when Mughira sent a delegation of forty men to Muawiya to promote the idea of him appointing Yazid as successor. At this, Muawiya said 'Do not hasten to make this known, but remain steadfast in your opinion.'"

Abdullah motioned for Rahman to sit but he declined politely. Abdullah sighed and continued, "Then he said secretly to Mughira's son, Musa, who led the delegation: 'How much coin did your father have to spend to purchase the soul of these men?'

Musa replied: 'Thirty thousand dirhams.'

Muawiya said: 'They did not value their souls much!'

When this delegation returned to Kufa, Muawiya was satisfied that he had the backing of a significant portion of the city and his resolve to take the pledge of allegiance for his son was strengthened. Then Muawiya sent a letter to Ziyad bin Abduh, who was his governor in Basra, to seek his counsel in taking the pledge of allegiance to Yazid. Ziyad was a top lieutenant of Muawiya. Muawiya had even attributed his obscure parentage to his own father, Abu Sufyan, thereby making him his illegitimate half-brother. But in spite of this, Ziyad was not comfortable with the idea of Yazid as Caliph. This concern did not stem from any piety on the part of Ziyad, but rather fear that the Umayyad Clan would fall from power because the people would not accept the rule of a frivolous youth like Yazid."

Abdullah squinted up at Rahman against the sunlight. "Do have a seat, my brother, my narrative is long and we will need our strength for later."

"We? You will be including me in your mysterious task, my brother?"

"I shall tell you all in due time. Would you like me to continue?"

"Please do, brother."

"Upon receiving Muawiya's letter, Ziyad summoned Ubayd Ibn Kab and said to him: 'Indeed everyone who seeks counsel has someone he trusts and every secret has a place of safekeeping... I have called upon you for advice on a matter that I would not entrust to paper. The Commander of the Faithful, Muawiya, has written to me seeking my opinion on taking the pledge of allegiance for Yazid from the masses; he fears their aversion but covets their obedience. Yazid is a man of leisure and indolence, and a depraved hunter of lust. So go to Muawiya and remind him of his son's character. Tell him: 'Proceed slowly in this matter, for it is more proper that your wish be accomplished. Do not rush, for attaining something late is better than losing it entirely!'

Ubayd bin Kab said: 'May I suggest something else?'

Ziyad said: 'What?' Ubayd Ibn Kab replied: 'Do not undermine Muawiya's opinion or make his own son hateful to him. I will go to Yazid and tell him that his father has written to you asking for advice about taking the pledge of allegiance, and that you fear that people will reject him because of the defects they hold against him. I will advise him that he should desist from those habits which the people dislike so that he will be in a strong position and will obtain his desires. If you allow me to do this, you will have given sound advice to the Commander of the Faithful and averted what you fear from the nation.'

Ziyad said: 'I see a good omen in this. If you are right then there is nothing blameworthy, and if you are in error then at least it does not appear duplicitous. Proceed and say whatever you think best.'

The wind began to blow dust in their faces as a sandstorm made its way closer to Kufa. Rahman covered his nose and mouth with the headdress that draped over his turban. Abdullah looked especially old as he sat stooping over his cane, his wrinkles cutting deep into his face as he frowned against the wind.

"Ubayd Ibn Kab approached Yazid and conveyed this message. Thereafter, Yazid attempted to exercise greater caution in exhibiting his immoral character before the public eye. For his part, Ziyad wrote to Muawiya and merely cautioned him to proceed slowly.

Muawiya also wrote to Marwan Ibn Al-Hakam, Saeed Ibn Al-Aas, and Abdullah Ibn Aamir, his key supporters in Medina, asking for their opinion on taking the pledge of allegiance to Yazid. They advised him to bide his time and not to rush lest he face opposition from the people of Medina."

Abdullah coughed into his cloak. He looked up, shaking his head and said, "It is amazing that Muawiya's own supporters displayed open opposition to the appointment of Yazid as his successor. In fact, he even faced opposition in his own household; his wife Fakhita detested the idea. She said to her husband: 'Mughira only advised you to appoint him as your successor because he wanted to make you an enemy of your own flesh and blood! Not a day passes that he does not wish for your destruction!'

Another person who opposed Muawiya's appointment of Yazid was Saeed Ibn Othman, the son of Othman Ibn Saffan, Muawiya's predecessor and the one in whose name Muawiya had assumed the

Caliphate in the first place. He said to Muawiya: 'O Commander of the Faithful! Why have you taken the pledge of allegiance to Yazid and not me? By God, you know that my father is better than his, my mother is better than his, and that whatever you obtained in this world was because of my father!'

Muawiya laughed and told him: 'Far from it, my nephew! As for saying that your father is better than his, a day of Othman is better than the lifetime of Muawiya; as for saying that your mother is better than his, the superiority over a woman of the Quraysh tribe to a woman of the Kalb is clear; but as for saying that whatever I obtained was because of your father, all dominion belongs to God and He bestows it upon whomsoever he wishes. Your father was slain but his clan of Al-Aas did nothing! It was my clan of Harb who rose up to avenge his blood, so it is you who are indebted to us! And as for saying that you are better than Yazid, by God I wish that my household were filled with men such as you rather than Yazid, but do not hold me to this. Ask me what you will instead and I will give it to you.'

"Muawiya may be selfish, but he is undeniably cunning." Rahman said, voice muffled by the fabric over his nose and mouth. "No one dares oppose him."

"Almost no one. There is a man who has opposed him and Yazid - but more on that later. Let me finish explaining how such a person as Yazid came into power when no one considered him for succession before. This is vital to understand the manipulation of the Umayyad clan."

Abdullah continued, turning his back against the wind, "Muawiya awarded Saeed Ibn Othman the governorship of the remote province Khurasaan.

Thus, the plot was perfected, allowing descendants of the Umayyad clan to usurp the reigns of power for the next 100 years. No longer was knowledge, wisdom, and justice conditions of leadership. Instead, politics of the vilest kind was at play.

In this way, the appointment of Yazid as his father's successor took place against a backdrop of apprehension amongst the leaders of the Umayyad clan, the haggling and reluctance of the advisers and governors and the coercion of the general public. Even Muawiya's most loyal supporters and closest allies were averse to this appointment. It is clear that from the very beginning, Mughira Ibn Shuba promised to deliver something which was not his to give. For although he secured the governorship of Kufa for himself as a reward for brokering this arrangement, Kufa was the first city to refuse to submit to Yazid and Basra was dilatory in responding; On the periphery of the State, in Hamdan there were uprisings, Hijaz revolted against the Umayyad clan for a number of years and in Yemen there was not a single supporter of the regime.'

"And even though Ziyad did not think it wise to make Yazid his successor, Muawiya persisted nonetheless, correct?" Rahman asked in a voice stifled by fabric.

"That's is so," Abdullah said, "At the very least he wanted a consensus amongst his own people about his son. I think that he was waiting for something. Yes, he was resolute about this, although he wanted to take further steps to ensure that things would go according to plan.

Once the people of the Levant had given their support for Muawiya's choice of successor, he wrote to the provinces demanding that they pledge allegiance to him. His greatest concern was Hijaz, so he wrote to Marwan Ibn Al-Hakam, his agent there, instructing him to gather the elites to demand the pledge of allegiance from them. But Marwan desired the Caliphate for himself after Muawiya and thought himself more entitled to it than the latter's son, so he tarried in carrying out his orders. In fact, he encouraged the leaders of Quraysh to withhold their allegiance from Yazid. So Muawiya disposed of him and appointed Saeed Ibn Al-Aos in his place, but he too was unable to obtain the pledge of allegiance from the People of Losing and Binding. This forced Muawiya to involve himself personally; he wrote letters to the leaders of the people – men such as Abdullah Ibn Abbas, Abdullah Ibn Zubayr, Abdallah Ibn Jafar and Hussein Ibn Ali - and ordered his agent, Saeed, to convey his message to them and forward their responses to him.

One of the things he told Saeed was: 'I understand what you have said concerning the people's hesitation in pledging allegiance to my son; I have written letters to their leaders, so hand these letters over to them that your resolve might be strengthened and your intentions recognized. Be cordial, but pay special attention to Hussein and do not do anything to upset him, for he is a close relative of the Prophet and has a lofty position in the eyes of the people that no Muslim man or woman could deny; he is a fierce warrior and I cannot protect you if you provoke him. As for Abdullah Ibn Zubayr, he shall spare no opportunity to pounce on you, so beware of him!'

For months, Saeed exhausted every means at his disposal to convince the leaders and their people to take this odious pledge of allegiance. In the end, Muawiya realized that the only way he could secure Yazid's succession was to travel to Medina himself, accompanied with an army and carrying bags of gold. He blockaded all roads between Syria and Hijaz and requested that a delegation of those to whom he had written visit him. He told them: 'You know well my conduct with you; I am your relative and Yazid is your brother and cousin. I had hoped that you would put Yazid's name forward to succeed me as Caliph and that you would go back and enjoin others to accept him as my successor, and take this money and divide it amongst the people.'

Abdullah Ibn Al-Zubayr, who also had aspirations for the Caliphate, interrupted him and counciled him the choice of following the precedent of Abu Bakr (namely recommending the position to someone not of his father's tribe) or following the precedent of Umar and convening a council of six persons – a council that did not include his son or any member of his father's family – to choose a successor.'

Muawiya was displeased. He said: 'Does anyone have any other options?'

There were some who remained silent and others who supported Ibn al-Zubayr, so Muawiya threatened them: 'He who gives warning is excused for exacting punishment. While I was addressing you all, one of you interrupted and quarrelled with me in front of the leaders of the people. But I shall pardon and forgive that. Consider this your warning.'

Then he informed them that he would gather the people and address them directly; if they interrupted him again he would kill them. He said: 'I am a man of my word. I do not make idle threats. I swear by God that if any of you interrupts a single word that I utter, he will have his head cut off before another word can be spoken. Each man is responsible for his own well-being!' Then he ordered the head of his guards to place two swordsmen at the head of each of those assembled. He said to them: 'If any of them moves to interrupt me, whether in agreement or disagreement, cut off his head!'

Muawiya then went out to the Mosque and ascended the pulpit, and referring to the delegation he said: 'Those men are the leaders of the Muslims and the best of them. No matter is accomplished without their support, no judgement made without their counsel. They have agreed to pledge allegiance to Yazid, so let you all pledge allegiance to him too!

And this, Rahman, is how the pledge of allegiance to Yazid was taken in Hijaz.

To whomever disagreed with his appointment as successor, Muawiya would send a bribe. One such person was Uqayba Al-Asadi, a poet from Basra, who loathed Yazid. Muawiya sent him a gift of ten thousand dirhams to buy the silence of his tongue and his conscience.

Muawiya did everything he could to make the people amenable to his wishes, giving gifts to his opponents and bringing near the averse, until they inclined towards him and responded positively to his entreaties.

Muawiya would try to win over the people during every Hajj for seven years. In the fifty-fifth year after Hijra, he summoned the people of the cities to send delegations to him. Groups came from Kufa, Basra, Mecca, Medina, Egypt, Jazira and all the provinces of the Empire. He then sought their opinion on appointing Yazid as his successor.

A man from Medina called Muhammad Ibn Amr Ibn Hazam stood up and said: 'O Muawiya! Yazid deserves whatever you desire to ordain for him. By my life, he is affluent in wealth and of fair lineage. But God will ask every shepherd about his flock, so beware of God O Muawiya! And look to whom you entrust the care of Muhammad's nation!'

Muawiya sighed deeply and said: 'O Ibn Amr, you are a well-intentioned man. You only spoke your mind and nothing else could be expected of you. But all that remains of the Companions of Muhammad is my son and their sons, and my son is dearer to me than theirs.'

So the people fell silent and went on their way."

THE TYRANT

The sky darkened to a deep orange color as the wind blew violently. Rahman bent over his friend to help him up, but Abdallah waved him away. "I am waiting for someone."

"Who?" Rahman asked over the sound of the gusts.

As if in response, the clopping and neighing of horses was heard nearby. The two men turned to find a man on a horse trotting toward them in the billowing sand storm with one hand holding the reigns of another horse at his side. His face was covered, so Rahman didn't recognize him as the village ironsmith until he jumped down and hailed them.

"Will you be riding in this weather?" the man hollered at Abdullah.

"I must - we cannot tarry any longer."

"Will you not have a bite to eat at my house before you embark, brother?"

Abdullah opened his mouth to decline politely but was seized by a violent fit of coughing. Rahman turned to the ironsmith. "If your residence is nearby, he should rest there for a while. If it is not, I invite you both to my house, which is over the bridge."

Abdullah shook his head but the ironsmith grasped him by the arm and led him down the road, yelling "My house is just a stone's toss away!"

They entered his home after the ironsmith tethered the two horses in a shack outside his house, where he kept a young cow and a mule. For a man with a steady job, he seemed to be incredibly poor. The walls of his house were crumbling and the the carpets on the dirt floor were frayed and faded. Despite this, the ironsmith welcomed the two men inside as if it were a palace and they were the kings.

"My friend Abdullah was just informing me about the affairs in Medina," Rahman said after thanking his host graciously. "Are you aware that Muawiya is planning on appointing his son Yazid as his successor?"

"I am," the ironsmith replied, handing Abdullah a glass of water and setting the tray in front of Rahman. "But what I don't know is what Hussein Ibn Ali Ibn Abi Talib says about all this."

They turned toward Abdullah, who was talking a sip of water with trembling hands. He looked too unwell to speak, let alone travel. Abdullah wasn't a frail man, however, and often spoke and moved with surprising agility if the need arose.

"Your meal is being fixed at the moment," the ironsmith informed Abdullah. "May you tell us what you know until it is done?"

"Very well," Abdullah said, after futilely resisting his hosts insistence for them to stay and eat. His breathing calmed now that he had rested and was safe from the billowing sand. "Would you like a detailed account or a summary?"

"Everything, please." Rahman and the ironsmith said simultaneously. It was an age where Arabs memorized narrations word for word, to keep from accidentally spreading misinformation.

"Among the people of Kufa are righteous servants of God," Abdullah began. "They could no longer tolerate Muawiya. After Hasan passed away they had hoped that Hussein would take up the cause and change their circumstances. The faithful gathered – amongst them the powerful clans - in the house of Sulayman Ibn Surd Al-Khuzaee, and they wrote to Hussein to offer their condolences for the loss of his brother. In one letter they wrote:

'In the name of God, the Most-Compassionate, the Most-Merciful,

To Hussein Ibn Ali Ibn Abu Talib, from his followers and the followers of his father:

We praise God, and bear witness that there is no god except He, and we ask Him to send blessings on Muhammad and his household. Word has reached us that your brother, Hasan, has passed away. May God have mercy upon him the day he was born, the day he died, and the day he will be raised yet again. May God forgive his sins and multiply his good deeds and join him with his grandfather and father in the Hereafter. May God reward you for your suffering and alleviate your distress after him. We anticipate God's reward for him, for indeed to God we belong and to him do we return from the affliction of the entire nation and what you have suffered in particular.

You have indeed suffered a great loss and have been burdened with overwhelming hardship. Be steadfast, O Abu Abdullah, in what afflicts you, for it is Divine providence. Indeed you – praise be to God – are the successor of those who came before you, and God will guide those who walk upon your path and are led by your guidance. We are your followers; when you suffer, we suffer; when you grieve, we grieve; when you are joyous, we are joyous. We await your command. May God elevate your status, empower you, and return to you what is rightfully yours. Peace, mercy and blessings of God be with you.'"

The ironsmith let out a low exclamation of awe. "That is a very eloquent and convincing letter!"

"But Hussein was not convinced. He did not want to cause a rift among the Muslims. He replied: 'I hope that my brother's stance in maintaining the peace, and my own in striving against oppression are both correct and rightly-guided. So cling to the ground, hide in your houses and do not think of taking action so long as the Son of Hind draws breath. But should anything happen to him while I live, I will give you my directions then, God willing.'

There was pressure on Hussein to rise up even at the time of Muawiya, but he would refuse and tell those who insisted: 'Between Muawiya and I there is a treaty that I cannot violate, until the time has passed. Once Muawiya is dead, we can consider taking action.'

Many people would come to Hussein when he was in Medina to ask him to rise up, demonstrating their readiness to assist him. But he would enjoin them to desist from engaging in rebellious activities. He told some of them: 'Let every man amongst you be like a rug in his own house so long as this man (meaning Muawiya) is still alive. If he perishes and you still live, we hope that you will let God choose for us and guide us aright; that He may not leave us to our own selves, for verily God is with those who are wary and those who do good.'

On one occasion, Musayyab Ibn Nujba came at the head of a delegation of men from Kufa to ask him to cast off his treaty with Muawiya. They said: 'We certainly knew your opinion and the opinion of your brother before.'

Hussein replied to them: 'I pray that God rewards my brother for his pure intentions and his desire to prevent further violence, and to reward me for my intention and desire to struggle against oppressors.'

Even though Hussein made clear in both his speech and writings during Muawiya's reign that he was opposed to any attempt to overthrow him, the fact that so many people frequented him, visited his home, venerated him, extolled his virtues, and asked him to rise up worried the Umayyad clan. This was not just because they feared

Hussein might heed these calls and actually rise up, but rather because they feared what would ensue following Muawiya's death.

People like Marwan Ibn Al-Hakam, who coveted the Caliphate and made no secret of this fact, worried that once Muawiya was dead, the people would not see anyone as the equal of Hussein.

Amr Ibn Uthman Ibn Affan once came to Marwan while the latter was still Muawiya's governor in Medina and said to him: 'People visit Hussein often. I think that he will deal you a calamitous day.'

So Marwan wrote to Muawiyah and said: 'I do not feel secure as long as Hussein remains a focal point for sedition. I think he will continue to be a source of problems for you.'

In truth, these men were all keen to see Muawiya remove Hussein by one way or another, just as he had with his brother, Hasan. They wanted to make sure that Hussein would not one day be an impediment to their own ambitions for power. But Muawiya could not preempt Hussein at that time, given Hussein's stature, and that he had given no indication that he intended to revolt. So Muawiya wrote to Marwan: 'Leave Hussein alone so long as he leaves you alone and does not display open hostility or disregard towards you. Remain vigilant but spare him not should stance change'"

A young boy who looked to be around twelve years old walked into the guest room carrying a large tray laden with rice topped with a mound of steaming lamb meat. Rahman and Abdullah both protested loudly at the expenses the ironsmith took for their sake, but the man insisted even louder, and swore upon God that it was his pleasure.

The ironsmith's son set down the tray shakily and joined them as they gathered around it. After eating in silence for a moment, Rahman turned to Abdullah and said, "I think people's hearts are inflamed by what is happening; how many in the ranks of the righteous have been abominably slain, how much property has been wrongly seized, and how many supporters of the Prophet's Household have been sent into exile! However, I think Muawiya showed political acumen when he did not heed the calls of his sycophants to have Hussein killed, banished, or imprisoned."

"That wasn't wisdom - he had no other choice!" Abdullah replied.

"How so?" asked Rahman.

"How could he make any move against Hussein considering the latter's social standing and his place in people's hearts, especially when he didn't do anything wrong! What pretext would Muawiya have had?"

"Do you think that Hussein really saw Muawiya as a legitimate ruler?" The ironsmith asked after swallowing his bite.

Abdullah shook his head. "None of the faithful – not one of them – thinks that Muawiya has the right to rule. He is neither the appointed legatee of God's Messenger nor someone to whom the people have willingly given their allegiance. He merely used violence and treachery; it was the people's failure to defend the truth that brought him to power."

"Do you think that Muawiya is afraid of Hussein?" Rahman inquired.

Abdullah: 'Yes. Because Hussein is the leader of the Hashemite clan and his personal merit and social standing are clear to all... he is the person most entitled to claim association with God's Messenger. The only reason he has not revolted against Muawiya and his brutality is because of the agreement which he cosigned with Muawiya along with his brother Hasan, otherwise the situation we find ourselves in today would certainly be very different."

"By God, I still cannot understand how Muawiya managed to secure the pledge of allegiance for his son, Yazid!" the ironsmith exclaimed.

Rahman: 'So how on earth did Muawiya manage to secure the

pledge of allegiance for his son, Yazid?'

Abdullah: 'Muawiya sent for Dhahhak b. Qays and said: 'I have decided to announce the pledge of allegiance for Yazid, so once the court is crowded with people and you see me silent, you must be the one to suggest that I take the pledge for him and insist that I do so.'

So the next day, Muawiya sent for the notables amongst the people and summoned them to his court. Once they had gathered, he spoke, emphasising Yazid's pre-eminence amongst the Quraysh and his political finesse.

Whereupon Dhahhak b. Qays stood up and offered the most unscrupulous flattery: 'O Commander of the Faithful! People must have a leader after you, and you must have a crown prince. We have known through experience both unity and division, and it is only unity that can prevent the shedding of blood, keep the roads safe and grant us good in this world and the next. The days twist and turn. One does not know what changes time will bring, or how events will transpire. Yazid resembles you in his manners and attitudes; he is the most sensible of us and the most well-endowed with knowledge. So make him your crown prince and give us a banner [to follow] after you, that he may be a shelter in which we seek refuge and ruler upon whom we can depend. This will content [our] hearts and protect [us] from tribulations.'

When Dhahhak fell silent, Amr b. Sa'eed al-Ashdaq stood up, echoing his peer: 'O people! Yazid is indeed capable, magnanimous and honourable. If you betake to his justice, it will protect you. If you seek his generosity, it will enrich you. He is the successor to the Commander of the Faithful and there is no substitute for him.'

Muawiya said: 'Be seated, Abu Umayya. You have been most kind and spoken well.'

The highlight of the event then followed, when Yazid b. al-Muqanna al-Kindi rose clasping a sword in his hand. Not to be outdone by his peers, he offered not just flattery, but an outright ultimatum to those who may even consider rejecting Yazid: 'O people! This is the Commander of the Faithful' – and pointed with his hand to Muawiya – 'and should he die then this' – pointing to Yazid – 'and who here disagrees, then this' – and he pointed to the sword.

The message was loud and clear.

Muawiya said: 'Be seated. You are clearly an accomplished public speaker!'

Then al-Hus'sein b. Numayr al-Sukuni stood up and said: 'O Muawiya! If you meet God without having taken the pledge of allegiance for Yazid, you shall certainly be held responsible for squandering this nation!'

Ensuring that no voices of objection remained, Muawiya then turned to Ahnaf b. Qays and said: 'O *Abu Baḥr*! What prevents you from speaking?'

Ahnaf said: 'You know Yazid better than we – how he spends his days and nights, his comings and his goings, his conduct in public and in private. So if you know that God and this nation will be satisfied with him, then do not consult anyone. But if you know anything else to be the case, then do not enrich him with this world while you are departing for the next. Now, if we have said our part, we hear and obey.'

Muawiya said: 'You have spoken well, O *Abu Baḥr*. May God reward you for hearing and obeying.' Swiftly dismissing that statement of objection, shy and timid as it were, Muawiya then ordered the people to pledge allegiance to Yazid. As expected, they all submitted to his rule without hesitation.

As the gathering dispersed, Dhahhak – the man who had encouraged Muawiya to entrust the affairs of the nation to Yazid – met Ahnaf at the door. He tried to justify his disgraceful stance to his friend, saying: 'O *Abu Baḥr*! I know that this man and his son are the most evil of God's creation, but they have locked up their wealth behind doors and bolts. Our only hope of bringing it out was with the words you heard.'

Ahnaf replied: 'Listen, you! Be silent, for it befits one who is two-faced to be disgraced by God!"

Abdullah b. Muslim: 'Don't you see, O Rahman, how Muawiya follows the practice of wanton despots like the kings of India, Rome and Persia, who take the pledge of allegiance for their sons without any consideration for ethics and morality, or the Prophet's legacy?

The ruler has wealth and power in his hands, so whoever obeys him he rewards and whoever holds back has his head severed. In this way, he took the pledge of allegiance for his son, whether willingly or by duress.

But Muawiya was not satisfied with merely appointing Yazid as his successor and sending word to his governors in the provinces to take the pledge of allegiance for his son. Rather, he employed all of the state's resources in pursuit of this goal; he would personally hold meetings from time to time with preachers and offer them bribes and gifts so that they would praise him and his son and encourage people to obey Yazid.

Sometimes he would hold public meetings in which he would permit delegations to enter, and he would tell his companions to ascribe to Yazid qualities that he did not possess. He held meetings all over the empire, all of them for the sole purpose of praising Yazid, hailing him as though humanity could never produce such a person ever again!

In one such gathering, he commissioned poets to proclaim: 'Yazid is the hope which you have been expecting and the one whom you have been awaiting; he is capable and strong; his justice is vast, his generosity limitless, a gifted youth... others have vied with him and fallen short, competed in honour and come up lacking, battled him and been vanquished – he is the successor to the Commander of the Faithful and unmatched in any way!"

Abdullah: 'It is strange indeed that some people claim the Prophet did not appoint a successor, leaving the entire nation in limbo, yet they acknowledge Muawiya's right to appoint an heir and preserve his bloody legacy. Did I not say to you before that if we wanted to understand our present situation according to the criteria brought by God's Messenger, then we are in one valley and the religion of Islam is in another?'

Rahman: 'You're right. But he is still the sovereign and ruler as you know.'

Abdullah: 'And this is exactly what I mean; he is the sovereign and the ruler, not the religion. We cannot consider what is happening now to be part of the religion or even remotely associated with morality. This is what God's Messenger meant when he said: 'Lo! Indeed the authority and the Quran will separate. Lo! So do not leave the Quran. Lo! Over you there shall be one who, if you obey him, he will lead you astray or, if you disobey him, he will kill you.'

His companions asked: 'So what should we do then O' Messenger of God?'

He said: 'Do as the followers of Jesus did. Become carpenters [i.e. make coffins for yourselves]. To die obeying God is better than to live disobeying Him."

Rahman: 'But tell me, did all the men of the Umayyad clan accept Yazid as Caliph? What about those who themselves aspired to the position of Caliph?'

Abdullah: 'Do you mean Marwan b. al-Hakam?'

Rahman: 'Yes.'

Abdullah: 'I told you already that he desired the Caliphate for himself and was making plans to that end. So when Muawiya wrote to Marwan, who you will remember was his governor in Medina, informing him of his choice of Yazid as a successor and ordering him to take the pledge of allegiance from the people, Marwan was furious. He set off for Damascus with his household and maternal uncles from the *Kināna* clan. There, he called upon Muawiya and, walking through the banquet, approached him until he was close enough for the latter to hear him. He greeted him and then launched into a scalding rebuke of Muawiya.

He said, 'O son of Abu Sufiyan! Set things right and stop appointing children to positions of authority! Know that you have equals amongst your own people and ministers who are capable of managing affairs.'

Muawiya was offended by Marwan's words, but he supressed his anger, took Marwan by the hand and began to praise him. He said: 'You are the equal of the Commander of the Faithful after him, and his supporter in every difficulty. You are second only to his appointed successor, and this is why I have placed you in charge of your own people and given you a greater share of tax revenue. I approve of your petition and appreciate your support; the Commander of the Faithful must enrich you and seek your satisfaction.'

With these words, Muawiya made Marwan his advisor, second only to Yazid, securing his homage and loyalty for the time being.

As was his usual practice, Muawiya showered him with gifts and wealth, until it was said that Marwan was the first man to be paid a thousand gold dinars every month, and members of his household were all given stipends in the hundreds.

When Marwan returned to Medina, he sent word to the leaders of his people and gathered them in the central mosque. There, he ascended the pulpit and enjoined people to obey the ruler and warned them against sedition.

Affirming his new allegiance, he said: 'O people! The Commander of the Faithful has become aged and enfeebled; he fears that there will be anarchy after him. But God has inspired him with a proper idea; he wants to appoint a crown prince to succeed him when he dies and be a refuge for you, so that God might bring about harmony through him and prevent the shedding of blood. He desires that this should be on the basis of consultation and mutual agreement with you, so what do you say?'

The crowd chanted: 'We see no problem in that, so long as God is satisfied with this.'

Marwan said: 'Verily he has chosen one with whom you will be satisfied, who shall follow the example of the rightly-guided and righteous caliphs, and that is his son, Yazid.'

Stunned, the people fell silent. But Rahman b. Abu Bakr stood up and said: 'By God, you have lied, O Marwan! And whoever has ordered you to do this has lied. By God, Yazid is not one who is agreed upon. Rather you desire to make him like a Heraclius over us!'

Marwan said: 'O people! The one who speaks is he about whom God revealed: 'As for him who says to his parents, 'Fie on you!''

Rahman b. Abu Bakr was enraged and raised his voice: 'O son of the blue-skinned slave whore! How dare you interpret the Quran against us while you are the fugitive son of the Prophet's expellee'?

Marwan had started a firestorm. The scene was one of chaos and anger. Abdullah b. Zubayr and Abdullah b. Umar, refused to pledge allegiance to Yazid. Members of the Umayyad clan present in the Mosque raised a tumult and shouted down Rahman b. Abu Bakr. Word of this reached his sister, A'isha, who was the Prophet's wife. She immediately came out of her house surrounded by her attendants and some women of the Quraysh and entered the Mosque. When Marwan saw her, he looked terrified and said: 'I implore you, O mother of the believers! Speak only the truth!'

A'isha said: 'I do not say except the truth and I bear witness that God's Messenger cursed your father and you with him! You are indeed the fugitive son of a fugitive, and yet you address my brother such?' Marwan fell silent and did not respond to her. Then A'isha returned to her home and the gathering dispersed.

Marwan wrote to Muawiya informing him of what transpired, in particular the actions of Rahman b. Abu Bakr. Upon reading this letter, Muawiya turned to those seated with him and said: 'Rahman is a senile old man. We must leave him and put up with his drivel. This is not his opinion; rather it is the opinion someone else has whispered in his ear.'

Abdullah: 'O Rahman; securing Yazid's position as Muawiya's successor was no easy task. Muawiya was assisted by the circumstances of the time after people had betrayed Ali and his son, Hasan, but Yazid was the spitting image of his grandfather, Abu Sufiyan, and played the same role in Islam that his grandfather had played during the Age of Ignorance. In other words, he wanted to revive the traditions of the pre-Islamic era and impose them over those of the religion in form and content. This is especially true when you consider that everyone knew this young man to be extremely conceited; he did not observe even the appearance of dignity – a gambling addict who was always drunk. He spent his days hunting and mating with anything that moved. Not to mention his frivolous and foolish behaviour with people! So as I said, the entire state from top to bottom had to be used if Muawiya was to have any hope of securing the Caliphate of Yazid and take the pledge of allegiance for him from the people.

To that end, Muawiya began writing personal letters to various figures, abusing his authority as an absolute ruler who felt no compunction against shedding the blood of anyone who disagreed with him, whether secretly or openly. I mean, was it not Muawiya who sent Busr b. Artaat to raid Muslim lands in the way that the pre-Islamic Arabs used to raid one another – killing men, women and children? Was it not he who killed Ammar b. Yasir, about whom God's Messenger said: 'He will be killed by the aggressing faction'? Was it not he who killed Muhammad b. Abu Bakr, placed his body in the hide of a donkey and burnt it?

It was with heinous acts such as these that Muawiya struck terror into people's hearts and made them fear his power. All the while, he flung open the doors of the treasury so that he could buy the loyalty of those willing to sell their souls to him.

One of those to whom he wrote was *Sa'eed b. al-'Āṣ*, now his governor in Medina. He commanded him to call people to pledge allegiance and inform him who amongst them obliged quickly and who hesitated and held back. When this letter arrived, he called people to pledge allegiance to Yazid and used coercive measures; forcibly taking the pledge of allegiance from many and raiding the homes of those who held back. But except for a few, most people were slow to pledge allegiance, especially the members of the Hashemite clan of whom not a single person responded to the summons. The most vocal dissenter was none other than Ibn Zubayr.

So *Sa'eed b. al-'Ās* wrote back to Muawiya: 'You commanded me to summon people to pledge allegiance to Yazid, son of the Commander of the Faithful, and to inform you of those whom obliged quickly and those who were hesitant. So I tell you that the people were slow to respond, especially the Household of the Prophet and the Hashemite clan. Not a single one of them responded to my summons and word has reached me that they consider pledging allegiance to Yazid to be a most loathsome thing. But the one who has shown the most hostility to this matter is Abdullah b. Zubayr, and I cannot overpower him except with men and horses, or unless you come yourself and form your own opinion about this.'

So Muawiya wrote letters to Abdullah b. Abbas, Abdullah b. Zubayr, Abdullah b. Ja'far and Hussein b. Ali and instructed Sa'eed to convey these letters to them and forward their responses to him.'

Muawiya's letter to Ibn Abbas read: 'I have heard that you are hesitant in pledging your allegiance to Yazid, the son of the Commander of the Faithful. I could, by my rights, have you executed for your role in the murder of Uthman because you were one of those who incited the people against him and stirred up strife. You have nothing that can keep you safe, or any guarantee of protection to rely upon. So when you receive this letter, betake yourself to the mosque, curse the killers of Uthman and offer your pledge of allegiance to my governor. I consider this fair warning. But you know yourself best."

Rahman: 'Such a harsh and threatening letter?'

Abdullah: 'Yes, but Abdullah b. Abbas' reply was ever harsher!'

Rahman: 'What did he write?'

Abdullah: 'He wrote to Muawiya, saying: 'I have received your letter and understood its contents; that I have no safety from you. But, by God, no one asks safety from you O Muawiya, they ask it from God, the Lord of the Worlds... as for executing me, if you do that you shall meet God with Muhammad as your prosecutor, and I doubt that anyone who has God's Messenger as a prosecutor shall be acquitted! And as for your accusation that I incited the people against Uthman and stirred up strife, you accuse me of something which you did not witness, for surely if you witnessed these events you would not have assigned me any responsibility for them. I swear by God that no one was more enraged by Uthman's murder than I, nor did anyone think it a graver sin than I. Had I witnessed it, I would have helped him or died defending him. I have already said that I wish whoever killed Uthman on that day had killed me to so that I would not have to live on without him... as for telling me to curse the killers of Uthman, he has children, comrades and relatives more entitled to curse than I. If they wish to curse his killers, let them do so, and if they wish to remain silent, let them do so.'

Abdullah b. Muslim paused for a moment, took a deep breath and sighed before saying to Rahman: 'Look, the Prophet's Household carried the banner of this religion when the Umayyad Clan, led by Abu Sufiyan and his son, Muawiya, bore the banner of faithlessness and error against that of *tawḥīd*. The Household of the Prophet were with God's Messenger from the very beginning; they endured all manner of afflictions, hardships, death and martyrdom. Some of them were slain while fighting beside the prophet, and after God's

Messenger it was they who safeguarded this religion and protected it from the plots of the hypocrites just as they protected it from the plots of the faithless. The righteous believers all know that the Prophet's Household are a refuge from error and that which saves us from destruction. This is especially so after the appointment of Yazid as his father's successor by force and the establishment of an imperial dictatorship; an event which the faithful saw as the beginning of the end for Islam. This was the view of Hussein b. Ali, when he said to Marwan afterwards: 'To God we belong and to Him we return, if the nation is afflicted with a shepherd like Yazid then may Islam rest in peace!'

When the people realized that they had been betrayed and that the Umayyad clan wanted to restore the Age of Ignorance, to uproot religion totally and complete their coup against God's Messenger, they began to come to Hussein and seek refuge with him. Muawiya regarded Hussein with apprehension. He was the head of the Prophet's Household and their leader; no one could compare to him, whether in personal qualities, knowledge or moral rectitude. Muawiya himself described Hussein as a lion who, if awoken, no one could overpower.

For this reason, Muawiya wrote to Hussein saying: 'Some matters about you have come to my attention that I encourage you to desist from. If these accusations are true, I will not ask you to confess to them, and if they are false you should be all the happier. Begin by protecting yourself and fulfilling God's covenant; do not do anything to estrange me from you or force me to harm you in any way. For when you dispute with me, I will dispute with you, and when you plot against me, I will plot against you. So beware of causing divisions in this nation or returning it to sedition by your hand, for sedition has ruined the people and afflicted them. Your father was superior to you, and all those who now seek shelter with you had gathered around him too. I do not think that they will avail you where they ruined him, so look to your own person and your own religion, and to the nation of Muhammad. Do not allow yourself to be used by the foolish and the ignorant.'

Upon receiving this letter, Hussein wrote in reply: 'I have received your letter in which you say matters have come to your attention from which you would like to dissuade me and that in your opinion it befits me to take another course of action. But it is only God who guides to good deeds and requites them.

Whoever brought these matters to your attention has only done so because they wish to stir up discord. I have no desire to wage war against you or dissent from you. My fear of God prevents me from doing so, for I doubt that God would be satisfied me if forsook your authority for rebellion. Nor do I think that He would excuse me unless you or your faithless supporters gave me just cause – a band of oppressors and confederates of Satan if there ever was!'

Then he added: 'Are you not the one who murdered Hujr b. ÝUday, the brother of Kinda, and the other pious worshippers who rejected oppression, who considered innovation a grave sin and who feared not the reproach of men but only that of God? You killed them unjustly and in aggression, after providing them with firm guarantees and repeated assurances that you would not pursue them for what had happened between you and them, nor for any desire of revenge you might have harboured. Did you not commit this crime brazenly against God, thinking nothing of this covenant?

Are you know the one who claimed Ziyad b. Sumayya, who was born upon the bed of a slave from Thaqif, then claimed that he was your father's son. But God's Messenger has said: 'The child belongs to the bed; the stones to the fornicator.' So you wilfully abandoned the practise of God's Messenger and followed your own desires over God's guidance, then you gave him authority over the Muslims, to cut off their hands and feet, gouge out their eyes and crucify them on the trunks of date palms, as if you are of this nation and they are not of you?

Are you not the one responsible for the Hadhramites, about whom the Son of Sumayya wrote: 'They follow the religion of Ali.' So you ordered him to execute whoever followed the religion of Ali, so he slew them and made an example of them. But the religion of Ali is the religion of his cousin, Muhammad, which your father detested and which you used to obtain this position of yours? If it was not for the Prophet, your highest honour would be nothing more than leading the summer and winter caravans in search of wine.

In your letter, you wrote: 'Look to your own person and your own religion, and to the nation of Muhammad. Beware of causing divisions in this nation or returning it to sedition by your hand.'

But I know no sedition in this nation greater than your authority over it, nor anything better for myself, my religion or the nation of Muhammad than to struggle against you... if I did so, it would bring me nearness to God and if I do not, then I ask God to forgive me for the sake of my faith, and I ask Him to grant me success and guide me.

As for your words: 'For when you dispute with me, I will dispute with you, and when you plot against me, I will plot against you.' Plot as you like, for I do not expect your plot to cause me any harm, nor can I think of anything I can do that would cause you greater harm than you plotting against me, for you have acted in haste and made plain your intent to break your oath – by my life, you have not fulfilled a single pledge thereof.

You have broken your oath by killing those persons whom you slew after making peace with pledges, oaths and treaties. You killed them while they were neither fighting you, nor acting in violation of your treaty. And the only reason you did this was because they would extoll our virtues and honour our dues. You killed them because you feared they would do something. Yet, had you not slain them you might have died before they acted, or they might have died before they found an opportunity to act. So be happy, O Muawiya, for retribution is near at hand and be certain that you will be held to account. Know that God has a book from which nothing great or small is omitted. God will not forget that you seized people on suspicion, or slew the supporters of Ali at the merest accusation, and then made your son your successor, while he is a foolish boy who drinks wine and plays with dogs. You have cheated yourself out of your own safety, ruined your flock and disregarded the advice of your Lord.

How can you give a wine-drinker authority over the nation of Muhammad when one who drinks wine is committing a grave sin? A wine-drinker cannot be trusted with a dirham, so how can you entrust him with the nationh! You will soon regret this when you read the scrolls of repentance and take your seat in Hellfire. So away with the wrongdoing lot!'

He closed his letter with the words: 'And peace on he who follows guidance.'

Rahman said to his friend: 'I cannot imagine a harsher letter! Hussein accuses Muawiya of heresy, says that he is an oppressor and enumerates his crimes against righteous men such as Hujr b. Udayy, Amr b. al-Hamq al-Khuza'ee and the Hadhramites, his broken pledges and treaties, just as he rebukes him for appointing Yazid as his successor as ruler of the Muslims! How did Muawiya respond to this?'

Abdullah: 'When Muawiya read Hussein's letter he said: 'It appears that I have underestimated him.'

Yazid said: 'O Father! Send him a response to belittle him and mention some fault of his.'

Muawiya replied: 'That would be a mistake. Do you think if I wanted to slander Ali truthfully I could? It is no good for someone like me to slander another falsely or with something he is not known for. Whenever I slander a man with something unknown to the people, it doesn't stick to him and the people refuse to believe it. I cannot expose Hussein's faults because by God I can find no fault of his to expose! Instead, I thought perhaps to write to him with warnings and threats, but I realized it was better not to. So I will not do that now.'

Rahman: 'The affair of this nation is strange indeed. The Umayyad clan managed to drive the Prophet's Household from their position of leadership and establish their own regime, then here they are trying to appoint a child – in the words of Marwan b. al-Hakam – as a ruler over this nation.'

Abdullah b. Muslim replied: 'Ali was right when he said: 'Lo! Indeed he is one whom truth avails not, [but] to whom falsehood does injury."

He continued: 'Appointing someone like Yazid as Caliph can only be accomplished through the use of bribery and coercion; buying men's consciences and threatening them with harm. And, as I told you already, all the tools of the state – from top to bottom – were employed to that end. So Muawiya didn't only give orders and write letters, no! He decided to go to Mecca and Medina to take care of things himself.'

He set out from Syria in force, accompanied by a thousand soldiers. When he came to Medina, the first person he encountered was Hussein b. Ali. When he saw him, he said: 'You are not welcome, you sacrificial camel whose blood God will soon spill.'

Hussein replied: 'Steady now, Muawiya! Such words do not befit me.'

Muawiya said: 'Oh yes, and worse! For you desire something but God detests what you desire.'

Then he left, not waiting to hear the Imam's answer.

Then he encountered Abdullah b. Zubayr, to whom he said: 'You are not welcome, you venomous snake! He sticks his head into a burrow and has it cut off for his sin. By God, he shall soon be seized by his sin and his back broken! Get him away from me!'

So Muawiya's bodyguards struck the face of Ibn Zubayr's mount and drove him off.

Then Muawiya met Rahman b. Abu Bakr, to whom he said: 'You are not welcome either, senile old food!' Then he ordered his bodyguards to strike the latter's mount and drive him off. He did the same to Abdullah b. Umar.

This is how Muawiya treated the great figures to teach others a lesson and demonstrate that he was going to proceed with his plan to give his son Yazid authority over the Muslims.

Then he went to visit A'isha. He asked permission to enter her home and she permitted him to enter, on the condition that he came alone and brought no one else with him. With her, she had her servant Dhakawn. Once Muawiya was seated, she said to him: 'O Muawiya, how can you be so sure I would not bring a man here to kill you as you killed my brother, Muhammad b. Abu Bakr?'

'You would not do that.'

'And why not?'

'Because I am in a sanctuary – the house of God's Messenger.'

A'isha fell silent. Muawiya began to justify his appointment of Yazid as his successor. He attributed it – as do all kings and rulers – to the will of God.

She said to him: 'O Muawiya! How can you justify killing my brother and burning his body? And coming to Medina and forcing the sons of the Companions to pledge allegiance [to you and your son], while you are one of the freed captives ('Tulaqaa') and not entitled to the Caliphate, and your father was one of the confederates (Ahzab)?

Muawiya replied: 'O Mother of the Believers! O she who knows God and His messenger best! You have guided us to the truth and prompted us to prompt ourselves. You deserve to have your commands obeyed and your words heeded. But the matter of Yazid's succession is part of the Divine Decree, and you know well that God's servants have no choice in their affairs. People have affirmed that allegiance to him rests upon their necks; and they have given solemn oaths to that effect. Do you think it proper that they should break these oaths?'

A'isha said: 'I have heard that you threatened my brother, Rahman, and Ibn Umar, my nephew Abdullah b. Zubayr and Hussein, the son of Fatima. One such as you cannot threaten men such as those. As for your solemn oaths, you should fear God in your treatment of those men and not act rashly towards them.'

Muawiya stood up to leave, but she continued: 'O Muawiya! It was you who slew Hujr and his righteous companions.'

He said: 'Leave that aside. Think instead about how I can be in matters where we share a mutual interest.'

From this, A'isha understood that he intended to proceed with his plan, but that he was ready to compensate with whatever she wanted in return. So she fell silent.

Of course, when Muawiya demanded that the leading figures of the people pledge allegiance to Yazid, or at least keep their objections to themselves, he would accomplish this through threats. He had said to Rahman b. Abu Bakr when the two were alone: 'With which hand or foot would you dare to disobey me?'

Rahman: 'I should think that a blessing for me!'

Muawiya said: 'By God, I will not rest until you are dead.'

Rahman replied: 'If you do that, then God will recompense you with curses in this world and cast you into Hellfire in the Hereafter.'

While in Medina, Muawiya once called for a dais to be set up where he held his court and had some special seats prepared around his. He came out after having perfumed himself and donned a Yemeni robe, sat on his dais, seated his scribes to one side of him and ordered his chamberlain not to let anyone enter – no matter how close a friend. Then he sent a messenger to Hussein b. Ali and Abdullah b. Abbas. It was Ibn Abbas who came first, and once he had entered the room and greeted Muawiya, the latter seated him on the dais to his left. He said: 'O Ibn Abbas! Indeed God has blessed you by making you a neighbour of this sacred grave and the house of God's Messenger.'

Ibn Abbas responded: 'Yes, and God has blessed us further by making us satisfied with what we have and averse to what we do not.'

Then Muawiya began to speak to him and dissuade him from answering, turning to matters such as how one person's lifespan differs from another according to their individual nature. Then Hussein arrived. When Muawiya saw him, he prepared a cushion that was to his right and invited him to sit there. Hussein came in and sat upon the cushion.

Muawiya said to the two of them: 'God's Messenger passed away and left what he had been granted of this world, choosing to relinquish that which had been placed at his disposal, out of piety, love of God, abstinence and demonstrating great fortitude. He was followed by two trusted men and a third who is to be thanked, at the same time there was a conflict which we were often preoccupied with, whether in quiet observation or open warfare.'

Then he began to praise his son, Yazid, saying: 'The matter of Yazid is as you anticipated and warned against. God knows that I act only in the interests of my flock; to close any gaps and seal any cracks by appointing Yazid, which will guarantee a bright future for the Nation. This is what I intend to do with Yazid. Of course, the two of you are distinguished by your familial connection to the Prophet, estimable knowledge and chivalrous nature. And upon comparing Yazid with the two of you, I see that he is nowhere near your equal, despite the fact he is knowledgeable in the Sunna, a capable reciter of the Quran and endowed with clemency beyond that of the most calm and tranquil of people!

'You both know that the Messenger, who was kept safe from error by the infallibility conferred upon him by his own message, gave precedence to someone else over Abu Bakr and Umar during the Expedition of Chains, not to mention other great Companions and the very first Emigrants present whom no one comes close to equalling whether in relation to the Prophet or piety and devotion. But he made this man their leader by his command, and thereby united them in prayer and safeguarded their share of the booty. In God's Messenger we have a good exemplar. So wait a moment, sons of Abd al-Muttalib, for you and I are of one family in our fortunes. I still hold out hope that, by bringing you here, you will be even-handed, as everyone knows that your opinions carry weight. Now reply to a relative who is beset by criticism, in such a way that it befits not anyone to malign you!'

Ibn Abbas moved to respond, but Hussein gestured to him and said: 'Hold on! It is my answer he wants most and it is better that I be the one to impugn him.' Then Ibn Abbas fell silent.

Hussein began by praising God and invoking His blessings upon his grandfather, the Prophet. Then he said: 'It's no use, Muawiya. No matter how much you praise the qualities of the Messenger. I see how you are trying to dress up the issue of succession to God's Messenger by playing with words. No never, O Muawiya! The dawn has stripped away the gloom and the sun has outshone the lantern; you have praised [Yazid] to excess and become so engrossed with him that your bias is clear to see, you have denied others their due [praise] to the extent of stinginess and gone beyond the bounds of decency. You have not given anyone so much as a share of his due, except that Satan comes and takes the lions share of it for himself!

You speak about Yazid's perfection and suitability to rule over the nation of Muhammad as if you want people to believe that you are describing something the likes of which they have never seen before. But Yazid has already shown us what he is like; so if you want to mention any qualities of Yazid, then mention those he has chosen for himself: look at him when he is amassing fighting dogs, racing pigeons, female musicians and entertainers, and I'm sure you will find him discerning. Give up this plot of yours, because it will only increase the burden of your sins when you meet God. By God, you continue you stir up falsehood in tyranny and wrath in wrongdoing, until the water skins were filled and a blink of an eye was all that remained between you and death. So now you are embarking on a deed that will be preserved on a witnessed day whence there shall be no time for evasion.'

Then he said: 'And I see you then turn to us, and deny us any inheritance from our fathers, when God's Messenger bequeathed to us an inheritance by virtue of birth. You came to us with it and your arguments; you committed outrages and did deeds. Then you said: 'It was and is' until the matter came to you, O Muawiya, by leaving its proper course whose destination was one other than you. So consider this, if you have sense!

You mention that God's Messenger appointed a man as a leader of the people – by which you meant *Amr b. al-'Āṣ* - but on the day he was appointed they scorned his leadership, detested his being given preference and enumerated his misdeeds. So the Prophet said: 'Very well, assembled Emigrants! No one shall be appointed a governor over you after today except me.

So how can you argue with us on the basis of an action of God's Messenger which has been abrogated (*mansūkh*), which is one of the most certain laws and the most fitting ruling for there to be consensus upon, or how can you follow someone while around you are those who do not believe in following him and who cannot be relied upon in their religion or respect for family ties? You are leaving them to extreme peril, wanting to confuse the people and thereby make the one whom you leave behind happy in this world, while destroying your own place in the Hereafter. This is indeed a manifest loss!'

Muawiya looked to Ibn Abbas and asked: 'What is this, O Ibn Abbas?'

Ibn Abbas said: 'By God, it belongs to the descendants of the Prophet, one of the People of the Cloak and one from the Purified Household. So ask him about what you want, for verily you may content yourself with the people, until God judges by His command and He is the best of judges.'

This is how Muawiya worked to secure Yazid's position as his successor, day and night, in public and in private, meeting with the heads of tribes for that purpose, addressing, debating and threatening them. These meetings were usually not held in public, lest the people become aware of these men's arguments against pledging allegiance to his son. But Muawiya did hold public gatherings as well. In some cases he would order that people be summoned for an important event. So people gathered in the Mosque, and amongst those present were Hussein b. Ali, Abdullah b. Zubayr, Abdullah b. Umar and others, who were seated around the pulpit. Then Muawiya got up, praised God and glorified him, before mentioning Yazid, his personal qualities and his recitation of the Quran.

Then he said: 'O people of Medina! I have resolved to take the pledge of allegiance for Yazid, and there is no village or city save that I have sent for its pledge of allegiance to him. Everyone has now pledged allegiance to him and accepted him as my successor. The only reason I have not taken this pledge from the city of Medina is because I know that this is his hometown and that I have no reason to doubt that you will be forthcoming. As for those who have so far refused to make this pledge, it was better for them if they do. For by God, if I knew of anyone superior to Yazid amongst the Muslims, I myself would have pledged allegiance to him already!'

Then Hussein stood up and said: 'By God, you have set aside he who is superior to Yazid in both his mother, his father and his own person!'

Muawiya said: 'You mean yourself?'

'Yes.'

'Then let me tell you something. You say your mother is superior, and by my life your mother is superior to Yazid's. Even if she was merely a woman of the Quraysh, the women of the Quraysh are better. So what about the daughter of God's Messenger? Yes, by my life, your mother is superior to his.

You say that your father is superior to his, and yet his father sought God's judgement, and God judged in favour of his father and against yours because God ruled in favour of Muawiya over Ali...' – meaning that Ali was slain while Muawiya became the Caliph of the Muslims.

Hussein said: 'Enough of your ignorance, for you prefer this world over the world that is to come!'

Muawiya continued unabated: 'You say that you are superior to Yazid in your own person, but by God Yazid is better for the nation of Muhammad than you!'

Hussein replied: 'That is a shameful lie! Yazid is a wine-drinker and a patron of amusements – is he superior to me?'

Muawiya said: 'Hold your tongue from reviling your cousin! If someone spoke ill of you to his face, he would not revile you such.'

Hussein said: 'If Yazid knew of me what I know of him, he would do right to speak about him as I do about him now!'

Once again, Muawiya resorted to threats: 'O Abu Abdullah, go safely to your family and fear God concerning yourself; and beware lest the people of Syria should hear the words I heard you utter, for they are your enemies just as they were the enemies of your father.'

Here we see that Hussein and others refused Muawiya's demand to pledge allegiance to Yazid and sabotaged his efforts to make his son appear desirable to the people. But Muawiya had decided to take the pledge of the allegiance in spite of all this opposition, and in his hand he had the means to accomplish this – the offices of the state and the wealth of its treasury. So whenever logic failed him, he used threats. And when threats did not avail him, he used persuasion. This is what he did with Rahman b. Abu Bakr, who said to him one day: 'By God, O Muawiya! Perhaps you have hope that I have left God to deal with you concerning your son, Yazid – meaning that I have left you to your own devices to do as you wish – but by God, I will never do that. We want this matter to be settled by consultation amongst the Muslims.'

Muawiya told him: By God, I know you and your foolishness better than you, and I have decided to do this.'

Rahman b. Abu Bakr said: 'Then God will seize you for it suddenly in this world and set aside punishment for you in the Hereafter.'

At which point, Muawiya said: 'O God! Rid me of this petulant old man. O wretch! Beware of God in your own self and don't let the people of Syria hear these words you utter.'

Rahman: 'We have been wary of God, so let us sit in our homes and do not bother us to pledge allegiance to Yazid, the wine-drinking monkey!'

Before he set off from Medina to Mecca, Muawiya bestowed presents on the people liberally; every tribe was given copious gifts, except the Hashimite clan. So when Abdullah b. Abbas met him, he asked: 'For what reason did you shun us?'

Muawiya replied: 'Because your companion, Hussein b. Ali would not pay allegiance to Yazid and you did not rebuke him.'

Abdullah b. Abbas said: 'O Muawiya! I ought to seclude myself on a beach somewhere, then you can do whatever you know and let all the people come out to fight against you.

Then they parted.

In Mecca, Muawiya employed a fresh approach; he spread rumours that Rahman b. Abu Bakr, Abdullah b. Umar, Abdullah b. Zubayr and Hussein b. Ali had pledged allegiance to Yazid in secret. He accomplished this by actually summoning them and sitting with them for a period of time without speaking to them about anything of import.

When they had returned to their houses, Muawiya ascended the pulpit, praised and glorified God and then said: 'O people! I find people's speech full of contradictions; they claim that Hussein b. Ali, Rahman b. Abu Bakr, Abdullah b. Umar and Abdullah b. Zubayr have not given the pledge of allegiance to Yazid. But in my eyes, these four men are the leaders of the Muslims and the best of them; I invited them to pay allegiance and found them to be those who hear and obey. They have accepted [Yazid as my successor] and pledged allegiance. They heard, responded and obeyed.'

And he had ordered those mercenaries who came with them from Syria to threaten to cut off their heads if they did not pledge allegiance publicly. This was something previously agreed with them, such that they had their hands clasped to their swords and drew them out. They said: 'O Commander of the Faithful! What is the meaning of you praising these four men? Permit us to chop of their heads, for we are not satisfied that they should give allegiance in secret. Rather they must pledge it publicly in full sight of the people.'

Muawiya said: 'Glory to God! How hasty men are to do evil, and how sweeter it is for them to remain as they are. Fear God, O men of Syria and do not hasten to sedition, for indeed killing invites retribution.'

Then the people of Mecca went to these four people and asked: 'O men! You were asked to pledge allegiance to Yazid in Medina, but you refused to do so. Now you are asked again and you agree?'

Hussein replied: 'No, by God, we have not pledged allegiance to him. Muawiya behaved treacherously with us and deceived us just as he has now deceived you!"

Abdullah b. Muslim: 'Do you see how Muawiya left Hussein and did him no harm despite his stern refusal to accept Yazid?'

Rahman: 'As I had heard it, Muawiya asked Marwan b. al-Hakam: 'Tell me what I should do with Hussein?'

Marwan told him: 'I think you should take him to Syria with you; this will cut him off from the people of Iraq and cut them off from him.'

Muawiya replied: 'By God, you only want to be rid of him for yourself and burden me instead! If I tolerate him, it shall be like tolerating something I detest, and if I harm him then I have violated our ties of family.'

But Muawiya did not really dear violating ties of family as much as he feared Hussein becoming even more prominent in the eyes of the people and them finding out the truth... exactly as had happened with Abu Dharr al-Ghifari when he was exiled to Syria. Once he was there, he began to spread the praises of Ali and the Prophet's Household. Muawiya was worried by his teachings, so he wrote to the Caliph and asked that Abu Dharr be returned to Medina.

In any case, by refusing to pledge allegiance to Yazid, Hussein became Muawiya's primary concern. So he did not only ask Marwan for advice on what to do with him, but also sent for *Sa'eed b. al-'Āṣ* and asked: 'O Abu Uthman! What should I do with Hussein?'

Sa'eed replied: 'By God, you need not fear Hussein for yourself. You need only fear him for Yazid's sake. You have left behind an heir whom will be thrown to the ground if Hussein wrestles him and left behind if Hussein races him. So leave Hussein in a date grove where he can drink water and fly through their air; he will not reach the heavens."

Abdullah b Muslim: 'So what did Muawiya do in the end?'

Rahman: 'He ordered Walid b. Utba, the governor of Medina, to prevent the people of Iraq from meeting Hussein. It was for this reason that Hussein told him: 'O he who wrongs himself and disobeys his Lord! For what reason do you bar me from a people who know my status, which you and your uncle, Muawiya, seem to be ignorant of?'

Walid said: 'Would that our clemency towards you not bid others to immoderation; you are forgiven the felony of your tongue so long as you hand remains still; do not threaten others with it lest it threaten yourself.'

This is how the Umayyad clan were able to encircle the Prophet's Household; they prevented those people who knew Hussein's merit from meeting him, withheld their stipends from the treasury and put to death anyone who made known his love for Ali and his family, not to mention expelling entire families from their homelands. These trials and tribulations continued to mount on whoever had any inclination towards the Prophet's Household; there was no righteous person save that he feared for his life and no evil one save that he felt safe in making public his impiety.'

Rahman: 'It seems then that the position of Hussein and his household had become very difficult by this point?'

Abdullah: 'Events have gotten to the point that they resembled the situation at the time of God's Messenger, when the Prophet and Abu Sufiyan faced one another – only now it is Hussein facing Muawiya.

Rahman: 'But things are different now. Abu Sufiyan at that time was the standard-bearer of faithlessness, but Muawiya still waves the flag of religion.'

Abdullah: 'It is true that Hussein and Muawiya are both speaking from within the same religion, but they are still polar opposites just as the Prophet and Abu Sufiyan were, and Ali and Muawiya likewise.

Just as Abu Sufiyan would speak in the name of the religion of his forefathers, and therefore would call himself a defender of their faith, while God's Messenger spoke about Divine Unity – so he was speaking about religion as well. What changed after the Prophet was that the Umayyad clan accepted Islam after their defeat and raised the slogan of 'There is no god but God and Muhammad is the messenger of God', while making the pilgrimage and offering prayers. So yes, their slogan is Islam, but the essence of their message is not.

Before they announced their conversion to Islam, the Umayyad clan, who were led by Abu Sufiyan, would say: 'Hubal be praised!' Of course, Muawiya does not say this; he says: 'God is greater!'

But they are the hypocrites about whom God has said: 'They are the enemy, so beware of them. May God assail them, where do they stray?'

They have turned prayer against itself, and the *adhān* and the pilgrimage! They have hollowed out the religion until it became an empty shell. Therefore, the goal of Hussein is not simply to seize power from them; what value does that have to the Prophet's Household who have sacrificed everything they have for the sake of God? Not a day passed for the Prophet, Ali, Fatima, Hasan or Hussein in which that they did not sacrifice for the sake of God's religion. Hussein will bear every hardship, every difficulty, every torment, every accusation and every threat... so that people may see the true essence of the religion.

Hussein opposes the appointment of Yazid as Muawiya's successor not for the sake of worldly power, or desiring any personal gain. No, he does so to protect the essence of the religion. Hussein wants to reform the religious, social and political system, so that the ruler does not merely see himself as the head of state, like any other emperor, tyrant or Caesar, but rather as the successor of God's Messenger.

The government today has become a worldly government; it has no connection to the religion. People cannot take the actions and attitudes of those people to be a part of the religion by which they can seek nearness to God! And this is the danger that Hussein senses now; and everything he says is only to explain this reality.

No one can be appointed a successor to the Caliph unless God has appointed him and the people have accepted him, let alone if he openly sins, commits indecency and contravenes the religion in his personal affairs – so what about in matters of government?'

Rahman: 'Do you think Hussein will stop at what he said in his meeting with Muawiya?'

Abdullah: 'I think not. Hussein's position and his words may have been sufficient for the ordinary people to realize that the Quran is in one valley and the government in another, and that the two have separated, but there is a section of scholars and nobles who have made no move as of yet and are not discharging their duties. So I do not think that Hussein will stop at that.'

Abdullah stood up: 'I'm sorry, but I must take my leave of you and the city of Medina if I am to join the pilgrims. There is still much for us to talk about, so I hope we can meet again soon.'

So the two friends bid each other farewell, hoping to see one another again.

TESTIMONY

A few months after their last meeting, Rahman travelled to Basra to visit some family he had there, and Abdullah b. Muslim had come to town a few days before on business. By chance, they happened to meet in one of the alleys of Basra and Abdullah invited his friend to come and visit him at his sister's house next to the river.

Once again they began to speak about current events. Abdullah: 'Did I not tell you that Hussein would not stop at what he said to Muawiya?'

Rahman asked: 'What happened?'

Abdullah replied: 'It was the season of the Hajj just two months ago and Hussein was performing the pilgrimage. He gathered the entire Hashemite clan and their supporters as well as the members of his own household and said to them: 'Do not call upon any of the Companions of the Prophet known for their piety and devotion who makes the pilgrimage this year unless you bring them to me.'

So in Mina, more than seven hundred men gathered around him in a pavilion. Most of them were from the Successors, with about two hundred from the Companions of the Prophet.

Hussein stood up to address them. He praised God and glorified Him, then he said: 'This tyrant has treated us and our followers as you have no doubt seen and heard already. Now, I wish to ask you something and you can tell me whether I speak the truth or not. I ask you by the right that God has over you, by the right that God's Messenger has over you and by my relation to your Prophet that you take up this position of mine, that you convey my words and summon your trusted supporters amongst your tribes, and call them to support what you know is our right. I ask you this because I am afraid that this matter will be blotted out and that truth itself might disappear, but God will complete His light even if the faithless should be averse.'

There was not a single verse that God has sent down in the Quran about the Prophet's Household save that Hussein recited it and explained it to those assembled, nor a single saying of God's Messenger about either his father, mother, brother or himself and his household, save that he narrated it to them.

Throughout, the Companions replied with cries of: 'O God, yes. We have heard this and we bear witness to it!' And the Successors said: 'O God, I have heard this from Companions whom I believe and trust.'

Hussein said to them: 'I adjure you by God – do you know that Ali b. Abu Talib was the brother of God's Messenger when the latter made members of the Helpers and Emigrants brothers; he made Ali his own brother and said: 'You are my brother and I am yours in this world and the Hereafter?'

They replied: 'O God, yes!'

Then Hussein said: 'I adjure you by God – do you know that God's Messenger purchased the place of his Mosque and his home, then he built it and built ten homes in it. Nine of them he kept for himself and one in the middle he gave to my father, then he closed every door that opened to the Mosque except the door of Ali. Some people complained about this, but God's Messenger said: 'I am not the one who closed your doors and opened his, rather it is God who commanded me to close your doors and open his.' Then the Prophet forbade anyone except him to sleep in the Mosque and his house in the house of God's Messenger, and his children were born therein?'

They said: 'O God, yes!'

Hussein said: 'Do you know that Umar b. al-Khattab asked for a window no bigger than his eye to remain between his house and the Mosque? But God's Messenger refused and said: 'God has commanded me to build a pure Mosque that no one dwells within save my brother, his children and I.'

They said: 'O God, yes!'

He said: 'I adjure you by God, do you know that God's Messenger stood Ali up on the Day of Ghadir Khumm and announced his *wilāya*, saying: 'Let those present convey this to those who are absent.'

They said: 'O God, yes!'

He said: 'I adjure you by God, do you know that God's Messenger said during the expedition to Tabuk: 'You are to me as Aaron was to Moses, and you are the wali of every believer after me'?'

They said: 'O God, yes!'

He said: 'I adjure you by God, do you know that God's Messenger, when he challenged the Christians of Najran to *mubāhila* brought no one other than my father, my mother, my brother and me?'

They said: 'O God, yes!'

He said: 'I adjure you by God, do you know that the Prophet gave my father the battle standard on the Day of Khaybar and said: 'I will give this flag to a man whom God and His messenger love, and who loves God and his messenger, who is relentless and will not flee.

God will open [the gates of the fortress] by his hands.'

They said: 'O God, yes!'

He said: 'Do you know that God's Messenger sent him to convey the verses of repudiation and said: 'No one shall relate [revelation] from me except myself or a man from myself'?'

They said: 'O God, yes!'

He said: 'Do you know that God's Messenger suffered no hardship except that he preferred my father to deal with and entrusted him with it, and that he never called for him by his name without saying: 'My brother, Ali'?'

They said: 'O God, yes!'

He said: 'Do you know that he would have a private meeting with God's Messenger every day, and a sitting with him every night? When my father asked him something, he would answer, and if my father was silent he would encourage him to speak?'

They said: 'O God, yes!'

He said: 'Do you know that God's Messenger preferred him to Ja'far and Hamza when he said to Fatima: 'I have married you to the best member of my household, the first of them to believe, the greatest of them in good sense and the most knowledgeable of them'?

They said: 'O God, yes!'

He said: 'Do you know that God's Messenger said: 'I am the master of the children of Adam, my brother Ali is the master of the Arabs, *Fātima* is the mistress of the women of Paradise, and Hasan and Hussein are the leaders of the youth in Paradise'?'

They said: 'O God, yes!'

He said: 'Do you know that God's Messenger ordered my father to wash him when he passed away and told him that Gabriel would help him to do so?'

They said: 'O God, yes!'

He said: 'Do you know that God's Messenger said in his final sermon: 'Indeed I have left amongst you two weighty things; the Book of God and my Household. If you hold fast to these, you will never go astray. And the Ever-gracious and All-aware has informed me that these two things will never part until they return to me at the Pool.'

They said: 'O God, yes!'

He said: 'Do you know that God's Messenger has said: 'Whoever claims to love me while he hates Ali has lied, for no one who hates Ali can love me.' And that someone there asked him: 'O Messenger of God, how is that so?' And that the Prophet told him: 'Because he is from me and I from him; whoever loves him loves me, and whoever loves me loves God, and whoever hates him hates me, and whoever hates me hates God.'

They said: 'O God, yes. We have heard this!'

Hussein did not neglect anything revealed about Ali b. Abu Talib or the Prophet's Household in the Quran, nor anything spoken about them spoken by the Prophet, save that he asked them to confirm that they had heard it. The Companions would say: 'O God, yes! We have heard this.' And the Successors would say: 'O God, I have heard this from someone I trust.'

Rahman: 'O Abdullah, was the dispute with Ali a personal disagreement or was it for the sake of power – did they not want Ali to sit in the place of God's Messenger, desiring power for themselves, and for this reason they excluded him?'

Abdullah: 'More than that! You see, the religion has an essence and an appearance. It is the essence that matters, not the appearance, which has no value unless it conveys people to the essence within. And the Prophet's Household were those entrusted by the Prophet with preserving his message – namely the essence of the religion, its roots and its branches, and not just its appearance – and Ali was the gateway to the knowledge of God's Messenger, the most knowledgeable of the Companions and the most well versed in the words of the Prophet. Remember also the words that the Prophet spoke about Ali; these were many indeed and he did not utter the like of them about anyone else... he never said that any other Companion was like the head of his own body, but he said of Ali: 'Ali is to me like the head of my body.'

He did not say of anyone else: 'I and he are of one tree.' But he said of Ali: 'Ali and I are from a single tree, but all other people are from varied trees.'

Nor did he say that just mentioning anyone else was an act of worship, but he said of Ali: 'Mentioning Ali is worship.'

He did not say about anyone else what he said about Ali: 'I am the city of Paradise and Ali is its gate, I am the city of wisdom and Ali is its gate, I am the city of knowledge and Ali is its gate – so let whoever comes to the city enter by its gate.'

No one denies these narrations, which clearly show that no one can reach the knowledge of God's Messenger except through Ali, nor to his wisdom except through Ali, nor can anyone enter Paradise except through Ali. The Prophet says explicitly: 'No one may cross the *Ṣirāṭ* save those to whom Ali has given written permission.' And he said: 'You are my brother, my deputy and my standard-bearer in this world and you are the keeper of my pool in the Hereafter.'

This means that those who opposed Ali wanted only the appearance of religion without its essence; this is why they opposed him, Hasan and Hussein. If not, then why would Muawiya appoint Ali's enemies to positions of power after his death, and send out word to all of his governors, saying: 'Keep watch for those who narrate Hadith about Ali and strike their names from the register [for stipends from the treasury.]' Or say: 'Seize them on mere accusation and execute them at the slightest suspicion.' He forbade people to relate traditions from Ali or about Ali, but why would he do this when Ali was no longer alive to compete with him for authority?

So this is more than just a dispute over power between one party and another. The narrations about the Prophet's Household or about the merits of Ali, Fatima, Hasan and Hussein – even those in which Hussein extols his own virtues, are not there because they wanted to praise themselves to achieve some position in the eyes of the people. Rather they exist only because the knowledge of God's Messenger is preserved with them, and so is his wisdom. Just as God does not accept anyone to believe in His unity without believing in His Messenger – because when He sends a prophet He wants him to be obeyed by His leave, and God wants His religion to be followed by way of Him and not by any other way – so too is the case for what happened after the Prophet. God's Messenger made this clear when he said: 'I am leaving amongst you two weighty things: the Book of God and the people of my Household.'

Rahman: 'And at that important meeting, did Hussein content himself with mentioning the merits of Ali, Fatima, Hasan and himself?'

Abdullah: 'No. The main issue for which he gathered them there was still to come! After he had mentioned the merits of the Prophet's Household and obtained the agreement of the Companions that they had indeed heard these words from the Prophet, and also the testimony of the Successors that they too had heard these traditions, Hussein put their responsibility in front of them and said:

'O people! Consider how God admonishes His friends with his censure of the Rabbis when He says: 'Why do not the rabbis and the scribes forbid them from sinful speech...' And when He says: 'The faithless among the Children of Israel were cursed on the tongue of David and Jesus son of Mary. That, because they would disobey and they used to commit transgression. They would not forbid one another from the wrongs that they committed. Surely, evil is what they had been doing.'

God only rebukes them because they witnessed the wrongdoing of the sinners and corrupters but did not forbid them from it, desiring to obtain some worldly benefit from them and fearful of their threats. God says: '...So do not fear the people, but fear Me.' He says: 'But the faithful, men and women, are comrades of one another: they bid what is right and forbid what is wrong...' God mentions enjoining the good and forbidding the evil as a duty imposed by Him because He knows that if this duty is performed, all other duties great and small will be performed as a result. This is because enjoining the good and forbidding the evil is the summons to Islam, along with the rejection of wrongdoing, opposition to wrongdoers, the fair division of booty and spoils, and the proper collection and distribution of alms and taxes. It encompasses all other duties!'

To this, Hussein added: 'And so you, O you who are known for your knowledge, revered for your goodness and famed for your sound advice, whom the people hold in awe for the sake of God – the noble esteems you, the weak respects you and those who should by rights be your equals defer to you, even if you have no power over them. You plead for those who seek redress for their needs, walk through the streets with the appearance and manner of kings – and did you not obtain all of this and more because you are seen to uphold God's dues? All of this, even though you fell short in most of His dues, and gave little regard to the rights of His Imams... even though you squandered the rights of the weak while seeking your own, by neither spending wealth, nor risking your lives for the One who gave you them, nor opposing any group for the sake of God. Yet, in spite of this, you expect that God should grant you Paradise, lodge you with His messengers and keep you safe from punishment!?'

Then he said: 'I fear for you, O you who expect God's blessings, that His retribution might yet befall you. For by God's grace you have attained a favoured station – one who is known for the sake of God does not defer to another, and amongst His servants you are deferred to for His sake – but then you have seen God's covenants broken and not stirred; you would stir for the honour of your forefathers, yet you allow the honour of God's Messenger to be besmirched. The blind, mute and crippled are ignored in the cities; you show no compassion, nor do you use your position for good, nor do you help those who do. Instead you keep yourselves safe by flattering and accommodating the tyrants! God has commanded you to forbid these deeds and desist from them yourselves, and still you neglect your duties.

You are the most gravely afflicted of people because of the position you have obtained as scholars, if only you knew. That is because all of the divine ordinances are enacted upon the hands of those who know God and have been entrusted with keeping his laws. You are the ones who have plundered this station, and you have plundered it by no other means than abandoning the truth and disagreeing about the Sunna after having seen clear proof.

If only you would endure hardship and bear the burden of your responsibilities for the sake of God, then His ordinances would be restored to you, emanate from you and return to you.

But instead you have used your position to empower the oppressors and surrendered God's ordinances from your grasp; the rulers act upon conjectures and pursue worldly desires, and you have allowed them to do so because of your fear of death, your admiration of life and your cowardice. You have abandoned the weak to their hands; some were enslaved and others left without any means to seek sustenance.

The rulers fluctuate in their governance according to their desires and hold others in contempt on a whim, in imitation of evil men and out of insolence towards the Almighty. In every land they have one of their own preachers crowing from the pulpit, the land has no protection from them and in it they have a free hand; the people are their chattel and they offer them no protection. Some are obstinate dictators who pounce mercilessly upon the weak, they are obeyed but do not know their Origin or their Return.

How astonishing it is! And how can I not be astonished, when the land is left to be tyrannized, the charitable to be oppressed and the governor of the faithful is cruel to them!?

But God will judge concerning that about which we have quarrelled and pass sentence on that which we have differed.'

Then Hussein raised his hands in prayer and said: 'O God, you know that what we have said was not spoken out of ambition for power, nor desire for worldly vanities, but only to show others the signposts of your religion, raise the banner of reform in your lands, protect your oppressed servants and to see your ordinances and traditions implemented.'

Then he addressed those gathered: 'Verily if you will not help us or treat us justly, then the oppressors will gain authority over you and strive to extinguish the light of your prophet. God suffices for us, in Him do we place our trust, to Him do we turn and to Him is the return.'

Rahman: 'What Hussein said was very dangerous! Do you not think that the Umayyad clan would see that as a move against them and a call to rise up against them?'

Abdullah: 'They can see it however they want, but Hussein wanted the scholars, the Companions of the Prophet and the Successors to do their duty in calling others to the truth and bear their responsibilities in defending the weak and oppressed. This, remember, is after Hussein realized that there was no hope of Muawiya and his supporters of heeding sound advice. And Hussein was following the practice of the prophets and the legatees in doing so; first, they go to the rulers, advise them and defend the rights of the weak. But if that has no effect, they then turn to the Nation and at the first stage demand that those scholars who consume the sustenance of the people in the name of defending the religion take action. This is what Imam Hussein said to them.

So insofar as these scholars claim to speak in the name of religion, they have obtained a position of rank and authority amongst the people. Now the time has come in which they must genuinely speak in the name of the religion; they cannot suffice themselves with merely explaining laws governing personal matters such as the rules of ritual purity and impurity. And here lies the rub; this is the focal point of the Imam's speech. It reminds me of what his father said: 'The responsibility God has charged the scholars with is that they should not endure the gluttony of the oppressor or the hunger of the oppressed.'

Rahman: 'It would appear that a time of great difficulty and tribulation is upon us.'

Abdullah: 'We stand at a crossroads. If the Umayyad clan can paralyze the will of the Nation, misguide people and thereby raise up the wicked and abase the righteous, then they will do as previous nations did. In that they swerved from the guidance, principles and values of the prophets, then distort the religion itself, hollow it out and reduce it to nothing more than an appearance which they can wear as they please.'

Rahman says: 'But God has promised that He will protect this religion. He says in the Quran: 'Indeed We have sent down the Reminder, and indeed We will preserve it." So we do not need to fear, do we?'

Abdullah: 'Yes, except that God will allow things to happen through cause and effect; our Lord will protect this religion with the Household of His Prophet, just as He said during the Battle of the Confederates: 'and God spared the faithful of fighting.' God did not send down any angels to fight Amr b. Wadd or attack the polytheists to set them to flight. No, rather he sent Ali and granted him victory over Amr b. Wadd. So God spared the faithful of fighting through Ali. When He says: 'Indeed We have sent down the Reminder, and indeed We will preserve it' he uses the plural form, "We", meaning Himself, His angels and His *people*. Just as He says elsewhere in the Quran: 'Indeed We have warned you of a punishment near at hand' and He means that He has warned people by sending down Gabriel to His messenger and the latter warning his people.'

Rahman: 'Sometimes I wonder to myself: 'Are those who rule by the name of God's Messenger, sit in his place, and claim to be his successors, really believers in God and His messenger in their heart of hearts, even though they are sinners who contravene some of the divine laws? Or have they forgotten everything connected to their afterlife and in doing so become like all the oppressors in history who used religion and its values for their own ends – as a cloak for their own power and wrongdoing?'

Abdullah: 'Only God knows the contents of men's hearts, but the way they behave outwardly shows that the world is all these men care about. As for the Hereafter, they have left that for the Prophet's Household. The only reason they ever speak about God and His Messenger is to serve their own ends. And this is exactly what many rulers throughout history have done; they tell people whatever will keep them quiet while doing the very things they condemn. Do you not see, for example, that Muawiya, who spent his last days gripped by illness, said to his family: 'Put makeup on my eyes and oil my head.' So they did that and made his skin shine with oil. Then they prepared the dais for him and he sat, saying: 'Prop me up so that no one can see my weakness.'

Only then did he say: 'Permit the people to come and greet me standing. Do not allow anyone to sit.'

So a man came in and greeted him while standing, seeing him oiled and made-up. When he left, he said to himself: 'This is the healthiest man I ever did see!'

He wanted to show people that his health was as good as it had ever been. So once the people had begun to leave, he said to his family:

'Showing myself as hearty for these malicious people shows them
that I am not worn down by the vicissitudes of time
But when fate puts on her tresses
no amount of trickery will avail'

He said to his two daughters when his illness became severe and they were looking after him: 'You are looking after a cunning fox who amassed wealth from his youth until he crawled.' Then he recited the verses of poetry:

'I have strived for you as one strives with hardship, and spared you roaming and travelling from place to place'

Rahman: 'What did he mean "from his youth until he crawled"?'

Abdullah: 'He meant that he had amassed wealth since he was young until the age when he crawled along with a stick in hand. But had they been mindful of the Hereafter, even a little, they would have thought about where they were going to and not what they were leaving behind.

So you see, when Muawiya's illness became severe and saw that he would soon die, he said: 'Water! Water! As if he could see something. So he drank a lot of water without being able to quench his thirst. This persisted for a day or two. And when he came back to his senses, he shouted at the top of his lungs: 'What have I to do with you, O *Hujr b. 'Adi*! What have I to do with you, O Amr b. al-Hamq! What have I to do with you, O son of Abu Talib!'

Yazid said to him: 'O Commander of the Faithful! Hasten to take the pledge of allegiance for me before you die. The time has drawn near. If you do not mention the pledge of allegiance for me now, I fear I shall face from the family of *Abu Turāb* the like of that which you faced!'

Muawiya began to boil, saying: 'May my day from you be long, O Hujr!'

Rahman: 'Did none of them have any conscience to reproach them for what they were doing?'

Abdullah: 'Yes, and this is why they would sometimes say things in service of the truth, but their desires and worldly ambitions would then push them once again into the arms of falsehood. For example,

Muawiya once recited the verses of poetry:

'O if only I had not spent an hour in kingship / nor stumbled night-blind through pleasures,

And I was like one with just two dates to eat, living a little / while before I visited the people of the graves."

Rahman: 'Did Muawiya not fear what would happen to him after death?'

Abdullah: 'Sometimes he would, but he thought that he could trick his way into Paradise, just as he tricked his way through this worldly life. Muawiya is the one responsible for the death of Ali, the cousin of the Prophet, his brother and his legatee, and he caused the death of hundreds and thousands of people at the Battle of Siffin. He oppressed the Prophet's Household, killed Hasan b. Ali with poison and oppressed Hussein even though the blood of the Prophet ran in their veins... On his deathbed he requested that the fingernail clippings of God's Messenger be placed on his eyes. He said: 'God's Messenger clothed me in a shirt once, and I have kept it. He cut his nails in front of me, so I took the clippings and placed them in a jar. When I die, please dress me in that shirt, take out those clippings and put them in my eyes and mouth. Perhaps God will have mercy on me for the sake of their blessings!'

Then he recited the poetry of al-Ashhab:

'When I die so will generosity and people's calls will cease save for the smallest number,

And most of those who have gone abroad will return and take hold of this world and the religion once again.'

Sometimes he would speak to his Lord, saying:

'If you dispute [with me], then disputing with you O Lord shall be

Punishment, and I cannot bear punishment.

Or overlook [my faults], for you are a Lord

who brushes the sins from the sinner as though they were dust.'

So Muawiya lived between the reproach of his conscience and his love of this world and worldly power. But it was ultimately his love of this world that won out. This is why as his illness progressed and his fear of leaving this world increased, he would reaffirm his intention to take the pledge of allegiance for Yazid.

One day, al-Dhahhak said to him: 'O Commander of the Faithful! People have quickly become confused, boisterous and seditious while you still live, so what will happen should the unthinkable occur? What do you think people's state will be?'

Muslim b. Uqba said to him: 'We see the people and hear their words, and we think that the matter of Yazid's succession is of the utmost importance to him and that it will satisfy the people too. So hasten to take the pledge of allegiance for him while you can still speak.'

He said: 'You have spoken truthfully, O Muslim! My opinion has not changed concerning Yazid – will the people settle for anyone else? I hope that the Caliphate will remain amongst my descendants until the Day of Recompense, and that the descendants of *Abu Turāb* may never have authority over those of Abu Sufiyan.'

The family of Abu Sufiyan saw this matter in a completely tribal manner, as they would have done during the Age of Ignorance. They still saw religion first and foremost as a source of power and therefore to be inherited by their own descendants rather than those of Ali and the Hashemite clan, who were all descended from the grandfather of the Prophet and included the descendants of the Prophet himself!

Look at his testament to Yazid! He says: 'My son, I have laid all things out for you, humbled your enemies and forced your allegiance upon the people's necks. Be attentive to the people of Mecca and Medina and treat them well, for they are your base and your origin. Whoever of them comes to visit you, treat him well. And whoever does not, make sure you send for him for the sake of maintaining ties with him.

But watch out for the people of Iraq, for they are a people accustomed to defaming the rulers and tire of them quickly. Every day they will ask you to change your governor over them, so do it.

And be attentive to the people of Syria and make them your closest friends, confidants and protectors. If you doubt anyone's loyalty, then throw them to the Syrians. And once they have finished with them, keep the Syrians close to you, for I worry that they might be led astray should they go abroad...' – meaning that he thought they should be kept in Syria so that they never hear anything contrary to the regime's version of events, and so can be used to fight against the righteous; Muawiya fears that they will become righteous, but he calls this 'being led astray'! – God has relieved you of the burden of Rahman b. Abu Bakr, because he has died. Now I only fear for you from Hussein, Ibn Umar and Ibn Zubayr. As for Hussein, I do not doubt that he will move against you, but those who killed his father and wounded his brother will suffice you against him. Indeed the descendants of Abu Talib have stuck out their necks so far that the Arabs will never allow them to be their leaders...' – do you see how Muawiya's words have no connection to the religion or moral values; he only speaks of Arabs, of tribes and of kingship!

Then he said: 'As for Ibn Umar, his faith prevents him from arguing with you. But Ibn Zubayr is a venomous snake. When he comes out to you, do not let him go for he has not the stamina for a prolonged struggle.'

Then he said: 'My son, for your sake I have preferred this world over the hereafter, usurped the rights of *Ali b. Abu Tālib* and born the burden of this upon my back.'

He added: 'This is my ambition for you and your children after you, so pay attention to the advice I am about to give you for you will praise God for its outcome, and by God's praise you will take matters firmly in your hand.

Pay attention. If you should encounter misfortune, then be aggressive and bold; do not display the weakness of a shrinking coward. I have taken care of everything for your succession and laid out the empire for you, my son! I have humbled the stubborn Arabs, lit the path, smoothed the way, amassed wealth and prepared the kingdom for you after me. So you must take care of matters near at hand, which are easily resolved, and you must show strength as soon as you are disobeyed.'

Do you see how Muawiya's sole preoccupation is worldly power and how to secure it, whether by crushing dissent or amassing wealth? There is no mention of moral values or right conduct; you will never find the houses of the Umayyad clan filled with discussion of what God desires or what the Prophet commanded. Instead, you will find them speaking as kings naturally do to their children, or as talking like all leaders and chieftains. And this is what the Prophet's Household wanted people to see so that they would know that their enemies have no connection to the religion, nor do they have any interest except worldly power and wealth.

After this discussion, Rahman and Abdullah bid one another farewell and parted company. They did not meet again until after Muawiya had died, when Abdullah b. Muslim went to perform Umra at the end of the month of Rajab. Muawiya had died in the middle of the same month, aged seventy seven. It was the year 60 AH.

Rahman: 'So, Muawiya has perished! Do you think something might happen?'

Abdullah: 'Things will happen.'

Rahman: [smiling] 'And I suppose you have knowledge of the unseen?'

Abdullah: 'No, but this is the logic of life. Hussein will not stay quiet in the face of falsehood and there is no covenant between him and Yazid as there was between him and Yazid's father. One of the main points of that covenant was, by the way, that Hussein would be given power and allowed to lead the Nation after Muawiya if his brother Hasan was not still alive. But Muawiya broke this agreement, while Hussein kept to his brother's word.'

Rahman: 'Do you think that it was right for Hussein to uphold their agreement when Muawiya did not afford him the same courtesy?'

Abdullah: 'That is the difference between the people of truth and the people of falsehood. The Prophet maintained the treaty of Hudaybiyya; if any of the polytheists came to him, he had to hand them over to the Meccans. But if a Muslim fled to Mecca, they did not hand him over to the Prophet. And even though the Meccans did not keep to this after the treaty of Hudaybiyya, the Prophet did. He even handed over one of the Muslims who had fled the persecution of the Quraysh, saying to the fugitive: 'Do not fear. God will grant you relief and an escape.'

Now Muawiyah is dead, Hussein has not pledged allegiance to Yazid and he is not bound by any agreement to keep the peace with him.'

Rahman: 'Do you think Yazid will try and force him to pledge allegiance?'

Abdullah laughed: 'It seems that you do not know who we are talking about! Of course he will try – he has no compunction in striking of Hussein's head should he not comply. As Marwan b. al-Hakam said, he is an inexperienced boy surrounded by men like Dhahhak b. Qays and Muslim b. Uqba who will encourage him to do so. But more dangerous than any of them is his father's old advisor, Sir John, who has no care for the Nation because he has no connection to it. Perhaps he even means to work for its destruction.

My friend, Yazid is a base and reckless man. He has no care for the religion save for kingship and frivolity. Strangest of all is what he did while his father was at death's door, overcome by his illness and speaking nonsense. He would say: 'How far is *Ghūṭa*?' And his daughter would tell him: 'O how you suffer, father!' And he would say: 'If you go to it, you will see how beautiful it is!'

While his father lay on his deathbed, Yazid would go out hunting in Hawran – a region in Syria – and tell Dhahhak, who was the head of Muawiya's police: 'Keep an eye on things here and do not hide anything from me about the Commander of the Faithful.'

Abdullah b. Muslim said to his friend: 'You know better than me the situation in Syria. Tell me, what has happened there since Muawiya's death?'

Rahman: 'Dhahhak b. Qays came to the central mosque after Muawiya's death and ascended the pulpit with Muawiya's shroud in hand and said: 'O people! Muawiya the son of Abu Sufiyan was one of God's servants, whom God gave authority over his servants. He lived by Divine Providence (qadar) and died at an appointed time (ajal). This is his shroud as you see it; we shall raise him up in it, lower him into his grave and leave him alone with his Lord. Whomsoever of you desires to participate in his funeral, then let him come after midday prayers.

Then he came down from the pulpit and the people dispersed, and once they had offered their midday prayers, they gathered and made ready for the funeral, then carried him to his grave.

Then Dhahhak wrote a letter to Yazid and said: 'To the servant of God, Yazid, the Commander of the Faithful. From Dhahhak b. Qays. Peace be with you. I write to you with both congratulations and condolences. I congratulate you on your accession to the Caliphate and offer you my condolences on the death of your father, the Commander of the Faithful, Muawiya. To God we belong and to Him we return. When you read this letter of mine, then make haste! We must take the pledge of the allegiance from the people again. God's peace, mercy and blessings be with you.'

Yazid came to Damascus, arriving three days after his father's burial. He went to his grave and lamented for a while, reciting poetry:

'Came the messenger with scrolls in haste
our heart overcome with apprehension at their sight
Said we: 'Woe to you! What is in these scrolls of yours?'
Pained, he said: 'The Caliph was yesterday interred.'
The ground shook beneath us or almost did
as though honour itself had been torn from its roots
The son of Hind has died and nobility with him too
just as they had always lived side-by-side
The fairest day who quenched the thirst of clouds
even if people contend with their good senses
They will never produce anything close, however hard they try
to do so, nor will they weaken what he did."

Abdullah: 'Did you know that these last two verses belong to the famous pre-Islamic poet *A'shā*, who uttered them in praise of God's Messenger? Though it is hardly surprising for someone who steals the Caliphate to steal the praise of God's Messenger with two verses in praise of him and use them to praise his own father! What did he do after that?'

Rahman: 'He got up from his father's grave and went to the Green Palace, where a place had been prepared for him. He sat on the throne and demanded that people pledge allegiance to him, which they did once again.

After that, he addressed the people and began to praise his father, saying: 'The Commander of the Faithful, Muawiya was like a loving father to you. He was the most noble and praiseworthy of the Arabs; the most important and famous of them; the one with the greatest deeds, the broadest merit and the most towering figure of them. His eloquence was flawless and his logic irrefutable until the day he left this world and went into the mercy of his Lord.'

Then a man at the back stood up and shouted out: 'By God, you lie! Muawiya was nothing like this – these are the qualities of God's Messenger, these are his manners, and neither you nor your father have any such manners!'

A commotion broke out as an attempt was made to seize the man, but they could not find him. A man called Atta b. Abi Siffi, one of Muawiya's lackeys, turned to Yazid and said: 'O Commander of the Faithful, pay no heed to your enemies. God has given you the Caliphate after your father. You are our Caliph and your son, Muawiya is your successor. We want no one else, nor will we seek any recourse to change.'

CRISIS OF LEGITIMACY

When an autocrat dies, anarchy naturally ensues. This is especially true of a tyrant who reigned for as long as Muawiya did and whose every dictate was unquestioningly obeyed. Much like his life, Muawiya's death threw the entire Muslim world into disarray; those who had endured the violence of the former regime saw an opportunity to rise up and demand a restoration of their rights, while those who had fled its persecution returned to their homes.

Taking the view that this crisis of legitimacy had already begun during Muawiya's reign, it is clear why such tense conditions prevailed in all quarters – most especially in Iraq, where Imam Ali had situated his capital. After all, it had only been possible for Muawiya to seize power from Ali by virtue of the latter's assassination; true legitimacy was and had always been with Ali and his sons. The people of Iraq had offered fierce resistance to the Syrian army. Their eventual submission to Muawiya was only given at the point of a sword; they neither believed that he was the rightful leader of the Muslims nor did they think he was a particularly desirable head of state.

As for the new ruler, Yazid, his authority was almost unanimously rejected by the People of Loosing and Binding (those with authority and respect) and most of the ordinary people too. The regime's only real supporters were the Umayyad clan, its henchmen and those persons who had some personal interest staked in the success of the dynasty.

The same was true with regards to the situation in the Hejaz.

So the new ruler, to whom allegiance had already been pledged more than once during his father's lifetime, sensed in the depths of his soul that his position as Caliph lacked legitimacy. For this reason, as soon as his father died, Yazid sent letters to all of his governors demanding that they take the pledge of allegiance once gain. In these letters, he singled out for mention those individuals who occupied a special place in the hearts of the people.

Letters were sent to Nu'man b. al-Bashir, the governor of Kufa, to Ubaydullah b. Ziyad, the governor of Basra, to Walid b. Utba, the governor of Medina and to Amr b. Sa'eed al-Ashdaq, the governor of Mecca, containing orders to take the pledge of allegiance from the people with the utmost urgency.

But amongst all the letters Yazid sent, that addressed to Walid b. Utba, which was dispatched with Abdullah b. Umar b. Uways, was truly unusual. At first glance, it read like any other letter: 'Muawiya b. Abu Sufiyan was one of God's servants. God ennobled him, made him Caliph, vested him with authority and established his rule. He lived by divine providence and died at an appointed time. May God have mercy upon him, for in life he was praised and died righteous and god-fearing; he was the best Caliph. But I need not attest to his good character before God, for God knows him better than I. And he has made a covenant with me and appointed me as his successor. When you read this letter of mine, take the pledge of allegiance from the people of Medina. Peace.'

As it would appear, this is an ordinary letter from a new ruler to one of his governors, and one which we would not expect to have any special outcomes had Yazid not secreted in it another message to Walid written on a tiny piece of paper. In this second message, he wrote: 'As for what follows, seize Hussein, Abdullah b. Umar and Abdullah b. Zubayr and take their pledge of allegiance forcefully, without showing any leniency or indulgence until they pledge allegiance. Should any of them refuse to pledge, you are hereby ordered to strike off their heads and send them to me.'

What is truly strange is that Yazid instructs his governor to strike off the head of someone for merely refusing to pledge allegiance, even if they do not openly voice their opposition, stir up rebellion or raise the flag of resistance! Yes, simply by refusing to give their allegiance to the new regime, a person's life was forfeit. This is even though God's Messenger never did such a thing and God has said in the Quran: "[This is] the truth from your Lord: let anyone who wishes believe it, and let anyone who wishes disbelieve it." And He says: 'There is no compulsion in religion.' God commanded His prophet to leave the Jews and Christians alone so long as they did not persecute people following the new religion.

More importantly, God has never ordered the faithful to cut off the heads of those who do not believe in him, and even has gone so far as to rebuke one of His greatest prophets, Jonah, because he lost patience with his people and invoked God's punishment upon them because they refused to believe in Him. But God said: 'And the Man of the Fish, when he left in a rage, thinking that We would not put him to hardship. Then he cried out in the darkness, 'There is no god except You! You are immaculate! I have indeed been among the wrongdoers!"

So how can a ruler who claims to be following the example of God's Messenger, less than forty years after the latter has passed away, allow himself to force people to pledge allegiance to him and order them executed should they refuse?

Moreover, the people whom he ordered executed in this manner were no ordinary people. No, each one of them was afforded almost heroic status by the Nation, not least "the Leader of the Youth of

Paradise", Hussein b. Ali b. Abu Talib, the son of Fatima and grandson of God's Messenger. He, about whom the Companions heard his grandfather extol many times, for example: 'Hussein is of me and I am of Hussein' and: 'Hasan and Hussein are the leaders of the youth of Paradise.' And: 'Indeed Hussein b. Ali in the heavens is greater than he is in the earth, for indeed it is written on the right-hand of God's throne: 'Hussein is the lantern of guidance and the ark of salvation.'

People had seen how the Prophet would treat Hussein; he would place Hussein and his brother on his shoulders and walk with them through the markets, saying: 'The best vehicle is your vehicle, and the best passengers are the two of you!'

In any case, the affection people bore God's Messenger and his Household was at that time focused on Hussein. So how can a frivolous youth like Yazid demand that Hussein pledge allegiance to him and threaten to cut off his head should he refuse?

Truly, the reign of Muawiya had been a dark time, in which the Nation had been completely led astray. During that time, all importance was given to the ruler, to the extent that when you read the history of that era, there are no reports about the people, only reports about Muawiya – an act, an order, an edict, and nothing more! It as though the Nation did not exist at all, for if it had, it would have certainly accomplished things. But Muawiya had led them astray, raised the status of his own tribe and devoted all of his attention to a single purpose; securing his own power, like any other Caesar or Khosrow!

It was a time in which darkness enveloped the land, and righteous persons were completely excluded from any and all positions of influence. But when Muawiya died, the Nation was on the verge of falling into a pit that was darker still, and in which they would suffer tyranny that was as yet unimaginable.

It was in conditions such as these that one of our two friends, *Rahman al-Ṣāliḥ* travelled to Kufa and visited the other, *Abdullah b. Mus-*

lim. And, as always, their conversation quickly turned to politics.

This was one week after Muawiya's death and information about what was going on in the centres of power was tightly controlled, especially with regards to the governor of Medina.

Rahman asked his friend if he had any news about what was happening.

Abdullah: 'I have heard that Yazid sent a letter to Walid b. Utba, in which he eulogized Muawiya and commanded Walid to take the pledge of allegiance from the people, especially from Hussein b. Ali, Abdullah b. Zubayr, and Abdullah b. Umar, and to strike off the heads of anyone who refused to do so.'

Rahman: 'And what did Walid do?'

Abdullah: 'Walid was mortified by the contents of Yazid's letter. And since he had no experience of dealing with orders such as these, he called for Marwan b. al-Hakam, who had previously been the governor of Medina for Muawiya. There was little love lost between these two men; Marwan would not come to Walid unless he was compelled to do so. But when Walid read Yazid's letter, he was forced to seek Marwan's advice. So he called him to the governor's palace and informed him of Muawiya's death, then gave him the letter to read, before asking: 'What do you think?'

Marwan read the letter and replied: 'You must immediately send for those persons mentioned and invite them to pledge allegiance. If they comply and offer their allegiance, not a single Muslim will oppose Yazid. So hurry before word of Muawiya's death spreads and they refuse you.'

Walid said: 'And if they should refuse...?'

Marwan replied: 'Then you go and cut off their heads before they realize that Muawiya is dead. If they realize he is dead, every one of them will take flight in a different direction and each will launch an insurrection in his own name."

Rahman: 'He gave the order to cut off their heads should they refuse with such ease!?'

Abdullah: 'As I told you, Marwan wanted the Caliphate for himself and he was planning ahead for that end. It was in his interest that Yazid should perpetrate some atrocity so that matters would quickly spiral out of control and Marwan could make his own play for power. He had no loyalty to Yazid whatsoever – you will remember that he was one of those who opposed pledging allegiance to Yazid in the first place. If it was not for Muawiya's threat to remove him from power and the latter's offer to shower him with wealth, he would not have taken the pledge of allegiance for Yazid from the people at all. This is in addition to the fact that he was an enemy of the Hashemite clan; he was one of those who had mustered armies to fight against Imam Ali during the latter's reign.'

Rahman: 'You mean that Marwan was neither thinking of his own place in the Hereafter, nor of Yazid's interests in this world?'

Abdullah: 'That's right. So he didn't just advise Walid to cut off Hussein's head, he insisted upon it! One of the things he said was: 'The family of *Abu Turāb* are our ancient enemies.' By this he meant that they were their enemies since the time of God's Messenger, when both he, Muawiya and Abu Sufiyan had fought against the Muslims (and continued to fight them now)! To this he added: 'O governor, if you do not hasten to take the pledge from Hussein b. Ali in particular, I cannot guarantee that you will not lose standing in the eyes of the Commander of the Faithful.'

Walid said: 'Wait a minute! Woe to you! Enough of such talk; you will speak well of the Son of Fatima, for he is the scion of the prophets!' He added: 'Heaven forbid, shall I kill Hussein if he does not pledge allegiance?!'

GOVERNOR'S MANSION

Even though Walid b. Utba was averse to confronting Hussein in light of the latter's esteemed position in the eyes of all Muslims, and especially the people of Hejaz and Iraq, he was still Muawiya and Yazid's governor in Medina and one of those loyal to the Umayyad Clan. He dwelt in a state of limbo; caught between his own interests with the regime, in addition to his own background and upbringing which was very much rooted in opposition to the Prophet's Household, and between his own mind and conscience which bid him to respect Hussein and not to follow Yazid's orders. In any case, he had to do something. So he listened to the advice of Marwan b. al-Hakam and immediately – in the middle of the night – sent for the grandson of Uthman b. Affan, Abdullah b. Amr, and said: 'Go to Hussein and Abdullah b. Zubayr and summon them to my presence.'

So this man went out in search of them and found them in the Prophet's mosque beside the grave of God's Messenger. He said to them: 'Respond to the summons of the governor Walid, for he requires your presence.'

They said: 'Go. We will come now.'

Once he had left the Mosque, Abdullah b. Zubayr said to Hussein: 'What do you think has caused the governor to summon us at such an hour? He does not normally hold meetings at this time.'

Summoning these two men to the governor's palace at this late hour was strange indeed and suggested that something important was taking place. Hussein replied: 'I suspect that the tyrant has perished, so they have sent for us to give allegiance to his son, before word reaches the people.'

Ibn Zubayr said: 'I do not think it could be anything else. What do you plan to do, O Abu Abdullah?'

Hussein said: 'I will go to him.'

Ibn Zubayr said: 'I fear for your safety should you be alone with him.'

Hussein said: 'I would not go to him unless I was able to refuse [to pledge allegiance.]'

And to ensure that the governor could not kill him, Hussein did not go directly to the governor's mansion as summoned. Rather, he first went to his home and gathered nineteen men, including his half-brother, Abbas and his son, Ali al-Akbar, and told them to bring swords concealed under their robes. He told them: 'I will go in to see the man. If you hear my voice become raised, then attack. Otherwise, do nothing until I come out to you.'

It was late at night and the streets of Medina were empty. Hussein and his companions walked quietly until they reached the governors palace. Hussein went in alone and left his men in a place where they could hear his voice should he raise it. He went in and sat next to Walid, then saw that Marwan was with him. As I said, there was little affection between Walid and Marwan, so at this point Hussein realized that he had been right to suspect that Muawiya was dead. These two pillars of the Umayyad house – with their intense dislike for one another – would not have been together at such an hour except for the gravest of reasons, such as the fear that the Caliphate might slip from their grasp, especially since the majority of the Muslims at that time were waiting for any opportunity to get rid of those who would turn the Caliphate into the hereditary title of the Umayyad clan, seize the people's property, aggress against their rights, put out the eyes of their opponents and kill those who stood against them.

Once Hussein was seated with them, Walid informed him of Muawiya's death and read Yazid's letter commanding him to take the pledge of allegiance from the people.

Hussein said: 'Someone like me does not pledge allegiance in secret. So when you have summoned the people to pledge allegiance, summon us with them, and then we will be on a single affair.'

It appeared as though Walid was satisfied with these words, but Marwan turned to him and said: 'Governor! If Hussein leaves you now without pledging allegiance, you will never have another opportunity such as this without an abundance of bloodshed between you. Either detain him until he pledges allegiance or cut off his head!'

Signs of anger appeared on Hussein's face, for he was the grandson of God's Messenger, the son of Ali and Fatima, and a man such as Marwan – whom his father, Ali, had described as the 'lizard son of a lizard' – had the impudence to order him arrested and compelled to give allegiance, or to strike off his head!

Hussein lept towards him and raised his voice: 'Governor! We are the Prophet's Household, the source of prophetic knowledge, the locus of the angel's visitation, the receptacle of revelation, by whom God has opened and sealed. Meanwhile, Yazid is a profligate sinner, a winebibber, a murderer of innocents and one cursed with impiety and indecency. Someone like me does not pledge allegiance to someone like him, but let us both sleep on it and see whom of us is more entitled to receive the pledge of allegiance and the Caliphate on the morrow.'

Hussein's men outside heard the commotion and burst into the meeting. Walid and Marwan were alarmed and allowed Hussein to depart with them unmolested.

Marwan said to Walid: 'You disobeyed me! By God you will not have another opportunity such as this, Hussein will never surrender himself to you again.'

So Walid – who still had some vestiges of a conscience left and knew Hussein's worth and position in the eyes of the people – said: 'Blame someone other than yourself, Marwan! You wanted me to do something that would have ruined my religion and my worldly affairs. Shall I kill Hussein simply because he says: 'I will not pledge allegiance'? By God, I do not think the man who meets his maker with the blood of Hussein on his hands shall weigh lightly on the Day of Resurrection, nor shall God have any regard for him or absolve him of blame. Rather he shall have a painful punishment!'

The meeting ended with Walid and Marwan exchanging rebukes with one another. As for Hussein, he returned safely to his home and told him men to return to theirs.

Hussein had uttered his brief speech in the presence of two pillars of the Umayyad regime; the former governor of Medina, Marwan b. al-Hakam and the current one, Walid b. Utba. Both of them had been appointed by Muawiya and relied upon by him to keep the city in line. Hussein's words were: 'We are the Household of the Prophet, the source of prophetic knowledge, the locus of the angel's visitation, the treasure-trove of knowledge and the house of revelation. By us does God open and seal. Meanwhile, Yazid is a winebibber, a profligate sinner, a murderer of innocents, and the likes of me does not pledge allegiance to the likes of him.' This is tantamount to an exposition of the principles on which Hussein would base his uprising, in which he would bear the banner of the prophets and their successors, and which – in line with his position as an Imam – would make him the inheritor of Adam, Abel, Noah, Abraham, Moses, Jesus, Muhammad and Ali.

His refusal to pledge allegiance, even under duress, was very important indeed, because God's *people* are distinguished by the fact that, once they have given their allegiance (even if they are forced to do so), they abide by its conditions. In the same way, even if they conclude a treaty under duress, they abide by its stipulations. This was the practice of God's Messenger with regards to the treaty of Hudaybiyya, which came at a time of extreme pressure, and in which he was forced to accept the conditions offered to him by the Quraysh. But despite this, he abided by it even though the Quraysh frequently disregarded it.

In the same way, Imam Ali accepted a ceasefire with Muawiya during the Battle of Siffin, and continued to abide by it, even though many of his companions were urging him to re-open hostilities with Muawiya. But he refused to do so, because he accepted the conditions of ceasefire.

Hasan b. Ali continued this practice in his peace-treaty with Muawiya b. Abu Sufiyan, which he was ultimately compelled to sign by the treachery of his own supporters. And Hussein also abided by the treaty which his brother had signed, even after the latter's death, and for this reason Hussein refused to pledge allegiance to Yazid under any circumstances, even in secret.

This quality is what distinguishes God's *people* from others, who have no compunction in doing one thing in private and another in public. So, for example, they would pledge allegiance privately and then publicly contravene that, or the opposite. Or they would tell people whatever the latter want to hear, then do the opposite themselves.

But God's *people* are true to themselves because they are true to their

Lord and this means they are true to the people as well. They have nothing they wish to hide from anyone. This is the meaning of what Hussein said: 'Someone like me does not pledge allegiance in secret.' For if he was willing to pledge allegiance in secret, there was nothing stopping him from pledging allegiance in public. By the same token, if he would not pledge allegiance in public, he would not do so in secret either.

In addition to the fact that Hussein's goal was to launch a corrective uprising which would restore the importance of the religion's essence as well as its appearance, which was starting to shake during the reign of Yazid, who would openly sin and commit indecency before leading prayers, a function which had by now become a symbol of worldly power rather than a display of reverence towards God. So when he stood up to lead prayers it was to affirm his authority and display his power. And when he went to make the Hajj pilgrimage, it was not to demonstrate his servitude to God and abase himself before his Creator, no, it was simply to show his own power and authority.

The same is true with regards to the religion's essence, which taught that people's rights must be respected, that justice must be done and that the weak should be protected from harm. Under Yazid, everything was turned on its head; the very sword that God's Messenger had once directed against the polytheist tyrants and oppressors, the sword which had been used to defend the oppressed was now turned against the oppressed, just as the appearance of the religion had now been turned against its essence.

Because Imam Hussein kept his intentions entirely pure, and was not seeking power but rather seeking the truth, he was ready to die defending this truth. And the authorities knew this about him; they knew that he would not give up his principles or his values, and that they could not buy him for any price; he would not surrender his beliefs.

Hussein sensed, in his heart of hearts, that the banner which had been carried by the prophets throughout history was now in his hand, and their duty which they had discharged in their own nations had now fallen to him. The time was right for him to awaken the Nation just as the prophets had awakened their own, and for him to lead a small band of his closest family and followers to face the dictatorial system at whose head sat Yazid b. Muawiya, who observed neither kinship nor covenant for the sake of God. From the moment he became crown prince, right up until the death of his father, he did not concern himself with even the pretence of justice or innocence from killing the righteous in public. Hussein knew that he would have to bear hardship just as the prophets had before him, and he knew that every manner of affliction which had befallen the prophets would befall him also.

So if there had been a prophet who had been forced to emigrate in the way of God, then Hussein would have to bear emigration for the sake of God. If there had been a prophet who had been persecuted, then Hussein would have to endure persecution. If there had been a prophet who had suffered attempts on his life, then Hussein would have to suffer attempts on his life. If there had been a prophet who had offered his son as a martyr in the way of God, then Hussein would have to offer his own sons as martyrs in the way of God. And if there had been a prophet whose family had been taken captive, then Husseins family too would suffer captivity.'

In Mecca, Rahman meets his friend, Abdullah, while performing the rites of Umra. Rumors on what transpired between Hussein and two pillars of the regime are already being heard, suggesting that Hussein as publicly and unambiguously stated that he will never pledge allegiance to Yazid. The regime is reported to be furious, because its supporters know that the Caliphate may soon return to its rightful claimants, and its rightful claimants are none other than the Household of the Prophet.

'Do you think it will come to a confrontation?' wondered Rahman.
'All knowledge is with God. What is certain is that God's Messenger foretold that Hussein would be slain, and I doubt that he will be

slain at the hands of anyone except the most detestable creature in God's eyes. There is usually a correspondence in the confrontation between truth and falsehood; the loftier the rank of the representative of truth, the baser the character of his opponent. Don't you see that Ali b. Abu Talib, being who he is, was slain by someone virtually unknown - Rahman b. Muljam – who was motivated by his lust for a woman in return for a thousand dirhams as payment for the dangerous crime he was about to commit?

Have you not heard the words of God's Messenger which he uttered to Ali as the latter went to face Amr b. Wadd: 'Faith itself has come out to face polytheism'? So to the extent that Ali embodied faith itself, Amr b. Wadd embodied falsehood and infidelity. So I do not doubt that Yazid b. Muawiya is going to kill Hussein.'

Rahman: 'Will he give no consideration to Hussein's position in the eyes of the people?'

Abdullah: 'If only he would consider Hussein's position in the eyes of God, we would have thought he might consider his position in the people's eyes too. This man wants to do something, something that will change the course of this religion forever and destroy its teachings once and for all. Not only that, but he is conceited in the extreme too. Don't you see how he demanded that Walid b. Utba either take the pledge of allegiance from Hussein or cut off his head?'

Rahman: 'Do you not think that Hussein, for his part, will avoid direct confrontation so that he will not be slain at Yazid's hand?'

Abdullah: 'Hussein is destined for martyrdom. The prophets gave glad tidings of martyrdom to their successors, and the Prophet gave glad tidings of it to his household as well.'

Rahman: 'And when did that happen?'

Abdullah: 'God's Messenger wept when Hussein was born. And when he was asked about it he said: 'This child of mine will be betrayed and slain!' Then he raised his hands in prayer and said: 'O God! Bless him when he is slain and make him a master of martyrs, and bless not his killer or those who will betray him!'

Rahman: 'If that is the case, Yazid will without doubt try to kill Hussein. Why has that not happened from the beginning? I mean why has the regime waited so long to kill him?'

Abdullah: 'For two reasons. First of all, Walid b. Utba was hesitant in carrying out Yazid's command from the very beginning, especially that some of the people around him did not think it prudent to harm Hussein. Not least of these was his wife, Asmaa b. Rahman b. al-Harith b. Hisham. She chided him for his treatment of Hussein, asking him: 'Did you speak abusively to Hussein?'

Walid said: 'He abused me first."

Rahman: 'And did Hussein abuse him first?'

Abdullah: 'No, but when Marwan advised him to strike off Hussein's head if he did not pledge allegiance, Hussein said: 'O son of a blue-eyed woman! Are you going to kill me, or him? By God you have lied and sinned gravely!'

Rahman: 'So what was the response of Walid's wife?'

Abdullah: 'She said: 'If Hussein abuses you, will you abuse him? And if he abuses your father, will you abuse his?"

Rahman: 'What was the second reason that the regime had not moved to kill Hussein until now?'

Abdullah: 'They were preoccupied with Abdullah b. Zubayr; they feared what he might do more than what Hussein might, because they saw Ibn Zubayr as a man like themselves – a man who had no compunction in deceiving the masses, engaging in assassinations or bribing some governors here and there, just as they might have done in a similar situation. So they devoted their attention to him rather than Hussein. Walid had to send a number of messengers demanding Ibn Zubayr's presence in the governors palace. But in the same night that Hussein had gone to him, Abdullah b. Zubayr refused to go and remained in his house instead. Whenever Walid's messengers came to him, he would say: 'Do not rush me, I will come to you!' Walid even sent some of his bondsmen after him to revile him, saying: 'O son of an old woman! Come to the governor or we will kill you!'

So Ibn Zubayr replied: 'I'm coming, I'm coming!'

Then he sent his brother, Ja'far b. Zubayr, to Walid. He told him: 'For heaven's sake, leave Abdullah alone. You've made him paranoid with all the messengers you have been sending after him. God willing, he will come to you tomorrow.'

So Walid desisted from sending his messengers, and this is how Abdullah duped them. That very night – on Saturday, three nights before the end of Rajab, sixty years after Hijra – he left the city and took the back roads to Mecca with his brother, steering well clear of the highway. The next morning, Walid sent for him, but no one could find him. Marwan said: 'I suspect he has gone to Mecca.' So Walid sent Habib b. Kuwayn after him with thirty horsemen loyal to the Umayyad clan. But they could not find Abdullah or his brother because they had not taken the direct route. So the regime was too busy hunting Ibn Zubayr to worry about Hussein.'

Rahman: 'So what happened in the end between Hussein and Walid b. Utba?'

Abdullah: Walid wrote to Yazid appraising him of the situation in Medina and informing him about what had happened with Ibn Zubayr. Then he mentioned Hussein and said: 'Hussein sees himself as under no obligation to obey us or maintain allegiance to us.'

When this letter reached Yazid, he flew into such a rage that he went blind. He wrote back to Walid, saying: 'From God's servant, Yazid, the Commander of the Faithful, to Walid b. Utba. When you receive this letter, take another pledge of allegiance from the people of Medina as an assurance from them. Leave Abdullah b. Zubayr aside; he will not escape us and will not succeed against us so long as we still draw breath. With your response to this letter there shall be the head of Hussein b. Ali. Once you have done this, I shall give you a free-reign, an abundant reward and the greatest prize of all. Peace.'

Rahman: 'So why didn't Walid do as he was told, in spite of Yazid's severe tone?'

Abdullah: 'Walid b. Utba did not see himself as any lower in rank or status than Yazid in the Umayyad clan, just as he saw no reason to kill Hussein so long as he was merely refusing to pledge allegiance while not engaging in any other seditious activities. It seems that what remained of his conscience restrained him from enacting Yazid's command. He commented on Yazid's letter: 'By God, I will not let God see me as the killer of Hussein, the son of God's Messenger, even if Yazid gave me the whole world and all it contains!'

Rahman: 'But how can you say that the regime was preoccupied with Abdullah b. Zubayr rather than Hussein, when the former had already escaped their grasp and fled to Mecca?'

Abdullah: Abdullah b. Zubayr was supported by many important figures in Medina, so Walid was busy monitoring them and having them imprisoned. Some of those he imprisoned on that day were Umar b. al-Khattab's cousin, *Abdullah b. Muṭīʿ al-ʿUdawī, Muṣʿab b. Rahman b. ʿAwf al-Zuhrī*, and many others. The situation was so severe that some men from the Udayy clan had to go to Abdullah b. Umar and ask him to intercede on their behalf to have their kinsman released.

It is said that some of them threatened to take up arms to release *Abdullah b. Muṭīʿ*. They told Abdullah b. Umar: 'Our kinsman, *Abdullah b. Muṭīʿ* has been imprisoned wrongly and without having committed any crime. By God, you will either get him out of jail or we will die trying!'

Abdullah b. Umar told them: 'Don't be so hasty to start sedition!' Then he sent word to Marwan b. al-Hakam inviting him to a meeting, then he asked him to leave alone *Abdullah b. Muṭī'* and release him from prison. One of the things he told Marwan was: 'I do not know if you have any recourse against our friend, nor any right to detain him. So if you claim that you had just cause to imprison him, then do so, but if you have only imprisoned him on the basis of suspicion, then we cannot allow our friend to be unjustly imprisoned.'

Marwan responded: 'We have only detained him at the behest of the Commander of the Faithful, Yazid, and you will have to take up the matter with him. We will do likewise and you shall have what you desire.'

But the Udayy clan did not wait to write to Yazid and receive his response. Instead, they assaulted the prison and released their kinsmen, as well as anyone else who happened to be in the cells with them.

It was these incidents that distracted the regime's attention from Hussein.'

Rahman: 'So tell me – what did Hussein do after that night?'

Abdullah: 'Hussein awoke the next morning and left his house. Then, there was Marwan b. Hakam blocking his way! Marwan said to him: 'Abu Abdullah, let me give you some advice which will lead you aright.'

Hussein said: 'And what is that?'

Marwan told him: 'I say to you: pledge allegiance to Yazid, for this is better for you in this world and the next.'

Hussein said: 'To God we belong and to Him we return... may Islam rest in peace should this Nation be afflicted with a shepherd such as Yazid!'

Then he said: 'O Marwan, do you advise me to pledge allegiance to Yazid while he is a profligate sinner? I have told you time and again. But I do not blame you for insisting, for someone who has been cursed by God's Messenger cannot be reproached for calling others to pledge allegiance to someone like Yazid.'

He added: 'Away with you, Marwan! We are the Household of the Prophet, the truth is in us and is pronounced upon our tongues. I heard my grandfather, God's Messenger say: 'The Caliphate is forbidden to the family of Abu Sufiyan, the freed prisoners of war and their sons. When you see Muawiya upon my pulpit, cut him open! And the people of Medina saw him on the pulpit of God's Messenger, but they did not do as they had been commanded, so now they are afflicted with his son, Yazid.'

Marwan became angry at Hussein's words and said: 'You will pledge allegiance to Yazid b. Muawiya, humbled!'

Hussein said: 'Away with you! We are the purified household about whom God has said: 'Indeed God desires to repel all impurity from you, O People of the Household, and purify you with a thorough purification.'

Marwan lowered his head and did not reply.

As he withdrew from him, Hussein said: 'Rejoice, Marwan! For you will see everything you despise about God's Messenger on the day you go to your Lord; my grandfather will ask you about my due and the due of Yazid.'

So Marwan went to Walid angry and told him about what Hussein had said.

Rahman: 'In your opinion, Abdullah, do you know how Hussein sees the end of his affair with them?'

Abdullah: 'I do not doubt that he knows he will die, and that he is God's sacrifice in this land. He is, after all, what God meant when he said in the story of Ishmael: 'Then We ransomed him with a great sacrifice.' And far be it from God to call a sheep 'a great sacrifice.' When Abraham saw himself slaughtering his son Ismael in a dream, but the knife would not cut, so he did not slaughter him. But God's Messenger was the master of the prophets, the seal of the messengers, so he is the one who will offer this sacrifice.'

Rahman: 'Has Hussein told anyone this?'

Abdullah: 'All of the Prophet's Household know what I say. As for Hussein himself, yes – he speaks of martyrdom. Sometimes he even says where he will be slain.'

Rahman: 'To whom does he tell these things?'

Abdullah: 'He told his half-brother, Umar b. Ali, who said: 'When Hussein refused to pledge allegiance to Yazid in Medina, I visited him and I found him alone. I said to him: 'May I be your ransom, O Abu Abdullah, your brother Hasan once told me...' but I choked up with tears before I could go any further. He embraced me and said: 'I know. He told you I would be slain.'

I said: 'No, never! O son of God's Messenger!'

He said: 'I ask you for the sake of our father, did he tell you I would be slain?'

I said: 'Yes.' And then I asked him to pledge allegiance.

Hussein said: 'My father told me that God's Messenger foretold that he and I would both be slain, and that the earth in which he was buried would be close to the earth in which I will be. Did you think you knew something I didn't?'

Then he said: 'I will not give the least bit of myself; surely Fatima will go to her father and complain about what her descendants suffer at the hands of his Nation. No one who harms her descendants shall enter Paradise.''

Rahman lets out a sigh.

Rahman: 'What a terrible state the Nation has reached, when the likes of Hussein b. Ali, the son of Fatima, the grandson of the Prophet, is under pressure to pledge allegiance to the likes of Yazid. The issue is grave indeed with regards to Hussein – does this mean that there will be a merciless confrontation between him and the soldiers of the Umayyad clan in Medina, or somewhere else, until they have killed him?'

Abdullah: 'No. It's not as you think. Hussein will not ask anyone for help; he is God's sacrifice who will be slain, but in the manner chosen for him by God. It is not as the Umayyad clan hope, especially when their goal is to stick Hussein's head on a pike to atone for the sins of God's servants, as the Christians believe about Jesus. No, what Hussein wants is to bring God's servants out of the confusion of darkness and save the religion from those who wish to turn the religion of God into the religion of the rulers, and turn the teachings of the master of the prophets to the teachings of the tyrants and sinners. I believe that the killing of Hussein will be a great earthquake, not just for this Nation, but for all human history!

In doing this, Hussein will become God's greatest proof over all mankind in every time and place; his day will be a day like no other. And this is what his brother Hasan once told him: 'There will be no day like yours, O Abu Abdullah!'

This is only natural; God stands with those of His servants who stand with Him, and insofar as Hussein is with God, then God is with Hussein.

When our Lord has mentioned the Men of the Ditch and the martyrs who were burnt at the stake for refusing to disbelieve in God, and they were ordinary believers like any others, then how will God see the martyrdom of the leader of the youth of Paradise, the grandson of God's Messenger, the son of Ali and Fatima and the brother of Hasan?

Rahman: Do you mean that what God revealed in Surat al-Buruj, when he said: 'By the sky with its houses, by the Promised Day, by the Witness and the Witnessed: perish the Men of the Ditch! The fire, abounding in fuel, above which they sat as they were themselves witnesses to what they did to the faithful. They were vindictive towards them only because they had faith in God, the All-mighty, the All-laudable, to whom belongs the dominion of the heavens and the earth, and God is witness to all things.' Do you mean this also applies to Hussein and his enemies?'

Abdullah: Exactly. A group of people will kill Hussein, but then God will fulfill the promise he mentions in this Surah: 'Indeed your Lord's striking is severe.' The pharaohs of this Nation will encounter what their predecessors did before. God has no inclination to any one person over another, His way of doing things does not change or alter; whoever does evil shall be requited with it and whoever commits a crime will be punished – 'Indeed your Lord is in ambush.'

Hussein ultimately decided to leave Medina for Mecca, but before doing so he sought God's guidance. He went to the Prophet's Mosque and offered two units of prayer. Then, when he finished them, he raised his hands in supplication and said: 'O God! This is the grave of Your prophet, Muhammad, and I am the son of Your prophet's daughter. You know why I have come here. O God, I love what is good and I hate evil, so I ask You – O Lord of Majesty and Generosity – for the sake of this grave and he whom it contains, only for that which You have chosen for me and for that which pleases You and Your messenger.'

Then he began to supplicate and weep. As draw drew near, he placed his head on the grave and dozed off. He had a dream in which he saw God's Messenger coming to him surrounded by a procession of angels. He came until he clasped Hussein to his chest, kissed him between his eyes and said: 'O my son, it is as though I see you soon stained with your own blood, slaughtered in a place of sorrow and tribulation, surrounded by a group of my Nation. You are thirsty but not given water, and yet those people hope for my intercession. What is wrong with them? God will not grant them my intercession on the Day of Resurrection!'

Then he said: 'My dear Hussein, your father, mother and brother have come to me and they are waiting for you.'

Hussein said: 'O grandfather, I do not need to go back to the world. Take me with you now and let me stay in your abode.'

The Prophet told him: 'In Paradise you shall have degrees that can only be obtained by martyrdom; God has written a great reward for you. You, your father, your brother, your uncle and your father's uncle shall all be raised together and you will enter Paradise together.'

Hussein awoke from his slumber and returned to his home. He gathered the people of his household and told them about his dream. On that day, there was no one in the east or west more grieved than the Prophet's Household, nor anyone who shed more tears than they.

With this dream, the picture was complete. Just as Abraham had seen himself slaughtering his son Ishmael in a dream and seen that has a divine command to slaughter his son, Hussein saw God's Messenger in the world of the unseen, and received an order from him that was obligatory for him to obey, just as he received the glad tidings that he would be God's sacrifice upon this earth. He only informed the people of his Household to prepare them for what he was going to do and what would happen to him and to them afterwards.

THE DEPARTURE

Rahman wanted to know the details of what had happened to Hussein and, because his friend - Abdullah b. Muslim – was one of the supporters of the Prophet's Household, Rahman would ask him about the news of Hussein and his family. In turn, Abdullah would ask Rahman about the news from the other side; the side of Yazid b. Muawiya. Insofar as Rahman was a resident of Medina and had some contacts amongst the agents of the state.

Rahman: 'What has happened since we last spoke?'

Abdullah: 'News of Hussein's rejection of the regime has spread quickly amongst the people. People had been expecting Muawiya to die any day now because of his age, and it had already been determined that his son Yazid would succeed him. As I said to you before, all the resources of the state were employed for years before Muawiya's death to ensure Yazid's succession. So people have been looking to see what position the Prophet's Household will take, especially since Hussein has long refused to pledge allegiance and openly stated that under no circumstances would Yazid be suitable for the Caliphate. As far as the people are concerned, Hussein is right not just because one of the condition of Hasan's peace treaty with Muawiya was that Hussein should succeed him, but because of the difference between his personality and the personality of his adversary and Hussein's clear desire to preserve this religion and protect the rights of the people.

For its part, the Umayyad regime wanted to force Hussein to pledge allegiance or do away with him if he refused. And because Hussein knew that this was their chosen course of action, he was keen to ensure that his death at their hands would not be in vain. Not only did he know the value of his own life, but his goal was not to contest the regime, it was to save the religion.

This is how Hussein and Yazid differed, not just on a single issue – because the substance of their dispute was not one thing – but rather in their fundamental aims and goals. Hussein wanted the hereafter and Yazid wanted this world; Hussein wanted to preserve the religion and Yazid wanted only to preserve his own power. This is clear from the way in which each of these two men took up their positions and the way in which they spoke about them.'

Rahman: 'The difference between them is still about two very different things, so why did they clash?'

Abdullah: 'The regime speaks using the name of the religion and derives its legitimacy by calling itself the "successorship" to God's Messenger. It portrays its authority as resting on God's religion and not on its status as a temporal, worldly government. This is what happened after God's Messenger passed away. The Prophet would legislate according to what was revealed to him by God, not according to what was most useful in constructing a government and setting up a state. After he passed away, whoever was the Caliph became a holy figure, and whatever he did was imbued with religious significance. People began to follow the Caliph as a means of obtaining nearness to God.'

Rahman: 'Can you give me an example of this?'

Abdullah: 'Look at the *tarāwīḥ* prayers as the Second Caliph organized them. He said: 'What an excellent innovation (*bid'a*) this is!' And this became part of people's religious practice, even though it was not the practice of the Prophet himself and innovation in religion is something explicitly forbidden by the Prophet and various verses of the Quran. But when Imam Ali wanted to erase this innovation, a group of people came out chanting: 'O sunna of Umar!' And there are many matters in which the practice of the Caliphs differs with the practice of God's Messenger. But it was the practice of the Caliphs that usually trumped the practice of the Prophet, and some Muslims took it up as their own religious practice.

So we see that many judges rule according to the precedents laid down by the Caliphs when they ruled over the nation, as though the government has a right to legislate and invent religious obligations; to permit what is prohibited and prohibit what is permitted. It is as if whoever sits on the throne is God's own ruler, such that if anyone else came and sat upon it, they too would become holy figures. But this is something God has not sent down any evidence for!

And when it is the behaviour of the ruler that defines the Divine Law rather than the values, principles, examples and laws brought by the prophets, then we might as well bid farewell to the religion in its entirety!

But Yazid gives no importance to the religion, whether in reality or in appearance; he sins openly in contempt of the explicit teachings of the religion. The danger here is that his own behaviour will also become a standard of religious practice, and that he will lead people astray by their following him and their belief that he represents the religion.

Therefore, Hussein's fundamental goal is to draw a distinction between these two things, so that people know that the ruler – despite whatever claims he might make – not only does not represent the religion should he contravene its teachings and values, but he could even represent faithlessness and in that case it is only right to oppose him.

Was not the first thing that religion taught that people should follow God's *people* and not their rulers?

God gives no value to the position of the regime insofar as it holds worldly power, or else Pharaoh would have been considered divine, and Haman, and whoever else is like them!

Rahman: 'Do you mean to say that we should not look at the ruler as someone divinely-ordained? Rather, we must take him to task should he violate the principles of truth, justice and faith. And moreover, that his way of practice should not be taken as an example for the people to follow?

Abdullah: Precisely! But I want to add something else, namely that the approach of these two men shows that they are following two very different routes, in destination, direction and morality. Hussein embodies every imaginable virtue, while Yazid embodies every possible vice – first and foremost of which is treachery.'

Rahman: 'Treachery towards whom?'

Abdullah: 'Treachery towards the Nation – the greatest and most dangerous kind of treachery!'

Rahman: 'So what about loyalty in Hussein? How does he display this?'

Abdullah: 'Hussein is one of God's *people*; his positions and actions are identical with the values and teachings of the religion. If you want to see loyalty itself, then go and look at Hussein! If you want to see bravery, honesty, purity, sincerity, justice, kindness, piety, humility, reverence for God and humbleness towards people, then go and look at Hussein!'

Rahman: 'Tell me about the details of Hussein leaving Medina.'

Abdullah: 'When Hussein resolved to leave Medina, he went out in the middle of the night. First he went to his mother's grave, offered prayers there and bid her farewell. Then he went to his brother, Hasan's, grave and did the same. Then he returned to his home as dawn approached.'

Rahman: 'Why did Hussein decide to depart for Mecca instead of anywhere else?'

Abdullah: 'For a number of reasons, one being that Mecca was Hussein's city; his father, grandfather and mother were born there, and the Holy Sanctuary was there – a place which granted safety to anyone who entered it. Not to mention the fact that Mecca was a place in which different tribes and people could meet, and that Hussein's closest friend had advised him to go to Mecca.'

Rahman: 'Who do you mean?'

Abdullah: 'Muhammad b. Hanafiyya, of course. He came to Hussein and said: 'O brother, you are the dearest and most beloved person to me, and I can find no one in the world more deserving of my counsel then you. Keep yourself and your followers away from Yazid b. Muawiya and away from his helpers as much as you can. Then send your messengers to the people and call them to yourself; if they pledge allegiance to you, then give thanks to God. But should the people gather around someone else, God will not see that as a deficiency in your faith or your intellect, nor will it harm your honour or chivalry. I fear that you might go to a city and a group of people will come differing amongst themselves – one group with you and another against you – and they will fight, and you will be on the front rank. Then the best of this Nation in his own person and parents will be the one whose blood has been worst squandered and whose family will be most abased.'

Hussein said to him: 'Where should I go, brother?'

Muhammad b. Hanafiyya said: 'Go to Mecca; if the House gives you rest, then that is what you want. If not, then go wherever you like, for example to Yemen. The people there are the supporters of your father, your brother and your father; they are the people broadest of land and soundest of intellect. Otherwise you must keep to the deserts and the mountains, moving from place to place, to see how matters will turn out for the people, then God will judge between you and the sinful people.'

Hussein said: 'O my brother! By God, even if there was no refuge or sanctuary for me in this world, I would never pledge allegiance to Yazid b. Muawiya. The Prophet has said: 'O God! Do not bless Yazid.' So may God grant you good for me, you have given be good and sound advice. I hope that you are right, for I have already decided to make for Mecca; my brothers and I and our families have made ready.'

Then Hussein asked for a pen and paper. He wrote: 'In the name of God, the Compassionate, the Merciful. This is the testament of Hussein b. Ali b. Abu Talib to his brother, Muhammad, known as Ibn Hanafiyya, the son of Ali b. Abu Talib. Hussein b. Ali bears witness that there is no god except God alone and without partner, and that Muhammad is His servant and messenger, who brought truth from Him, and that Paradise is real and Hellfire is real, and that the Hour will indeed come without doubt, and that God will raise those in the graves.'

'Lo! Indeed I do not go forth to do evil, for vainglory, to oppress or cause corruption. I go forth only to seek reform in the Nation of my grandfather, Muhammad. I intend to enjoin the good and forbid the evil, and follow the method of my grandfather, Muhammad, and that of my father, Ali b. Abu Talib. Whoever accepts me in truth, God is more entitled to the truth. And whoever rejects me, I shall wait for God to judge between me and the people with truth, and to judge between me and them, and God is the best of judges.'

'This is my testament to you, O brother! My only hope of success lies with God. In Him do I place my trust and to Him do I turn. Peace be upon you and those that follow guidance, there is no power or means except by God, the High, the Awesome.'

Then he rolled up the letter, sealed it with his signet ring, handed it to Muhammad b. Hanafiyya and bid the latter farewell.

Abdullah b. Muslim: Hussein – as I said – was the epitome of loyalty, nobility, chivalry and bravery. He did not leave Medina without bidding farewell to his relatives, both dead and alive. Nor did he do what Abdullah b. Zubayr did; Hussein took the main road from Medina to Mecca.

Hussein was seen walking between two men, entering the Prophet's Mosque, uttering the verses of the poet, *Yazid b. Mafza' al-Himyarī*:

'I have not crossed the world at the crack of dawn
as a raider, nor have I been called Yazid
A day that gives injury to avoid death
and fate lies waiting for me to swerve'

Everyone who heard his words knew that he would not give the slightest part of himself to the regime, whether under threat of death or offers of wealth and prestige.'

Rahman: 'I want to ask you about something I heard – is it true that Umm Salama – the wife of the Prophet – knew in advance about the martyrdom of Hussein from her husband?'

Abdullah: 'It's true. She has said: 'I went to the Prophet one day and found him weeping.' I asked him: 'O prophet of God, has someone grieved you?'

He said: 'No.'

She said: 'Then why do you weep?'

The Prophet said: 'Gabriel has just left me. He told me that Hussein would be slain on the banks of the Euphrates!'

Then he asked: 'Would you like to smell the dust of that place?'

I said: 'Yes!'

So the Prophet stretched out his hand, holding a lump of soil. He gave it to me and I could not stop myself from crying.'

When Hussein decided to leave Medina, he came to Umm Salama. She said: 'My son! Do not grieve me by going to Iraq! I have heard your grandfather say: 'My son Hussein will be killed in the land of Iraq, in a place called Karbala.'

Hussein said to her: 'O mother, I know this better than you and I will surely be slain – there is no avoiding this. I even know the day on which I will be slain and by whose hand; I know the spot of ground in which I will be buried; I even know who amongst my household, family and followers will be slain. If you like, O mother, I can show you the exact spot!'

Then he pointed towards Karbala and the earth shrank until he showed her where he would be buried, where his camp would be, where he would stand and fight, and where he would be martyred. Umm Salama wept profusely but left the matter in God's hands. Hussein said to her: 'O mother! God wishes to see me slaughtered; slain aggressed against and oppressed, and my children either murdered unjustly or fettered in chains, calling for help but finding no helper.

Then he took a piece of earth, placed it in a vial and gave it to her. He said: 'Place it with the vial which my grandfather gave to you; when they overflow, you will know that I have been slain.'

So Hussein knew that he would be made the great sacrifice of the Prophet's Household on this earth, and the great offering to God in the heavens. There was no avoiding what the Pen had written; Hussein knew that there would be no return after his emigration to Mecca and this is why he had informed the women of the Clan of Abd al-Muttalib that he would be leaving. They gathered around him, weeping. He said to them: 'I adjure you for the sake of God not to display disobedience to God and His Messenger in this matter!'

They said: 'Then for whom shall we save our wailing and weeping? This day to us is like the day in which the Prophet died, and Fatima, Ali and Hasan, and Zaynab and Umm Kulthum. So we adjure you by God, may God take us in your place, O you who is beloved by the righteous!'

His aunt, Umm Hani - who was by now very advanced in years – came to him. When Hussein saw her, he said: 'O my aunt! Why have you come when you are in this condition?'

She said: 'How could I not come, when I heard that the one who cares for widows is abandoning me?'

She began to weep and recite the verses of Abu Talib about the Prophet:

Bright, the clouds were watered by his face
refuge of the orphans, protector of the widows
The firmament of the Hashemite clan orbits him
for they are blessed abundantly in his presence

He said: 'O my aunt, everything that has been ordained will surely come to pass. The matter has been decided'

Then Umm Hani left, weeping, visibly grieved by Hussein's departure from his grandfather's city.

Hussein left Medina on Saturday night, two days before the end of Rajab, sixty years after the Hijra.

Half a century had passed since God's Messenger had passed away, and still the people of his Household lived in difficult circumstances. They were the ones who had built the state and erected its edifice; they had brought people out of darkness and into light; by their hands, people had been guided to God's true religion. But events had disrupted the balance of things; the Prophet's Household had been excluded from government, and in their place ruled the grandsons of those who had resisted the Prophet at every turn and tried to destroy him and his religion time and again. They now held the reins of power in their grasp, while the grandson of the Prophet was threatened with death in his own grandfather's city!

When Hussein left Medina, he was accompanied by his sisters Umm Kulthum and Zaynabm his son's children and his brothers - Abu Bakr, Ja'far, Abbas - and all the members of his household in Medina. Everyone except Muhammad b. Hanafiyya, who remained in Mecca.

On the road, he recited the verse from the Quran: 'So he left the city, fearful and vigilant. He said, 'My Lord! Deliver me from the wrongdoing lot."

History was repeating itself; the inheritor of the prophets in Medina had become like Moses when he had to flee Egypt in fear of Pharaoh. Hussein also fled so that he would not be compelled to pledge allegiance to the Pharaoh of his time. Just as Moses fled fearful and vigilant, so too did Hussein. And just as Moses asked to be delivered from the wrongdoers, so too did Hussein.

This is one of the similarities between Hussein and the previous prophets.

For his part, Walid b. Utba tried to bring Hussein to force him to pledge allegiance, but when his men found his house empty, he said: 'Praise God, who made him leave and spared me the shedding of his blood.'

Hussein followed the main road, which the majority of people would take from Medina to Mecca. One of his family members said to him: 'Should we not depart from the main road as Ibn Zubayr did, so that those they send after us will not find us?'

He said: No, by God. I will not depart this path until God decrees the outcome dearest to Him.'

On the road, he would recite the Qur'an and murmur it to himself.

Sometimes he would speak to his sons about what they must do, instruct them and mention the sayings of God's Messenger. Sometimes, he would recite the verses of poetry:

When a man does not defend his intentions, honor
or family, he is ignoble and frivolous
And despite how Yazid will wrong us on the morrow
we plunge into death's waters east and west
And go forth striking with a strike like fire
whenever a lion sees him it flees in fright

The two friends met once more. This time, Rahman asked Abdullah if anything unusual had happened during Hussein's journey from Medina to Mecca. "You know that Hussein is one of God's men and that he carries the banner of Monotheism, which all of God's prophets had carried before him. The least that can be said of his standing are the words uttered by his grandfather about his father during the Battle of the Trench: 'Faith itself has come out to face polytheism itself.'

There is no doubting that God's men have a special position with their Lord compared to everyone else; they do nothing save for the sake of God. For the sake of their Lord, they eat, drink, move and speak, and for that reason God guides them to the right path. Is it not God who says: 'We made them imams, guiding by Our command, and We revealed to them the performance of good deeds, the maintenance of prayers, and the giving of zakat, and they used to worship Us.' And is it not He who says: 'whoever believes in God and the Last Day. And whoever is wary of God, He shall make a way out for him,'

Just as God commanded the angels to lend their services to Abraham when he was cast headlong into the fire, but he refused their assistance. Gabriel said to him: 'So ask God to help you!' Abraham replied: 'It suffices me that He knows my condition.'

It is easy for God to command the angels and jinn to offer their assistance to Hussein and to defend him from his enemies, but with one difference: It had not been determined in God's knowledge that Abraham should burn and die, whereas Hussein is God's sacrifice in this life. He will surely be slain!

Rahman: I don't understand... so did the angels offer something to Hussein?

Abdullah: When Hussein departed Medina for Mecca, he met a host of angels dressed for battle, bearing lances, mounted on horses of Paradise. They greeted him and said: 'O representative of God on earth! God supported your grandfather, His messenger, with us in many battles. And indeed God will support you with us.'

Hussein told them: 'The place of my martyrdom and burial is Karbala. Come to me when I am there.'

They said: 'O representative of God on earth! God has commanded us to hear and obey you – shall you fear any enemy you meet while we are with you?'

He said: 'They have no means of bringing me harm, nor shall they do me any harm until I reach my appointed place.'

And waves of faithful jinn came to him and said: 'Master! We are your helpers, so command us as you see fit. If you tell us to kill every one of your enemies right now, we will do it.'

Hussein said to them: 'God grant you abundant good! Have you not read God's book which he sent down to His messenger, when He says: "Even if you had remained in your houses, those destined to be slain would have set out toward the places where they were laid to rest.' If I stay here, then how will mankind be tested and how will they be measured? Who is it that will rest in my grave, when God has chosen that spot for me on the day He made the world, and made it a place of visitation for those who love Him, that He might accept their deeds and prayers, respond to their supplication and grant them safety in this world and the next.'

They said: 'Were it not for the fact we are honour-bound to obey you, we would have certainly ignored you and slain your enemies before they could even reach you.'

Hussein said: 'By God, we are better able to destroy them than you, but [we will not] so that he who perishes might perish by a manifest proof, and he who lives may live on by a manifest proof.'

Hussein followed the path which had been laid out for him; He did not so much as move without full awareness of what he was doing. He was the one to whom God had entrusted custodianship of His earth and made him His representative to His servants. The weight of the prophetic message weighed on his shoulders and it fell to him to reform the path and the people who walked it. He knew that his mission required him to make the ultimate sacrifice, to be cut by swords, stabbed by spears and pierced by arrows for the sake of God. But he considered martyrdom in order to protect God's religion a blessing to give thanks for rather than a trial to be endured. This is the same as his father, the Commander of the Faithful, whom he remembered saying: 'O Messenger of God! Did you not tell me at the Battle of Uhud, when so many Muslims were martyred, and I was grieved for not having been granted martyrdom: 'I give you glad tidings of martyrdom later.' And he said to me: 'If that is the case, how is your endurance?' And I said: 'O Messenger of God! This is not something I need to endure, this is something I need to give thanks for!'

Hussein's eyes were set upon the Hereafter and what God has promised those who are martyred for his sake; everyone else had their eyes set on this world, including everyone who had advised him not to come out and rise up, or to go into the mountains. They were desirous of the life of this world, while Hussein wanted to give this world for the Hereafter and his life for his message.

Rahman: Did Hussein not meet anyone on the road who advised

him against what he was planning?

Abdullah: Of course! Hussein met *Abdullah b. Muṭīʿ al-Qurishī* at a well of his. He asked Hussein: 'Where are you headed?'

Hussein said: 'Now, to Mecca. Later, wherever God would have me go.'

Abdullah b. Muṭīʿ told him: 'God bless you, O son of God's Messenger. But I want to give you my advice.'

Hussein said: 'And what is that?'

'Once you have gone to Mecca and want to set out to one of the provinces, beware of Kufa for it is an ill-fated land. There your father was slain and your brother betrayed and beset by an attack that almost killed him. Instead, you should stay at the Holy Sanctuary in Mecca, for you are the master of the Arabs and by God not a single person in Hejaz will turn away from you. By God, if they want to kill you, they will have to take us as slaves first!'

Rahman: And was Hussein's departure from Medina, and that of Ibn Zubayr beforehand, a setback for the authorities in Syria because they had been expecting Walid to force them to pledge allegiance? Or did they think this was something normal?

Abdullah: No, it was certainly not seen as something normal. Orders came from Yazid to Walid to take the pledge of allegiance from all the people in Medina and from Ibn Zubayr and Hussein in particular. Yazid was very troubled when both of them escaped, and Marwan informed him of that in a letter he had sent to him, also highlighting how weak and tolerant Walid had been towards Hussein. So Yazid removed Walid as governor despite his close familial relationship with him because arrogance is a common trait in tyrants; when one of their orders is not carried out, they punish the agents under their control in the harshest manner possible. For this reason he removed Walid as governor of Medina and appointed *Amr b. Sa'eed b. al-ʿĀṣ al-Ashdaq* in his place. He was a man like Yazid himself - gravely arrogant.

The first act Amr undertook when appointed governor was to ascend the pulpit in the Prophet's Mosque. As soon as he had reclined upon it, he suffered a nosebleed. Amongst the people gathered there was a Bedouin augur, who said: 'Ah! By God he will bring us blood!'

A man stood up and began to mop up Amr's blood with his turban. The Bedouin said: 'Ah! By God that blood will swallow us all.'

Then he stood up to speak with a forked staff in his hand. The Bedouin said: 'By God, the people will split apart.'

One of the things Amr said in his speech was that Ibn Zubayr had sought refuge in Mecca. By God, if we have to, we will attack it. And if he enters the Ka'ba, we will burn it with him in it!'

PROPHET'S SON AT THE HOUSE OF GOD

After a journey of five days and nights, Hussein reached Mecca with his retinue and his dependents. It was Thursday night, three nights after the beginning of Sha'ban. He stayed amongst the people of Ali, in the house of Abbas b. Abd al-Muttalib.'

People, both inhabitants of Mecca, those performing Umra and travellers altogether, began to frequent Hussein and gather around him in circles, hearing his Hadith and asking him questions about religious and worldly affairs.

As for Abdullah b. Zubayr, he had been ill at ease since Hussein arrived in Mecca – or worse – because he knew that people would not come to him so long as Hussein was nearby. But he did not make known his displeasure; he would visit him from time to time. It was difficult for him to bear the presence of Hussein because he desired that people pledge allegiance to him, but no one would pledge allegiance to him so long as Hussein was there because Hussein held an even higher position of esteem in their eyes and they were more ready to obey him than Ibn Zubayr.

With Hussein in Mecca, the scales had turned against the government. They could not kill him while he was there, because the people surrounded him, frequented him and attended his gatherings. Not to mention the presence of the Holy Sanctuary; no one could prevent people from going to it and circling around it, especially when God had said: 'the native and the visitor being equal therein' and: 'Who is a greater wrongdoer than him who denies access to the mosques of God lest His Name be celebrated therein?' And this is what Hussein told Yazid's governor of Mecca when the latter asked him: 'What brought you here?' He said: 'I am seeking refuge with God and with this House.'

In addition to the fact that Mecca was Hussein's city, and he was like a son to the House of God built by his ancient ancestor, Abraham, and purified of idolatry by his grandfather, God's Messenger, and his father, Ali b. Abu Talib when they retook it from the polytheists. The houses of the Hashemite clan were still there; word of Hussein's refusal to pledge allegiance to Yazid and his subsequent arrival in Mecca had stirred up faith in the hearts of the people both there and in other cities.

Hussein spent his days in Mecca doing one of three things; either speaking to the people and giving them moral admonition, or circling the Holy House and praying in the Mosque, or visiting the graves of his forefathers, especially his grandmother *Khadīja*. He would visit her grave, pray there and supplicate to God a great deal.

With Hussein in Mecca, both *Abdullah b. Muslim* and *Rahman b. Ṣāliḥ* decided to remain in Mecca for the time being, without having agreed on this between themselves beforehand. So they kept meeting one another from time to time and discussing the situation. One day, Rahman told his companion in the vicinity of the Ka'ba: 'What is going to happen with Hussein and Yazid b. Muawiya?'

Abdullah: What I know for now is that the faithful in every place have begun to gather together and discuss the matter of Hussein, despite the fact that they live under the shadow of the Umayyad house; it has only been a short time since Muawiya died, the government is strong and it still has the loyalty of its governors in every city. It has been built along the lines of the Roman and Persian empires – a state that rests on foundations of autocracy, coercion, murder, exile and striking everyone who opposes it. But despite that, many of the faithful have been roused by Hussein's bravery, refusal to pledge allegiance and arrival in Mecca. Of all the lands, the one which has been most deeply affected by this is the capital of Iraq – Kufa, the city which Ali b. Abu Talib made his capital and in which Hussein lived with his father until he was slain in the Mosque by Rahman b. Muljam al-Muradi.

Rahman: Speaking of Kufa, what is the news from there?

Abd God b. Muslim: Those of the faithful who support the Prophet's Household and desire to see them return to power have started to gather in the house of Sulayman b. Sard al-Khuza'ee, a companion of the Prophet who fought in some of his battles, like the Battle of the Trench. On one occasion, with his home full of the nobility of Kufa, he stood up to speak, praised and magnified God, invoked His blessings upon the Prophet and his Household, then mentioned the Commander of the Faithful, Ali b. Abu Talib and invoked God's mercy upon him, mentioning his noble achievements – and we all know that Muawiya forbade speaking about Ali or mentioning his merits, not to mention instituting his public cursing and reviling from the pulpit, calling it a sunna! – then Sulayman said:

'You will have all heard that Muawiya has gone to his Lord with his deeds, and God will surely recompense him for them. In his place has sat his son, Yazid, and this Hussein b. Ali has refused to pledge allegiance to him and set out for Mecca. You are his supporters (Shi'a) and the supporters of his father; if you know that you will help him and fight against his enemies, then write to him. But if you fear you are too weak or that you will fail, then do not dupe the man out of his own life!'

A group of people spoke up: 'No, we will support him, fight his enemies and be slain before him.'

So Sulayman took a pledge from them [that they would do this] and said: 'Now write him a letter from all of you saying that you will do this for him and ask him to come to you.'

They said: 'Would it not suffice that you write a letter to him?'

Sulayman replied: No, your group must write to him.'

Rahman: Were people free to gather to discuss their affairs, debate openly and relate the merits of Ali?

Abdullah: They could do that because Muawiya was dead and Yazid did not yet have complete control over things. Moreover, the governor of Kufa, Nu'man b. Bashir, despite being a partisan of Uthman who openly proclaimed his hatred for Ali and reviled him, was not like men such as *Busr b. Arṭā* or Muslim b. Uqba, who were hasty to shed blood. This, in addition to the fact that the strength of the faithful in Kufa could not be underestimated.

Rahman: And did the Kufans write to Hussein as Sulayman bid them?

Abdullah: The letters and messages from the people of Kufa began to flood to Hussein like a great deluge. Every day he heard from another group who came from his father's city, bringing letters for all different kinds of people asking Hussein to come to them.

Rahman: Was this something that only happened in Kufa?

Abdullah: No, actually the letters came from all over the Muslim world – Basra, Yemen, Rayy and others too. But more letters came from Kufa than anywhere else.

Rahman: What did these letters say?

Abdullah: I'll read one for you – written by the group around Sulayman b. Ñard – it says:

'In the name of God, the Compassionate, the Merciful. To Hussein

b. Ali from *Sulayman b. Ṣard, Musayyab b, Nujba, Rafā'a b. Shaddād, Habib b. Muẓahir* and his followers from the faithful and Muslims of Kufa.

Praise be to God who has slain your enemy, the obstinate tyrant who aggressed against this Nation, deprived it of its rights, usurped its affairs, monopolized its booty and appointed governors over it without its consent, then killed its best men and kept alive its worst, and made God's wealth the property of its richest members. So away with him, as God did away with *Thamūd.*

We have no leader, so come to us that God might gather us upon guidance through you. Nu'man b. Bashir is in the governor's palace, but we do not gather with him for Friday Prayers, nor do we go out with him for the festivals. When we hear you have set out to us, we will expel him from Kufa and send him back to Syria. Peace.'

Letters came to Hussein one after another, becoming more abundant with each passing day. Sometimes, someone would come from Kufa carrying close to fifty letters, each signed by two or three people, asking him to hasten to them.

One letter that came to him read: 'Come quickly! The people are waiting for you! They have no leader except you, so hurry, hurry, hurry! Peace.'

Another from Kufa read: 'We are with you and with us are a hundred thousand swords!'

One letter came to Hussein signed by *Shabath b. Rab'ey al-Rubū'ī, Hajjār b. Abjar al-'Ajalī, Amr b. al-Hajjāj al-Zubaydī, 'Udhra b. Qays al-Aḥmasī, Yazid b. al-Harith al-Shaybānī and Muhammad b. Umayr al-Tamīmī.* It's text read:

'The leaves have turned green, the fruit has ripened and strength overflows. If you wish, come to us, for you will be coming to an army that is ready for you. Peace.'

In other letters, they wrote: 'We have devoted ourselves to you. We do not attend Friday prayers with the governor. Come to us!'

Another said: 'We will die for you. We neither attend Friday prayers nor congregational prayers [with the governor] for your sake.'

Another still said: 'We have separated from the people. We do not pray beside them. We have no leader. Should you come to us, we hope that God will gather us upon faith through you.'

Yet another said: 'We have devoted ourselves, so come to us. We are a hundred thousand people in whom tyranny has spread, neither adhering to God's book nor the Messenger's sunna. We hope that God will gather us upon truth through you, and repel oppression from us with you. You have more right to this affair than Yazid and his father who have usurped the Nation's wealth, drank wine and played with monkeys and mandolins, and meddled with the religion.'

The letters followed one another continuously. In one day alone, Hussein received six hundred letters. Altogether he received as many as twelve thousand letters.'

Rahman: Does Hussein respond to every letter they send him?

Abdullah: Until now, Hussein has kept himself to receiving letters. He has not written any response as of yet.

Rahman: Do you not think that these letters and messengers, with everything that they say, at the very least saddle Hussein with a duty to respond to them?'

Abdullah: That's correct, because the contents of these letters are far from ordinary. First, they openly proclaim that they have withdrawn from Friday and congregational prayers, because they do not think that the governor and the followers of the Umayyad clan are worthy to gather with and pray behind.

Second, they say that they have gathered together on the leadership of Hussein and that they will have no leader except him.

Third, they ask that Hussein repels injustice, wrongdoing and tyranny from them.

Fourth, they ask that Hussein guides them to the right path and unites them on the truth.

Fifth, they announce their readiness to fulfil their duties with him, even if that means death. And you know that Imam Ali did not accept the position of Caliph except for the reasons he gave in his sermon of Shaqshaqiyya: 'But, by He who split the grain and created life, if people had not come to me and supporters had not exhausted the argument and if there had been no covenant of God with the learned to the effect that they should neither endure the avarice of the oppressor nor the hunger of the oppressed, I would have cast the rope of Caliphate on its own shoulders, and would have given the last one the same treatment as to the first one.'

All of these matters have gathered together now; there are those in the arena who show their readiness to support the truth; these letters, which affirm that their authors are ready to give their assistance; the spread of oppression, tyranny, impiety, and God's covenant with the learned that they should not accept the avarice of the oppressor nor the unger of the oppressed – all of these things mean that Hussein now bears a tremendous responsibility.

Rahman: So why does Hussein not respond?

Abdullah: I suspect that he is waiting, not just for the proof of his rightness to be complete or for the sake of preparation; he is waiting for something in the realm of the unseen.

Rahman: Did you not say that Hussein already knew that he was the sacrifice of the Prophet's Household and the martyr of this Nation?

Abdullah: Yes, but Hussein will not go forth to die for death's sake. Hussein follows a clear plan for the sake of specific divine goals.'

Rahman: 'What are those goals?'

Abdullah: 'They are the very same goals which the Prophets had, as mentioned in the Quran: 'Certainly We sent Our Messengers with manifest proofs, and We sent down with them the Book and the Balance, so that mankind may maintain justice.' Their goals are to spread fairness, repel wrongdoing, to obtain justice for the oppressed, guide the misled, carry out God's commandments, bring about reform amongst the people and develop the land... and these are the goals of Hussein as much as they were the goals of the prophets who came before him.

Rahman: Do you mean to say that Hussein's goals are a mixture of religious and worldly ones?

Abdullah: Exactly.

Rahman: But did you not say that Hussein desired only the Hereafter, not this world?

Abdullah: That's right, but this does not mean that he does not want this world for others, or that he does not wish to bring about reform amongst the people, or that he does not want to establish justice for them. No, he only wants this world insofar as this world is where we sow our seeds for the next world by doing righteous deeds in it for the sake of God's satisfaction with us, to benefit God's servants and restrain the tyrants and wrongdoers... but his goal in doing so is not worldly benefits; when Muawiya went against Ali, it was clear that he only wanted this world, while when Ali fought him he did so not to obtain any worldly benefit for himself, but to prevent Muawiya from making the wealth of the state the sole property of the wealthy, from oppressing God's servants and spreading corruption in the land.

Rahman: It appears that the Umayyad clan are resolved to stand against the Hashemite clan at every stage in history! Abu Sufiyan against God's Messenger, Muawiya against Ali and Yazid against Hussein!

Abdullah: Glory to God! This is how our Lord tests his servants. He tests the best of them with the worst of them and the worst of them with the best of them. He created the opposition between night and day, darkness and light, good and evil. If He did not create things this way – just as Hussein said before – then how would God test mankind?

Rahman: Do you think that Hussein's inclination towards good and Yazid's towards evil is like that of God's Messenger and Ali to good and that of Abu Sufiyan and Muawiya towards evil? Does this mean that it comes down to their different natures – I mean, that the nature of Abu Sufiyan and Muawiya is to work for worldly wealth and temporary benefits, while that of God's Messenger, Ali and their Household is to work for goodness, nobility and morality?

Abdullah: No, actually it comes down to differing goals and the way in which each side responds to their own innate inclinations. The Prophet's Household respond to their inclinations towards good, while their enemies respond to their inclination towards evil.

And both sides gather other people like them around themselves; Hussein does not seek out those who seek worldly benefit, wicked men or slaves of this world and people like that do not incline towards Hussein. By the same token, Yazid does not gather men around him unless they share his avarice for this world and its trinkets, his base character and lack of moral scruples.

Hussein does not want worldly benefits for himself. Even what he possesses he desires for the sake of the people. The opposite is true with Yazid; he and all the rulers like him want all the benefits of the people for themselves. For this reason, we see men like Hussein ready to give themselves to save the people from these tyrants. On the other hand, men like Yazid are ready to slaughter as many people as necessary for their own benefits. Hussein holds on to his principles and forgets his own needs for the sake of these principles and values, because he wants what is best for people. On the other hand, Yazid is not ready to give up the slightest benefit to himself for the sake of people's wellbeing.

Rahman: Does the same distinction hold between Ali and Muawiya?

Abdullah: Yes, exactly the same. Hussein is an extension of Ali just as Yazid is an extension of Muawiya. Hussein's path is that of Ali and Yazid's is that of Muawiya. The fundamental difference between Ali and Muawiya was the difference between leadership and authority. Ali wanted to lead people to what was best for them in this world and the next, while Muawiya wanted to use the people and have control over them, and he said as much when he entered Kufa after Ali had been killed and he signed the peace treaty with Hasan. Muawiya ascended the pulpit and said: 'By God, I have not fought you in order that you pray and fast, nor that you make the pilgrimage or pay alms. You already do that. No, I have fought you to have control over you and God as granted me that though you may detest it.'

Ali's struggle with Muawiya was more than a struggle between two different people, it was a struggle between two different worldviews. Just as the difference between them was made clear by the way in which they each conducted themselves in the person affairs and their politics. Hussein is free of any fault, as Muawiya said to his son: 'By God I can find no fault with him!'

And if Muawiya could find no fault with Hussein, then every fault imaginable can be found in Yazid. For this reason, the nobles of the Umayyad clan were very hesitant to accept Yazid as his father's successor even while his father still lived. Some of them even opposed him openly to the extent that Muawiya was compelled to banish some of his closest allies and had to kill more than one personality in order to ensure Yazid's succession.

Rahman: Who did Muawiya have to kill to ensure that his son would be the next Caliph?

Abdullah: Muawiya killed many people. As for the best of people, he killed Hasan b. Ali by duping his wife – *Ja'da b. Ash'ath* – into poisoning him, promising her that she would be allowed to marry

Yazid and that she would be rewarded with a hundred thousand dirhams. He fulfilled his promise of money, but he did not marry her to his son.

As for other people, he killed Rahman, the son of *Khālid b. Walid*, one of his knights who was a staunch opponent of Ali and the Hashemite clan. Muawiya had used him in his campaigns against the Romans, and the Syrians hoped that he would be the next Caliph. This became clear when Muawiya addressed them to appoint his successor and the people indicated their preference for Rahman. This troubled Muawiya greatly, but he kept this to himself. Then he called for one of his physicians, a Jew known as *Ibn Āthāl*, to give Rahman poison. He did so and Rahman died in the year forty-six.

Meanwhile, you see that Hussein is confronted with letters asking him to go them, but he bides his time because he does not wish to see anyone die for him to obtain political power, because he fundamentally does not want political power. The difference between these two men is not merely that one is better than the other – it is like the difference between darkness and light, good and evil, righteousness and corruption, faith and hypocrisy, Paradise and Hellfire.

This is the contrast that exists between these two sides.

Rahman: So the difference in outcome between Hussein and Yazid will also be clear, because Hussein responds to his inclinations towards good and so sacrifices himself for the sake of his ideals, while Yazid has no compunction in committing every imaginable sin in the pursuit of worldly power, just as happened between Ali and Muawiya. Ali gave up worldly power for the sake of his ideals, while Muawiya used every trick and stratagem at his disposal, whether bribery or assassination, to secure his power.

Abdullah: But the difference is that things are clearer now; Hussein clearly represents the message of the Prophet in its nobility, goodness, faith, honesty, purity, justice and altruism, while Yazid embodies worldly power in its avarice, hypocrisy and base qualities.

And to the extent that Hussein possesses knowledge and merit, his enemy is neither a righteous, noble or wise man. He is a frivolous boy who spends his days and nights drowning in wine and music, constantly surrounded by women, except when he hunts for sport, spending week upon week between monasteries, wildernesses and forests.

If Hussein is a mountain of virtue, Yazid is a valley filled with iniquity.

Rahman: Let us say, for the sake of argument, that Hussein pledged allegiance to Yazid for a while – what harm is there in that?

Abdullah: And if Moses worshipped Pharaoh for a while? And if God's Messenger had obeyed Abu Sufiyan for a while? And if he had accepted idol-worship for a while?

Rahman: Has the matter really reached that level?

Abdullah: More than that, and this is what the following days will show.

DECISION

A few days after their last meeting, Rahman and Abdullah meet again in the grounds of the Holy Sanctuary.

Rahman: What news of Hussein? Do you think he will go on like this and not answer the people of Kufa? The number of letters and invitations he has now received exceed twelve thousand, some of them from more than one person. This is something unprecedented! Is he going to give a response?

Abdullah: Yes, we've never heard of so many letters being written to one man asking him to rise up, lead them and stand at their head once this position has been vacated amongst them. As for this, Hussein has responded.

Rahman: What did he do?

Abdullah: Some of the last people to come to Hussein were *Hani b. Hāni al-Sabuʿī and Sa'eed b. Abdullah al-Hanafī*, both from Kufa. Imam Hussein asked them about what was happening there, and which people had agreed on inviting him to the city and separating themselves from Yazid's governor. They said: 'All of the leaders of

Kufa' and mentioned names like Shabath b. Rab'ey, who was considered the preeminent jurist of Kufa, *Hajjār b. Abjar, Yazid b. al-Harith, Yazid b. Rawīn, Amr b. Qays, Amr b. al-Hajjāj and Muhammad b. Umayr b. 'Aṭārid.*

Afterwards, Hussein got up, made ritual ablutions and went to the Holy Mosque. There, he offered two prayers between the Pillar and the Station of Abraham. Upon finishing his prayers, he asked his Lord to show him the best course of action in response to the letters from Kufa.

Rahman: What do you mean he asked his Lord to show him what was the best course of action to take?

Abdullah: This is one of the teachings of God's Messenger, that whoever wants to do something should ask his Lord to grant him the best outcome by offering to units of prayer and asking his Lord to choose the best outcome for him.

Rahman: Then what did Hussein decide?

Abdullah: The last people who came to see Hussein were still waiting for his answer and they came back to him a few days after he had gone and offered this prayer to God. He came out to meet them and said: 'I saw my grandfather, God's Messenger, in a dream. He commanded me to do something and I am going to do it. God has resolved to grant me good; he is the guarantor of that and well-able to deliver it, should He will it so.'

Then he asked for a pen and ink and wrote a letter to the people of Kufa. It read:

'In the name of God, the Compassionate, the Merciful. From Hussein b. Ali to the assembly of faithful and Muslims.

Hani and Sa'eed brought me your letters and were the last persons to do so. I have given thought to everything you have related to me and mentioned therein. The majority of you have said: 'We have no leader, so come to us that God might unite us upon truth and guidance through you.'

I am sending to you my brother, my paternal cousin, and trusted member of my household, Muslim b. Aqeel. He will inform me of the truth of your affair and write to me about your situation. If he writes to me that your leaders, notables and scholars are unanimous in their opinion, as your letters and messages to me have claimed, then I will come to you with all haste, God-willing. By my life, the Imam is none other than he who acts according to God's book, upholds justice, proclaims the truth and dedicates himself to God. Peace.'

Then he called for Muslim b. Aqeel and told him: 'I am sending you as my representative to the people of Kufa and these are the letters they wrote to me. God will decree for your affair whatever He desires and whatever pleases Him best. I hope that you and I will be ranked amongst the martyrs, so go with God's blessing to Kufa. When you arrive there, stay with the most trustworthy of its people and if you see the people there united then hasten to send word to us, that I may act upon that God-willing.' Then he gave him some advice to be God-fearing, discreet about his mission and kind to the people.

During their daily meeting near the Ka'ba, Rahman asked his friend about what was happening in the house of Hussein and who was going to him.

Abdullah: You know that Hussein has become the axis of the people's movement and the object of their hopes. The oppressed and downtrodden of the faithful see in him a flag raised for the truth and a clear call to restore their rights. They know that the Prophet's Household were and still are the true and rightful leaders of the Nation. And the leader of the Prophet's Household is none other than Hussein. People only fell silent and surrendered to tyranny because they had lost all hope of victory over their enemies. But today all the hopes of the people to obtain their rights and throw-off the yoke of oppression have been gathered in Hussein. They believe that Hussein embodies the spirit of his grandfather, God's Messenger, in this time now. This is why you see the people of Hijaz, whether alone or in groups, going to Hussein's house to meet him, to show their love for him and the fact that they stand with him. And even if Hussein does not say much – he never does! – the simple fact he has refused to pledge allegiance and withdrawn to Mecca is enough to show his contempt for the regime. For this reason, Hussein can never leave his home to visit the Holy Sanctuary, whether for circumambulation or prayer, without hundreds of people walking with him in the streets. And when the vicinity of the Ka'ba is crowded with worshippers, anyone who sees him there will know that he has the hearts of the people with him.

As for Kufa, you know the situation there. All that is new is that Hussein has sent his letter to them, and he has sent other letters to Basra and Rayy.

Rahman: What did he write in those letters?

Abdullah: Their import was a summons to hold fast to the truth, restore the place of the Quran and the Prophet's sunna and throw off all innovations which had not been endorsed by God, such as turning the Caliphate into biting kingship, ruling according to one's whims, expelling virtuous men from every centre of government and replacing them with vicious ones, which meant the exclusion of the Religion and all of its teachings and principles too.

All of this is what happened a long time ago, when things were progressing far away from what God and his Messenger had commanded.

Rahman: Who did Hussein write these letters to?

Abdullah: In Basra, he wrote to the people's tribal leaders, like *Ahnaf b. Qays, Mālik b. Masmaʿ, Mundhir b. Jārūd, Qays b. Haytham, Masʿūd b. Amr and Amr b. Ubaydullah b. Muʿammar.*

Rahman: Do you have a copy of these letters or part of them?

Abdullah: I do. In his letter to the chieftans in Basra, Hussein wrote:

'In the name of God, the Compassionate, the Merciful. From Hussein b. Ali. God chose Muhammad above all His creation and honoured him with prophethood, bestowed upon him His message, and Muhammad guided God's servants and conveyed the messages of His Lord to them. Then God took him unto Himself, and his household and people were the rightful possessors of his position after him, but a people usurped our rights. We submitted and remained quiet to avoid discord and to seek harmony. I write to you in this letter, calling you to God's Book and the sunna of His prophet. For indeed the sunna has been slain and innovation given life in its place. If you hear my words and follow my command, I will guide you to the right path. Peace and God's mercy be with you.'

Throughout the Islamic world, signs of unrest became more apparent by the day. News came from different quarters indicating that there were the beginnings of an uprising amongst the Nation against deviation from the teachings of the Prophet, against tyranny and oppression, against efforts to hollow out the religion and ignore its principles while holding on to its appearance.

Hussein's decision to rise up spurred things forward, all indications seemed to show that something big was about to happen.

It was the middle of *Shawwāl* and the two friends, Rahman and Abdullah, were still meeting from time to time after *'Ishā'* prayers at the Ka'ba.

Rahman: 'What has happened with Muslim b. Aqeel and his journey to Kufa?

Abdullah: Muslim left Mecca for Medina in secret in the middle of *Ramaḍān*, so that the Umayyads would not know of his journey. He went to Kufa by way of Medina in order to put his affairs in order and see his family. Then he hired two guides from the Qays tribe and went with them, but they lost their way by night and were afflicted by severe heat and thirst. The two guides became so enfeebled that they could not walk. They said to Muslim: 'Keep going that way, you might make it.' The two of them remained in the desert.

Muslim followed their directions and were in not for his own strength he would not have escaped death; it was not long before the two guides died. But Muslim, accompanied by *Qays b. Musahhar al-Sayḍāwī*, in the nick of time, came across water and found their way again. Muslim stopped at the watering hole and sent a letter to Hussein, seeing what had happened to them in the desert as an ill-omen for their endeavour. He sent the letter with Qays b. Musahhar. It read:

'In the name of God, the Compassionate, the Merciful. To Hussein b. Ali from Muslim b. Aqeel. I set out from Medina with two guides I had hired, but they lost the way and died of thirst. We would have perished too had we not found water at the last moment. O son of God's Messenger, I inform you that we have found water in a place called al-MuÃayq, but I see an ill-omen in what befell us. If you think it best, then relieve me of my duty and send someone else. Peace.'

In response, Hussein wrote: 'In the name of God, the Compassionate, the Merciful. From Hussein b. Ali to Muslim b. Aqeel. I have heard God's Messenger say: 'None of us, the People of the Household, sees an ill-omen in anything nor does anyone see an ill-omen in him. When you read my letter, then proceed as I have commanded you. Peace.'

When the response reached Muslim, he set off immediately towards Kufa without any further delay.

Rahman: Then when did he arrive in Kufa and where did he stay there?

Abdullah: Muslim b. Aqil arrived in Kufa five days into Shawwal and moved from one place to another. In the beginning, he stayed in the house of *Mukhtār b. Abi Ubayda al-Thaqafī*. Then he moved to the house of *Muslim b. 'Awsaja*. Once there, the faithful began to visit him to offer their greetings to him; whenever a group came to him, he would read Hussein's letter to the people of Kufa for them, and they would hasten to pledge allegiance whether alone or in groups. Sometimes the head of a tribe would come to him and pledge allegiance on behalf of his tribe, but in most cases it was the people themselves that came to give their allegiance.

Rahman: Did this happen openly or in secret?

Abdullah: It wasn't completely out in the open, nor completely kept secret. It was something in between, in that the ones who came to him were people that he trusted.

Rahman: How were the groups who came and greeted him and what did they say?

Abdullah: When Muslim first arrived in Kufa, whenever he would read Hussein's letter to the people they would begin to weep and cry.

'Ābis b. Shubayb al-Shākirī was one of the first people to meet Muslim. And amongst a group of people, he stood up, praised and magnified God, sent blessings on the Prophet and his family, then said: 'I cannot tell you about the people for I do not know what is in their hearts, neither will I mislead you about them. But by God, I shall tell you where I stand, and by God I will respond to you if you call on me; I will fight your enemies beside you and I will strike out with my sword in front of you until I go to meet my Maker, wanting nothing from that except God's reward.'

'Ābis b. Shubayb had an old friend with whom he used to meet and they always had similar positions on things. This old friend was *Habib b. Muẓāhir al-Asadi*. And when *'Ābis* had finished speaking these words, Habib turned to him and said: 'God have mercy on you, you said it better than I ever could.'

Then he turned to Muslim b. Aqeel and said: 'As for me, then by the

God whom there is no god besides, I am of the same view as him.'

Rahman: And did Muslim's arrival remain hidden from the agents of the regime?

Abdullah: I'm afraid not. Because so many people were going to see him, word of his presence spread and soon everyone knew who he was. So he moved to the house of *Hani b. 'Urwa*, where he received the pledge of allegiance from close to eighteen thousand men.

Rahman: Then what was the position of the regime towards him? Is not the governor of Kufa one of Yazid's men?

Abdullah: Of course, the governor is none other than *Nu'man b. Bashir al-Anṣārī*, a man who detested Ali and the people of Kufa for supporting him. He was one of Muawiya's veterans from *Siffīn* and a close friend of his. Now, he rules Kufa on behalf of Yazid. But he is motivated primarily by an amibition for status and power - he is not a fighter or a killer. He tries to settle things in Yazid's favour through persuasion and affability towards the people sometimes, and by threatening them at others. Once word reached him that Muslim had arrived in Kufa and people were pledging allegiance to him, Nu'man called people for congregational prayer and addressed them in the central Mosque. In his speech, he told them: 'Fear your Lord, O servants of God! Do not hasten to sedition and division, for therein do men perish, therein is blood shed and property usurped. Lo! Indeed I will not fight anyone who does not fight me, nor will I attack anyone who does not attack me. I will not revile you, sow discord amongst you, nor arrest you on the basis of dislike, suspicion or accusation. But if you show immoderation towards me, break your oaths of allegiance or disobey your leader, then by Him other than whom there is no god, I will strike you with my sword so long as it remains in my hand, even if I have not a single helper amongst you. But I hope that those of you who know the truth outnumber those who will be felled by falsehood.'

Abdullah b. Muslim al-Haḍramī, one of the allies of the Umayyad clan, stood up and said: 'Nothing will fix this except violence, and your words to your enemies are the words of the weak and enfeebled!'

Nu'man said: 'I would rather be weak in obedience to God than mighty in disobedience to Him; I will not violate that which God has preserved.'

Rahman: From what you say, it seems as though the allies of the Umayyad clan in Kufa are divided amongst themselves with regards to Muslim. Some of them want to see a ruthless and bloody response, while others are seeking to avoid just that.

Abdullah: It's exactly as you say. Of those who are with the Umayyads just to seek stability, worldly wealth, status and power, not one of them is convinced that the Umayyads represent the truth. But then there are those people motivated by a hatred of the Prophet's Household to take a harsh line and fight them; they want to use their swords without delay.

Rahman: Do you think that these ruthless people will prevail over the likes of Nu'man b. Bashir?

Abdullah: With regards to Nu'man, he is no different from anyone else in that he is against the Prophet's Household. Rather he differs in that he just wants peace and stability as I told you; he wants power, wealth and an easy life... I do not think he will take a harsh line, especially when he told one of those demanding he do just that: 'The son of the Prophet's daughter is dearer to me than the son of *Buḥdal's*.'

Rahman: And what did he mean by the son of *Buḥdal's* daughter?

Abdullah: He meant Yazid b. Muawiya; his mother was *Maysūn*, the daughter of *Buḥdal al-Kalbī*.

Rahman: Did Nu'man dare to say such a thing about Yazid?

Abdullah: You know that the nobles of the Umayyad clan, including Muawiya's governors, were not happy about pledging allegiance to Yazid. Many of them thought that they were more entitled to the Caliphate than him, and some saw no good in his accession to the throne. So while they had no desire to see the Prophet's Household return to power, because their own disobedience towards God, wrongdoing and tyranny had deprived them of the opportunity to follow the Prophet's Household, neither did they hold any affection for Yazid b. Muawiya – all they had in common was a hatred of Ali b. Abu Talib. So sometimes they would utter words such as these.

Rahman: Is it possible that word of this will reach *Yazīḍ*?

Abdullah: Absolutely! The Umayyad clan has spies, agents and henchmen who oppress the people to prop up their regime. In fact, it was hearing these very words that caused Yazid to say: 'I have heard that Nu'man is weak and speaking inappropriately.'

Rahman: How do you see the situation in Kufa now?

Abdullah: If things continue as they are, Muslim b. Aqeel will soon be in control of the city. The balance is tipped in his favour; the people want change and the faithful have found a leader for their movement; the ruler has no desire to see bloodshed, and you know that in a war of words the truth will always prevail. The Prophet's Household are the people of truth, their words are light, their commands are guidance, their advice is godfearingness and it shapes people's souls to incline towards good.

But should the balance change and the governors of the Umayyad clan take up the sword, hasten to shed blood and follow Muawiya's policy of using every trick and stratagem at their disposal; whether betral, assassination or torture, then things may take a turn for the worst. If that happens, Kufa will not be a safe place for the people of truth.

Rahman: "Do you mean that people will turn coat, even after so many have pledged allegiance to Muslim b. Aqeel?"

Abdullah: Those are still a minority compared to the entire population of Kufa, who number in the hundreds of thousands. So they are by no means a majority. Yes, if all of those who pledged allegiance were soldiers like *'Ābis b. Shubayb* and *Habib b. Muẓāhir*, then this number would be sufficient. But this is not the case.

Perhaps some of them will change sides – the mob will follow anyone and changes its allegiance with the changing of the winds. But for the supporters of falsehood to triumph, this does not mean that the people of truth will change sides. If the faithful moved now, and if the Umayyad clan used all the tactics employed by Muawiya, mobilizing the hypocrites with wealth and weapons and putting their own affairs in order, then perhaps things will go against the faithful. But this does not mean that the faithful will change sides, only that the balance of power will be altered.

Rahman: So you are still not optimistic about their chances?

Abdullah: We will not know the outcome until the last moment; it all depends on matters progress. People still live under the yoke of the Umayyids and in the shadow of their regime; all the resources of the state are in their hands; their police and army still control the situation. Changing this will not be easy, especially when people are tempted by worldly gains – they are not like they were in the time of the Prophet.

Don't you see how some of the Prophet's companions – who had lived a difficult life before Islam – changed when they were enriched by the success of Islam, and they started to fight for the sake of wealth and booty? Have you not heard the words of Ali when one day he gave a sermon in which he complained about the positions of others towards him: 'When I took up the reins of government one party broke away and another turned disobedient while the rest began acting wrongfully as if they had not heard the word of God saying: 'This is the abode of the Hereafter which We shall grant to those who do not desire to domineer in the earth nor to cause corruption, and the outcome will be in favour of the Godwary.' Yes, by God, they had heard it and understood it but the world appeared glittering in their eyes and its embellishments seduced them.'?

I do not believe that it will be easy to change the people such that they will give up their servitude to this world day and night and begin again to search for that which will bring them near to God by sacrificing their lives and wealth for him. Most people are not like the Prophet's Household who show asceticism towards this world, not wanting anything except good for others, not seeking anything for themselves.

We will soon see the outcome of these matters.'

REVERSALS

The agents of the Umayyad clan felt they were losing their grip on power. Once they saw notable figures such as *Mukhtār b. Abu Ubayda al-Thaqafī, Hani b. 'Urwa al-Mudhḥajī, 'Ābis b. Shubayb al-Shākirī, Habib b. Muẓāhir al-Asadi* and others, gathering around Muslim b. Aqeel, with the possibility of Hussein coming to the city, they began to write to Yazid asking him to make changes to the highest echelons of government in Kufa.

Abdullah b. Muslim al-Bāhilī, Umar b. Sa'd b. Abu Waqqāṣ al-Zuhrī, Muhammad b. al-Ash'ath al-Kindi, Muslim b. Sa'eed al-Haḍramī - all loyal supporters of the Umayyad clan – wrote a letter to Yazid, in which they said: 'To God's servant, Yazid, the Commander of the Faithful, from his followers amongst the people of Kufa. Muslim b. Aqeel has come to Kufa and Hussein's supporters have pledged allegiance to him. They are numerous indeed, so if you intend to retain control of the city you must send a strong man to implement your commands, and deal with your enemies as you would. Nu'man b. Bashir is a weakling or is making a show of weakness. Peace.'

When this letter reached Yazid, he summoned one of his father's advisors, a Roman called Sir John. He said: 'Muslim b. Aqeel is in Kufa taking the pledge of allegiance for Hussein. I have heard Nu'man is weak and speaking inappropriately. What is your advice? Who shall I make my agent in Kufa?'

It was not unusual for this man to advise Yazid, and he was a man of real influence in the Muslim state who worked to advance Roman interests; he appointed and deposed governors as he wished, as is the practice of every ruler who did not have the interests of the Muslims at heart. He sought assistance from foreigners, who advised him on courses of action that were not in the interest of the religion of the people, because they were fundamentally enemies of that religion.

Sir John said: 'Should I give you advice that you will not like?'

Yazid said: 'Even if I do not like it!'

Sir John said: 'Make Ubaydullah b. Ziyad your governor in Kufa.'

Yazid detested Ubaydullah b. Ziyad and had actually wanted to remove him from his post in Basra. He said: 'He is no good. Find me someone else.'

Sir John said: 'If your father was alive, would you accept his advice and do as he told you?'

Yazid: 'Of course.'

Sir John said: 'This is a document appointing Ubaydullah b. Ziyad as governor of Kufa. Muawiya had ordered me to draw it up, so I did as he requested. It has his seal, but he died and it remained in my possession. I only failed to inform you of it until now because I knew how much you disliked the man.'

Yazid said: 'Then see that it is delivered.'

So Yazid ultimately accepted Sir John's advice and joined Basra and Kufa under Ubaydullah's authority, sending him his letter of appointment to Kufa.

In it, he wrote: 'From God's servant, Yazid, the Commander of the Faithful, to Ubaydullah b. Ziyad. Peace be with you. There are days when the praiseworthy are reviled and the reviled are praised. To you belongs whatever is your due. But you have been raised up so high that you are as the poet says:

You were raised up beyond the clouds and higher still
Until the only seat for you was that of the Sun.

Of all the times that could have been afflicted by Hussein, it is your time, and of all the lands, it is yours, and of all the governors, it is you. In this, you will either be released or remain a dutiful servant. My supporters in Kufa have informed me that Muslim b. Aqeel is gathering followers and sowing disunity amongst the Muslims. Many of the supporters of Abu *Turāb* have amassed around him. So when this letter reaches you, you are to go to Kufa and take care of matters for me there. I have added it to your domain and made it one of your duties. Make finding Muslim b. Aqeel your first priority; win him over, kill him or expel him, and know that I will accept no excuses for failure. Make haste! Peace.'

Then he gave this message to *Muslim b. Amr al-Bāhilī* and told him to deliver it to Ubaydullah in Basra.

When Rahman meets Abdullah again, they begin to talk about events in Kufa.

Abdullah: Have you heard about what happened in Basra?

Rahman: No.

Abdullah: Hussein's letters have reached the people to whom they were addressed; the tribal leaders.

Rahman: And what did they do in response?

Abdullah: Some of them did their duty. For example, when Hussein's letter reached *Yazid b. Mas'ūd al-Nahshalī*, he gathered all the *Tamīm, Hanẓala* and *Sa'd* clans in his house. Once everyone was present, he said: 'O men of *Tamīm*, how do you see my place amongst you and my standing with you?'

They said: 'Bravo! By God, you are the foremost in distinction, the source of honor, the axis of nobility – there is no one more noble than you!'

Ibn Mas'ūd said: 'Good, for I have gathered you all here to seek your advice and assistance on a matter that concerns me.'

They said: 'We will give you our advice and opinion on whatever you ask. Speak!'

He said: 'Muawiya has perished, and has been brought low in perishing. And lo! Indeed the back of tyranny and wrongdoing has been broken, the pillars of oppression have crumbled, but he thought that by taking the pledge of allegiance for his son he had settled the matter and secured his legacy. He tried and – by God! – he failed, he sought advice and was betrayed. Now his winebibbing and immoral son, Yazid, has stood up to take his place and claim the Caliphate of the Muslims for himself. He appoints governors over them without their consent, despite his lack of common sense and knowledge, and the fact that he does not even know the truth even of where he puts his feet! So I swear to you by God, ready to give my life, that struggling for the sake of the religion is better than fighting against the polytheists!

Then there is Hussein b. Ali, the son of the Prophet's daughter, a man of great nobility and vision, a man with merit that cannot be described and knowledge that cannot be exhausted! He is more entitled to the Caliphate because of his pre-eminence in the religion, his age, stature and blood-relation to the Prophet. He is gentle with the young and kind to the old; a flock would be ennobled by having him as a shepherd, and a people by having him as a leader. Through him, God will raise His authority and deliver His admonition. So do not be blind to the light of truth, nor grope about in the depths of falsehood. *Ṣakhr b. Qays* was left helpless by you at the Battle of the Camel – wash away this stain by rising up for the grandson of the Prophet and assisting him!

By God, no one will fall short in assisting Hussein save that God will bequeath him abasement in his children and meagreness in his tribe. Here you see me dressed for battle and donned my armour. Whoever is not slain will one day die, and whoever flees will not escape death forever. So respond as you should, may God have mercy upon you!'

Then the *Hanẓala* clan spoke and said: 'O *Abu Khālid*! We are the arrows in your quiver and the horsemen of your tribe. If you shoot us from your bow, you will strike your target, and if you send us forth, you will conquer. By God, you will not delve into something save that we have already delved into it, nor will you encounter any hardship save that we have already encountered it. We will assist you with our swords and protect you with our bodies. So do as you wish.'

Then the Sa'd clan spoke: 'O *Abu Khālid!* We hate nothing more than to disagree with you or depart from your opinion. Sakhr b. Qays had told us not to fight, so we praised God for our affair and retained our honour. So let us discuss this and give you our opinion.

Then the *Tamīm* clan spoke: 'O *Abu Khālid!* We are the tribe of your father and your sworn allies; we will not be satisfied if you are angry, nor will we stand by if you go forth. The matter rests with you. Call us and we will answer. Command us and we will obey. Do as you see fit.'

Having heard what each of the clans had to say, he wrote a letter to Hussein, saying:

'In the name of God, the Compassionate, the Merciful. I have received your letter and understood what you have called me to, and that you have summoned me to take my share in the blessings of obeying you and seize the prize of supporting you. God does not leave His earth without someone in it to do good and guide others to the way of salvation. You are God's authority over His creatures, His trustee in His earth. You are a branch of the tree of Muhammad. Come forth and none would be more joyous than I, for I have placed at your disposal the clan of *Tamīm*. And I have left them more desperate to obey you than a thirsty camel is to drink water. And I have put at your disposal the clan of Sa'd, having washed the filth from their hearts with the water of a storm cloud that strikes out with its lightning and is illuminated.'

When Hussein read the letter, he said: 'Why? May God grant you safety on a day of fear, and quench you on a day of great thirst.'

Rahman: You said that people responded differently to the letters from Hussein, were there any who did not answer Hussein's call?

Abdullah: Yes! *Mundhir b. Jārūd* – one of those to whom Hussein wrote – immediately went to show the letter to Ubaydullah b. Ziyad, who was still in Basra. He did this because his daughter was Ubaydullah's wife, not to mention the fact that he was afraid that this letter was a ruse concocted by Ubaydullah to test his loyalty. So he brought the letter to him and Ibn Ziyad became angry: 'Who is Hussein's messenger to Basra?' He demanded.

Mundhir said: 'His messenger is a non-Arab (mawla) called *Sulayman*.'

Ubaydullah said: 'Bring him to me!'

Sulayman was hidden amongst some of the non-Arabs in Basra. Mundhir brought him to Ubaydullah. The latter said nothing to him, he just stepped forward and cut off his head. Then he ordered his body crucified. He was the first messenger to be killed in Islam.

As for Ahnaf b. Qays, he did nothing save to write a reply to Hussein, in which he said: 'So be patient! God's promise is indeed true. And do not let yourself be upset by those who have no conviction.'

There was also a group of non-Arabs in Basra who began to organize themselves in support of Hussein. One devout woman, known as *Māriya b. Sa'd*, who was a follower of the Prophet's Household, turned her house into a meeting place for the faithful, wherein they would discuss the affairs of the Nation, the Imamate and the condition of the people. A group of them resolved to set out for Mecca to meet Hussein, others wrote letters to Hussein telling him to come to them.

Another member of the faithful in Basra called *Yazid b. Nabuṭ* gathered his sons, who numbered ten, and asked them: 'Who of you will come with me, for I am going to Hussein?'

Two of his sons, Abdullah and Ubaydullah, agreed to accompany him. He told his companions: 'I have decided to go to Hussein and I am going soon.'

They said: 'We fear you will come to harm at the hands of Ibn Ziyad's thugs!'

He said: 'By God, even if they trample me under foot, it is nothing for me.'

This shows that the happenings in Kufa, the widespread unrest and the activism of the faithful had spread to Basra too. The righteous men and women were busy there; some decided to go to Hussein and others to write to him and invite him to Basra as the Kufans had done before them.

Rahman: Didn't the regime do anything in response to all of this?

Abdullah: In fact, it did everything that it could. When Yazid's letter reached Ubaydullah b. Ziyad, ordering to go to Kufa and placing it under his authority with Basra - making the man responsible for governing Iran and Iraq one in whom the Umayyad clan's hatred for the Prophet's Household was deeply rooted – and this tyrant wanted to depart from Basra, he gathered the people in the central mosque and addressed them, making them tremble and shake with terrible threats.

He said: 'By God, I am not a stubborn or hateful man, but I am a shackle to whoever opposes me and poison to whoever attacks me. Never challenge a bowman to an archery contest.'

Then he fell silent for a moment, before saying: 'O people of Basra, the Commander of the Faithful has appointed me as governor over Kufa, and I intend to travel there. In my stead, I have left my brother Uthman b. Ziyad in charge of you. So beware of dissension and agitation! For by the One whom there is no god except He, if I hear that anyh of you has disobeyed me, I will kill him, his chieftain and his heir. I will punish even the slightest infraction with the utmost severity so that you will be obedient subjects. So let there be amongst you not a single opponent or dissenter. I am the son of Ziyad, and I resemble him most of anyone. I do not betake after anyone else.'

Rahman: Were these empty threats intended to scare the people into line, or did this man mean what he said?

Abdullah: These were not just threats; Ibn Ziyad was a man whose deeds matched his words, as he has demonstrated in the past. He gave many gifts to his police and kept his people into line by using the same methods as Muawiya had. He had people arrested on accusation and executed on suspicion. He had spies in every place and guards watching everyone who came and went from Basra. He commanded his brother to keep the people under lock and key, to question their beliefs and to arrest the innocent as well as the accused. In this way he cast a fear without equal into the hearts of the Basrans.

Rahman: After Yazid's letter to him, did Ubaydullah hesitate in going to Kufa, or did he go with all haste?

Abdullah: He ordered his people to make preparations for the journey as soon as he read the letter, intending to go to Kufa the next day.

Rahman: Ubaydullah's methods in Basra sound just like those of

Pharaoh in the Qur'an: '...and I will crucify you on the trunks of palm trees!' – don't they?

Abdullah: The tyrants all have one teacher – Satan. That is why their methods are always the same throughout history: "You are either with us or against us!" There is no middle-ground; whatever they believe, the people must believe. This is just as Pharaoh says: 'I only make you think what I do, and I guide you only to the way of rectitude.'

Rahman: But those people speak about God as though they are His deputies who speak in His name, and those to whom He has entrusted care of the earth. Whatever they do, they ascribe it to God's will, and in every other word they utter they swear oaths by God, just as sometimes they speak in the name of the people and consider Yazid, who was appointed by his father, as the rightful ruler, using violence and bribery to secure his rule, while the faithful neither appointed him nor chose him. Is this not the very same thing that Pharaoh did?

Abdullah: Pharaoh considered himself to be the highest lord. All tyrants really think that they are gods, or at the very least speaking on behalf of God. If our rulers today thought they could say what Pharaoh did, they would have done so. But they are hypocrites who conceal in their hearts what Pharaoh did, while paying lip-service to the message of the prophets. In their hearts, they tell the people "We are your highest lord" and in practice they act as though they are, but they make a show of remembering God... they kill God's *people* while using the words of His prophets.

Rahman: So the danger of these people to the religion must be greater than that of the faithless and the idol-worshippers!

Abdullah: It was not for no reason that our Lord sent down a complete Surah in the Quran about the hypocrites! He says of them: 'They are the enemy, so beware of them. May God assail them...' This is because the threat of the hypocrites is twofold. You see that the state is being run by a foreigner who works as an advisor for

Yazid, as he did for his father – Sir John, the Roman, who does not believe in God's religion. Yazid neither appoints or dismisses anyone without his say-so. Don't you see that when he initially refused to appointed Ubaydullah b. Ziyad as the governor of Kufa, he told Sir John: 'Give me someone else.' Meaning either this one or someone you deem suitable.

In any case, what matters is that the decision ultimately rests with this foreign advisor. When he is not satisfied with someone, he can choose someone else. The danger here is that such people are trying to destroy everything that the Prophet built. And this is why false innovation has appeared and the practice of the Prophet has been put to death.

The worst innovation of all is that the Caliphate of God's Messenger has been turned into a biting kingship, and that the whims of the ruler have become the measure of truth and falsehood, not the teachings of the prophets. Therefore the danger of the hypocrites is twofold in that from one angle they are distorting the religion from within, and from another they are trying to destroy whatever remains of the edifice that God's Messenger erected!

Rahman: Do these people want to bring an end to religion, or do they want to continue making a show of religiosity and ruin it from within?

Abdullah: I do not doubt that they wish to destroy it and everything connected to it, whether great or small. Muawiya said as much on one occasion.

Rahman: When!?

Abdullah: Listen, *Muṭraf b. Mugheira b. Shu'ba* said: 'I went with my father as a delegation to Muawiya, and my father would go and speak to him and then leave. One night, my father came from his presence but would not eat food. I saw he was troubled and I thought it was because of something that had happened to us or our efforts. I asked him, 'Why do I see you so troubled this night?'

He said, 'Son, I just came from the presence of the foulest man upon the earth.'

- 'Who do you mean?'

- 'Muawiya.'

- 'How so?'

My father said, 'When I was alone with Muawiya, I told him: 'You have attained your heart's desire, O Commander of the Faithful! Perhaps now you can do justice and spread goodness, for you have grown old. Perhaps you can even show some concern for your brothers in the Hashemite clan and maintain your ties of family – by God, you have nothing to fear from them now!'

Muawiya told me: 'Oh no, far from it – Abu Bakr ruled and did what he did, but no sooner did he perish than he was forgotten in all but name. Then Umar ruled, strived hard and ruled for twenty years, but no sooner did he perish than he too was forgotten in all but name. Then our brother, Uthman ruled, followed by a man with a lineage like no other – he dealt as he did and then was dealt with. But, by God, no sooner did he perish than he and his fate were both forgotten. And every day, God's Messenger is mentioned five times – I bear witness that Muhammad is God's Messenger – so what deeds can possibly be remembered against that? No, by God. Not unless we bury his memory too.'''

Rahman: Now I understand the depth of the wound Hussein bears and why he feels he must revive the religion of Islam, restore God's laws and bring the message afresh. Is Hussein's goal in refusing to pledge allegiance to bring down the government of the Umayyads and to raise the government of the Prophet's House?

Abdullah: This issue is bigger than merely setting up a government. Of course Hussein wants to raise-up truth and spread justice, but that doesn't mean he can necessarily achieve these aims by simply ruling. All of God's prophets wanted to raise-up the truth, spread justice and implement God's laws on earth, but not only by setting up a government with them at its head. No, by guiding people and encouraging them to do their individual duties and play their own roles in bringing this about, by curbing the oppressor's tyranny, confronting evil men and assisting good ones... and all of this can only be achieved through the people.

Rahman: But in the end, a movement of people must crystallize into some kind of regime?

Abdullah: Yes, of course. Their movement must set up a just system, but not necessarily a regime or changing one leader for another. It was never the goal of God's Messenger to remove Abu Sufiyan from power in Mecca to install himself or someone else he liked in his place. Rather, his goal was to guide the people and thereby change their lives from all angles.

The difference between Hussein and Yazid is that Yazid wants nothing other than power, while Hussein wants to guide the people.

Rahman: You mean to say that Yazid has no program he wishes to implement?

Abdullah: I don't mean that. Yazid has a specific program he wishes to implement, namely his own interests. His only message is one of hypocrisy – he wants power for its own sake.

Rahman: Didn't you say that they wanted to destroy the religion. Isn't that their program, then?

Abdullah: Yazid, like all tyrants in history, wants absolute power. Such absolute power naturally runs contrary to submitting to God's power, which is the essence of the prophetic message, just as it also runs contrary to the idea of people's rights. This is because such tyrants want absolute power and their goal is to destroy every view except their own and crush whoever disagrees with them.

Pharaoh was against Moses – why? Because he wanted his own authority to be that of the highest lord, and because the Israelites would not accept that, he punished them. And when Moses said to him: 'We are the Messengers of your Lord. Let the Children of Israel go with us, and do not torture them!' he had resolved to have him killed.

Pharaoh wanted the Israelites to be his slaves, to think nothing besides what he thought, to accept whatever he claimed, namely that he was their god. This is the message of all tyrants throughout history, and this is their program.

As for the program of the prophets and people, is it a complete and holistic one. Good governance is only one part of this program, and not the ultimate goal or ambition of it. Hussein himself said in his testament to Muhammad b. Hanafiyya, 'I do not go forth to do evil, for vainglory, to oppress or cause corruption. I go forth only to seek reform in the Nation of my grandfather.' So he does not want to act for the sake of "evil" - meaning to stir up discord or "vainglory" – seeking power and position; no, he wants to reform the Nation of his grandfather. This is reform in its fullest sense; part of it is connected to their faith, piety and self-purification, part of it with countering tyranny and oppression, and setting up a just system.

But as for restricting this issue to regime-change, that is not one of Hussein's goals, just as that was not the goal of his grandfather, father or any of the prophets and people. They had no desire for worldly authority and even if their uprisings resulted in them being granted it, they only used it to raise-up truth. And when their uprisings did not result in political and military victory over their enemies, they nevertheless did what they could to guide people and bring about reform.

For this reason, at the same time as the prophets were sent 'so that mankind may maintain justice' they were also ready to be slain for the sake of God. The Quran says: ''Do you await anything to befall us except one of the two excellences?' In their eyes, there were two equal outcomes: either they would be victorious, or they would be slain.

Rahman: Do you mean to say that these are the two outcomes Hussein sees open to himself now as well? And that his present refusal to pledge allegiance, his response to the people of Kufa, and his dispatch of messengers to the leaders of the faithful, does not mean that he is seeking necessarily to overthrow the Umayyads?

Abdullah: Exactly! Hussein wants what the prophets wanted before him, his goal is their goal in bringing about the realization of the truth, the destruction of falsehood, implementing justice, reviving people's souls, guiding mankind, raising up the good amongst men and restraining the evil; encouraging the faithful to do their duties in defending the truth, assisting the oppressed and suffering and punishing the oppressors.

So, unlike the tyrants, who act in place of the people, deciding for them – no, even thinking for them, eating for them, drinking and enjoying life for them, without giving any chopice to the people... the people are completely the opposite of this. They do not wish to act in place of the people. When some say to them: Come, take power, decree whatever you wish and do as you like, they are seeking to make them partners in their actions. Therefore, the people forbid themselves the pleasures of this world that the ordinary people might have them instead. Their slogan is: 'Say, 'I do not ask you any reward for it!' Because God has made asceticism their duty in the levels of this low world, and they observe this duty for Him.

When one of them is pledged allegiance to as a leader of a people, and complete authority comes to rest in his hand, he does not suffice himself with issuing decrees and he forces no one to obey him. Rather he enjoins himself to live like the weakest members of his society, so that the poor man would not be overcome by his poverty. This includes all areas of life under that authority; in other words, they never see themselves as needless such that they become afflicted by tyranny as the Quran says: 'Indeed man becomes rebellious when he considers himself without need.' Under their authority, any duty remains the duty of the group and not that of the individual, by the same token, any rights are the rights of the group and not of the individual. For this reason, none of God's people allow themselves to do wrong to a single person, or even a single grain of barley, as Imam Ali once said: 'By God, even if I am given all the domains of the seven (stars) with all that exists under the skies in order that I may disobey God to the extent of snatching one grain of barley from an ant I would not do it.' In their eyes, all property belongs to God, and authority belongs to the people.

The ruler of Iraq comes to Kufa.. Thirsty for blood and revenge

Appointing Ibn Ziyad as the governor of Kufa and Basra meant only one thing; that the regime was prepared to shed the blood of innocents to preserve its power.

Ibn Ziyad understood his mission well; what was expected of him was to lead a merciless and bloody campaign of repression against the Prophet's Household. Perhaps the pillars of the regime saw this a fitting time to deal with them once and for all. God's Messenger had left this world not fifty years past, Imam Ali had been slain, and his enemy, Muawiya, had changed the very nature of the state and society in the course of his twenty year reign, in accordance with the goal of the Umayyad clan to hollow out the religion and turn the very symbols and rites of the religion against the religion itself. He did this by making a big show of the religion's slogans, while acting against its dictates. Of the Prophet's Household, there remained only Hussein and a small number of his brothers, children and cousins. For this reason, wiping them out entirely, using Hussein's refusal to pledge allegiance to Yazid as a pretext to slay him and everyone who followed him, meant the fruition of the plans of the Umayyads – namely, destroying the message of the Prophet by destroying his Household who were its defenders, and then destroy the religion altogether.

As we know, when a regime purges its enemies, this is not restricted to shedding their blood. Rather, it extends to include the waging of a media war against its enemies' goals as well, and therefore the destruction of their enemies' project as a whole. This is what Muawiya did. After Imam Ali was slain, he ordered that Ali be slandered from the pulpit, forbade that people mention any traditions about him or relate them from him. In fact, just mentioning his name was treated as a serious crime worthy of punishment. For this reason, Imam Hussein named all of his sons Ali - Ali the Elder, Ali the Middle and Ali the Younger, because only the Imam himself was capable of naming his children Ali - the state had otherwise erased this name from public discourse.

In this way, the destruction of Hussein did not only mean shedding his blood and killing him; it also meant the destruction of his view of religion and his view of the prophetic message. This was destruction in the truest sense of the word.

In their daily meeting, *Rahman al-Ṣāliḥ* and *Abdullah b. Muslim* exchanged news of current events, after the regime began to follow the strategy of tyrants by responding to words with blades, using violence and coercion against anyone who opposed them. Soon the conversation turned to events in Kufa and Basra.

Rahman: What news from Iraq?

Abdullah: After Ibn Ziyad appointed his brother, Uthman, as his deputy in Basra, he set off with twelve nobles, including *Mundhir b. Jārūd al-Abdī, Sharīk b. A'war al-Harithī, Muslim b. Amr al-Bāhilī*, and hundreds of horsemen and retainers; it is said they exceeded five hundred in number.

They rode hard from Basra, so as to reach Kufa as quickly as possible and purge the pockets of support for the Prophet's Household from it and be ready to confront Hussein from there.

But the battle lines had not yet been drawn, so some of those with Ubaydullah b. Ziyad were not loyal supporters of the Umayyads, in fact they were the opposite. For example, *Sharīk b. A'war al-Harithī* was one of those who hoped Hussein would reach Kufa before Ibn

Ziyad and settle the matter for him.

Rahman: Isn't this strange, though? That Ibn Ziyad was surrounded by men who supported the Prophet's Household?

Abdullah: Not at all! Man's soul is fashioned to love good and despise evil, but this does not mean that men's places in the world always follow the fashioning of their souls. Perhaps an oppressor may have men close to him who hate him more than anyone and love his enemies, but who do not act according to what they love and hate.

In any case, those who rode with Ubaydullah to Kufa were not as eager as he was to reach their destination. Some of them even hoped to delay Ibn Ziyad en route so that Hussein would arrive before them and secure the city for himself.

Ubaydullah was so determined to reach Kufa and enjoyed such good health at that time, that many of those who rode with him fell from their mounts because of exhaustion. The first to fall was *Sharīk b. al-A'war*. They had expected Ibn Ziyad to stop and wait for them to recover themselves and remount their horses, hoping that in doing so Hussein would have an opportunity to reach Kufa first. But Ibn Ziyad did not stop for a single one of them.

It is said that some of the men with him feigned illness en route, to delay Ibn Ziyad and force him to travel at a more relaxed pace. But he showed no concern to any of the men with him, even those whom he depended upon – when they fell from their horses, he did not stop for them. When his bondsman, *Mihrān*, fell at Qadisiyyah, Ibn Ziyad merely told him, 'If you recover and come with us, you may rest in the governor's palace, and you shall have a hundred thousand [dirhams].'

Mihrān said, 'By God, I can't!'

So Ubaydullah left him where he lay and *Mihrān* fell behind.

Rahman: And when Ubaydullah b. Ziyad reached Kufa?

Abdullah: I've been told he tricked the people; he entered the city in such a way as to give the impression that he was Hussein b. Ali whom the faithful were awaiting. He entered Kufa from the direction of Hejaz, wearing white robes and a black turban, veiled as was the practice of the people from Hejaz, and riding a grey mount and carried a bamboo cane, with his five hundred men behind him. He chose to enter the city in the evening, just as Joseph's brothers went weeping to their father in the evening, so that their father would not be able to tell whether they were crying or merely pretending to cry. Ibn Ziyad did not pass a single group of people save that he greeted them with peace and waved his staff to them, and they thought that he was Hussein. They said to him: 'What a pleasant sight you are, O son of God's Messenger!'

Some people even kissed his hand and feet.

Ibn Ziyad was angered when saw how the people loved Hussein, saying to his companions: 'How terribly these people have been corrupted!'

As the procession neared the governor's palace, *Muslim b. Amr al-Bāhilī* turned to the people who had come to him thinking that Ibn Ziyad was Hussein and said: 'Hold on, woe to you from the face of the governor. This is not who you think it is, nor who you hope him to be!'

Ibn Ziyad went to the governors palace. Word had already reached Nu'man b. Bashir, the governor of Kufa, that Hussein had come with a large force. So when Ibn Ziyad reached the door of the palace, Nu'man thought he was Hussein and locked the door and shouted: 'I will not surrender what has been entrusted to me to you, nor do I have any need to fight you!'

Ibn Ziyad's face blackened and he called out: 'O Nu'man! You have fortified your palace and abandoned your city. Open the door, you have not been conquered, and your night has grown long!'

At this point, the people who thought this was Hussein realized that it was none other than Ibn Ziyad and began to cry out: 'By He whom there is no god except him! It's the son of *Marjāna*!'

Some others who did not believe them shouted back: 'Woe to you! It is Hussein!'

They shouted back, 'No! It is the son of *Marjāna*!'

Nu'man opened the door of the palace for him, Ibn Ziyad went inside and they slammed the door in the people's faces.

Rahman: What happened to the people?

Abdullah: They despaired; from that day on they were filled with grief and laments.

Rahman: Aside from displaying their sorrow, did no one do anything?

Abdullah: Yes, some of those who thought Ibn Ziyad had been Hussein began to pelt him with pebbles. But this did not bother him much.

Once inside the palace, Ibn Ziyad's replacement of Bashir went smoothly. Ubaydullah removed him from office after giving him a harsh rebuke for failing to use sufficiently harsh measures against the people, as Yazid b. Muawiya had expected from him.

The next day, people were summoned and they gathered in the central mosque. Once it was full, Ubaydullah b. Ziyad ascended the pulpit, praised and glorified God, then said: 'The Commander of the Faithful has made me the governor of your city and your borders; he has made me responsible for dividing your booty, to give redress to your plaintiffs, to look after your poor, to be kind to those of you who hear and obey and to be harsh with anyone who disobeys or is of doubtful loyalty. I will see to it that his commands are followed with regards to you and I will implement his edicts amongst you. To those of you who are good and obedient, I will be like a kind father. But my shout and my sword shall be directed against anyone who disobeys my command or opposes my edicts. Let each man take responsibility for himself. Truthfulness should avert evil from you without threat of punishment' Then he came down from the pulpit.

With this sermon he showed people that he had been given a free hand to use both money and violence to achieve his goals; he will divide the war booty amongst them and treat the obedient well, but he will seize those of doubtful loyalty harshly. He said: 'Let each man take responsibility for himself.' This is a clear threat of death for anyone who would oppose the regime of the Umayyad clan.

As for Nu'man b. Bashir, he set off home towards Syria.

For his part, Ibn Ziyad did not suffice himself with delivering a sermon in the central mosque, threatening the people with death and wooing them with promises of money. No, he undertook a number of practical steps to ensure his position was secure; first, he dealt harshly with the prefects, gathering them and saying: 'Write for me the names of any strangers, as well as the supporters of the Commander of the Faithful, the Kharijites, and those of doubtful loyalty whose views are opposition and discord.' Whosoever's name you give me, you are not responsible for him. But if you do not write anyone's name, then you are responsible for guaranteeing order in your district and that no one will oppose us therein nor rebel against us. Whoever does not do so, I cannot be held responsible for his fate; his wealth and blood will be forfeit. Any prefect who finds a rebel in his district and does not hand him over to us for justice will be crucified at the door of his house, the entire district will have its stipends stopped, or he will be appointed to Oman!'

Secondly, he bestowed more gifts upon the police and increased the number of foot soldiers and horsemen in the city, sending many of them to question people and search their homes. This spread a sense of fear and apprehension throughout the city, as though a psychological war was being waged. Every day, word was spread that the Syrian army was coming to Kufa; a crier was ordered to call out to the Arab tribes: 'Better that you pledge allegiance to Yazid before he sends men from Syria to kill your men and take your women!'

This is how Ubaydullah b. Ziyad began his campaign against those opposed to pledging allegiance to Yazid, supported Muslim b. Aqeel, or wrote letters to Hussein. He also ordered that the local tribal chieftains and military commanders be lavished with gifts. In addition to this, he formed small groups of men and ordered them to go to the tribes, posing as supporters of Hussein b. Ali and asking to be given the pledge of allegiance for Hussein. Whoever gave his allegiance to them, they forwarded his name and those of the people around him to Ibn Ziyad. And of those who refused to pledge allegiance, they would slay one or two of them to increase their hatred of the Prophet's Household.

SHOWDOWN

Ubaydullah's orders to the prefects in Kufa had spread fear and sown confusion amongst the people, as had his placement of men at crossroads to question people, furnished with lists of those individuals whom the regime wished to detain. He had given clear instructions that strangers were to be arrested and that guards were to be posted at all points of entry and exit to the city. Throughout the day, Ibn Ziyad gathered those persons who were loyal to the Umayyad cause, giving them orders and instructions. He went to the treasury and emptied its coffers in the form of gifts and bribes to local leaders. The prisons of Kufa became crowded with new inmates.

His first orders were to arrest anyone who posed a threat to the regime, so it was only natural that one by one, his cells became filled with people.

For his part, Muslim b. Aqeel heard about what was happening. Under cover of darkness, he left the house he had been staying in and moved to the house of *Hani b. 'Urwa al-Madhḥajī*, who was one of the nobles of Kufa, an elder of the *Murād* tribe and its chieftain. When he entered his house, Hani stood up and said: 'What has brought you here?'

Muslim said: 'What I have done. This Ubaydullah b. Ziyad has come to Kufa, so I have come to you to ask for you to grant me shelter and asylum so that I can observe developments.'

Hani said: 'May God have mercy on you. Had you not already entered my house, I would have preferred that you leave. But that would hardly be proper, would it? You may stay here with God's blessing.'

So Muslim went into the house and lodged there, but that is not all he did. He had not gone to hide in the house of *Hani b. 'Urwa* just to keep himself safe, no, he had gone there to continue his work. His trusted and closest companions would still come to him and pledge allegiance to Hussein through him.'

By this time, the number of people who had pledged allegiance to him since he entered Kufa exceeded eighteen-thousand.

With such a large number of people pledging allegiance to Hussein, whether individually or in groups, announcing their loyalty to Hussein and their readiness to defend him and his household, Muslim b. Aqeel wrote a letter which he sent with *'Ābis b. Shubayb al-Shākirī* to Hussein, in which he said:

'In the name of God, the Compassionate, the Merciful.

The initial signs were correct. Eighteen thousand people have pledged allegiance to me, so when you read this letter make haste to come. The people are with you and they have no desire for the continued rule of Abu Sufiyan's clan. Peace.'

In the shade of the Ka'ba, Rahman and Abdullah meet again and discuss the situation.

Abdullah: Do you know what has happened in Kufa?

Rahman: No.

Abdullah: There are now two governments in the city; one is the official government headed by Ubaydullah b. Ziyad, in whose hands rest all the resources of the state to face the Prophet's Household, the other is that of Muslim b. Aqeel, with such a large number of people having pledged allegiance to him, in hiding, a movement of the faithful, striving to win as many supporters for Hussein as possible.

Rahman: Will there be a showdown between these two governments?

Abdullah: As things stand, Muslim b. Aqeel does not have the means to confront Ubaydullah b. Ziyad militarily. His task is only to assess the situation and write to Hussein about events there. According to the letter of Hussein to him and the people of Kufa, he has not been charged with leading any sort of uprising.

Rahman: But what if Ubaydullah was to launch an attack against Muslim?

Abdullah: There's something to be said for every eventuality. I suspect that Muslim would defend himself, as he has not gone there to gather money or weapons for any armed confrontation with the regime. This is because the Prophet's Household follow the same approach as the prophets who came before; they do not hasten to start a war, nor do they see fighting as a way to guide people. In their eyes, the sword is only there to defend against the sword, and power to defend against power.

Rahman: But God's Messenger made war, as did Imam Ali.

Abdullah: And before them, the prophets fought battles too: 'How many a prophet there has been at whose side a multitude of godly men fought.' But they did not fight people to force them to believe in God or His religion. God's Messenger did not even demand that the people of Medina believe in him when he emigrated there, nor did he compel the people of Mecca to believe in his religion when he conquered them. And the Prophet considered those who remained neutral and did not fight him as people whose hearts were to be won over; he showered them with gifts to win them over, so that perhaps they would incline to God's religion by their own choice.

This does not mean that the prophets and people surrender positions of power to their enemies, rather they repel aggression with the like thereof: 'So should anyone aggress against you, assail him in the manner he assailed you.' As Imam Ali once said: 'Return the stone to whence it came, for only aggression can repel aggression.' They were at peace with whoever was at peace with them, and they resisted whoever wished to force faithlessness, idolatry, wrongdoing, tyranny and sinfulness upon them. And Muslim b. Aqeel is no exception to this rule; reports from there indicate that Muslim has not taken up arms even at the most opportune times, when the government was at its weakest. He is not trying to capture the governor's palace, nor declare war on Ubaydullah b. Ziyad when the latter first arrived, even though he has ample men and weapons. This is because God's people fight for the sake of God, while those who have no faith fight for the sake of idols; the people hold fast to their principles and morals, even in the most dire of circumstances, and reject the notion that 'the end justifies the means.' Rather, they believe that 'the ends determine the means and limit them.'

Do you not see that Imam Ali gave up many opportunities for victory [over Muawiya] first because he refused to initiate hostilities, second because he held fast to his moral principles and gave them priority over victory. He said openly to some of his followers: 'Do you enjoin me to seek victory through wrongdoing (jawr)?' He also said: 'Whoever wins through sinning has not won at all.'

During the battle of Siffin, he had the chance to remove one of his bitterest and most dangerous enemies, *Amr b. al-'Āṣ*, but the man undressed himself and began to flee, so Imam Ali - out of respect for modesty – turned away and let Amr flee in the shadow of Dhul al-Fiqar with his private parts exposed to the wind. Had Ali pursued him to strike him down, no one would have blamed him. But Ali was not like other men in his personal qualities, morality, bravery and generosity.

When he told his companions that Ibn Muljam would be the one to kill him, they said: 'So why don't you kill him first?' He said: 'God does not punish a servant until the servant commits the sin.'

Other times he would say: 'But then who would kill me?' Or: 'Can there be retribution before the crime?' And when one of his Companions said to him: 'O Commander of the Faithful! Tell us who will spill your blood? We will destroy his entire clan!' He replied: 'Then by God would you not have slain my killer!'

The same is true of Muslim b. Aqeel; he refuses to seek victory through wrongdoing and so does not hasten to take anyone's life, nor does he use methods such as treachery or assassination.

And this is exactly what happened when he had a chance to assassinate Ubaydullah b. Ziyad but didn't; *Sharīk b. al-A'war al-Baṣrī*, who had accompanied Ibn Ziyad from Basra, fell ill and lodged with *Hani b. 'Urwa*. He expected Ubaydullah b. Ziyad to visit him in Hani's home, while Muslim was also lodged there in hiding.

When Ibn Ziyad sent word that he would pay a visit, *Sharīk* told Muslim b. Aqeel: 'Your only goal is to remove this tyrant, and God has placed him in your power. He is coming to visit me in my sickness, so go and hide in the cellar until he feels safe with me, then come out and kill him. Then you need only go and sit in the governor's palace; no one will oppose you. And if God cures me, then I will go to Basra and take care of matters there for you and obtain the pledge of allegiance for you from its citizens.'

Hani said: 'I do not like that Ibn Ziyad should be slain in my house!'

Sharīk said: 'And why not? By God if [Muslim] kills him, it will be a sacrifice for God!' Then he turned to Muslim and said: 'Do not fail in this!'

While discussing this, someone told them: 'The governor is outside!'

So Muslim hid in the cellar and Ubaydullah b. Ziyad came in, greeted *Sharīk* and asked him about his complaints.

A while passed, and *Sharīk* thought Muslim too slow in coming out to kill Ubaydullah, so he began to recite some poetry:

Is there a cool drink to quench one who is thirsty
even if it would mean the end of me!
If you think you might cause calamity for my health
You cannot always avert such calamities.

He began to repeat these verses of poetry, then he took off his turban and placed it on the ground, then he placed it again on his head, then he placed it on the ground. Then he said: 'Quench my thirst, even if it means my death!' And he repeated this two or three times.

Ubaydullah turned to Hani and said: 'Do you think he is feverish?'

Hani said: 'Yes – may God make you prosper! – he has been like this since morning.'

Then Ubaydullah got up and left. Muslim came out of the cellar and *Sharīk* rebuked him: 'What stopped you from killing him?'

Muslim said: 'Two things. First of all, God's Messenger said: 'Faith has prevented assassination; a believer does not assassinate...' and secondly, Hani did not want someone to be slain in his home.'

Sharīk said: 'By God, had you slain him you would have slain a sinful traitor and succeeded on your mission.' Then he added: 'I have never seen anyone forgo such an opportunity save that he was overtaken by regret and grief, but you know best.'

This is how Muslim b. Aqeel refused to dispose of his enemy through assassination and betrayal, even though it was an easy strike for someone like Muslim and would have a great effect on his mission. Ubaydullah b. Ziyad, as *Sharīk* had said, was a sinful and treacherous man; completely ruthless in the pursuit of his goals. But despite that, Muslim b. Aqeel's faith prevented him from assassinating this tyrant and seeking victory through wrongdoing.

Rahman: What happened to *Sharīk al-A'war*?

Abdullah: He died three days later. Ubaydullah b. Ziyad led his funeral prayers and had him buried next to his father in the graveyard.

Rahman: Day by day, people are learning that this religion has two struggles; one against faithlessness and idolatry led by God's Messenger, and God scorned any outcome save the victory of His prophet, and another struggle against hypocrisy and hidden faithlessness, which is led by the Prophet's Household.

Abdullah: And it was the Prophet's Household who stood beside the Prophet in the first struggle. Ali was the raised sword of the Prophet, his indispensable assistant and his foremost supporter. God used him to save the Prophet on the night of the emigration to Medina, repel the evil of the Quraysh at the Battle of Badr and spare the faithful from fighting at the Battle of the Trench. The Prophet's Household are the ones who know the value of their Prophet and the value of this religion; they stand beside it, sacrifice for it, not desiring any reward for what they endure. And they did not receive anything for their pains except grief, persecution, exile and death. They are men whom neither trade nor sale distracts from God's remembrance; they fulfil their pledges to God. Some have fulfilled their vows, others wait, and they do not change places.'

While Abdullah b. Muslim and Rahman were speaking, a person sat behind them and listened to what they were saying. Then he spoke up.

Man: I ask you both, by God and by the Ka'ba, what are you speaking about?

Abdullah: There is no need for oaths. We are speaking about Hussein and Yazid; about the Prophet's Household and the Umayyad Clan; about the true believers and the hypocrites.

Man: O man! This is a dispute within the Nation between one Muslim and another. So this is a situation about which our Lord has said in His Book: 'If two groups of the faithful fight one another, make peace between them. But if one party of them aggresses against the other, fight the one which aggresses until it returns to God's ordinance.'

Abdullah: The verse you mentioned does not apply to the present situation.

Man: Do you not think that Abu Sufiyan, Muawiya and Yazid are believers?

Abdullah: Look, if we took the history of those three men who you mentioned, and the history of the Prophet, Ali, Hasan and now Hussein, what would we see?

When God sent His prophet with the message of this religion, Abu Sufiyan b. Harb stood against him; he was the leader of those who conspired against God's Messenger and the commander of those who fought against his message. There was no attacks launched against the Muslims save that Abu Sufiyan played a key role in uniting the tribes against the Prophet and gathering funds for the war against him.

He spent a long time leading the Quraysh against the Prophet, assailing the Emigrants and the Helpers. And he persisted until God finally conquered Mecca for His prophet. Abu Sufiyan professed Islam to save his own hide, and when he looked at the armies of the Muslims, he said to Abbas b. Abd al-MuÔÔallib: 'By God, O Abu al-*Faḍl*! The kingdom of your nephew has become grand indeed this day!'

Abbas told him: 'You mean his prophethood.'

So even after he accepted Islam, he saw it as a kingdom rather than prophethood. And for that reason he said: 'Yes, I mean.'

As for his son, Muawiya's faith, it was like that of his father after the conquest of Mecca. And it was the least faith known to the Muslims after the conquest of Mecca. Even his mother, Hind b. Utba would call out amongst the people after Abu Sufiyan embraced Islam: 'Kill the foul worthless wretch; he shamed himself before the leaders of a people. Will you not fight and defend yourselves and your land?'

And even after he embraced Islam, for a while Abu Sufiyan saw the victory of Islam over Ignorance as a victory over himself. He looked at the Prophet in the mosque once and said: 'Would that I knew how he defeated me!'

The meaning of his words were not hidden from the Prophet, so he went to him and struck him between the shoulders and said: 'I defeated you with God, O Abu Sufiyan!'

Even at the Battle of Hunayn, when the Muslims initially fled, Abu Sufiyan said: 'Why do I see them standing before the ocean?' Hoping that the Muslims would be defeated.

And while campaigning in Syria, whenever the Romans came forth, he would say: 'Come on, O *Banū al-Aṣfar*...!' and when they withdrew, he would say: 'Woe to *Banū al-Aṣfar*.'

Man: But when the Prophet conquered Mecca, He said: 'Whoever is in the house of Abu Sufiyan is safe, whoever enters the Ka'ba is safe, and whoever bars his door is safe.'

Abdullah: This is a merit of God's Messenger and not a merit of Abu Sufiyan! The Prophet did not see his struggle with Abu Sufiyan in personal terms, as though he was defending the interests of his people. Rather he was defending God's religion, and for this reason he considered everyone who went to this man's house, or barred his own door or went to God's house, as being safe. The Prophet fundamentally did not want to fight – he told Ali to call out: 'Today is a day of mercy! A day in which sanctity is observed!'

So the Prophet put Abu Sufiyan at the head of those whose hearts needed reconciling to the faith, those upon whom he bestowed many gifts that the resentment they harboured towards Islam's victory would depart from their breasts. In spite of this, the Muslims were still wary of Abu Sufiyan; they would not pay attention to him or sit with him, until he became so fed up of this that he pleaded with the Prophet to make Muawiya one of his scribes.

After the death of the Prophet and the pledge of allegiance to Abu Bakr in the tent (*saqīfa*) of the *Sāʿada* Clan, Abu Sufiyan tried to start a war between the Muslims. He came to Ali and Abbas and said: 'O Ali! And you, O Abbas! What has happened to abase the tribe of the Quraysh and reduce its stature!? By God, if you wish it, I will fill the streets with men and horse against him, and seize it from him in its entirety!'

He wanted to start a war so that the door would open to the Umayyad Clan returning to its position of leadership. For this reason, Ali refused and said: 'No, by God. I do not wish that you fill the streets with men and horse.' Then he added: 'O Abu Sufiyan! The faithful are a people who advise one another, while the hypocrites are a people who dupe and betray one another, even if it this betrayal strikes near to their own homes and persons.'

And after Uthman b. Affan's reign as Caliph began and the Umayyad Clan succeeded therein – insofar as the Caliph was one of them and a close cousin of their leaders – the Umayyad regime began to only consider the interest of the Umayyad Clan and its supporters in its decisions. Marwan b. al-Hakam was the vizier of the First Caliph; he showered his family with gifts and withheld them from everyone else, confirmed Muawiya b. Abu Sufiyan as the governor of Syria, as well as adding other regions to his authority. He acted only to keep his own family and supporters happy, as well as those whose help they desired and whose opposition they feared.

When Uthman was killed, it came clear that all of those who had benefited from the offices of the state and its wealth were either members or agents of the Umayyad Clan.

And when people pledged allegiance to Ali b. Abu Talib, the entire state was in the hands of the Nationyads. Muawiya used whatever wealth he had at his disposal and mobilized whatever allies he had to face Ali and start a war with him, ultimately resulting in the latter's murder.

Then the people of Iraq and Iran pledged allegiance to Hasan b. Ali, but Muawiya assassinated some people and bought others, such that Hasan was unable to govern. Muawiya made peace with him on a number of conditions, the first being that he submit the position of leadership to Muawiya provided that the latter acted in accordance with the Quran, Sunna and the precedents of the righteous Caliphs. The second condition was that authority would devolve to Hasan after him, and after Hasan to Hussein, and Muawiya had no right to appoint any successor. The third condition was that Muawiya should only make good mention of Ali, that he must desist from slandering him and invoking prayers against him in congregational prayers. The fourth condition was that safety be granted to the companions and followers of Ali, and that Muawiya must not harm any member of the Prophet's Household.

But Muawiya did not observe a single one of the conditions laid down in this treaty, save that leadership should be his. In addition to this, he induced Hasan's wife, JuÝda b. al-AshÝath, to poison her husband with the promise of a hundred thousand dirhams and marriage to Yazid. He fulfilled his promise of money, but not of marriage.

The Umayyads went to such extremes that they even prevented the burial of Hasan b. Ali next to the grave of his grandfather, as he had written in his will, when Marwan b. al-Hakam led a band of his stooges to prevent Hasan's funeral procession from approaching the grave of God's Messenger and shot arrows at them, so that Hussein was forced to bury his brother in Baqi. This is how the world treated the Prophet's Household, both living and dead.

Man: They have all gone to their Lord, so let us not speak of them anymore.

Abdullah: Yes, they have all gone to their Lord. But have Moses and

Pharaoh not also gone to their Lord? So why must we read about their fight in the Quran, and to know the truth for its people or to curse the oppressors... and Nimrod and Abraham have gone to their Lord too, and Cain and Abel before them... does God say that they have gone to their Lord so let us not speak of them anymore?'

The problem is not those who have gone, the problem is that Muawiya was preparing to take the pledge of allegiance for Yazid for several years, sometimes by using the sword, and by assassination and bribery at others. He knew his son was a foolhardy, boisterous drunkard of a youth, who was not fit to be so much as an officer of the law, let alone the Caliph of the Muslims who sat in the place of God's Messenger!

So the conflict that began with God's Messenger announcing his mission to Abu Sufiyan continues to this very day three generations on.

Man: Do you mean to say that the Prophet's Household are in the right?

Abdullah: And you, do you mean to say that their enemies are? Let me ask you a question: Did God's Messenger enjoin people to be good to his household, or did he enjoin them to take the gift he bestowed upon his daughter, Fatima? {ah}? Did he enjoin them to kill Ali in his prayer niche, or poison Hasan, or besiege Hussein?

Did he not say: 'Fatima is a part of me; whoever distresses her has distressed me, and whoever distresses me has distressed God'?

Did he not tell Ali: 'Loving you is faith and piety, hating you is faithlessness and hypocrisy.'

Did he not say: 'Hasan and Hussein are my two fragrant flowers of this world.'?

Did he not say: 'Hasan and Hussein are the leaders of the youth of Paradise'?

Did he not say: 'Hussein is of me and I am of Hussein, whoever loves Hussein loves God'?

Did he not say: 'The Imams of my household are like stars, whichever of them you follow, you will be guided.'

Did he not say: 'The similitude of my household is like that of Noah's Ark, whoever boarded it was saved, and whoever did not was drowned.'?

Had God's Messenger actually enjoined people to mistreat his household, could they have done worse than they do now? Our Lord says in the Quran: 'Say, 'I do not ask you any reward for it except love of [my] relatives." And God's Messenger made the sending of blessings upon his household a part of obligatory prayers.

Man: And who is responsible for that?

ÝAnd God: Go yourself and see who is responsible for that! When God's Messenger and his household are the measure of truth and justice, whoever falls short of that, he is responsible for everything that has happened and will happen.

The man falls silent, they get up and the gathering is at an end.

ALONE AGAINST THE EMPIRE

After Ubaydullah b. Ziyad was spared by Muslim b. Aqeel's moral scruples, because the latter would not agree to have him assassinated, events took a different turn. Muslim had become the axis of the movement of those faithful who sought to throw off the yoke of oppression, organizing their affairs and gathering allies for them, and taking the pledge of allegiance from them on Hussein's behalf. The situation changed when Ibn Ziyad emptied the contents of the treasury into the pockets of the leaders of tribes and clans, and sent his allies to every house in the city furnishing promises and threats, and spreading rumours that a large Syrian army would soon arrive in the city. They warned people that they would lose their stipends and that the innocent and the guilty would be punished alike, and threatened them with death if bribes would not work. They used every means at their disposal to goad people into forsaking Muslim b. Aqeel. They would even send a wife after he husband, a mother after her son, a brother after his own brother, to cling to them until they were securely latched to their cause, or they would lure them to join the side of Ubaydullah b. Ziyad. At the very least, they would tell some of the weak that this was a battle between two regimes, the incumbent regime and an opposition, so it was better that they stayed in their homes; if one side wins, you have a chance to curry favour with them, and if the other wins then you are at least safe. They raised the slogan: 'We have nothing to do with the struggles of sultans!'

This is how the situation of Muslim b. Aqeel was transformed. In a short space of time, he went from the leader of thousands to a fugitive from the regime. While each passing hour saw Ubaydullah b. Ziyad increase his number of soldiers and police, giving them clear orders on what to do, on the other side, Muslims companions were fragmented and divided against themselves. Most of them had returned to their homes; those who came for the sake of worldly wealth, they had turned coat and joined Ubaydullah b. Ziyad. Muslim went into hiding and Ubaydullah became obsessed with finding him; he knew that killing or capturing Muslim would put the supporters of the Prophet's Household in a weak position, and perhaps even destroy their power in the city of Kufa altogether.

Muslim had hidden in the house of *Hani b. 'Urwa. Hāni*, in addition to being advanced in years and senior in rank, was the headman of the *Mudhḥaj* tribe, who had four thousand soldiers in total. And because Muslim had changed his location several times, he had hidden his hiding place from Ubaydullah well. And before raiding any houses, Ubaydullah had to be sure where Muslim was; was in in the home of *Sulayman b. Ṣard al-Khuza'ee*, the house of *Mukhtār b. Abu Ubayda al-Thaqafī*, the house of *Muslim b. 'Awsaja* or the house of *Hani b. 'Urwa*?

Here, Ibn Ziyad devised a stratagem, as the tyrants of the Umayyad Clan often would. They observed no rules or principles in how they waged war, nor did they at times of peace or weakness.

One of Ibn Ziyad's men was a shady character from Syria called MuÝqal, who was unknown to the people of Kufa. Ibn Ziyad gave him three thousand dirhams and instructed him: 'Take this money and go; find Muslim b. Aqeel for me, advise him not to be hasty and tell him to move with the utmost caution.'

So the man came to the central mosque of Kufa, but he did not know where to begin his search. He looked at those present there and saw someone with the appearance of a righteous man; someone who prayed a great deal and with sincerity and concentration. He said to himself: 'Perhaps this man is one of Ali's supporters, for they pray a lot and display sincerity in it. I think this is one of them.'

He sat beside the man and waited for him to finish his prayers, then he approached him and said: 'May God make me your sacrifice, I am a man from Syria, a client of the *Kilāb* Clan. God has blessed me with the love of the Prophet's Household, and I have three thousand dirhams that I would like to convey to one of them. I have heard that someone has come to this city calling people to Hussein b. Ali. Can you tell me where he is, so that this money reaches him and he can use it in some of his affairs or dispose of it as he sees fit?'

The man said to him: 'Why did you come and ask me out of all the people in the mosque?'

MuÝqal said: 'I saw upon you the marks of one who is righteous, so I hoped that you might be someone who adheres to the Prophet's Household.'

The man replied: 'You picked me out well. I am one of your brethren; my name is *Muslim b. 'Awsaja*. I am pleased to meet you and apologize if I seemed suspicious. I am a man who loves the Prophet's Houshold, so give me your word and a vow before God that you will keep what I tell you secret from everyone.'

MuÝqal did as I was bid, then *Muslim b. 'Awsaja* said: 'Go for now, but come to my house tomorrow and I will take you to your master' – meaning Muslim b. Aqeel – 'and introduce you to him.'

Mu'qal went that night and came to *Muslim b. 'Awsaja* in his house the next day; he went with him until they came to Muslim b. Aqeel. MuÝqal told him the same story, gave him that money and pledged allegiance to him.

He kept coming to Muslim b. Aqeel every day, so the latter's news was never hidden from him; he knew everyone who came to see him. When night came, *Mu'qal* would go under cover of darkness to Ubaydullah b. Ziyad and tell him everything he said and heard. Of course, he also informed him that Muslim was staying in the house of *Hani b. 'Urwa* and had not changed his location.

Armed with the knowledge of Muslim b. Aqeel's location and the identities of those who would frequent him and meet with him, Ibn Ziyad launched a two pronged offensive. From one angle, he summoned *Hani b. 'Urwa* without giving any hint as to his motives in doing so (and not letting on to anyone that he knew of Muslim's location), from the other he had men ready at the houses of those who met him, so that they could detain them all at once after he dealt with Hani.

As for how he summoned Hani, he asked *Muhammad b. al-Ash'ath* and *Asmaa b. Khārija*: 'Why do I not see *Hani b. 'Urwa* and why does he not visit me?'

They said: 'O governor, he has been ill for some time.'

Ibn Ziyad: 'How can that be? I have heard he sits at the door of his house all day, so what prevents him from coming to us and doing his duties? Go and tell him not to neglect his duties; I dislike that such a noble of the Arabs should behave in this way with me.'

So they went to Hani and told him that Ibn Ziyad had been asking after him. He said: 'My complaint prevents me.'

They said: 'He hears that you sit all day at the door of your house; he thinks you overdue – a ruler does not tolerate aloofness.'

Then they insisted that he ride with them to Ibn Ziyad. So *Hāni* called for his robes and dressed himself, then he called for his donkey and mounted it. He was some-and-ninety years old and lame, so it took some time for him to mount his donkey and go with them to the governor's palace. When they arrived at the door, he seemed to sense something was afoot. He turned to *Hassān b. Asmaa b.*

Khārija and said: 'O nephew, I sense something is amiss.'

Hassān said to him: 'Glory to God, uncle! I do not worry for you, so do not let yourself worry; you are not guilty of anything.'

So when he entered the presence of Ibn Ziyad, the latter recited the verses of poetry:

'I desire his life but he desires my death, who would excuse such a friend?'

When he heard this, Hani said: 'What does that mean, O governor?'

Ibn Ziyad said: 'What could be graver than taking Muslim b. Aqeel into your house and gathering men to pledge allegiance to him?'

Hani said: 'I have done nothing of the sort, nor do I know of anything to do with this.'

Ibn Ziyad summoned a servant and told him: 'Call MuÝqal for me.' MuÝqal came in and Ibn Ziyad asked Hani: 'Do you know this one?'

When Hani saw him, he knew that he had been one of Ibn Ziyad's spies. Hani said: 'By God, I tell you the truth when I say that I did not invite Muslim b. Aqeel to my home, nor did I know anything about him until I found him sitting at the door of my house! He asked me to lodge him, so I felt too ashamed before my Lord to refuse; I was responsible for him as a guest, so I lodged him in my house and sheltered him. You already know what he has been doing there, so if you wish I will tell him to leave my house and go somewhere else, then I will no longer be responsible for him or his safety.'

But Ibn Ziyad feared that if he allowed *Hani b. 'Urwa* to leave, Muslim b. Aqeel would slip from his grasp, so he said: 'No by God, you will not leave here until he is brought before me!'

Hani said: 'No by God, I will not bring him to you – shall I bring you my guest that you might kill him!?'

Ibn Ziyad said: 'By God, you will bring him.'

Hāni replied: 'No, by God, I will not.'

In that gathering sat *Muslim b. Amr al-Bāhilī and Sharīḥ al-Qāḍī.* Muslim b. Amr said to Ubaydullah: 'Let me speak with him.'

Muslim b. Amr turned to Hani and said: 'Come over here so I can talk to you.'

They went to one side and stood close together such that Ibn Ziyad could see them and – if they raised their voices – hear what they were saying, but if they spoke in whispers he could not.

Muslim b. Amr said to him: 'Hani, I adjure you by God. Do not kill yourself and bring ruin upon your people and your family. You know that Muslim b. Aqeel is the cousin of the Umayyad Clan; they will neither fight him nor do harm to him. Give him to Ibn Ziyad and there is no blame or disgrace upon you for that. You are merely delivering a fugitive to the proper authorities.'

Hāni b. 'Urwa replied: 'No, by God, it is shameful for me to do so. Should I offer up my guest and neighbour while I still live and hear and see and have means at my disposal? By God, even if I am alone and without a helper, I will not give him up unless I die first!'

Muslim b. Amr began to plead with him again, but Hani kept saying: 'No, by God, I will not.'

Ibn Ziyad heard his words and said: 'Bring him to me!' Hani was brought in front of him and he told him: 'By God, you will either bring him to me or I will strike off your head!'

Hani replied: 'Then there will be many swords flashing around your palace.'

Ibn Ziyad said: 'I feel sorry for you – do you threaten me with swords?'

Then Ibn Ziyad told his minions to restrain him and bring him closer. They brought him before Ibn Ziyad and he began to strike Hani in the face with his stick. He kept striking his face, his cheeks and his brow until his nose was broken, blood was spilling over his robes and the skin of his cheeks hung over his beard, and until the stick itself had broken.

But despite his old age, he wrestled his hand free, lunged towards the soldier who stood there and tried to take his sword from him. But Ibn Ziyad's guards piled onto him and seized him again.

Ibn Ziyad said to the guards: 'Take him and throw him in one of my cells, make sure he is under guard.'

When they took Hani from the room, *Asmaa b. Khārija* – who had gone to Hani with *Muhammad b. al-Ash'ath* and brought him to Ibn Ziyad – stood up and said: 'Treacherous messengers, were we? You told us to bring you a man and we brought him to you. Then you beat his face, shed his blood on his beard and threaten to kill him because he refused to give up his guest!?'

Ubaydullah said: 'Are you still here?'

Ibn Ziyad had him seized, beaten and imprisoned in another part of the palace while Asmaa called out: 'To God we belong and to Him we return, I inform you of my own death, O Hani!'

As for *Muhammad b. al-Ash'ath*, he joined himself to this evil act, saying: 'We are pleased with whatever the governor thinks best, whether it is for us or against us. The governor is only there to instruct us.'

Word of Hani's imprisonment soon spread, and rumours that Ibn Ziyad had killed him were rife. The men of Hani's tribe, the Mudhîaj took up arms and encircled the governor's palace. So Ubaydullah told the judge, *Sharīḥ* - who was one of the nobles of Kufa – to go and see *Hani b. 'Urwa* himself and tell his people that he still lived. When *Sharīḥ* went to him, Hani said: 'O *Sharīḥ*! Do you see what they have done to me?'

Sharīḥ said: 'I see you still live.'

Hani replied: 'Alive, am I? Despite what you see?'

Then he asked *Sharīḥ* to tell the tribe of *Mudhḥaj* not to depart from around the palace, because if they leave then Ibn Ziyad would surely kill him.

But *Sharīḥ* returned to Ubaydullah and said: 'I saw Hani alive, though I saw signs of ill-treatment too.'

Ibn Ziyad said: 'Do you deny a governor the right to punish his flock? Go out and tell those people that their companion lives!'

Sharīḥ did as Ibn Ziyad bid him. He went out to the *Mudhḥij* and said: 'When the governor heard of your concerns for your companion, he told me to go and see him. Hani bid me inform you that he lives, and that word of his death is false.'

Amre b. al-Hajjaj and his companions said: 'If Hani is not dead, then praise be to God.' whereat they left.

After the *Mudhḥaj* tribe returned to their homes, Ubaydullah b. Ziyad called the people to congregational prayers. His guards, servants and police went out with him. He ascended the pulpit and said: 'O people of Kufa! Protect yourselves by obeying God, obeying the Messenger and obeying your leaders. Do not fall into disputation lest you divide yourselves and perish, then you will be given cause to regret, suffer abasement and be cut off. Let none of you expose himself to danger - consider this fair warning.'

But before he could finish his sermon, he heard a hue and cry. He said: 'What's going on?'

Someone said: 'O governor, beware! Muslim b. Aqeel has come out in force with his supporters!'

Ubaydullah b. Ziyad hurriedly descended from the pulpit and fled the Mosque, took refuge in the governor's palace next door and barred himself therein.

Rahman and Abdullah meet again near the Ka'ba towards the end of the month of *Dhul al-Qi'da*.

Rahman: What is the latest news?

Abdullah: The situation in Kufa hangs in the balance

Rahman: What do you mean by that?

Abdullah: At any moment, events in Kufa might turn to the benefit of Ibn Ziyad or go in favour of the Prophet's Household. Ubaydullah b. Ziyad still holds power, and he has men from every tribe with him who he has furnished with money and materiel for the moment of confrontation. But those who pledged allegiance to Muslim b. Aqeel are still holding fast to their promises, even though *Hani b. 'Urwa* still languishes in Ibn Ziyad's prison and the *Mudhḥaj* tribe make no move to free him or give any indication of support. If a large tribe with as many soldiers as *Mudhḥaj* does not move to free their leader and are duped by Ibn Ziyad's ploys and lies, this means that others might yet fall prey to them.

Rahman: Do you think it possible that those who pledged allegiance to Muslim b. Aqeel might fail to support him?

Abdullah: Absolutely! Ibn Ziyad uses the same tactics as Muawiya used before; he uses wealth and weapons, and he still has control over the police and the army. Word has reached us that he has filled his prisons with four thousand people he suspected of supporting Muslim.

Rahman: And what about Muslim b. Aqeel? Why doesn't he take the initiative and move?

Abdullah: You mean, why doesn't he draw his sword and fight?

Rahman: Yes.

Abdullah: You don't know the Prophet's Household. They are brave beyond comparison, but they never start a fight with anyone, even with the faithless. So how can they open hostilities with someone who professes Islam – although I think that the imprisonment of *Hani b. 'Urwa* gives ample cause for the Muslims to rise up to free him, just as Abraham fought to free Lot. But let us wait and see.

After Hani was imprisoned and news of this spread, Muslim called his supporters and four thousand men came to join him, filling the streets around his home. He marshalled them and advanced on the governor's palace with the aim of freeing *Hani b. 'Urwa*. Ubaydullah b. Ziyad barred his doors and had only thirty of his police and ten men of Kufa in the building with him. He was overcome with despair and was sure that he would be dead before any help could arrive from Syria. In desperation, he used every means at his disposal, sending his agents to every quarter of the city promising people wealth and important offices and threatening them with the men and horses coming from Syria.

He appointed *Muhammad b. al-Ash'ath b. al-Qays, Kathīr b. Shihāb al-Harithī* and a number of other important figures to tempt people away from Muslim's cause, frighten them with news that an army from Syria was nearby, threaten to cut off their stipends and to punish the innocent along with the guilty.

From another angle, Ibn Ziyad ordered those who were with him to go to the palace walls and rain arrows upon the besiegers, to prevent them from approaching. They continued doing this until night fell, then Ibn Ziyad ordered them to each go to one side of the palace and shout threats to the people below.

Al-Qa'qā' b. Shawr, Shabath b. Rab'ey, Hajjār b. Abjar and *Shimr b. Dhil al-Jawshan* ascended the walls and began to shout out: 'O people of Kufa! Beware of God and do not hasten to stir up dissension! Do not divide this Nation and do not bring down the horses of Syria upon yourselves, for you have already tasted their lances!'

They also said: 'O people! Go back to your families and do not hasten to evil. Do not risk your own lives, for the armies of the Commander of the Faithful, Yazid, are coming from Syria! God has given the governor a pledge that if you undertake this war and do not turn aside, your descendants will receive no gifts and you will be butchered by the men of Syria – the innocent with the guilty, until there is no trace of rebellion amongst you save that it has tasted the consequences of its actions!'

And when some of Muslim's companions heard this, they began to slink away. Father's would come to their sons, men to their brothers and cousins and tell them: 'Come away, there are enough people here!' Women would come to their sons, brothers and husbands and cling to them until they came away.

As the Sun dipped beneath the horizon that day, Muslim looked around him and saw that there were five hundred men. The rest of the four thousand had dispersed under cover of darkness. He offered Maghrib prayers with only thirty men behind him, the rest had scattered from around him. When he saw this, he left the Mosque on foot and they walked with him towards the Kinda Gate. Then when he turned to them, he saw that no one remained with him and he had no one to guide him through the streets.

He turned left and right and saw how people retreated from him. He said: 'Glory to God, they lured us here with their letters and then delivered us to our enemies.'

That was on Monday the seventh day of Dhul al-Hijja, sixty years after the Emigration. This was the day before Hussein left Mecca for Kufa; sixteen days after Muslim had written to him and said: 'The indications were true, eighteen thousand people from Kufa have pledged allegiance to me. Make haste as soon as this letter reaches you, for all the people are with you. They have no desire for the family of Abu Sufiyan.'

When the people dispersed from around Ibn Ziyad's palace and

Muslim left the mosque alone, the companions of Ubaydullah heard what was happening and realized that the clamour had died down. They went up to the walls to see what remained of the mob outside, but could neither see nor hear anyone. At first, they thought this was some sort of trick; that people were hiding behind walls and pillars. So they cast down candles and torches until they were sure that the mosque was empty and there was no sign of Muslim and his followers. Ibn Ziyad hastened to call a congregation immediately, and ordered criers to call out in the streets: 'Lo! I am absolved of responsibility for any harm that comes to any man of the police, prefects or army who does not offer his *'Ishā'* prayers in the mosque!'

And the police, prefects and the supporters of the Umayyad Clan really responded to this summons, gathering in the mosque in such numbers that it was filled by them. Ibn Ziyad came with his guards, led the *'Ishā'* prayers and then addressed the crowd: 'We bear no responsibility for any harm that should befall a man who keeps Ibn Aqeel in his home.'

Then he called for the head of the police, Hasseen b. Numayr: 'O Hasseen, may your mother be deprived of you if a door on any street in Kufa opens and this man steps out without you bringing him to me! I give you responsibility for encircling the people of Kufa, so send your watchmen to the head of every street. Tomorrow you will tighten the noose and search until you bring me this man!'

With this threat and the order to place watchmen on roads, search houses and spread the word that the Syrian army would soon arrive, people stayed in their homes and the streets were completely empty.

Muslim b. Aqeel began to walk through that dark night, wandering aimlessly, not knowing where to go. He was not familiar with the city, nor aware of any home where he might find refuge with the supporters of the Prophet's Household. Kufa was a big city; he had entered secretly and spent his time there moving from one house to another. Now he meandered hopelessly through the streets. It is said he was wounded from brief encounter with some of Ubaydullah's police – although this is not confirmed – but he was certainly despondent. Yesterday he had been like a prince in the city, but today he was a stranger with nowhere to go.

He left the Kinda quarter for that of Jabala and walked until he reached the door of a house. He stood there to rest a little and think about what he needed to do. He was hungry, thirsty and tired.

The house's owner was a woman called *Ṭūʿa*, she had been a slave of *al-Ashʿath b. Qays* and borne him a son, so he freed her and she married *Usayd al-Haḍramī*, giving him a son she called *Bilāl.* But *Bilāl* was an irreligious youth who drank wine with his friends.

Because *Bilāl* had not yet returned home, his mother came out to see where he was. Ibn Aqeel greeted her and she returned his greeting. He said: 'O servant of God, may I have some water?'

She went into the house, brought him a vessel of water and quenched his thirst. Then she went back into the house and Muslim sat at the door. When she came out again, she saw him still sitting at the door and said: 'O servant of God! Did you not drink water?'

He said, 'Yes.'

She said, 'So go to your family.'

Muslim stayed silent. Then she came back and said the same to him. He still didn't say anything. Then she said to him: 'Glory to God! Get up and go to your family, may God be kind to you! It is not right you sit at the door of my house, nor will I permit such a thing!'

Muslim got up and said: 'O servant of God, I have no friends or abode in this city. Could you not lodge me a while and perhaps one day I can repay the kindness?'

She said, 'And what is that?'

He said, 'I am Muslim b. Aqeel, the people have deceived me and misled me.'

She was shocked, 'By God... you are Muslim b. Aqeel?'

He said, 'Yes.'

She said, 'Then come in, and be welcome!'

She lodged him in her home, in a room apart from the other rooms which she lived in. She furnished it with a carpet for him and offered him dinner, but he did not eat. Not an hour had passed before her son, *Bilāl*, returned. And when he saw her going in and out of Muslim's room at lot he asked her: 'By God, I am suspicious of how much you frequent this room tonight. Is something amiss?'

She said, 'Leave it alone, my son. You need not worry.'

He said, 'By God you will tell me.'

She said, 'Look after your own matters and do not ask me anything.'

He kept pestering her, so she took a promise from him: 'Do not tell anyone what I am about to tell you.'

After he swore he would tell no one, she informed him that Muslim b. Aqeel was lodging in that room.

Ubaydullah b. Ziyad had announced that whoever brought him Muslim b. Aqeel would have a handsome reward, and *Bilāl* needed money to buy more wine with his friends. So the devil began to whisper to him that he should inform the government about Muslim and claim the reward. He quickly slept with this thought in mind and waited until morning to go to the governor's palace.

As for Muslim b. Aqeel, he spent his night in that room, standing, sitting, bowing and prostrating, beseeching his Lord and praying to Him sometimes, and reciting the Quran at others. He was not thinking of himself at that time, rather his thoughts were with Hussein and the letter which he had sent him, the change of fortunes in

Kufa and the betrayal he had suffered at the hands of those who had pledged allegiance to him.

That night, he remembered what had befallen his uncle, Ali, from the people of Kufa, and his cousin Hasan, the eldest grandson of the Prophet. But he thought most of Hussein, and how he could get word to him of the reversal they had suffered.

But the sun had not yet risen on the eighth day of Dhul al-Hijja, the day before the *Day of 'Arafa*, and *Bilāl* had already hastened to Rahman b. Muhammad b. al-AshŶath and informed him that Muslim b. Aqeel was in his mother's house.

So Rahman went to his father, *Muhammad b. al-Ash'ath*, who was sitting in the court of Ibn Ziyad, and whispered the news in his father's ear. Ibn Ziyad saw the expression on Muhammad's face and said: 'What do your son tell you?'

Ibn al-Ash'ath said: 'He told me that Muslim is in our quarter of the city!'

Ibn Ziyad did not hestitate: 'Go now and bring him to me at once!'

Then he sent word to *Amr b. Harīs* who often led the prayers in the mosque on his behalf: 'Send sixty or seventy men with *Ibn al-Ash'ath*, all of them from the tribe of Qays. Make sure that none of them are from the Quraysh, lest they harbour some tribal loyalties.'

His instructions were clear; Ibn al-AshŶath must bring Muslim b. Aqeel to him either killed or captured.

A company of armed men mounted their horses and rode to *Ṭū'a's* home. Muslim b. Aqeel was awake at that hour, so when he heard the sound of the men he knew that they were about to attack him. He took up his sword to go out and meet them but they had already broken into the house. Muslim beat them back, striking at them with his sword, until he had driven them out of the house. They came in again, but he drove them out a second time. Leading the attack was *Bakīr b. Hamrān al-Aḥmarī*. They exchanged blows, then

Bakīr's blade struck Muslim's mouth and split his lips. But Muslim, though wounded, struck back and dealt *Bakīr* a deadly blow to his head, then struck his neck with such force that he almost cleaved him in two.

When the attackers saw Muslim's strength, they climbed onto the roof of the house and began to pelt him with stones and flaming bundles of stalks. So he came out into the street and launched a ferocious attack against them. According to witness' accounts, he was able to fell a number of them.

Muhammad b. al-Ash'ath called out: 'O Muslim! I will grant you safety! You need not die!'

But Muslim kept up his attack, leaving his opponents dead and wounded in the streets. As he went, he recited the poetry:

'I swear I will not be slain except as a free man
even if death is to me a thing unknown
Every man will one day meet harm
as cool water is mixed with water bitter and warm
The light of the Sun has returned to stay
I will not let myself be duped or betrayed'

Muhammad b. al-AshÝath said: 'This is no lie or trick; they will not kill you or otherwise harm you, you need not die!'

But Muslim paid no heed to his words and kept fighting until he was covered in wounds and his strength began to fail. They pelted him with arrows and stones. He said to them: 'Woe to you! Do you pelt me with stones and arrows as you do the faithless, while I am descended from the righteous prophets! Woe to you! Do you not observe the rights of God's Messenger and his relatives!?'

In spite of his weakness, he attacked them again and put them to flight in the alleys. Then he withdrew and pressed his back against the door of one of the houses. Muhammad b. al-AshÝath called out: 'Wait! Let him be until I tell him what he wants to hear.'

He approached Muslim until the two stood face-to-face and said: 'O son of Aqeel! You need not die here, you are given safety and your blood will be spared, on my life!'

Muslim replied: 'Oh son of al-AshÝath! Do you think that I will give you my hand while I can still fight? No, by God, I will not.'

Then Muslim attacked him and drove him back to his companions and returned to his place. He stood and said: 'O God, thirst has overcome me.'

Muslim's determination, courage and strength – like that of his uncle, Ali - put many of Muhammad b. al-AshÝath's men to flight, such that he had to send word to Ibn Ziyad asking for more. Ibn Ziyad reproached him, saying: 'I send you after one man and you lose so many? What will happen when I send you after the other one?' – by which he meant Hussein.

Ibn AshÝath replied: 'O governor! Do you think you've sent me after a greengrocer, or a shopkeeper? Or do you not know that you've sent me after one of the swords of Muhammad b. Abdullah, a ferocious lion of a man, to bring down a gallant hero?'

And when reinforcements arrived, Muhammad b. al-AshÝath called out to his companions: 'This is shameful! How can one man terrify you so? Attack him together all at once!'

When Muslim saw this, he said amazed: 'Did you bring all these men just to kill Muslim b. Aqeel? O my soul, go forth to death from which there is no escape!' He attacked them again, reciting:

'It is death, so do – woe to you! – whatever you will
for you will no doubt drain the cup of death!
Be steadfast for the command of God, exalted and magnificent
The verdict of His judgement all Creation permeates'

But they fled again from him and he returned to rest against the wall. Ibn Ziyad grew impatient and sent word to *Muḥammd b. al-Ash'ath*: 'Woe to you! Give him safety, or else I will have your heads!'

So they called out promises of safety, but he refused to accept. So they devised a stratagem and dug a pit in the road for him, hiding it with straw and mud. Then the next time they fled from him and he pursued them, he fell into that pit and they surrounded him. *Muhammad b. al-Ash'ath* struck him across the face.

They offered him safety again, and he took a pledge from them. He said to those around the pit: 'Am I granted safety?'

They said: 'Yes.'

But by this point he could not walk, so they seized him and brought a donkey for him to ride.

As soon as he was their captive, they seized his sword. Muslim said: 'So this is the first betrayal, where is your pledge of safety? To God we belong and to Him we return!'

Then he began to weep and one of Ibn Ziyad's henchmen - *Ubaydullah b. al-Abbas al-Salamī* - said to him: 'Someone who seeks what you do should not weep when such a fate befalls him.'

Muslim said: 'By God, I do not weep for myself, nor do I mourn that I will be killed, though I do not for one moment desire it. Rather I weep for my kinsmen who are coming to you – I weep for Hussein and his family!'

He then turned to Muhammad b. al-AshÝath and said: 'By God, I do not think you can give me the safety you promised, for Ibn Ziyad is a treacherous man. But I ask you, do you have it in you to do a good deed?'

Muhammad b. al-Ash'ath: 'And what might that be?'

'Send someone to Hussein and warn him of what has happened, for he may already be on his way with his household. Have him say that Ibn Aqeel has sent him and that he is currently a prisoner and does not expect he will live past evenfall. Tell him I said: 'Go back, may my parents and my household be your sacrifice! Do not let the people of Kufa dupe you; they are the companions of your father, and he looked forward to being released from them by death. The people of Kufa have lied to us, and you cannot rely on them.'

Muhammad b. al-AshÝath said: 'I will do that, and I will inform Ibn Ziyad that I granted you safety.'

By now Muslim b. Aqeel was exhausted, thirsty and bleeding from multiple wounds, especially those to his face. When they brought him to the door of the governor's palace, they came across a man bearing a container of cool water, which he placed at the door. Muslim said to him: 'Give me some water.'

Another one of Ibn Ziyad's henchmen – Muslim b. Amr – spoke to him, as if he was the gatekeeper of Hades itself: 'O son of Aqeel! Do you see how cool this water is? You shall never taste a drop of it until you taste the boiling waters of Hell!'

Muslim replied: 'Woe to you! Who are you?'

Ibn Amr said: 'I am someone who knew the truth when you denied it, who advised the Imam when you betrayed him, and who obeyed when you rebelled. I am *Muslim b. Amr al-Bāhilī*'

Muslim b. Aqeel said: 'May your mother mourn you! How cruel and hard-hearted you must be! You, O son of *Bāhila*, are more deserving of the boiling waters of Hellfire than I, for you have preferred obedience to the clan of Sufiyan over obedience to the Household of the Prophet!'

It seems that Muslim's condition affected the consciences of others who were present. One of them, *Amr b. Harīth*, sent a servant to him with a jug of water and a cup. The servant poured water into the cup and handed it to Muslim. But when Muslim took it to drink, the cup filled with blood and he threw it away without drinking. The servant poured water afresh, but the cup filled with blood again and he had to throw it away. The third time, one of his front teeth fell into the cup. He said: 'Praise God, if there was any provision left for me, I would have drunk it.'

Inside the governor's palace, Ibn Ziyad sat haughty and proud upon his throne, surrounded by his chiefs, officials and guards with swords drawn. He gave leave for Muslim to be brought before him that he might demonstrate his greatness to Ibn Aqeel, his wounded prisoner. But when Muslim was brought in, he did not offer a greeting of peace to him. One of the guards said: 'Greet the governor!'

Muslim said: 'Be quiet, you motherless fool! By God, I have no governor except Hussein. As for this one, people only greet him if they fear him... and what good will it do me to greet him with peace when he wants to kill me?'

Ibn Ziyad said: 'Whether you greet me or not, you are still a dead man.'

Muslim said: 'Worse men than you have killed better men than me.'

Ibn Ziyad said: 'Traitor! You dare rebel against your ruler, divide the Muslim and stir up sedition?'

Muslim replied: 'You lie, Ibn Ziyad. By God, Muawiya was not a Caliph agreed upon by the Nationh. Rather, he defeated the Prophet's legatee through trickery and usurped the Caliphate, and the same is true of his son. As for sedition, you are the cause of it, you and your father – Ziyad, son of *'Alāj* of the *Thaqīf* tribe. I hope that God will grant me martyrdom at the hands of His most evil creature, for by God I have not rebelled, nor disbelieved, nor turned coat. Rather I obey the true Commander of the Faithful, Hussein b. Ali, the son of Fatima daughter of God's Messenger. We are more entitled to the Caliphate than Muawiya, his son and the family of Ziyad.'

Muslims response was so swift and forceful that Ubaydullah was left looking weak in front of those assembled, so he resorted to lies: 'Sinner! Did you not drink wine in Medina?'

Muslim answered: 'Someone who kills those whose lives God has made sacrosanct, spills the blood of innocents in anger, enmity and suspicion, while busying himself with play and amusements as if he heeds nothing – that person is more like to be a winebibber than I!'

Ibn Ziyad said: 'You bestowed the Caliphate upon yourself, but God has held you back and given it to those who deserve it.'

Muslim said: 'And who deserves it, O son of *Marjāna*?'

'Yazid and his father.'

'Praise God, God suffices as a judge between us and you!'

'Do you think you are in the right?'

'No, by God, I don't think. I know.'

'May God curse me if I do not kill you in the worst way imaginable!'

'You are always killing in the worst way, following the foulest conduct, harbouring the most evil thoughts, and uttering the most reprehensible prattle! Do what you will, O enemy of God!'

Then Muslim added: 'By God, if I had ten men I could trust and I had a drink of water, you would have seen me a long while in this palace. But if you've decided to kill me, as you have to, then let me make a last will.'

Ubaydullah said: 'You may make a last will as you see fit.'

Muslim studied the faces of the people there and saw Umar b. Sa'd. He said to him: 'You and I are related; there is no man here from the Quraysh save you, so come hither that I might speak to you.'

Umar b. Sa'd looked to Ubaydullah b. Ziyad as if asking his permission. Ibn Ziyad told him: 'Go and see to the needs of your cousin.'

Umar b. Sa'd approached Muslim, who told him: 'In Kufa, I owe a debt of seven hundred dirhams; take my sword from them, sell it and repay the debt. See to my body once I am dead; ask for it from Ibn Ziyad and bury it in the ground. Send someone to Hussein b. Ali to let him know what they have done to me, for Hussein and his companions – no more than ninety men and women – are on the way. Send them back and write to them about my fate, so that they will turn away from here and not suffer what I have suffered.'

Muslim b. Aqeel and Umar b. Sa'd were to one side of the gathering. No one heard what transpired between them. Muslim had wanted it this way, but Umar b. Sa'd got up and sat beside Ubaydullah b. Ziyad and asked him: 'Do you know what he said?'

Ibn Ziyad said: 'Keep your cousin's secrets.'

Umar b. Sa'd insisted: 'It's more important than that.'

Ibn Ziyad replied: 'What is it then?'

Umar b. Sa'd said: 'He told me that Hussein and his entourage are on their way; they are ninety people, men and women.'

Ibn Ziyad said: 'You were wrong to reveal his secret. But since you are the one who informed me of this, it must be you who goes and fights them.'

He added, 'As for his wealth, we will not prevent him from disposing of it as he wishes. As for Hussein, if he does not wish us harm, we do not wish it for him. But if he wishes us harm, we will not go easy on him. As for this one's body, we will not accept your intercession on his behalf. He does not deserve anything from us, for he has fought us, rebelled against us and tried to kill us.'

Ibn Ziyad turned again to Ibn Aqeel and said: 'Woe, O Ibn Aqeel! Tell me why you came to this land, sowed division amongst its people and turned them against one another?'

Muslim b. Aqeel answered: 'I did not come to this land to do that. It was you who raised up evil and buried good; you ruled people without consent and bid them do what God did not command. You treated them as a Khosrow or a Caesar treats his subjects. So we came to enjoin them to good, forbid them from evil and call them to the judgement of the Quran and the Sunna. We had the right to do that, the Caliphate was still our right after the Commander of the Faithful, Ali b. Abu Talib was murdered and our right it will remain. It has been wrested from our grasp because you were the first to take up arms and rebel against the Imam of guidance, you were the first to divide the Muslims, usurp the Caliphate and fight its rightful bearers with injustice and aggression. We know no other similitude for you and us save God's saying: 'And the wrongdoers will soon know at what goal they will end up.'"

So Ibn Ziyad began to revile Ali, Hasan and Hussein.

Muslim said: 'You would do better to revile yourself and your father than them, we – the Prophet's Household – are charged with enduring tribulation.

Ibn Ziyad called out: 'Where is he the one whose head Ibn Aqeel struck with his sword?'

So they brought *Bakīr b. Hamrān al-Aḥmarī*, with whom Ibn Aqeel had traded blows at the beginning of the fight and taken a wound to the head. When they brought him, Ubaydullah said: 'Take Ibn Aqeel up to the top of the palace and strike off his head with your hand so that may heal your heart.'

But when Ibn Ziyad announced the execution of Muslim, *Muhammad b. al-Ash'ath* – who had guaranteed Muslim's safety – stood up and said: 'O governor! I granted him safety!'

Ibn Ziyad said: 'What authority do you have to give safety? Did I send you to give him safety? I sent you to bring him to me!'

While *Ibn Hamrān* was leading Muslim away to the roof to kill him, Muslim turned to Ibn Ziyad and said: 'But God, if you were really from the Quraysh and we were related thus, you would not have killed me. But you are your father's son, so do whatever you want, you enemy of God.'

Once they had taken Muslim up to the roof, he said to them: 'Let me offer a short prayer, then do what you like.' But they would not allow it. He said: 'There is no way to do that.'

At that time, Muslim was invoking God's name, asking for forgiveness for his sins and sending blessings on the Prophet, his household, God's angels and His messengers, and saying: 'O God, judge between us and a people who have deceived us and abased us.'

His executioner brought him to a spot where they overlooked the onlookers assembled below. He struck off his head and cast his body down from the roof of the Palace, followed by his head. Then he went down to Ubaydullah b. Ziyad. The latter asked him: 'Did you kill him?'

'Yes.'

'Did he say anything while you were going up?'

'Yes. He was invoking God's name and asking Him to forgive his sins. And when I drew near to kill him, he said: 'O God, judge between us and between a people who deceived us, abased us and killed us.' I told him: 'Come closer. Praise God who has granted me retaliation against you.' Then I struck him once, but it did no good – he wasn't dead. He told me: 'Do you think a scratch is going to suffice for all that blood of yours I shed?''

Ibn Ziyad said: 'Proud even unto death?'

The man said: 'Then I struck him again and killed him.'

At that time, a great many people had assembled outside the palace, waiting to see what would happen to Muslim. Some were saying: 'They'll keep him here until Yazid sends word.' Others said: 'He's going to be executed for sure.' Then his killers threw his body from the top of the palace and after it came his severed head.

He was slain on Wednesday, the ninth day of Dhul al-Hijja, the Day of *'Arafa*, sixty years after Hijra.

THE AMBASSADOR

After Ubaydullah b. Ziyad had dealt with *Muslim b. Aqeel*, *Muhammad b. al-Ash'ath* went and spoke to him about Hani b. ÝUrwa. He said to him: 'You know the stature of *Hani b. 'Urwa* in this city, and his position in his clan. They know that *Asmaa b. Khārija* and I were the ones who brought him to you, so I adjure you by God – O governor – that you release him into my custody, for I am averse to his people's enmity. They are the strongest clan in the city and the most numerous of the Yemenites.'

Ubaydullah b. Ziyad fell silent for a moment, as if he had agreed. But he changed his mind and scolded *Muhammad b. al-Ash'ath*, and decreed that Hani would be executed in the market. He said: 'Take him out to the market and strike off his head!'

They took him out to the cattle market with his hands bound. He was calling out: 'O *Mudhḥaj*! Where are the MudhÎaj? O MudhÎaj? Where are you O *Mudhḥaj*?' But when he saw that no one would help him, he managed to remove his hands from the fetters, then began to look for something to defend himself, saying: 'A staff, a knife, a stone, a bone... is there nothing with which a man can defend himself?' The police pounced upon him and held him fast. The executioner – a Turkish slave and bondsman to Ibn Ziyad called Rushayd – came and said: 'Stick out your neck.'

Hani replied: 'I'm not about to give that away, nor will I help you take my life.'

Rushayd struck him, but failed to kill him.

Hani called out: 'To God is the Resurrection! O God, to Your mercy and satisfaction! O God make today an expiation for my sins! For I am only enraged for the son of your Prophet Muhammad's daughter!'

Then Rushayd leapt upon him and struck him until he died.

Then Ibn Ziyad ordered that the heads of Muslim b. Aqeel and Hani b. ŶUrwa be brought and given to two of his henchmen – Hani b. Abu Hayya and *Zubayr b. Arwaḥ* - to bear them to Syria. He wrote a letter to Yazid in which he said:

'Praise God who secured the due of the Commander of the Faithful, and sufficed him against the burden of his enemy. The Commander of the Faithful – may God ennoble him – is hereby informed that Muslim b. Aqeel took refuge in the home of *Hani b. 'Urwa al-Murādī*, that my spies sought them out, my men infiltrated their ranks, and I lured them into the open. God gave me power over them, so I went forth and struck of their heads. I have sent these to you with *Hani b. Hayya al-Hamadānī* and *Zubayr b. 'Arwaḥ al-Tamīmī*. These are two obedient men, so let the Commander of the Faithful ask of them whatever he desires. They are knowledgeable, honest, discerning and pious. Peace.'

The head of Muslim b. Aqeel was the first head of the *Hāshimite* Clan to be sent to Damascus.

When Yazid received the heads and the letter, he read out the letter gleefully and ordered that the heads be taken and placed over the city gates.

As for the bodies of Muslim and Hani, they were dragged through the markets by their feet for the rest of the day, then Ubaydullah b. Ziyad ordered that they be crucified upside-down in the markets of Kufa near the garbage tip. Muslim's body was the first body of the Hashemite Clan to be crucified and put on display.

The two bodies remained crucified in the markets until the wife of *Maytham al-Tammār* took them down in the middle of one night, and buried them in the vicinity of the central Mosque, where they rest until this day. But only the wife of *Hani b. 'Urwa* knew of this.

It is said that the tribe of *Mudhḥaj* mounted their horses, came, brought down the bodies and buried them.

But Ubaydullah b. Ziyad did not stop at killing Muslim b. Aqeel and *Hani b. 'Urwa*. Now he turned his attention to everyone who had supported Muslim and helped him; he ordered them arrested and many were executed.

Every day, Ibn Ziyad would sit in public court and order that each man accused of helping Muslim b. Aqeel be brought before him. Of each, he demanded two things: First that they swear a solemn oath that they did not help him. Second, that they go with the force of men he was preparing to face Hussein with. And whoever refused, he would strike off his head.

One of those men brought before him was *Abd al-A'lā al-Kalbī*, another was *Ammara al-Azadī*. His head of police, *Kathīr b. Shihāb* had arrested them and it was he who identified them to Ubaydullah b. Ziyad. He asked them: 'What brought you out into the open?'

They said: 'We came out to see what people were listening to, then your friend *Kathīr b. Shihāb* seized us.'

So Ibn Ziyad demanded that they swear a solemn oath to him that they had nothing to do with Muslim b. Aqeel, but they would not swear. Then he ordered that *Abd al-A'lā al-Kalbī* be taken to the

SAbu' cemetery and executed. So they took him and killed him. Then he ordered that Ammara al-AzadĐ be taken to his people and executed in plain sight of them.

Farazdaq recited eulogies for both Muslim b. Aqeel and Hani b. *'Urwa* in poetic verse. He said:

'If you do not know death, then look to Hani in the market and the son of Aqeel

To a hero whose face the sword did smash and another who fell from the heights of the slain,

They were beset by the vicissitudes of time and became the talk of those walking in all directions,

You see a body discoloured by death and a spatter of blood that has gushed forth,

A youth more modest than the most bashful girl and sharper than a glistening blade,

Around him circle devils and all of them are deluded and deluders,

Do names ride horses ambling in anticipation, while the *Mudhḥaj* reclaimed him absent-mindedly,

So if you do not seek revenge for your brother, then be whores satisfied with little.

THE CONFRONTATION

With the execution of Muslim b. Aqeel, a new stage of Hussein's uprising began, and the doors to many possibilities were flung open.

Even though Ubaydullah b. Ziyad was able – at least in appearance – to secure Kufa against the movement of the faithful led by Muslim, he was not truly able to supress their revolt altogether. He had merely thrown ashes on the flames.

It is true that he carried out atrocities, killing some men and imprisoning others, but he could not put out the fires in people's hearts, especially because of the way in which he had killed Muslim b. Aqeel, *Hani b. 'Urwa* and other members of the Kufan elite. Moreover, he had used treachery and assassination to attain his ends, while Muslim b. Aqeel had refused to assassinate Ibn Ziyad on more than one occasion when he had an opportunity to do so. All of this led the faithful to become more and more averse to Umayyad government as a whole, and the Nation to become divided against itself more than ever before. Though from the outside it was not always clear, the believers were on one side and their enemies were on another.

It was not possible to stay neutral once Ibn Ziyad had committed such crimes against the faithful and made an example of the people by punishing the innocent along with the guilty.

How many young men he ordered executed in front of the homes of their families and relatives; eventually killing became the only logic the regime knew when it came to dealing with the opponents of Yazid b. Muawiya.

Muawiya had died knowing that Yazid's succession, for which so much blood and gold had been spent, could not be secured so long as there was someone like Hussein b. Ali in whose personality all virtues were gathered, and who – in the eyes of the people – embodied God's Messenger, with all of his virtues and merits, perfectly. Meanwhile, on the opposite side stood Yazid b. Muawiya, thirty-five years old, with no experience of leadership and bereft of any capable advisors save a group of criminals motivated by Umayyad resentments like Ubaydullah b. Ziyad.

This is how the struggle between the hypocrites of the Umayyad Clan and the righteous Hashemites came to a head; there was no room for compromise – the two sides were about to clash.

On the side of truth stood Hussein b. Ali, the inheritor of the prophets – Adam, Abel, Noah, Abraham, Moses, Jesus and Muhammad, and the successor to his own faither, Ali. With him, stood the Prophet's Household and a band of righteous believers. On the side of falsehood stood Yazid b. Muawiya, the inheritor of Cain, Nimrod, Pharaoh, the Pharisees, his grandfather, Abu Sufiyan and his father, Muawiya – the sly fox; a treacherous and ruthless man as ever was.

The struggle between Hussein and Yazid was not merely a struggle between two men, except to the extent that these two men represented two contradictory tendencies. And it is this very struggle that has taken place throughout history between the prophets and their enemies, between the martyrs and the tyrants.

To the extent that Hussein was defending God's religion and its teachings and values, such as justice, kindness and faith, and to the extent that he exemplified qualities such supporting and assisting the truth, Yazid was driven to the same extent by a love of power and leadership, and unconcerned with moral principles to the extent that he did not display the slightest concern for humanity – whether respect for the sanctity of human life or for the protection of people's property and dignity – and he used deceit, treachery and vanity in shaping the destiny of the Nationh.

So the contrast between Hussein b. Ali and Yazid b. Muawiya was one of morality and of two different ways of life; the battle between the two sides was the battle between good and evil, righteousness and corruption, faith and hypocrisy... at its core was the battle between Cain and Abel, which will continue to the end of the world, and which is represented in every age by men on both sides; the faithful against the hypocrites, the righteous against the sinners, the learned against the ignorant, the truthful against the liars, the martyrs against the murderers.

To the extent that Hussein was ready to sacrifice himself and those people who were nearest and dearest to his heart for the sake of truth, justice and goodness, his enemies were ready – to the same extent – to slaughter people, shed blood, usurp their rights and take captive their women and children for the sake of their authority and their own personal interests and desires.

This is the least that can be said about the enemies of Hussein; they were in truth a band of ruthless criminals... and, as is usually the case when a criminal becomes the head of state, they behave like mobsters with the people, with the difference that they bestow upon themselves an air of sanctity in the sense that they are the legitimate ruler of a state. This is how things were with Yazid and the Caliphs of the Umayyad Clan.

We cannot merely call Hussein's enemies worldly kings, nor can we simply dismiss their policies as defending their own power against their enemies. In fact, the least we can call them is rapacious beasts, who obey every cruel and vindictive impulse they have. They do not care if they wantonly trample the rights of the innocent or shed their blood as if it were a pastime. It was only in this way that they could feel that they had power and authority. Each of Yazid's agents 'Violated the blood of the Muslims to no end, slaying those whose lives God had sanctified in anger, enmity and suspicion, all the while engaging in idle play and diversion as if they had done nothing.' Just as Muslim b. Aqeel had said.

This is why in the entirety of human history we can find no clearer depiction of the struggle between truth and falsehood, between good and evil, between true faith and utter hypocricy, than the struggle that took place sixty one years after Hijra between Hussein and his enemies.

Truly, I say to you that in the confrontation between Hussein and his enemies, the human soul is displayed in two conflicting forms; the form of the soul contented (al-nafs al-mutmaÞinna) with its faith, which observes its morals and is true to God in its conduct, and 'the soul which bids to evil', which is true to nothing, whether God, people or its own self, and is absorbed in pleasures and desires power, never hesitating to sin.

These two conflicting forms of the human soul are the driving force behind human history, whether individuals, communities or nations, in every time and place.

Hussein is the ideal for all those people in history with contented souls, beginning with Adam and ending with Muhammad, just as Yazid embodies all the enemies of the prophets, from Cain the kinslayer to the rejector of truth Muawiya b. Abu Sufiyan.

For this reason we find no one in history who reproaches Hussein's actions, even amongst his enemies, just as we find no one who praises Yazid for his, even amongst his own supporters. That is sufficient proof that this is as much a conflict between two different ways of life as it is a conflict between two persons; and this is represented even in their outward appearance. All the enemies of Hussein were disfigured on the outside as much as they were on the inside.

Yazid b. Muawiya's face was scarred by smallpox, Ubaydullah b. Ziyad was of unknown parentage and a stammerer, and Shimr b. al-Jawshan was afflicted by leprosy.

On the other hand, Hussein and his companions were as bright as the full moon in the midst of night; their faces resembled those of angels, and their personalities were like those of the prophets, facing men whose faces were like those of demons and whose personalities were like those of devils.

ROAD TO KARBALA

Before word of Ibn Ziyad's counterrevolution against Muslim b. Aqeel in Kufa and the reassertion of Umayyad power could reach Mecca, where Hussein was based, events revealed great excitement in the Muslim world. In Mecca, the people of Hijaz and those who had come to fulfil the rites of Hajj were gathering daily in the presence of Hussein, who could scarcely leave his home without people swarming around him wherever he went. Basra had also begun to boil; the faithful there began meeting in secret to prepare themselves for any change of situation.

Just as the greatest enemies of Yazid began to move, for example, Abdullah b. Zubayr based himself in Mecca and his supporters began to gather followers, events sent the regime into confusion. Yazid began to change his governors in the provinces, including Mecca and Medina. He also initiated an opposing movement to try and get ahead of events, as all tyrants in history are wont to do; the tyrants began to use violence and punish the slightest infractions with the most serious punishments. Usually, it was they who decided to choose confrontation and not their opponents, just as was the case between Cain and Abel, between Nimrod and Abraham, Pharaoh and Moses, between the Pharisees and Jesus and between Abu Sufiyan and Muhammad.

Who was it that decided to kill the other; Cain or Abel?

Who was it that decided to burn the other; Nimrod or Abraham?

Who was it that decided to imprison, kill or exile the other; Pharaoh or Moses?

And who was it who decided to crucify the other; the Pharisees or Jesus?

And who was it who decided to assassinate the other; the Quraysh or Muhammad?

In the same manner, it was Yazid who decided to confront Hussein. He wrote letters to his governors demanding that they compel Hussein to give allegiance or face the consequences. He also wrote letters to some of the leading figures of the Hashemite Clan and demanded that they prevent Hussein from continuing on his current course, and most of these contained clear threats against Hussein.

One of the people who Yazid wrote to at the mere settling of Hussein in Medina was Abdullah b. Abbas, as he was a companion of Ali b. Abu Talib and a relative of his. And in his letter, he tried to rouse the Hashemite Clan against Hussein. In this letter, Yazid wrote: 'Your cousin, Hussein, and God's enemy, Ibn Zubayr, have turned away from pledging allegiance to me and gone to ground in Mecca to stir up sedition, putting themselves in grave danger.

As for Ibn Zubayr, he will soon be spent and tomorrow the sword will slay him.

But as for Hussein, I desire to excuse you – the Prophet's Household – for his actions, for it has reached me that some of his followers in Iraq are exchanging letters with him and offering him the Caliphate while he offers them leadership. You know the great love, respect and familial connection we share. But Hussein has severed that. You are the leader of your household, the master of the people of your land, so go to him and dissuade him from sowing division. Save this Nation from discord! If he listens to you and desists, I guarantee him safety and great generosity, and I will treat him as my father treated his brother. If he desires more, I will guarantee whatever God makes you see fit. Give him your guarantee and undertake that for him, and he shall have firm assurances and solemn oaths from me to put his mind at ease. Hasten to reply with whatever need you might have from me. Peace.'

He closed his letter with the following verses of poetry:

O rider who departs in the morning, mounted upon camels for a dangerous undertaking,

He roused the Quraysh at a distance shrine, and between me and Hussein lies God and family ties.

And a position in the courtyard of the House he has sought, God's covenant and a source of protection,

You harassed your people out of pride for your mother, a mother – by my life! – chaste, pious and noble!

Such that no one approaches her grace, daughter of the Prophet, as everyone well knows,

I surely know, or suppose I do, and sometimes supposition proves true,

Then what you claim will abandon you, and you will die surrounded by eagles and vultures,

O our people! Do not start a war when all is peaceful; hold fast to the rope of peace and seek protection therein

War has deceived those who came before you; generations by which nations have been destroyed,

So be fair to your people and do not perish out of pride; for pride often goes before a fall.

The letter clearly shows that Yazid considered Hussein's moving from Medina to Mecca by itself and exchanging letters with the people of Kufa, a serious crime which the Hashemite Clan must oppose. In the same vein, he accuses Hussein of wanting to sow sedition and threatens him with death and destruction. He also considers himself the axis of the Nation's unity, and from there portrays Hussein's movement as striving for division. At the end of the letter he offers to buy off Hussein with wealth, thinking that Hussein shares his own motivations, seeks only to fleece money out of him through threats, and thus can be bought with wealth and temptations. Finally he gives Ibn Abbas the choice whether to increase or decrease the offer of wealth to Hussein, if he thinks this will motivate the latter to obey him.

As for Ibn ÝAbbas, he responded to Yazid's letter with the following:

'I have read your letter concerning Hussein and Ibn Zubayr's arrival in Mecca. As for Ibn Zubayr, he has no connection to us in his views and motivation. In spite of that he writes to us concealing his rancour and feigning affection. So we are of one mind concerning him.

As for Hussein, when he arrived in Mecca and left the sanctuary of his grandfather and the homes of his forefathers, I asked him why he came. He told me that you agents in Medina treated him badly and hastened to speak to him immoderately. So he came to God's sanctuary seeking asylum therein. I will inform him of what you mentioned, and I will not fail to give good counsel concerning that through which God will unite opinions, extinguish the flames [of rebellion], subdue discord and spare the blood of the Nation.

I enjoin you to fear God in private and in public; do not go to bed at night desiring calamity for a Muslim, nor while plotting to do some wrong to him, nor while laying traps for him – for how many a man has laid a trap for others only to fall into it himself, and how many a man has harboured hopes which he is not granted – so take hold of your prize in reciting the Quran, and I enjoin you to fast and stand in prayer. Do not let the vanities and falsehoods of this world distract you from them. For whatever distracts you from God will only cause harm and vanish, but whatever means of obtaining felicity in the Hereafter occupy your mind will endure and avail you. Peace.'

Clearly, Ibn Abbas informs Yazid of his position with regards to Hussein's movement from Medina to Mecca, considering that to be the result of the regime's position towards him, especially the governor, and the position of Marwan b. al-Hakam, both of whom mistreated Hussein and spoke to him immoderately, threatening to kill him if he did not pledge allegiance.

By the same token, he considers Hussein's departure from the city of his grandfather to God's sanctuary something completely natural, and the right of every Muslim in the world. This is in addition to his responding to Yazid's threats of death and destruction with wise counsel to fear God and not be hasty in dealing with Hussein.

Hussein made his decision to rise up based on a number of facts:

First, to demonstrate conclusively that there are those who will support the truth.

Second, because God has enjoined the scholars not to endure the avarice of the oppressor or the hunger of the oppressed.

Third, because of the advice his father – Imam Ali – gave to him and his brother, Hasan, before he departed this world: 'I enjoin you to fear God, and not to go after this world even if it entices you, nor grieve for anything of it that escapes you. [I enjoin you] to speak the truth and act for the rewards of the Hereafter. Be an enemy to the oppressor and a helper of the oppressed.'

Fourth, because of the Umayyad Clan's persistence in tyranny, aggression and wrongdoing, beginning with Muawiya compelling the people to pledge allegiance to Yazid as Caliph of the Muslims, the man about whom Hussein said: 'May Islam rest in peace if the Nation is afflicted with a shepherd such as Yazid.'

It was because of a combination of these facts that Hussein took the decision to rise up; not to become a ruler here or there, but rather to do his duty, the very same duty that motivated the prophets, the people and the righteous to rise up in their own nations and take up the cause.

Word of Hussein's decision to head for Iraq spreads like wildfire amongst the people, especially the Hajj pilgrims, and Rahman *al-Ṣāliḥ* goes quickly to visit his friend, Abdullah b. Muslim. He enters his house and finds him distressed and weeping. He asks: 'What do you think about Hussein's decision?'

Abdullah: The moment of truth has come, and I think the days are pregnant with terrible events for this Nation.

Rahman: We all know Hussein's position, and the truth about Yazid is clear to everyone. The entire regime is in the hands of this man, so how can Hussein go to Iraq and rule there?

Abdullah: It appears that you do not really know Hussein at all! These are men who do not seek this world and its vanities; even if it came knocking at their doors they would throw it out on its face, as their father did. They are the Prophet's Household, the wellspring of revelation, the locus of visitation for angels, the treasuring of knowledge; revelation came down in their homes!

Do you think that when God's Messenger fist took up his mission in Mecca, he wanted to be a prince over its people? They offered him as much, but he refused. Do you think he was after money? They offered him the jewels of the Ka'ba, but he refused. Do you think he wanted all the daughters of the Quraysh? They offered him that, but he refused that too.

Hussein's grandfather told his uncle, Abu Talib: 'O uncle! By God if they placed the Sun in my right hand and the Moon in my left so that I give up this cause, I would not give it up until God makes it victorious or I perish [in the process.]'

Rahman: But God's religion has triumphed, so why must Hussein go forth?

Abdullah: Come on! The people are put to tribulation by the Umayyad Clan and take their religion from them; the final religion is on the verge of becoming nothing more than a hollow shell, and the teachings with which God sent his prophets to establish justice in the world are about to become nothing more than a cover for hypocrisy and tyranny.

This is why Ali said: 'Lo! Verily the tribulation I fear most for you is that of the Umayyad Clan!'

Don't you see? If the Umayyad Clan rebuilt their idols at the Ka'ba and forced the people to worship them, ever last believing man and woman would rise up against them and refuse to follow them!

Rahman: Of course!

Abdullah: Do you think that tyranny in the name of religion, making monopoly out of God's property and taking His servants as chattel is any less dangerous that placing idols in the Ka'ba again?

Did not the Prophet tell the Ka'ba: 'Greetings to the House! How great you are and how great is your sanctity in the eyes of God. But by God, the believing man or woman is more sacred than you!'

Isn't it strange that the Prophet, sent by the Lord of the Worlds, did not demand that anyone pledge allegiance to him – it was their own free choice. And yet today, the Umayyad Clan compel people to pledge allegiance to Yazid as the successor to God's Messenger, while he has no connection to the Prophet whether in his religion or lineage, in his manners, morals or knowledge?

Do you think that that God's Messenger was sent so that the Nation could be ruled by one such as Yazid? So that someone like him could govern people and take charge of their affairs, their destiny, their dignity, their wealth and every matter great and small in religious and worldly affairs?

Rahman: So is Hussein sallying against the regime to do away with this man, Yazid, and take his place?

Abdullah: God's people do not take stances based on personal enmity towards anyone; they want to awaken the people, not to take hold of power and a crown. Did Abraham want to sit in the place of Nimrod? Did Moses want to sit in the place of Pharaoh? Did God's Messenger want to obtain the rank of Abu Sufiyan?

The prophets are after something else, namely to guide the people and motivate them to uphold justice and prevent wrongdoing, so that wealth will not be in the hands of people who use it to drive people away from religion and religious values.

Rahman: But if Hussein rises up and goes to Iraq, might he not be slain?

Abdullah: Hussein is not undertaking a political adventure, nor is he rising up as some bargaining ploy. No, Hussein believes in his religion; if the people accept him and help him, they help themselves because they will be free in this world. But if they waver, and the regime has power over Hussein, he will hold fast to the truth. It does not matter to him whether this ends in his life or death, rather death is more desirable to him than life.

Rahman: So you think Hussein will definitely go forth?

Abdullah: It certainly seems that way.

Rahman: Has anyone advised him to do anything else, or tried to prevent him from going to Iraq?

Abdullah: Many have advised him not to go forth.

Rahman: Did Hussein heed any of them?

Abdullah: No.

Rahman: Why not?

Abdullah: Because Hussein's logic differs from theirs. Many came to Hussein thinking that he seeks political power, and intends to overthrow the Umayyad Clan no matter the cost. They tell him, 'You won't succeed, the regime is too strong to fall by your hand, when you have so few men and even fewer whom you can rely upon.'

You know that Hussein is the grandson of God's Messenger and the son of the Commander of the Faithful. He is fifty-eight years of age, while Yazid is no more than thirty five. Hussein is wiser and more experienced than his foe; he has lived through great events from when he was born until today. So whatever they tell him, he knows already, but his logic differs from theirs. Hussein does not take up arms to seize power, as they think.

Rahman: So will Hussein go forth to be killed?

Abdullah: No. This isn't a question of Hussein is either seeking power or seeking death; Hussein is doing his duty and this will have one of two good outcomes; either he will win or he will be martyred. And this is what all of the prophets have done before him. If a prophet is sent to a people, do they want to rule them or to guide them?

The problem in the Nation today is that there are those who seek power so that they can become kings in the name of religion; the danger in these people lies in the fact that their actions take on a religious significance in the eyes of the people and the positions they adopt are given an air of legitimacy. And this is the very hypocrisy of which we must always be vigilant both in ourselves and in others.

All of those who came to Hussein have told him that the situation in Kufa is still confused and that his going to Iraq may not lead to his attaining power. But Hussein is fundamentally not searching for power. He is just looking to do his duty.

When Abdullah b. Abbas heard that Hussein wanted to head for Iraq, he went to see him. After he entered his presence and greeted him, he said: 'May I be your sacrifice, O son of God's Messenger! People say that you are going to Iraq, tell me what are you going to do?'

Hussein said: 'Yes, in these days I have decided to do that – if God wills, and there is no power save with God.'

Ibn Abbas said: 'I beg you, by God, do not do that. If you were going to a people who have killed their governor, taken control of their lands and expelled their enemies, then this is something sensible indeed. But if they have invited you while their governor still rules, and his agents control the land, then they have invited you to start a war. You know that this is the land in which your father was slain and your brother betrayed; allegiance has been pledged to Yazid b. Muawiya and Ubaydullah b. Ziyad controls the wealth there – people today are the slaves of dirhams and dinars. You might be killed, so beware of God and remain here in this sanctuary!'

Rahman: Don't you think Ibn Abbas gave Hussein good advice?

Abdullah: Good advice for someone who wants to seize power, yes. He is saying do not go to Kufa until the people have overthrown their governor, expelled him and taken power, so that when you go there you will become their leader. Otherwise, you might be killed on the way. But Hussein is not after power, nor does he fear death, just as the prophets did not seek power or fear death.

In response to Ibn Abbas, Hussein said: 'By God, I would rather be slain in Iraq than slain in Mecca and have the sanctity of God's

House and the Prophet defiled. Whatever God has decreed will happen, and so I seek goodness from God and look to what will come.'

Some days later, Abdullah b. Abbas came to him again and said: 'O son of the daughter of God's Messenger! I have thought of something, if you will listen to me?'

Hussein said: 'What have you thought of?'

Ibn Abbas said: 'Go to Yemen, for it has fortresses and mountains; it is a land as broad as it is wide. You have followers there. You can hide and bide your time until you have gathered your strength, then you can write to the people and let them know where you are.'

Hussein said: 'O cousin! I know that you mean well, but I have made up my mind to go to Iraq. It cannot be avoided. Let it go, Ibn Abbas, for I would be ashamed if I met my Lord if I do not enjoin good and forbid evil amongst our Nation.'

Ibn Abbas fell silent for a moment, then said: 'O son of the daughter of God's Messenger, if you have made up your mind then do as you must, but do not take your women and children with you, lest you be killed before their eyes while they are helpless.'

Hussein said: 'They have been entrusted to me by God's Messenger and I trust no one else with them, they will come with me.'

And it appears that some of the women heard what Ibn Abbas said and they began to cry loudly, one of them called out to Ibn Abbas: 'O Ibn Abbas! Do you advise our chief and master to leave us behind and go alone! No, by God, we will either live with him or die with him – shall there be any time for us without him?'

When Ibn Abbas saw that Hussein would not take his advice, he said to him at last: 'By God, if I thought that if I threw myself upon you, clung onto the hem of your robes and taken hold of your hair in my fingers until the people gathered around the two of us... if I thought it would do any good, I would have done it. But I know that

God will see His affair comes to pass.'

Then his eyes welled up with tears and he began to weep. As he bid farewell and left, he was saying: 'Alas Hussein!'

As they met at night near the Ka'ba, Rahman sits beside Abdullah b. Muslim. The two are silent for a while. Then Rahman turns to his friend and says: 'Everyone is talking about Hussein's departure.'

Abdullah: Do they support him or oppose him?

Rahman: The ordinary people are with Hussein; they see that we are in a dark night and something must change in this Nation.

Abdullah: That's right, but do you know the first thing that must change in this Nation is its perception and the expression of its will, so that the people can move themselves and change things. It's no good to just support something with your heart while sitting still and silent where you are. This is what distinguishes Hussein from everyone else. He does not say anything save that he does it, and whatever he does, he does according to the way of his grandfather, God's Messenger without ever diverting from the path.

Rahman: So in the end Hussein is definitely going forth for his uprising?

Abdullah: Hussein is utterly convinced of his position and has no hesitations about it. If Abraham had hesitated in breaking the idols, Hussein would have hesitated in this, and if God's Messenger had hesitated in his rejection of idol-worship, Hussein would have hesitated in this. But just as God's Messenger announced his repudiation of the idol-worshippers on the day of the greater pilgrimage, Hussein too has announced his repudiation of the hypocrites during this pilgrimage.

Rahman: What positions have the nobles and worthies taken?

Abdullah: There are those who try to prevent Hussein from going to Iraq, and they are of four kinds:

First are those who sympathise with Hussein, second are those who sympathise with the Umayyad Clan, third are those who do not understand the objectives Hussein is pursuing – so they speak with a logic that is completely different from that of Hussein...

Rahman: Do you mean to say that these kind of people do not understand Hussein and he does not understand them?

Abdullah: Hussein understands them, but they are the ones who do not understand him.

The fourth kind are those who are pleased with Hussein's decision to depart, but make a show of displeasure, so that they will not be held responsible for his blood if he is killed.

Rahman: Who do you mean by this kind?

Abdullah: I mean the likes of Ibn Zubayr, for he once came to Hussein to encourage him to rise up against Yazid. One of the things he told him was: 'I do not understand why we have left those people to their own devices, while we are the sons of Emigrants and more entitled to rule than them. Tell me, what do you plan to do?'

Hussein told him: 'By God I have debated with myself about whether I should go to Kufa, for the leaders of its people have written to me asking me to come to them, but I ask God to show me what is best.'

Ibn Zubayr said: 'If had followers like yours, I would not ignore them.' But then he feared that he might be accused [of desiring Hussein to leave] so he said: 'Although, if you stayed in Hijaz and pursued things from here it would be better – God-willing. So once you have strengthened your position you can expel Yazid's agents from this land, and I will stand by your side and support you. If you want my advice, you should pursue your mission from this sanctuary, for it is the place in which people from the four corners of the empire meet, and – by God's permission – this will not prevent you from achieving your goals. I hope you will heed my advice.'

Rahman: And what did Hussein say in response?

Abdullah: He told him: 'My father told me that there will be a sacrificial animal in Mecca that will profane its sanctity – I have no desire to be that sacrifice. We will not profane it, nor will we allow it to be profaned on our account. I would rather be slain on a dusty mound that be slain here.'

Then Hussein left Ibn Zubayr and said to those with him: 'There is nothing of this world dearer to him than me leaving Hijaz, because he knows that he will get nothing from me and that the people will always turn to me rather than to him. So he would like me to leave this place so he can have it to himself.'

Rahman: So these kind of people advise Hussein not to go to Iraq, but what about those who advise him not to go because of their love for him? How are they, what do they say and what does Hussein tell them?

Abdullah b. Muslim: Abdullah b. Ja'far b. Abu Talib is one of them, he is Hussein's cousin and the husband of his sister, Zaynab. He was in Medina, but when he heard that Hussein wanted to go to Iraq, he wrote to him:

'In the name of God, the Compassionate, the Merciful. To Hussein b. Ali from Abdullah b. Ja'far.

I adjure you by God not to leave Mecca, for I fear that this matter upon which you have decided will be the end of you and of your household. If you are killed, I fear that God's light will be put out. You are the banner of the rightly-guided. You are the hope of the faithful. So do not be hasty in going to Iraq – I will obtain a guarantee of safety for you from Yazid, and from the entire Umayyad clan, for yourself, your property, your children and your household. Peace.'

As should be clear, this man loves Hussein dearly and he fears that the Umayyad Clan will kill him and wipe out the descendents of God's Messenger entirely.

Hussein wrote back to him:

'In the name of God, the Compassionate, the Merciful. I have received your letter, read it and understood its contents. I inform you that I have seen my grandfather, God's Messenger, in a dream. He has informed me of something which I am to do, whether it is in my favour or against. By God, cousin, even if I was in some burrow deep in the earth they would bring me out of it and kill me, and by God they would violate my sanctity just as the Jews profaned the Sabbath. Peace.'

Rahman: Does the letter of Abdullah b. Ja'far show that some of the Prophet's Household disagreed with Hussein about going to Iraq?

Abdullah: The Prophet's Household are united in their belief in the Imamate of Hussein – there is no arguing that he is their leader and their master. They love him, and if he has resolved to go then they will defer to his judgement. This is why when Abdullah b. Ja'far read this letter, he sent his two sons, ÝAwn and Muhammad to go with Hussein's caravan, without any consideration for what might happen to him or them.

Someone else who advised Hussein not to go out of love for him was Abdullah b. MuÔĐÝ. He told him: 'May my mother and father be your sacrifice! I beg you in God's name to look to your own safety and not go to Iraq. Your life is sacred in the eyes of God, for you are a near relative of God's Messenger. And if the Umayyad Clan, they will not hesitate to violate anything sacred thing, nor will the fear killing anyone after they have killed you. By God, if they kill you, they will take everyone else as slaves and chattel.'

Another sympathizer who told Hussein not to go to Iraq was *Amr b. Rahman al-Makhzūmī*. He had come to him and said: 'I hear that you intend to go to Iraq, but as a friend I ask you not to go. You will be going to a land filled with Yazid's agents and deputies. They have the treasury and people are slaves to dinars and dirhams – I do not doubt that those who have promised to help you will end up fighting you, and those who love you more than the ones they fight beside.

Hussein told him: 'May God grant you good for your counsel, but whatever has been decreed will be, whether I take your advice or neglect it.'

Amra, the daughter of *Rahman al-Anṣārī* also advised Hussein not to leave, telling him that he was only going to his end. She said: 'I bear witness that A'isha told me that she had heard God's Messenger say that Hussein will be killed in the land of Babylon.'

When he read her letter, he remarked: 'So I have no choice but to go to my end, then.'

Rahman: Hussein's answer to this letter is great indeed. If God's Messenger foretold that he would be killed in Iraq, then he has no choice but to go there, because when God's Messenger foretells something, it is revelation from heaven.

But tell me who told Hussein not to go because they sympathised with the Umayyad Clan rather than Hussein?

Abdullah: *Amr b. Sa'eed b. al-'Āṣ* was one of them. He is the deputy in charge of the two sanctuaries. He wrote to Hussein haughtily: 'I ask God to give you back your senses, turn you aside from that which will bring about your ruin, and guide you to what will make you prosper. I have heard that you have decided to leave for Iraq. But I warn you, by God, against division. If you fear [I intend you some harm], I have sent you my brother, *Yaḥyā b. Sa'eed*, so come to me with him and you shall have safety, friendship, goodness and generosity from us.'

Hussein wrote back, saying: 'One who calls to God and righteous conduct and says 'I am of the Muslims' does not sow division. You call me to goodness and generosity, but the best safety is that which is granted by God and on the Day of Resurrection, God will not grant safety to those who feared him not in this world. We ask God for such fear in this world that will grant us safety on the Day of Resurrection. If you truly wanted goodness and friendship for me with this letter of yours, then may you be granted good for that in this world and the Hereafter. Peace.'

Rahman: So who are those who thought one thing while Hussein thought something else, and that perhaps didn't understand Hussein's goal in setting forth for Iraq?

Abdullah: Muhammad b. Hanafiyya, for example. He thought that Hussein wanted to go to Iraq because he feared for his safety should he remain in Mecca, while in Iraq he had followers and supporters who had asked him to come and lead them. He told Hussein that he feared for him more in Kufa than he did for him in Mecca. He even said: 'I think you should remain in Mecca and be the mightiest of those in the sanctuary, either that or go to Yemen for there you will be fortified and the Umayyad Clan will not be able to reach you.'

But Hussein responded that he had seen God's Messenger in a dream and he had commanded him to go to Iraq even if he is killed there, for God had willed that he would see him slain. But when he asked about his household, Hussein told him: 'God has willed to see them prisoners.'

The same is true with regards to Abdullah b. Abbas. He thought that Hussein wanted to go and establish his government in Kufa and then extend his control over Iraq from there, then receive the pledge of allegiance as Caliph of the Muslims. As if Hussein wanted to set up a counter government to that of the current regime.

But Hussein wanted to go to Iraq in order to do his duty in enjoining good and forbidding evil, returning the Nation to the right path, guiding the people with the guidance of God and His messenger and showing the difference between politics which use religion as a cover, and God's religion – as brought by the Prophet – which must be followed and acted upon, not for the sake of worldly gains but for the sake of God's satisfaction.

So Hussein only went forward to revive God's ordinances which had been set aside, spread justice amongst the people and keep God's religion safe from being misused by evil men and hypocrites.

Rahman: Can you tell me about what Hussein and Ibn Zubayr disagree about, while both of them have refused to pledge allegiance to Yazid?

Abdullah: Just as governments differ between those that seek to spread justice for the people and treat them well, without looking at the slogans they raise, and whether religious or unreligious, and those governments that have no interest in justice, who only want all the benefits of power for themselves. Such governments only mention the name of "the people" or "God" for their own interests. The same is true for those who come out to oppose governments; some come out to oppose an oppressive regime, crying out for justice, and let their only intention is to usurp the positions of those in power and nothing more. They seek power, position, supremacy, a crown and a sceptre, and wealth. But there are others who come out against oppressive governments and are sincere in their calls; they want nothing for themselves.

Abdullah b. Zubayr is of the first kind; he only differs from Yazid in that he wants to take his place. He does not differ from Yazid in his means or ends. While Hussein follows the path of the prophets, whose slogan was: 'We want neither thanks from you, nor reward' and 'Say, I ask you no reward for it.'

The difference between them is that if Hussein attains power, he will do as his father did, who had no interest in the vanities of this world once he received the Caliphate. So he denied himself its pleasures. He even forbade that a man should walk behind him and took no bodyguards for himself, despite his many enemies he had earned through fighting three bloody civil wars. Nor did he take male or female slaves in his home or abode. His family enjoyed a standard of life that was less than that of the ordinary people.

As for Abdullah b. Zubayr, if he attains power, he will do exactly as the other oppressors have done before him. He wants power for himself and his faction, while we see that Hussein wants to go to Iraq, even with death staring him in the face. But that does not trouble him because he has no interest in this world in the first place, as he told Abdullah b. Umar when he came to him and warned him of the hardships the people of obstinacy would assail him with, for they were completely ruthless. Perhaps they would even kill him.

Hussein said: 'O Abu Rahman! Do you not know that one of the most trifling things for God in this world is that the head of John the Baptist was given to a whore of the Israelites?'

Rahman: What is the position of the Prophet's companions, like *Jābir b. Abdullah al-Anṣārī* and *Abu Sa'eed al-Khudrī*?

Abdullah b. Muslim: Both of them are sympathetic to Hussein. *Jābir b. Abdullah* came to him and said: 'You are the descendent of God's Messenger and one of his two grandsons. I only think it best that you come to an accommodation (*ṣulḥ*) [with the Umayyads] as your brother [Hasan] did, for that is a sensible position to take.'

Hussein told him: 'O *Jābir*, my brother did that by God's command and the command of His messenger, but I too will act by God's command and the command of His messenger.'

Rahman: Was *Jābir b. Abdullah* satisfied with Hussein's answer?

Abdullah: Yes; he knew that Hussein would not falsely attribute something to God or His messenger. For how could he, when he is God's trustee upon the earth and the proof of His authority over His servants? *Jābir* knew that Hussein possessed this rank.

Rahman: What of the wives of God's Messenger?

Abdullah: Umm Salama sent for him; she had brought him up when he was little and she loved him and sympathised with him above all people. The Prophet had entrusted her with some of the earth of Karbala, and she had placed it in a container. She asked Hussein: 'My son! Do you intend to go?'

Hussein said: 'O mother! I intend to go to Iraq'

She said: 'I pray to God for you if you plan on going to Iraq.'

Hussein said: 'Why, mother?'

She said: 'I heard God's Messenger say: 'My son, Hussein, will be slain in Iraq.' And I have some of the earth from the place where you will be slain sealed in a container – God's Messenger gave it to me.'

Hussein said: 'By God, I shall be slain thus. And even if I don't go to Iraq, they will kill me anyway. I will not flee from what has been set down, nor from the certain decree, nor from God's commandments.'

Umm Salama said: 'Woe! Will you go even though you will be slain?'

Hussein said: 'Mother! If I do not go today, I will go tomorrow, and if not tomorrow then the day after that. There is no escape from death. I know the place where I will be killed, and the hour in which I will be killed, and the grave in which my body will be buried. I know them as well as I know you. I see them as I see you. I will show you them, if you would like.'

Umm Salama said: 'I would like that.'

Hussein wiped his hand over her face, and he spoke nothing more than God's name before God opened her eyes and the earth shrunk before her, and God showed her where he and his companions would lie. And he took another piece of that earth and placed it in a container for her. Then he told her: 'When they overflow with blood, you will know that I have been slain.'

On the seventh day of Dhul al-Hijja in the sixtieth year after Hijra, *Rahman al-Ṣāliḥ* meets *Abdullah b. Muslim* in one of the alleys of Mecca. He tells him: 'Everyone is saying that Hussein is about to leave today. But I ask you: Is there no other option for him while this journey poses such danger to his life and perhaps the life of the Prophet's Household too?'

Abdullah: If there was another option, Hussein would have taken it. But there is no doubting that commitment to religion is deeply rooted in this man's heart. He is utterly convinced that forsaking religious ordinances is the greatest tribulation facing this Nation now and in the future. And what kind of Muslim who believes in his religion can allow this to happen, let alone Hussein, the inheritor of the prophets and the grandson of God's Messenger!

Hussein sees Yazid's presence at the head of a regime as a danger to the religion as a whole; the Caliph must look after people's religious and worldly affairs; their material and spiritual interests, but Yazid isn't fit to be so much as a police officer. So isn't religion in danger of being utterly destroyed at his hands?

It is Yazid who has given Hussein two choices: to pledge allegiance or be slain. But Hussein has chosen something else, namely to rise up, because he cannot abide the falsehood of the regime. How can Hussein testify that Yazid is fit to be a leader? Is this not misguiding the people? And in return for what? For a comfortable worldly life?

Yazid doesn't possess a single admirable quality for Hussein to praise, whether in religion, nobility, knowledge, skills or concern for the people's well-being. Anyone who accepts the Caliphate of Yazid denies all the principles of the religion and ignores the rights of the people in every sphere of life.

It is not in Hussein's character to submit to falsehood; neither his sense of honour nor his faith would allow him to do so.

Rahman: But Hussein himself did not venture forth against Muawiya?

Abdullah: Yes, he didn't go out and fight Muawiya, but neither did he pledge allegiance. And Muawiya did not force him to choose between pledging allegiance and being slain. Whereas Yazid has given Hussein precisely this choice. This is what he wrote to his governor in Medina and what Marwan b. al-Hakam advised on the night the governor summoned him to the palace. This is something different. Hussein is a sincere believer who observes all the moral precepts of Islam; he is a treasury of virtue and is as loyal as he is brave. His loyalty meant that he could not fight Muawiya after his brother's death, because his brother had made a peace treaty with Muawiya that included him, so he had an agreement with Muawiya, and Hussein did not see himself as released from it until Muawiya was dead.

The ascencion of Yazid to the Caliphate marked the beginning of a new kind of kingship, and submitting to it meant turning this state into a practice that the Nation would be bound to for generations, without any hope for change. This, in addition to the fact that it would become a part of people's religious beliefs and practice.

Don't you think that the Umayyads have made tyranny appear an almost natural state of affairs? Through those men who sold their consciences for gold and silver, they have made the tyrant seem holy, or rather the successor to God's Messenger. This meants a return to the Age of Ignorance in the fullest sense of the word!

When our Lord has commanded us to disassociate from tyrants, and counted the renunciation of lords and gods besides God as a prerequisite for proper belief in Divine Unity with the words: 'There is no god but God'. And when all the prophets were sent to confront the tyranny of their age – even Adam who was sent to confront the tyranny of Satan. And when our Lord has said in His book: 'Allah is the Guardian of the faithful: He brings them out of darkness into light. As for the faithless, their patrons are the tyrants, who drive them out of light into darkness. They shall be the inmates of the Fire, and they shall remain in it [forever].' So these men have made the tyrant into a holy figure, so as long as he rules, he is accepted, his actions become part of the religion – no matter how unjust or oppressive he is. In other words, they have reduced religion to a cover for oppression and injustice, such that religion and tyranny are joined together in spite of all the sins that the tyrant commits. And now they are tyring to make this into a practice which will be passed down from one generation to another, not to mention the way in which Yazid was chosen went against the Sunna of God's Messenger, and the practice of the First, Second, Third and Fourth Caliphs... as if this religion is a system without any system, standards or ordinances whatsoever!

Was not Muawiya's appointment of Yazid as his crown prince nothing more than brazen haggling in which each party demanded the price of their satisfaction, in plain sight of the people, whether this was wealth, position or flattery... if Muawiya had wanted to appoint a monkey as his crown prince and spent the same money and gave the same positions to these people, then his supporters would have tried to make that monkey the Caliph of the Muslims!

But the real danger of Yazid becoming Caliph of the Muslims is that he has not come as a king who will pass on his kingdom to his children, but rather as the successor of God's Messenger. And the faithful did not see the Prophet, who was more entitled to the faithful than they were to their own selves, forcing them to pledge allegiance to him – he gave them the choice – after forsaking all the ordinances of the religion and casting aside every measure of morality.

The strangest thing is that Hussein was asked to give allegiance to this man in the first place, proclaim him the leader of the Muslims and testify that he is the successor of God's Messenger, who has a divine right to the Caliphate, leaving Hussein no choice in the matter – he must either surrender and pledge allegiance, or he must be slain.

But Hussein has chosen a third way, namely to proclaim a sacrted uprising against tyranny and oppression, fully aware that he will become the Master of the Martyrs of this Nation.

THE REVOLUTION

On the eve of the eighth of Dhu al-Hijja, while the pilgrims to God's sacred house were preparing themselves to spend the following night at Mina before heading for the plain of Arafat the day after, an important piece of news was spreading amongst the people; Hussein wanted to make a public statement of his intentions. He had not addressed the people directly until now, only exchanged words with this person or that, or letters which he had sent to groups here and there. This, coupled with the prevailing atmosphere of repression and the struggles going on in the provinces, meant that the majority of both the pilgrims and the residents of Hejaz hastened to hear Hussein's words.

Groups of people raced to get to the house where the Imam was staying, and once the alleys and courtyards surrounding it were full of people, Hussein came out – the embodiment of excellence – walking as the Prophet himself would have walked. The expression on his face revealed that he had made a grave decision, his steps reverberated with the weight of what he was about to undertake and his eyes glistened with the anticipation of martyrdom. Husayn, before anyone else, knew what was to come and what each step meant for his person and his household.

Whoever saw Hussein in those moments saw in him the innocence and purity of Abel, the strength and determination of Noah, the faith and courage of Abraham, the kindness and mercy of Jesus, the message and mission of Muhammad, and the merits and virtues of Ali. As he stood above them, they waited silent and still with anticipation. Then he began to speak:

'In the name of God, the Compassionate, the Merciful. Praise be to God and what God wills, there is no strength save through God. God bless His messenger, his family and grant them peace!'

He fell silent for a moment or two, then he said: 'Death hangs upon the son of Adam as a necklace hangs around a young girls neck. I long to see my ancestors as Jacob longed for Joseph, and the spot on which I am to be slain has been chosen for me. I see myself as if dismembered on the barren plains between *Nawāsīs* and *Karbala*. From me will be filled empty stomachs and hungry sacks. There is no escape from a day written by the Pen. God's pleasure is our, the Prophet's Household's, pleasure. We will be steadfast in His trials and He will grant us the reward of the steadfast. God's Messenger shall never be separated from his own flesh and blood, for they are as one in the Holy Presence, they are a consolation for him and through them his promises is fulfilled.'

Then he said: 'Lo! So whoever would sacrifice himself for us or is determined to meet God himself, then let him come with us, for I shall go in the morning, God willing.'

Rahman al-Ṣāliḥ and *Abdullah b. Muslim* were amongst the first to come and hear Hussein speak. It may have been a brief statement, but it was an open declaration of a revolution whose outcome was anybody's guess.

Rahman turned to his friend and said: 'Unlike me, you have been with the Prophet's Household from the beginning – and if it were not for the grace of God I would still be astray! – So you know Hussein better than I. Tell me, what does he mean?'

Abdullah: First, Hussein said that he faces two kinds of death; the death that seeks him – which Yazid has resolved to carry out – and the death which he seeks – which he himself has resolved to carry out. Yazid has sent a number of agents to Hejaz to assassinate Hussein, even if – as Yazid says – he is clinging to the cloth of the Ka'ba! But Hussein has chosen the second path, because he has already said in private that he will not allow the sanctity of the Ka'ba to be violated, for he feels responsible for the sanctity of this place. The Prophet's Household do not profane a holy place with anyone's blood, nor do they allow others to profane a holy place with theirs. This, in addition to the fact that the death which seeks a man humbles him but the death which a man seeks ornaments him as a necklace ornaments a young girl.

Second, Hussein revealed his own innermost feelings; he misses his grandfather, God's Messenger, his father, the Commander of the Faithful, his mother, *Fātima Zahra* and his brother, Hasan. He misses them as Jacob missed Joseph once his eyes had gone white with grief for him.

Third, he announced that he will face a violent death and hence he is intended to be a sacrifice to God, who chose him for this before He created the heavens and the earth.

Fourth, he clearly disclosed what will be done to him, and in doing revealed the viciousness of his enemies, when he said: 'I see myself as if dismembered on the barren plains between NawÁsĐs and Karbala.' He even specified the locaton! And just as hungry wolves tear bodies to pieces and fill their stomachs with their flesh and blood, that is what Hussein's enemies will do to him. He also made clear that this was the Divine Decree by saying: 'There is no escape from a day written by the Pen.'

Fifth, Hussein explained his intentions; that he does not act for his personal interests, nor is he seeking the vanities of this world; the Prophet's Household are satisfied with that which satisfies God –

this is the highest level of faith. Hussein said that he would forbear, endure and never shrink from that which pleases his Lord: 'We will be steadfast in His trials and He will grant us the reward of the steadfast.'

Sixth, he announced that the outcome for him and for the people of his household will be – without a shred of doubt – Paradise. 'Indeed God has bought from the faithful their souls and their possessions for paradise to be theirs: they fight in the way of God, kill, and are killed. A promise binding upon Him in the Torah and the Evangel and the Qur'an. And who is truer to his promise than God? So rejoice in the bargain you have made with Him, and that is the great success.'

If God's Messenger is in the holiest station, then Hussein is there with him, because 'God's Messenger shall not be estranged from his own flesh and blood, rather it shall be gathered together for him there.' Considering that true life, happiness and success rests only in the Hereafter and not in this world, then God's Messenger will be gladdened by his household, God will fulfill His promise through them, and his descendants will dwell with him in the highest reaches of Paradise.

Seventh, Hussein opened a door for anyone who wishes to join him, with one condition only; that they be ready for death: 'Lo! So whoever would sacrifice himself for us or is determined to meet God himself, then let him come with us...'

Eighth, he specified the time he would set out; the morning of the next day – '...for I shall go in the morning, God willing.'

Rahman: If Hussein knew how vicious his enemies were, then why did he let them know when and to where he was going!?

Abdullah: That Hussein already knew the outcome of his undertaking is the greatest evidence that he did it only for the sake of God; he did not go out in insolence and vainglory, nor to do wrong or cause corruption in the earth. If he wanted the vanities of this world he could have negotiated from the position he was in. Remember that struggling in the way of God is one of the most important teachings of this religion; being slain in the way of God is the highest level of faith, and God's Messenger has said: 'There is a good deed above every good deed until a man is slain in the way of God, when someone is slain in the way of God there is no good deed superior to it!'

Did not Imam Ali write at the end of his letter of appointment to *Mālik al-Ashtar*: 'I ask God... to seal our lives with martyrdom and [everlasting] felicity'?

And did he not write: '*Jihād* is one of the gates to Paradise which God has opened for his closest people.'?

Rahman: But when Hussein knows that he will be slain, this is different! Is he expected to struggle even though he knows that he will be slain?

Abdullah b. Muslim: But when God said: 'Indeed God has bought from the faithful their souls and their possessions for paradise to be theirs' he did not make staying alive a condition for *Jihād*. In fact He said: '...they fight in the way of God, kill, and are killed.' So struggling in God's way is not conditioned on believing that you will be victorious – it could, in fact, lead to martyrdom.

Did not God's Messenger plunge into battle with only a handful of companions and a smattering of arms, facing experienced foes? How many times did the Prophet go out for *Jihād* with a very small number of men, how many of the best companions were slain in battle – including the Prophet's own uncle, Hamza, the master of martyrs?

Do not forget that Hussein is an Imam, so if *Jihād* is a duty for everyone, then it is an even greater duty for the Imam!

Rahman: And why is that?

Abdullah: Because one of the duties of the Imam is protecting God's bounds (*ḥudūd*). And if the Imam, who bears the prime responsibility in the nation and is the axis of the religion, does not do his duty, then can we expect that anyone else will do their duty?

Rahman: Do you mean to say that Hussein will undertake a course that will lead to the shedding of his blood and the blood of his family in order to protect God's religion and its bounds?

Abdullah: Exactly! Our Lord has described the faithful as those who are penitent, devout and observant of God's bounds. After mentioning the covenant between Himself and the faithful, God says: '[The faithful are] penitent, devout, celebrators of God's praise, wayfarers, who bow [and] prostrate [in prayer], bid what is right and forbid what is wrong, and keep God's bounds - and give good news to the faithful.'

Rahman: So you think Hussein will be martyred without a doubt?

Abdullah: That's the way of it. Hussein has resolved to rise up to save the religion of his grandfather, just as Yazid has resolved to destroy Hussein. There is going to be a clash between them.

Rahman: But who is to say that Yazid will defeat Hussein and not the other way around?

Abdullah: As for Hussein's being victorious, in God's knowledge he is certainly victorious and there is no doubt about this. But this doesn't mean that he will win power, for one simple reason, because he does not want that, just as he does not use the same means as Yazid does.

From the beginning, you see that he has clearly announced that he is going to be slain. If Hussein wanted to win, meaning to overcome his enemy and win power, he would have promised people victory rather than death. Hence the balance of forces is not in Hussein's favor; he cannot win against this empire that Yazid inherited from his father with such a small force, not to mention the fact that all the people want is to live an easy life and remain forever on the earth; they fear death.

Treasuries filled with gold and silver are at Yazid's disposal; he buys the consciences of the weak-willed, while Hussein demands selflessness from people. In the short-term, Hussein will not defeat Yazid, but in the long-term he will win no matter the immediate outcome. You know that Hussein and his companions are completely the opposite of their enemies; while the oppressive regime uses the wealth of the Nationh to buy consent, Hussein wants only those who are resolved to die for the cause – he would not spend a single dirham to buy a single person!

See how his emissary to Kufa, Muslim b. Aqeel, came empty handed? He had to borrow money for even the most mundane things!

While the regime promises people victory to motivate them to sacrifice themselves for their ruler, Hussein speaks only to his companions of death and martyrdom; namely his own and that of whoever chooses to follow him.

While tyrants do not even leave their own palaces during wartime; sending armies to fight on their behalf, Hussein himself is setting out tomorrow, accompanied by his own household and his own flesh and blood. This is what Hussein wants – to show people the difference between genuine faith and hypocrisy, between the true believers and those who merely claim to believe.

Hussein does not intend to conquer any lands or win any power; his uprising is not a political adventure, nor a cynical ploy to obtain his desires. Rather, he rises up to defend what is right. So if the people help him they have helped their own rights and their own selves, but if they turn away, he will defend the truth by himself, even if it means his own violent death!

Rahman: And you will go with him in the morning?

Abdullah: Why shouldn't I? Is there any greater success than this? What a great reward it is for a man to travel with the son of the daughter of God's Messenger, the leader of the youth of Paradise! If we were not alive at the time of God's Messenger to fight for the revelation, we are today alive in the time of Hussein to fight for the sake of its interpretation!

The First Step

The Eight of Dhul al-Hijjah is the day on which people prepare for the rites of Hajj and go to lodge in Mina on the night of ÝArafah, before going to the plain of Arafat the next morning, or going from Mecca to Arafat directly on the next day.

As the Hajj pilgrims ready their provisions for the day of ÝArafah and the night of Muzdalifah, then go to Mina and spend the night, there is a great deal of commotion in Mecca. Preparations to go to Arafat happen every year, but this year was different because of Hussein's announcement – and the Muslims thought of Hussein as their leader – of his uprising; so all of the pilgrims were waiting for Hussein to move so that they could learn from him, follow him and walk behind him, but what Hussein did was to come, circumambulate the Ka'ba, run between Safa and Marwa, then take off his *iḥrām* having gone from the *iḥrām* of Hajj to that of Umra mufrada.

News of Hussein putting off his *iḥrām* to go to Iraq caused a storm of questions: 'Why did Hussein not delay for a couple of days to complete his pilgrimage and then go to Iraq?'

'What is it that the son of the daughter of God's Messenger knew that no one else did that caused him to hasten his uprising? Especially when there had been no positive news from Kufa to whence he was going? In fact the opposite was true; word had reached Mecca that Ubaydullah b. Ziyad, a cruel tyrant who knew only the language of violence, had come from Basra and taken over governing the city from Nu'man b. Bashir who had refused to take up the sword against Muslim b. Aqeel?'

Some of those close to Hussein were asked about this sudden decision of his, and their response was that there were confirmed reports that the new regime in Damascus had sent a number of agents to assassinate Hussein when people were moving from Arafat to Muzdalifah, then blame thieves and brigands for his murder.

And when they were asked: And what if they fail? Can Hussein not take some bodyguards with him, so that he would be surrounded by a group of men from his household who were known for their bravery, like his brother Abbas or his son Ali the elder?

They responded: The mission of those agents is to kill Hussein somewhere in a way that the government is not held responsible. So they are ordered to kill Hussein however they need to; if they cannot do so secretly, then in any way they can, even if they kill him while he clings to the cover of the Ka'ba.

And when they were asked: 'So he is afraid of death?'

They said: 'Never! Hussein is the one who only last night announced his own death and took joy in the fact that it would reunite him with his ancestors whom he misses as Jacob missed Joseph! He is merely avoiding a base death for a noble one!

This is in addition to the difference between assassinating someone and the same person rising up for a cause then being killed in its pursuit; the cause is victorious and hence he will have discharged the message with which God has charged him. This is the meaning of the Imam's words: 'God has willed to see me slain.' So if Hussein putting off his *iḥrām* and changing his Hajj to an Umrah has shaken the Islamic world so, then imagine what will happen if the Umayyad's violate the sanctity of his life? Especially when this is not a conflict between two people, but between two ways of life. There is no doubt that Hussein represents God's Messenger in this confrontation, for if God's Messenger was still alive, he would have done what Hussein is doing now.

The two friends, Rahman and Abdullah are in Hussein's caravan, witnessing events as they unfold. One of the most important things they saw immediately before Hussein departed Mecca was that he had asked for a pen and paper and written a short letter to the Hashemite clan, which he sent to Muhammad b. Hanafiyyah. It read:

'In the name of God, the Compassionate, the Merciful. From Hussein b. Ali to Muhammad b. Ali and to the Hashemite clan. Whoever joins me will be martyred and whoever stays back will not attain victory. Peace.'

The letter was absolutely clear in stating that Hussein was asking the entire *Hāshemite* clan to rise up with him against the Nationyads, and that each one of them bore full responsibility for confronting hypocrisy, the abuse of religion and tyranny.

It was morning when Hussein's set out from Mecca towards Iraq; as they were making preparations to depart, it was surrounded by people weeping and lamenting. There was no one in Mecca not overtaken by grief.

When people had massed around him beginning him to stay, he recited the poetry of the brother of al-Aws:

I shall go, for death is no shame for a youth
when he intends good and struggles for Islam
Supports the righteous men with his life
separates from the ruined and opposes the wicked
If I live, I will not regret, and if I die I shall not suffer
It is enough shame to live under oppression.

Then he recited the verse of the Quran: 'and God's commands are ordained by a precise ordaining.'

Eighty-two men left Mecca with Hussein; his sons, brothers, household and companions.

To each of his companions, Hussein gave ten dirhams and a camel to bear his provisions and carry him. His daughters and sisters rode in howdahs. They set out on a Tuesday, on the eighth of the sacred month of Dhull-Hijjah.

In total, Hussein had spent a little over a hundred-and-twenty days in Mecca after his emigration from Medina.

Hussein's departure from Mecca left Yazid's governor there, *Amr b. Sa'eed b. al-'Āṣ*, dumfounded. He did not know how to react. He had been involved in Yazid's plot to assassinate Hussein after the latter left Arafat for Muzdalifah. So he ordered the head of his police force, his brother, *Yaḥyā b. Sa'eed* to prevent Hussein from leaving for Iraq. *Yaḥyā* came with armed men and blocked Hussein's way, saying: 'Go home. The governor bids you go home. Go home or I will prevent you from leaving.'

Hussein refused, the two groups clashed and the police lashed out, shouting: 'O Hussein! Do you not fear God? You are leaving the community and dividing this Nationh!'

In response, Hussein recited the verse: ''My deeds belong to me and your deeds belong to you: you are absolved of what I do and I am absolved of what you do.'

It almost came to blood between the two groups and word of this reached Amr b. Sa'eed. He feared that things would get out of hand, so he sent word to his brother to withdraw.

While Hussein, his family and his companions were leaving Mecca, Abdullah b. Abbas met Abdullah b. Zubayr, who desired the Caliphate for himself and secretly hoped that Hussein would leave Mecca so that Yazid and the Umayyad regime would shed his blood and give him a pretext to rise up and make himself Caliph of the Muslims. When Abdullah b. Abbas met him, he said:

'Woe to you, digger of graves!
The stage is yours now, so be joyful!

Wrangle as much as you like
The trap has sprung already, so what do you fear?

This is Hussein who is leaving, so be glad!'

Abdullah b. Zubayr told him: 'By God, you think you are more entitled to this affair than everyone else!'

Ibn Abbas said: 'Verily I see someone who is in doubt, while we are in certitude. But tell me, why do you think you are more entitled to this than the rest of the Arabs?'

Abdullah b. Zubayr said: 'Because of my superiority to them.'

'And what gave you this superiority? If you have any superiority it is because of us, so we are superior to you.'

The argument became heated, so the nephew of Abdullah b. Zubayr said: 'O Ibn Abbas, leave us alone! By God, you *Hāshemites* will never like us!' So Abdullah b. Zubayr struck him with a shoe and said: 'You speak while I am present?'

Ibn Abbas objected: 'Why do you strike the boy? He does not deserve that! It's the hypocrites and schemers that need a beating!'

'Meaning who?'

'Meaning you.'

Abdullah b. Zubayr, wanting to calm the situation, said: 'Won't you forgive a single word?'

'We forgive people who settle down, not people who growl.'

Abdullah b. Zubayr said, as if pleading for forgiveness: 'Where has virtue gone?'

'To us, the Prophet's Household, and we don't place it anywhere save where it belongs such that we would be blamed, nor do we deny it to those who deserve it such that we would do wrong to them.'

'And am I not of you?'

'Only if you put aside envy and respect the proper bounds.'

At this point a number of men from the Quraysh got involved and put an end to the argument.

Hussein's caravan set off from Mecca, his companions filled with a resolve like no other, despite the many dangers they would face – least of all that Yazid b. Muawiya would send an armed force from the provinces to confront Hussein at the outset of his journey. However, two things averted this danger:

First, the bravery for which Hussein and his companions were well-known; the family of Ali were famous for their courageousness and endurance in battle, their physical strength and their martial prowess. There had not been enough time yet for one of the governors to array a force of sufficient size, even though Ubaydullah b. Ziyad was working tirelessly to that end.

Second, the people's hearts were with Hussein and small numbers of people continued to join him wherever he went. This, even though he never once promised anyone victory or spoils – the opposite, in fact; he was always talking about killing, martyrdom, paradise and reward.

Of those who joined Hussein in *Abṭaḥ* - a riverbed in the valley of Mecca, full of pebbles which begins where the mountain cuts across the valley of Mina and ends at the cemetery known as *Mu'allā* - was Yazid b. Nabud who had come from Basra with two of his sons, Abdullah and Ubaydullah, and a few others. He had travelled hard to reach Hussein in Mecca, only to arrive and realize that Hussein had already left. He set out in pursuit until he reached his caravan. When he finally saw Hussein he said: 'In God's grace and His mercy - let them rejoice in that!' and greeted him: 'Peace be with you, O son of the Prophet!'

Then he sat with the Imam and told him of those he had brought for him, then Hussein prayed for him and he was allowed to join the caravan.

Opposing Forces

While Hussein's caravan was en route to Iraq, Abdullah b. Muslim and Rahman – who were both in his caravan – gathered news about the regimes activities in Syria and Iraq. Abdullah was particularly gifted at seeking out information because of his connections all over the Muslim world; meeting people coming from Syria and Iraq and asking them what was happening there.

They heard that when word reached Yazid b. Muawiya of Hussein's departure from Mecca for Iraq, he wrote to Ubaydullah b. Ziyad: 'Word has reached me that Hussein b. Ali is coming to Iraq; of all the provinces, it is yours that has been afflicted with him, and of all my governors, it is you who bears this burden. With this you shall either win your freedom or earn your slavery; so post lookouts, arm your men and lay ambushes; make use of your spies and take every precaution; arrest people on the slightest doubt, seize them on suspicious and send me daily reports of whatever transpires.'

This is how the regime made preparations for Hussein's arrival; taking harsh measures and striking out at dissidents with full force, seizing people on mere accusation and imprisoning them on suspicion. The prisons of Kufa were filled with four thousand men, including *Mukhtār al-Thaqafī, Sulayman b. Ṣard al-Khuza'ee* and other nobles and men from Kufa. Merely inclining towards the Prophet's Household by itself was enough to land you in jail.

Hussein, on the other hand, was pursuing his objective and knew with certainty that every word he spoke and every step he took would be an example for the faithful throughout history – how could it not be, when he was the grandson of God's Messenger, his successor and the leader of all the faithful?

In *Tan'īm*, Hussein encountered a caravan that was coming from Yemen. One of its members was *Jubayr b. Raysān al-Himyarī*, Muawiya's governor in Yemen, in order to reach Syria. It carried dyes and copperware; Hussein took them and said to the owners of the camels: 'I will not force you, but whoever wishes to come with us to Iraq, we will give him his wage and our good company, and whoever wishes to leave us at this place, we will give him his wage until here.'

He fulfilled his promise to those that left, and gave the wage to those who came with him. Three people chose to accompany Hussein; he gave each ten dinars and a camel.

When *Rahman al-Ṣāliḥ* saw this, he said to his friend Abdullah: 'I didn't think Hussein was in need of dye and copperware! So why did he take them?'

Abdullah: These are the property of the Muslims and so they should reach the needy people of them; Yazid has usurped the Caliphate and made God's property his personal estate and God's servants his cattle. He has no right to this property. Hussein, on the other hand is the Imam of the Nationh and entrusted with protecting the rights of the people. He set out from Mecca for no other reason save justice, so when he has an opportunity to do justice right in front of him he will do it; he doesn't care about the consequences. Do you not see while you are journeying with him that Hussein gives to the Bedouins everything that he would like for himself?

He only does this so that others know that they too have a duty to enjoin what is right in word and deed, and forbid the evil likewise. When the ruler usurps power and has no right to manage the property of the Muslims, it is the duty of the people to prevent him from doing so. And if we see no right for Yazid to possess the Caliphate or lead the Nationh, do we think he has the right to manage the people's property, booty, taxes and the like thereof?'

In *Safāḥ*, Hussein met the famous poet, Farazdaq, who was travelling in the opposite direction, from Iraq to Mecca. He said to Hussein: 'May God grant you your every hope, O son of God's Messenger! What has caused you to hasten from the Hajj?'

Hussein said: 'Had I not hastened, I would have been taken.'

Then he asked: 'O Farazdaq, how were the people when you left Iraq?'

'You have asked an expert! You, O son of God's Messenger, are the dearest person to the people; their hearts are with you, but their swords are with the Umayyids. God's decree descends from heaven and He does whatever He wills.'

'You are right, this affair belongs to God and God will do as He wills. Every day, our Lord is engaged in some work. Verily people are slaves to this world and religion is but a coating upon their tongues. They surround it so long as their lives are comfortable, but when they are put to tribulation, the ranks of the righteous thin.'

'O Farazdaq, they are a people who have clung to obeying Satan but given up obedience to the Most Merciful; they have brought about corruption in the earth and effaced God's bounds; they drink wine and devour the wealth of the poor and needy. I am the most fitting to support God's religion and struggle for His sake, that His word be elevated.'

'If God decrees what we love, then we will praise Him for His blessings, and His help is sought in giving thanks. But if the Decree obstructs our hopes, then whoever's intentions were right shall not be reprimanded, for piety is His bed.'

Then Hussein spurred on his mount and left Farazdaq.

Hussein walked with his family, his brothers and his sisters, and at their head was Zaynab bt. Fatima, but her husband, Abdullah b. Ja'far b. Abu Talib – Hussein's cousin – was not with them. He loved Hussein dearly and was afraid for the latter's life. When he heard Hussein was departing Mecca, he wrote: 'I advise you sincerely that if you proceed with this course of action you will perish and your lineage with you!' And sent the letters with his two sons, ŶAwn and Muhammad.

When Hussein read the letter, he said to those around him: 'I saw God's Messenger in a dream and he commanded me to do something which I am doing now.'

When someone asked him about this dream, he said: 'I have not spoken to anyone about it, nor will I until I meet my Lord.'

ŶAwn and Muhammad, in accordance with their father's wishes, went with Hussein and accompanied his caravan to Iraq.

When they reached Rammah, the caravan rested at one of the oases of the Arabs. There, Hussein met *Abdullah b. Muṭīʿ*, who was leaving Iraq. He greeted Hussein and told him: 'My parents be your sacrifice, O son of God's Messenger! Why have you left God's sanctuary and the sanctuary of your grandfather?'

Hussein said: 'The people of Kufa wrote to me requesting that I should come to them, hoping to revive the truth and destroy innovation.'

'By God, I adjure you not to go to Kufa! By God, if you go you will surely be killed and if they kill you they will fear nothing ever again! The very sanctity of Islam will be violated, and the sanctity of the Quraysh and the Arabs!'

Hussein replied: 'O Abdullah! All of that to avoid death? Rather you should say that nothing will afflict us save what God has written for us. By God, death following the truth is better than life following falsehood, and fighting Yazid for the sake of the religion is more important than fighting the infidels!'

This is what transpired whenever Hussein set down somewhere and met travelers from here and there; he would explain the righteousness of his cause, not just to ascribe whatever he was doing to God and make his enemies fully accountable, but also to explain the principles upon which the faithful should base any uprising they launch in the future.

One person they met was a Kufan man called Abu Harrah al-AzadĐ. He said to Hussein: 'O son of the daughter of the Prophet! Why have you left God's sanctuary and the sanctuary of your grandfather, Muhammad?'

Hussein told him: 'O Abu Harrah! The Umayyad Clan took my wealth, but I endured. They insulted my lineage, but I stayed quiet. Then they sought by blood, so I left. By God, Abu Harrah, the rebellious group will kill me, and so that God may cover them in shame and bloodshed, and give power over them to those who would abase them, until they are the lower than the people of Sheba, who were ruled by a woman, who ruled over their blood and property!'

And when Hussein came to *Shuqūq*, a man approached him and he asked him about Iraq. The man told him of the situation there and recited the following poetry to Huayn:

If this world is counted for anything
then the abode of God's reward is higher and more noble,
If wealth is to be left for those who would amass it
then why does the man left with it become stingy?
If our sustenance is a decreed portion
then it is better for a man to be less greedy
And if bodies have been made to die
then it is better for a man to die by the sword for God
Peace be with you, O progeny of Ahmad
For I think I shall soon depart from you!'

The man spoke to Hussein as if he was telling him something he didn't already know, so Hussein asked him: 'Where are you from?'

- 'Kufa.'

'By God, O brother of the Kufans, had I met you in Medina I would have thought you affected by Gabriel in our house and the coming down of revelation to my grandfather. O brother of the Kufans, is it possible for one who has learned from us to know something we do not? This will never be.'

In *Hājiz*, Hussein wrote a letter to the faithful in Kufa and sent it with *Qays b. Musahhir al-Ṣadāwī*. It read:

'In the name of God, the Compassionate, the Merciful.

From Hussein b. Ali to his brethren, the faithful and Muslims of Kufa.

Peace be with you. Muslim b. Aqeel has written to me informing me of your sound opinion, and your consensus on supporting us and pursuing our rights. I have asked God to bless this endeavor and to grant you the greatest reward for that. On Tuesday the eighth of Dhull-Hijjah I set out from Mecca to come to you. When my messenger reaches you, ready yourselves, for I am coming to you in the coming days – God-willing. Peace and God's blessing and mercy be with you.'

Rahman: Truly this world is treacherous; a man inherits all the traits of his grandfather and displays the traits of revelation, receiving his knowledge from his father – who is the gate to the city of prophetic knowledge. But rather than becoming a leader of the people, he must wander the wilderness and the desert, from place to another, not to reach any pasture, but to do his duty, defend the weak and oppressed and fight for the truth!

Abdullah: That's how it is for God's prophets and legatees, brother. They are 'Among the faithful are men who fulfil what they have pledged to God. Of them are some who have fulfilled their pledge, and of them are some who still wait, and they have not changed in the least.'

Hussein reached *'Aqīq*, one of the stations where the Hajj pilgrims from Iraq don the *iḥrām*; he met a shaykh from the *Banū 'Ikramah* called *Amr b. Lūdhān*. The latter asked him: 'O Abu Abdullah, where are you going?'

'Kufa.'

'I ask you for the sake of God, go back. You go to nothing but fangs and the blades of swords. If those who have written to you do the fighting and make preparations for you to come to them, then that would be a good idea. But in this state, as you mention it, I do not think it is.'

Hussein said: 'O servant of God, I am not lacking in sense, but God's command cannot be overcome. By God they will not leave me alone until they have spilled my blood, but when they do this God will subject them to he who will abase them until they become the most abased of nations.'

The two friends, Rahman and Abdullah, heard Hussein's conversation with the shaykh. Rahman turned to his friend and said: It seems as though Hussein's mind is made up. There's no going back now. All he talks about is God's command and decree, and that the regime will not leave him until he is dead and his blood is well and truly spilled.

Abdullah: It is as you say, things as they stand all point to this fact, even if we still don't know what has happened in Kufa. Let's wait and see what the situation will be there.

On his way to Kufa, Hussein did not avoid the main roads that were frequented by travelers, he set down at the usual stopping points where they would rest, and he was not in haste to reach Kufa. This was in total contrast to Ubaydullah b. Ziyad who had no sooner been made governor of Kufa than he raced there from Basra to reach it before Hussein. The reason for this difference was that Ubaydullah was after power, while Hussein wanted to do is duty to respond to those who had invited him to be an Imam.

In any case, Hussein met Bedouins and travelers on his way to Kufa, whether they were coming from there or going to there. Most of those coming from Kufa warned Hussein against going there in light of the Umayyads' firm grip on power there and the preparations that were being made to confront the Prophet's Household.

Hussein and his companions reached *Zarūd*, where they met two men of the BanǓ Asad who had just completed their Hajj pilgrimage and hurried to catch up with Hussein. When they approached him, they saw a man coming from Kufa, but no sooner had this Kufan man seen Hussein's procession than he had veered off the main road, even though Hussein had stopped as if to ask for news from him.

One of them said to the other: 'Let's go after him and ask if he has any news, it might be that he knows something of Kufa.'

So they went after him and asked him for his lineage. He said 'I am of the Asad tribe.' And they said: 'We are of the Asad as well. Who are you?'

'I am *Bakīr b. Muth'aba*.' And they introduced themselves to him. Then they asked him for news from whence he had came.

He said: 'I did not leave Kufa until Muslim b. Aqeel and Hani b. ÝUrwa were killed. I saw them dragging them by their feet through the markets.'

Then he went on his way.

Then these two men went after Hussein again and caught up with him in ThaÝlabiyyah that evening. They greeted him and told him: 'God have mercy upon you, we bring news. We can tell you now, or we can tell you in private.'

Hussein looked to his companions and said: 'There are no secrets from them.'

They said: 'Did you see the rider who approached yesterday?'

'Yes, I had wanted to ask him for news.'

'We pursued him and pressed him for news for you. He was of the Asad, like us, sensible and honest, virtuous and clever. He told us that he had not left Kufa until Muslim b. Aqeel and Hani b. ÝUrwa were killed, and that he had seen them being dragged through the markets by their feet.'

'To God we belong and to Him we return, may God have mercy upon them both...' He repeated this a number of times.

'We implore you in God's name, for your sake and the sake of your family, to go back. You have no helpers or supporters in Kufa; in fact, we fear that they may fight against you!'

Hussein looked at Muslim's brothers and said to them: 'What is your view, for Muslim has been slain?'

They said: 'To God we belong and to Him we return, by God we shall not go back until we have avenged our brother or joined him in his fate.'

Hussein turned back to the two men of Asad and said: 'There is no goodness left in life after them.'

That is when they knew that Hussein was determined to continue. They said: 'May God be good to you.'

'God be merciful to you.'

Then Hussein gathered his followers and said: 'You may have an opinion about the news that is reaching us; a people have decided nothing less than to betray us, so whoever wants to go back, let him go now.'

So most of those who had joined him along the way departed and only those who had come with him from Mecca remained with a small number of those who had accompanied him thereafter. In total they had just thirty two horsemen.

After news of Muslim's death arrived and the people who had come with worldly ambitions had left Hussein, leaving him with only his family and very best companions, the entire camp was racked by sobbing. Tears flowed from every eye. But in spite of their sorrow, the weight of responsibility which they felt left them no choice but to continue on the way to their goal.

Though the reality of their situation had become clear to all of those who were with Hussein, some of them still thought it possible that the balance of power would shift in their favour and Ubaydullah b. Ziyad would fail to keep control of Kufa, and people would do their duty when Hussein reached them.

Some of those with him said: 'By God, you are not like Muslim. When you reach Kufa and people see you, they will hasten to you and never turn away.'

But Hussein held out no hope for that; he stayed quiet and went on his way.

After Muslim's martyrdom, Hussein would often repeat the words: 'To God we belong and to Him we return' or the verses of poetry:

> I shall go, for death is no shame for a youth
> when he intends good and struggles for Islam

Supports the righteous men with his life
Separates from the ruined and opposes the wicked
If I live, I will not regret, and if I die I shall not suffer
It is enough shame to live under oppression.

Then Husayn ordered the young men to store up large quantities of water and the caravan left *Tha'labiyyah*.

Rahman and Abdullah were present there. Rahman turned to his friend and said: 'The Umayyads have killed Hussein's messenger, and he who sheltered him – *Hani b. 'Urwa* – and who he was a guest of. And yet Hussein does not harm their messenger, but instead shows him every courtesy and allows him to return safely to whence he came!'

Abdullah: My brother, the Prophet's Household exemplify virtue and the Umayyad clan exemplify viciousness. What you see is not a difference between two persons – as I told you before – but the difference between two different ways of life, between the followers of the true prophets and the avaricious hypocrites. And as you see, those people respect nothing and fear nothing; they will stop at nothing to preserve their own power. They disregard God's bounds and give no credence to morality or virtue. Their love of power has blinded them and made the world appear attractive in their eyes, and its trinkets have delighted them... do you not see how they rule in the name of God's Messenger, Hussein's own grandfather? And were it not for the sword of Ali, Hussein's father, they would not even be Muslims! They did not embrace Islam for any reason save worldly ambition or fear for their own lives.

Rahman: But why will Hussein not go back even after certain news that his allies have been either killed, imprisoned or exiled, and that Kufa is firmly in the grip of the Umayyad clan, and so leave things to them?

Abdullah: Will Hussein leave his grandfather's religion as a plaything for these hypocrites? Shall he abandon this Nationh to the whip of the Umayyads so that they can oppress people in the name of religion and in the name of his grandfather's teachings? Shall the leader of the youth of Paradise stay quiet so that they can commit whatever outrages and indecencies they please in the name of God's Messenger?

Hussein knew already that these were the ones who killed ÝAmmar b. Yasir, to whom all had heard the Prophet say: 'You will be killed by the rebellious faction.' They have no compunction against shedding the blood of tens of thousands of innocent Muslims. They will not leave him alone and they will fight him no matter what. This is what he himself has said on more than one occasion; shall he leave them to do that unimpeded?

On the way, a man returning from Hajj saw a tent erected on the road to Kufa. He asked: 'Whose is this?'

Some people told him: 'It belongs to Hussein b. Ali.'

So he went inside to see Hussein and found him reciting to Quran with tears upon his cheeks. He said: 'May my father and mother be your sacrifice, O son of the daughter of the Prophet! What has brought you to this barren and deserted place?'

Hussein told him: 'These letters the people of Kufa sent to me.' He fell silent for a moment and then said: 'And I do not see them...' – meaning the Umayyad clan – '...doing anything other than killing me, and if they do that then there shall be nothing God hath declared sacred save that they violate it.'

After hearing of Muslim and HÁni's death, Hussein asked for a pen and paper and wrote a letter to the nobles of Kufa, in which he said:

'In the name of God, the Compassionate, the Merciful.

From Hussein b. Ali to *Sulayman b. Ṣard, Musayyab b. Nujbah, Rafāʿa b. Shaddād, Abdullah b. Wāl* and the congregation of the faithful.

I know that God's Messenger said when he was alive: 'Whoever sees a tyrant permitting what God has prohibited, violating God's covenant, contravening the practice of God's Messenger and acting with sinfulness and enmity towards God's servants, then does not reproach him with word or deed, God has the right to put him in the same place [as the tyrant.]

And I know that those are a people who have held fast to obeying Satan and turned away from obeying the All-Merciful; they have caused corruption in the earth and cast aside all laws and bounds; they have misappropriated common property, permitted what God has prohibited and prohibited what he permitted. I am more entitled to this affair [than they,] because of my relationship by blood to the Prophet. Your letters reached me and your messengers came to me professing your allegiance and promising that you would not betray me. If you fulfill these pledges, then you have indeed hit the mark, but whoever violates them only violates his own self and God will suffice me of you. Peace.'

He sent this letter with one of his milk-brothers, *Abdullah b. Yaqṭar*, to the people of Kufa.

PREPARATION FOR WAR

Once he had done away with Muslim b. Aqeel, Ubaydullah b. Ziyad immediately set about preparing the people of Kufa to confront Hussein and his companions. He ordered a public announcement to be made: 'Lo! I shall not protect anyone who does not go forth to fight Hussein!'

He increased the stipends of those who received payments from the state by one-hundred-percent, as well as arresting many of the nobles who he could not compel to fight Hussein. But he did not kill them because he feared that their tribes would rise up against him.

Then he ordered *Huṣayn b. Numayr*, the head of his police force, to take four thousand armed horsemen to the regions surrounding the city and spread them between *Q̱ādisiyya and Khaffān*, and *Q̱aṭqaṭāna* and *La'la'*, and to set up checkpoints to control access to and from the city of Kufa in order to prevent people from reaching Hussein and prevent the companions of Hussein from entering Kufa. They did not anyone come or go.

At the same time, he sent *Hurr b. Yazid al-Riyāḥī* with a thousand men to search for Hussein under orders to either halt him or bring him as a captive to Kufa. He told him: 'When you find Hussein, take him prisoner. Do not let him go back, but bring him to Kufa and clap him in irons.'

This is how Ibn Ziyad controlled the area that fell between *Wāqiṣa* and the roads to Damascus and *Basra*.

Before these forces reached Hussein, the Imam met some Bedouins and asked them about the situation. They said: 'By God, we know nothing save that we are not free to come and go.'

Insofar as the entire region had fallen under the control of Ibn Ziyad, all of the roads had become unsafe. For this reason, *Abdullah b. Yaqṭar*, who was bringing Hussein's letter to the people of Kufa, fell into the hands of *Huṣayn b. Numayr* at *Qādisiyya*. Abdullah destroyed Hussein's letter to prevent it falling into the hands of the enemy, *Huṣayn* arrested him and sent him to Ubaydullah. There, Ubaydullah interrogated him about his lineage.

He said, 'I am a client of the Hashemites.'

'What is your name?'

'Abdullah b. YaqÔar'

Then he asked about the letter he had been carrying, what happened to it and who gave him it, but he refused to speak.

Ibn Ziyad told him: 'You will either tell me who gave you that letter and escape my grasp, or you will ascend the pulpit and curse Hussein b. Ali and his father and then I'll see what I think of you.'

'As for telling you whose letter it was, this I will not do. But I will ascend the pulpit.'

So Ibn Ziyad gathered the people in the mosque and ordered *Abdullah b. Yaqṭar* to ascend the pulpit. Then, when he stood above the people, he said: 'O people! I am the messenger of Hussein b. Fatima, the son of the daughter of God's Messenger, and I have been sent to you that you might rise up with him against the son of *Marjāna*, the son of *Sumayya*, the son of one whom God has cursed!'

But before he could finish his words, Ubaydullah sent his thugs to bring him down from the pulput. He ordered him thrown from the top of the governor's palace. His bones were shattered, but he still lived, delirious from pain. He was attacked by a man called *Abd al-Malik b. Umayr al-Lakhmī*, who slaughtered him while he was in that state.

As for *Qays b. Musahhar al-Ṣaydāwī*, he also fell into the hands of Hasseen b. Numayr's soldiers. Like *Abdullah b. Yaqṭar*, he tore up Hussein's letter and was brought before Ubaydullah b. Ziyad.

Ubaydullah asked him: 'Who are you?

'I am a follower of the Commander of the Faithful, Hussein b. Ali.'

'Why did you destroy the letter that was with you?'

'So you wouldn't know what it said.'

'And who was this letter from and who was it for?'

'From Hussein to a group of people in Kufa whose names are unknown to me.'

Ibn Ziyad grew angry and said: 'By God you will either stay here until you lead me to the people to whom this letter was addressed, or you will ascend the pulpit and curse Hussein, his father and his brother, or I will cut you to pieces!'

Qays said: 'As for those people, I know them not. But I will do as you ask.'

Qays was taken to the mosque and the people were called for congregational prayers. Once they had gathered, Qays stood up, praised and magnified God and sent blessings on Muhammad and his household, invoking God's mercy repeatedly on Ali and his sons. Then he cursed Ubaydullah b. Ziyad and his father, before saying: 'O people! This is Hussein b. Ali, the best of God's creation, the son of Fatima, the daughter of your Prophet, and I am his messenger to you. I left him in Hejaz, so respond to him!'

When Ibn Ziyad was informed of what he said, he ordered him taken up to the roof of the governors palace and thrown to the ground. So they took him up and threw him down headfirst. His neck broke, blood flowed from his ears and he died.

Worrying news and tragic events

From the time that Hussein left Medina and during his stay in Mecca, the news reports that reached him indicated that the faithful had gathered around him. All indications were that people had begun to stir for the sake of God and reject the falsehood represented by the Umayyad regime whose power rested upon tyranny, perfidy and violence.

But after Hussein left Mecca, events had undergone a complete reversal. Now the successive pieces of news reaching him were all worrying and unhappy, just as all the course of events had begun to turn against his uprising.

In *Zubāla*, a village with markets that is so called because of it is in a region where water collects and falls between *Wāqiṣa and Tha'labiyya*, Hussein received word of *Abdullah b. Yaqṭar's* death, just as he had already received word of the death of *Muslim b. Aqeel* and *Hani b. 'Urwa*. Hussein. He now sat down and wrote a letter which he read to all of those around him:

'In the name of God, the Compassionate, the Merciful. The terrible news of the deaths of *Muslim b. Aqeel, Hani b. 'Urwa* and *Abdullah b. Yaqṭar* have reached us. Our followers have betrayed us. Whoever amongst them would endure the blades of swords and gnashing of teeth, then let him rise up with us. And whoever of you desires to leave, then let him go without worry. He bears no responsibility towards us.'

This was like a thunderclap for those present, not because of the killing of Muslim or Hani, because they had already heard this news, but the killing of *Abdullah b. Yaqṭar*, Hussein's milk-brother, who had been nothing more than a messenger from him to some of the people in Kufa, was a terrible shock. It showed that the regime was ready to go to any length, no matter how vile or terrible, to oppose Hussein. That is because messengers in all cultures and all nations are not to be killed; even in pre-Islamic Arabia, enemies would not kill messengers. If it happened that a messenger was killed, this was considered a declaration of war, which gave the side to whom the messenger belonged casus belli against his killers.

The reason why Hussein announced the killing of *Abdullah b. Yaqṭar* was because he knew that the Bedouins accompanying him had only come because they thought they were following him to a land where the people were ready to obey him. He did not want them to come with him unless they knew that they were going to face death and bloodshed; he only wanted those who were ready to die with him.

And after repeating these words, there remained with Hussein only his household and retainers who said: 'By God, we will not go back unless we avenge our brethren or taste death one after another!' They numbered less than eighty men, most of whom were those who had set out from Mecca with him and a few who had joined the caravan along the way.

One of those who had joined them was *Zuhayr b. Q̱ayn al-Bajalī*, a nobleman who had been a partisan of Uthman and felt no loyalty to Ali or his children. He had just completed his Hajj and was heading to Kufa and the thing he hated most was to meet Hussein and travel with him, or to set down at the same resting place. So when Hussein travelled, Zuhayr b. Qayn hung back, but when Hussein rested,

Zuhayr went on ahead. But one day it so happened that Zuhayr had to set down at the same time as Hussein in *Zurūd*. That was on the twenty-first of Dhull-Hijjah. Hussein set down on one side and Zuhayr set down on the other.

While Zuhayr and his companions were sitting at eating, Hussein's messenger came to them and greeted them. He said: 'O Zuhayr, Hussein b. Ali sent me to bring you to him.'

Then he asked everyone present what they were eating, but they sat in silence, as if they had birds perched upon their heads, and it was clear that this man did not want to answer Hussein's summons.

His wife, whose name was Dilham bt. Amr stood up and told him: 'Glory to God! Will you refuse the invitation of the grandson of God's Messenger? Won't you at least go to him, hear what he has to say and then go?'

So Zuhayr got up, clearly displeased, and reluctantly went with the messenger. Not an hour had passed before he returned with a happy expression on his face, calling for his tent, provisions and mount, then went to Hussein. He told his wife: 'Go to your family, I do not want you to suffer any harm on my account.'

It was clear to everyone present that Zuhayr had resolved to join Hussein's caravan. His wife went to him, weeping and bidding him farewell, and said: 'God be your support and helper, God be good to you, I ask you to remember me when you are with Hussein's grandfather on the Day of Resurrection.'

Then Zuhayr said to his companions: 'Whoever amongst you wishes may follow me, otherwise this is goodbye.'

He added: 'I will tell you something: We were on the expedition to Balanjar, God granted us victory and we won great spoils. It was then that *Salmān al-Fārisī* asked us: 'Are you pleased with God's victory and the spoils you have won?'

We said: 'Yes.'

Then he told us: 'When you meet the leader of the youth of Paradise, then you will be happier for fighting alongside him than you are with these spoils."

Then Zuhayr said: 'As for me, I leave you in God's care. I am going with Hussein.'

Hussein's caravan continued to Khuzaymiyya, where it spent a day and a night. In the morning, Hussein's sister, Zaynab, came to him and said: 'Abu Abdullah, yesterday I heard a voice say:

'Lo! O eye, attend my struggle
for who will weep for the martyrs after me
For a people driven forth by death
the distance to fulfill my promise.'

Hussein told his sister: 'O my sister! Whatever God has decreed will happen.'

This was just one of the many signs that Hussein's caravan was destined for martyrdom in God's way, and that everyone in it would be slain. Even Hussein, when they were in ÝAqaba told his companions: 'I can only see myself slain, for I had a dream in which dogs were snapping at me, and the most vicious was a spotted dog.'

In *Sharāf*, Hussein bid the young men to store up a lot of water.

Rahman: Why is it that Hussein has told the young men to carry so much water? Are there not other oases on our way? Will we not be following the banks of the Euphrates for the last part of our journey?

Abdullah: The caravan is still destined for death, so we must prepare for anything.

Rahman: Is one sure of his own death occupied with such things?

Abdullah: Hussein will not surrender, and there is a big difference between someone who is sure of an ignominious death and someone who is going forth to a noble one. There is no doubting that Hussein will defend himself, his cause and his household, so he cannot afford to neglect the essentials of survival. Do you not see that Hussein is not looking for a fight? He has brought his entire household; women and children, young and old, and that is why he bears arms. Hussein does not want a fight, but if he is forced into one then he will fight and will follow the instructions his father gave to his brother, Hasan, when he said: 'Do not open hostilities but respond if they are opened against you, for the one who starts a fight is a rebel, and the rebel will suffer a violent death.' This is in addition to the fact that Hussein is thinking of his family and dependents; even if the men are all slain, the women and children will need water.

Rahman: If Hussein does not want a fight, then perhaps he will not die after all because the people will not want to kill him?

Abdullah: I do not think so. God's people do not aggress against anyone, it is always their enemies who aggress. As I told you, Abel meant no harm to his brother Cain, he even told him so: 'Even if you extend your hand toward me to kill me, I will not extend my hand toward you to kill you. Indeed I fear God, the Lord of all the worlds.' But in spite of that, Cain still aggressed against him and killed him. Abraham did not try to set Nimrod alight with fire, but Nimrod still cast him headfirst into the fire. Moses did not want Pharaoh to drown, it was Pharaoh who pursued Moses and brought on his own destruction. God's Messenger himself called his own people to guidance in Mecca and did not even carry a dagger to protect himself. And yet the Quraysh persecuted him and aggressed him, torturing and killing his followers and driving them out of Mecca.

The people of falsehood are the people of aggression, whereas the people of truth – of whom Hussein is the leader today – do not aggress against anyone.

Rahman: So why does Hussein bear arms?

Abdullah: He is following God's instructions: 'Prepare against them whatever you can of power.' The believer does not accept abasement under any circumstances, do you not recall the words of God's Messenger: 'Verily God has delegated all affairs to the believer, but He does not allow him to abase himself.'

Rahman: And what about water? Does he expect that we will be denied water?

Abdullah: Anything is possible. The enemy we are facing does not fear God in anything, so we must expect that they will commit every crime imaginable. Did Muawiya not deny water to Ali and his companions, even though amongst them were the likes of Ammar b. Yasir, the martyr son of a martyr? Did he not deny them access to water during Siffin, but when Ali gained control of the water he did not deny it to anyone?

People are the sons of their fathers. Hussein is the son of Ali, and Yazid is the son of Muawiya. So everything else will follow from this fact.

Hussein's caravan continued along its way, until in the middle of the day one of Hussein's companions called out: 'God is greater!'

Hussein turned to him: 'God is greater! What did you see?'

The man said: 'I saw a date palm.'

Two men of the Asad tribe that knew the area well said: 'We have never seen a date palm in this region!'

Hussein turned to them and asked: 'So what do you think he saw?'

They said: 'He must have seen the banner of some horsemen.'

'By God, I think you are right.'

Hussein turned to them and said: 'Is there some refuge to which we can betake and put it at our backs so we can approach this people from one direction?'

'Of course, this outcropping to your side is defensible, put it to your rear and if you get there before they do, then it will be as you wish it.'

So Hussein hurried to that place and put the mountain at his back before the other people could arrive. Only a short while later, some banners appeared, borne by a force of a thousand horsemen; their spearheads were like a swarm of bees and their banners were like the wings of birds. They were lead by Hurr b. Yazid al-TamÐmÐ; he and his horsemen wheeled until they faced Hussein and his companions in the midday heat.

Hussein called out to them: 'For us, or against us?'

Hurr replied: 'Not with you.'

Hussein and his companions put on their turbans and unsheathed their swords. But when Hussein saw that their opponents were suffering from extreme thirst, he bid the young men to help them instead, saying: 'Bring them water, quench their thirst and ensure their animals are watered.'

Hussein's companions did as he bid and gave water to Hurr and his men and their mounts; they filled bowls and buckets with water before placing them in front of the horses. Once each horse had drunk down four or five gulps, they took it and gave it to another, until all the horses had been watered like their riders. A man called *Ali b. al-Ta'ān al-Muḥāribī* was one of the last companions of Hurr to arrive, when Hussein say how thirsty he and his horse were, he told him: 'Kneel for the *rāwiya...*' and *rāwiya* was the word for waterskin (*siqā'*) in the dialect of Hejaz, but the man did not understand what Hussein meant, so Hussein said: 'Cousin, make your camel kneel.' So he knelt down the camel.

Then Hussein said: 'Drink up!'

But whenever the man wanted to drink, the water spilled from the waterskin, so Hussein said: 'Fold it up!' But the man did not know what to do, so Hussein came himself and folded up the waterskin for him, then he drank it and gave some water to his mount.

Once all of Hurr's men had been given water, the time for prayer set in, so Hussein ordered his *mu'adhdhin, Hajjāj b. Masrūq al-Ju'fī* to give the call to prayer.

When it was time to begin the prayer, Hussein came out wearing a pink cloak, and two slippers on his feet. He asked Hurr: 'Do you wish to pray with your companions?'

Hurr said: 'No, you prayer and we will pray with you.'

So Hussein ordered his *mu'adhdhin* to pronounce the *iqāma*, then they prayed together.

Once prayer was completed, Hurr's companions went back to their lines and each man took the reins of his animal and sat in its shadow.

Hussein stood up and rested on the hilt of his sword, praised and glorified God and then said:

'O people! To you and to God I say that I would not have come to this land until your letters came to me and your messengers visited me, telling me: 'Come to us, for we have no Imam, perhaps God will gather us upon guidance through you.

So if you are of that mind, I have come to you and if you give me such pledges and assurances as will satisfy me, I will enter your city. But if you will not and you detest my coming to you, then I will go back to whence I came.'

But the men remained silent and uttered no word.

Then Hurr entered his own tent, which had been set up for him and sat thinking about this. Just then, a letter arrived from Kufa, from

Ubaydullah b. Ziyad, saying: 'When you read this letter, arrest Hussein and do not leave him until you have brought him to me, and I have bid my messenger not to leave you until you have carried out these orders. Peace.'

When Hurr had read the letter, he sent for his trusted companions and told them: 'Ubaydullah b. Ziyad has written to me with orders to do injury to Hussein, but by God, my conscience will not allow me to do that.'

Amongst Hurr's companions was a man called *Abu al-Sha'thā' al-Kindi*. He turned to the messenger and said: 'May your mother be deprived of you! Why did you come?'

'I obeyed my Imam, fulfilled my pledge of allegiance and brought the letter of my commander.'

Abu al-Sha'thā' replied: 'You have disobeyed your Lord, obeyed your Imam, ruined yourself and earned disgrace. Your Imam is the worst Imam. God says: 'We made them leaders who invite to the Fire, and on the Day of Resurrection they will not receive any help.'

While they were in the midst of their discussion, the time came for *'Asr* prayer. Hussein again bid his muÝadhdhin to make the call to prayer. Then Hussein came and prayed with the soldiers too.

When he finished his prayer, he stood up, praised and magnified God and said:

'O people! If you respect the rights of others, this is more pleasing to God. We, the Prophet's Household, are more entitled to be entrusted with your governance than those who claim what is not theirs, and those who act unjustly and with enmity towards you.

And if you dislike us and are ignorant of our rights, and your opinion [now] is not what you expressed in your letters or what your messengers conveyed to us, then we will depart you.'

Hurr stood up and said: 'Abu Abdullah, by God we know nothing about these letters of which you speak.'

Hussein turned to *'Aqaba b. Sam'ān* and said: 'Bring out the sacks of their letters to me.'

So *'Aqaba* brought out the letters from the people of Basra and Kufa and spread them out in front of Hussein.

Hurr said: 'O Abu Abdullah! We are not the people who wrote these letters; we are under orders to find you and bring you to Ubaydullah b. Ziyad.'

Hussein smiled and said: 'Death is closer to you than that.'

Then he turned to his companions and said: 'Mount up!'

So they mounted their animals and waited for the women and children to mount theirs, then Hussein told them: 'Come with us.' But when they wanted to leave, Hurr's soldiers barred their way.

Hussein told Hurr: 'May your mother be deprived of you, what do you intend to do?'

Hurr became angry at the mention of his mother, but he suppressed his anger and said: 'By God, if anyone of the Arabs but you had said that to me in your situation, I would have said the same back to him. But by God, how can I mention your mother in anything but the best way possible?'

Hussein: 'So what do you intend to do?'

'By God, I will take you to Ubaydullah b. Ziyad.'

'Then by God I will not go with you.'

'Then by God I will not leave you.'

And they repeated this exchange two or three times, then Hurr said: 'Abu Abdullah, my orders are not to fight you. I have only been ordered not to leave you until I have taken you to Kufa. If you refuse to come with me, you must take a route that will take you to neither Kufa or Medina, as a compromise between me and you, so that I can write to Ubaydullah b. Ziyad. Perhaps God will see fit to send me something that will relieve me of your tribulation!'

Then he pointed to a path and said: 'Take this path and incline away from *'ADhilb and Qādisiyya*.' And *'ADhilb* was about thirty-eight miles away.

He added: 'O Hussein, I remind you of God with regard to your own person. If you fight, you will be slain, and if you are fought, you will perish. That's what I think.'

Hussein said: 'Do you try to frighten me with death? Have you received word that you will slay me? I don't know what I should say to you, but I shall say as the brother of Aws said to his cousin when he met him on his way to help God's Messenger and he said to him: 'Where are you going? You're a dead man!' He replied:

'I shall go, for death is no shame for a youth
when he intends good and struggles for Islam
Supports the righteous men with his life
separates from the ruined and opposes the wicked
I offer my life, which I do not aim to save
to receive my due in a violent battle,
If I live, I will not regret, and if I die I shall not suffer
It is enough shame to live under oppression.'

So Hussein took a path that neither led to Kufa nor to Medina, his caravan escorted by Hurr and his soldiers.

When night came, Hussein turned to his companions and said: 'Does anyone here know the way well?'

Terammāḥ b. 'Uday al-Ṭā'ī said: 'O son of the daughter of God's Messenger! I know the way!'

Hussein said: 'Then lead us.'

So *Terammāḥ* went ahead and urged his camel on, singing:

'O my camel, do not be alarmed by my goading
go with us before the daybreak,
With the best youths, the best journey
the family of God's Messenger in whom pride we take,
Luminaries with faces bright
who thrust with tall spears
And strike out with sharp swords
until they are adorned with beads of sweat
Noble, free and generous
God's grace brought him to me
May God make him his commander so long as time endures
and enhance him with good reputation
O master of benefit together with harm!
Furnish my master Hussein with victory
Against the tyrants who remain in disbelief
against the cursed serpents of Yazid
Who remains still a friend of wine
strings and cymbals together with horns
And [against] the son of Ziyad, the illegitimate son of the illegitimate father.'

Hussein halted in *Bayḍa* and Hurr's force accompanied him. Hussein stood up to address his companions and the soldiers. He began by saying what he had mentioned in his letter to the people of Kufa after the killing of Muslim b. Aqeel: 'O people! Indeed God's Messenger said: 'Whoever sees a tyrant permitting what God has prohibited, violating God's covenant, contravening the practice of God's Messenger and acting with sinfulness and enmity towards God's servants, then does not reproach him with word or deed, God has the right to put him in the same place [as the tyrant.]'

Lo! And verily those are a people who have held fast to obeying Satan and turned away from obeying the All-Merciful; they have caused corruption in the earth and cast aside all laws and bounds;

they have misappropriated common property, permitted what God has prohibited and prohibited what he permitted. I am more entitled to this affair [than they are].

O people! Your letters have reached me and your messengers have come to me, conveying your pledge of allegiance that you will not surrender me [to my enemies] or betray me. If you complete this pledge of allegiance, you will have hit the mark, for I am Hussein, the son of Ali, and the son of Fatima, the daughter of God's Messenger; My self with your selves, my family with your families and my sons with your sons. In me you shall have an exemplar.

But if you do not do that and you break your pledge and removing your allegiance to me from your knecks, then by God this is an evil deed. And you have done the like of it with my father, my brother and my cousin. Deceived is he whom you mislead. In which case you will have missed the mark and squandered your share. Whoever breaks his pledge only betrays himself and God will suffice me of you. Peace and God's mercy and blessings be with you.'

At this time, Hussein's companions numbered less than a hundred, while Hurr had more than a thousand soldiers at his command and Ibn Ziyad was about to send reinforcements to them. And whenever new soldiers arrived, Hussein would remind them of the state of the Nation and their moral responsibility, and explain to them his own decision to continue on this way. He would address them periodically, beginning as he always did by praising and magnifying God and invoking blessings on the Prophet, then mentioning the merits of the Prophet's Household, their blood relation to God's Messenger and expounding his own position as the Prophet's successor.

On one occasion, he said: 'Lo! Our situation is as you see it. Lo! Verily the world has changed and deteriorated, its virtue has regressed, and it has fallen until all that remains of it is leftovers, and a harsh existence like poor grazing. Do you not see that the truth is left aside, while falsehood carries on unimpeded?

Let the faithful desire meeting their Lord truthfully, for verily I see only happiness in death and weariness in living with oppressors.'

Then stood Zuhayr b. Qayn, who had joined Hussein's caravan on the road. He said: 'O Abu Abdullah, we have heard your words. By God, even if the world would last forever and we could live eternally therein, we would rather go out [to battle] beside you than remain in it.'

Hilāl b. Nāfi' al-Bajalī stood up and said: 'By God, we are not averse to meeting our Lord, for we are firm in our intentions and our insights! We are an ally to your allies and an enemy to your enemies.'

Next was *Bureir b. Khaḍīr*: 'By God, O son of God's Messenger! God has blessed us with the opportunity to fight by your side and be cut to pieces with you, then your grandfather will be our intercessor on the Day of Resurrection.'

The rest of Hussein's companions made similar statements, and Hussein invoked God's blessings upon them.

Hussein continued to *'ADhilb al-Hajānāt*, whereat he encountered four people coming from Kufa on mounts; *Nāfi' b. Hilāl al-Murādī, Amr b. Khālid al-Ṣaydāwī*, his servant *Sa'd* and *Majma' b. Abdullah al-'Ā'idī*, all from the tribe of *Mudhḥaj*. Hurr wanted to prevent them from reaching Hussein and told Hussein: 'These did not come with you, so I will either detain them or send them back to Kufa.'

Hussein replied: 'I will not allow you to do that. They are my supporters and helpers, and you agreed that you would not obstruct me until you receive word from Ubaydullah b. Ziyad.'

So Hurr left them alone and they were able to join Hussein. He asked them about events in Kufa, so *Majma' b. Abdullah* told him: 'My master, the nobles have been given hefty bribes, had their pockets filled, their affections won and their advice sought, so they have become a single force arrayed against you. As for everyone else; their hearts incline to you, but tomorrow their swords will be drawn against you.'

'Tell me, have you any word of my messenger to you?'

'Who is that?'

'*Qays b. Musahhir al-Ṣaydāwī*.'

'Yes. Hasseen b. Numayr seized him and sent him to Ibn Ziyad, who told him to curse you and your father from the pulpit. So he went up the pulpit, invoked God's blessings upon you and your father, and cursed Ibn Ziyad and his father, before calling the people to rise up with you and informing them that you were coming. Then Ibn Ziyad had him taken and thrown from the top of the governor's palace.'

Hussein's eyes watered and he could not hold back his tears. He recited the verse: 'Among the faithful are men who fulfil what they have pledged to God. Of them are some who have fulfilled their pledge, and of them are some who still wait, and they have not changed in the least.' Then he said: 'O God! Make paradise our abode and theirs, and gather us with them in the resting place of your mercy, and grant them your abundant reward. By God, I hope that God intends good for us, whether we receive victory or death.'

Then he raised his hands in supplication and said: 'O God! Grant us and our followers a noble abode with you, and gather us and them in your mercy, and you have power over all things!'

At this point, *Terammāḥ* turned to Hussein and said: 'By God, I think you do not have enough men. Even if only these who are following you with Hurr were to attack you, it would be a massacre. Before we left Kufa, on a single day I saw the back of Kufa filled with such a multitude of men that I never did see before. I asked about them and was told that they had assembled for inspection before being sent against you. So I plead with you for the sake of God, if you can avoid taking another step towards them, do it.

I wanted you to stop in a land where God would detain that I might see what you have to say and that the weight of your actions might become clear to you, so come and I will take you to AjÁÞ, our mountain where we have long fortified ourselves against the kings of *Ghassān* and *Himyar*, from Nu'man b. Mundhir, the Black and the Red. By God, we have never been subjugated. I will come with you and lead you to the village, then we will send for men of the *Ṭayy* tribe in Aja' and Salma. By God, not ten days will pass before men and horses come from *Ṭayy*. Then stay with us for as long as you see fit. And if someone comes to do battle with you, I guarantee you twenty thousand men who will protect you with their swords. By God, no harm will ever come to you while they still draw breath!'

Hussein replied: 'May God grant you and your people good, but between the people of Kufa and me is an agreement from which we cannot withdraw, and we do not know the final outcome of affairs between these people and us. If God protects us, then he has always blessed us and sufficed us, and if what must happen comes to pass, then victory and martyrdom, God willing.'

Then *Terammāḥ* made another demand which he insisted for the Imam to accept: 'Come with me on a fast horse, and I will take you in the night to the *Ṭayy* tribe and take care of everything you need; I will gather five thousand warriors to defend you.'

'Is it chivalrous for someone to save himself while his household, brothers and companions perish?'

One of his companions said: 'The Umayyads cannot do anything so long as they do not find you!'

But Hussein paid no heed to these words and merely invoked God's blessings on *Terammāḥ*.

Then *Terammāḥ* said: 'I have a family to provide for in Kufa, let me go and give them their provisions and then – God willing – I will come back to you. If I arrive in time, I will surely be one of your helpers!'

Hussein said: 'If you are going to do that, you had better make haste!'

Then *Terammāḥ* bid him farewell and went to his family.

Hussein set off from *'ADhilb al-Hajānāt* and continued until on the first of Muharram he set down at the fortress of the *Banū Muqātil*, whereat he saw tents struck up. He asked to whom they belonged and was told: 'They belong to *Ubaydullah b. al-Hurr al-Ju'fī*.'

The Imam sent one of his companions, *Hajjāj b. Masrūq al-Ju'fī* to him to invite him to meet Hussein, so *Ibn Masrūq* went to *Ubaydullah b. al-Hurr*'s tent and greeted him. The latter asked: 'What news?'

Hajjāj said: 'God has gifted you [His] generosity, should you accept it.'

'And what is that?'

'This is Hussein b. Ali, who invites you to support him. If you fight for him, you will be rewarded. And if you die, you will be a martyr.

Ubaydullah said: 'I only left Kufa because I did not want to be there when Hussein arrived, for if I fought him that would be a grave sin in the eyes of God and if I stood with him I would be the first to be killed without being of any avail to him. By God I will not see him and he will not see me. So go and tell him that.'

Hajjāj went to Hussein and told him about what *Ubaydullah al-Ju'fī* had said. So Hussein got up and went to him with a group of his brothers. After praising and magnifying God, he said: 'O son of Hurr! The people of this city of yours have written to me and told me that they are united in support of me, and asked that I come to them. So I have come!'

Ubaydullah answered back: 'By God, I only left Kufa so I would not be there when you arrived and would not have to help you; you have no helpers in Kufa!'

Hussein told him: 'O son of Hurr, know that God will hold you to account for what you have earned and the sins you have sent ahead in days gone by, but I am calling you right now to a penance that will erase all of your sins; I am calling you to support us, the Prophet's Household. If we are given our due, we will praise God and accept it, but if we are denied it, you will be amongst those who supported us in our cause!'

Ubaydullah replied: 'By God, O son of the daughter of God's Messenger, if you had any helpers who would fight beside you in Kufa, I would have been the most severe of them against your enemies. But I saw your followers in Kufa hiding in their homes in fear of the Umayyad clan and their swords. So I adjure you by God not to ask this of me, and I will help you however I can. This is my horse, bridled and ready, and by God I have not pursued anything upon it save that I made it taste death. Take this, for it is my sword, and by God I have not struck anyone with it save that he died.'

'O son of Hurr! We did not come to you for your steed or your sword, we came to you to ask for your help. If you will be stingy towards us with your life, then we need nothing of your possessions! I need no assistance from those who are astray, and if you will not give us your help, then do not oppose us. And if you are able to avoid hearing our cries, then I advise you to do so, for I heard God's Messenger said: 'Whoever hears the cry of my household and does not help them to obtain their rights, God will throw him headlong into Hellfire."

In the gathering of Ibn Hurr at that time was a man called Anas b. *Harith al-Kāhilī*, who had left Kufa for the same reason as *Ubaydullah b. Hurr*. Hussein's words had a profound effect on him, so he went out of Ubaydullah's tent and caught up with Hussein. He said: 'By God, I left Kufa for the same reason as him, because I neither wanted to fight with you or against you. But God has struck my heart with the desire to help you, and emboldened me to go with you.'

'Then come with us, rightly-guided and under God's protection.'

This man was an elderly Companion, who had seen the Prophet and heard his words. When he joined Hussein, one of the things he told Hussein's companions was: 'I heard God's Messenger say, while Hussein was in his home: 'Verily this son of mine will be slain in Iraq. Lo! So let whoever sees him help him!'

When Rahman heard Hussein's discussion with Ubaydullah b. Hurr, he turned to Abdullah and said: 'Why did Hussein tell him: 'God will hold you to account for what you have earned and the sins you have sent forth in days gone by...'? True, people are not perfect, but why did Hussein stress to Ubaydullah in particular that he had committed sins in the past, and why Ubaydullah did not answer him?'

Abdullah: Ubaydullah b. Hurr was an officer in the army of the Commander of the Faithful, Ali, at the battle of Siffin, but his faith was weak. Muawiya sent a bribe to him with the promise of more, so he abandoned his men and fled to Muawiya in secret. He remained in Syria until people thought he had died. His wife even observed her mourning period and remarried a man called *'Ikrama*. But when word of this reached him, he went to the house of *'Ikrama* to take her back, but the man sent him away harshly. So he was forced to go to Imam Ali in the mosque of Kufa where the latter was praying. Once the Imam finished his prayer, Ubaydullah sat beside him. Ali recognized him and began to reprimand him for his treachery. Once he had finished, the man said: 'Does my treachery mean that I will be denied your justice, O Commander of the Faithful?'

The Imam said, 'No.' So he told him his story and how his wife had remarried. So Ali sent someone to seek out the woman, but it so happened that she was pregnant, so she remained in the house but both men were forbidden from approaching her. He ordered that when she gave birth, the child would belong to *'Ikrama* but she must return to Ubaydullah b. Hurr. Hussein mentioned God's holding him to account referring to his former betrayal.

In any case, the man did not enjoy the good fortune of being cleansed of his sins by helping Hussein, having already betrayed his father before.

And in the fort of the *Banū Maqātil*, *Amr b. Qays al-Mashriqī* came to Hussein with his cousin. They knew Hussein from before, so they greeted him and Amr said: 'O Abu Abdullah, is this dye I see or is your hair always this color?'

The Imam said: 'It is dye. Grey hair comes quickly to us Hashemites!'

Then he turned to them and asked: 'Have you come to help me?'

Amr said: 'I am a man with many dependents and many things which people have entrusted to my care. I do not know what will happen and I do not want to squander what people have trusted me with.'

His cousin said the same, so Hussein told them: 'Go and be sure you neither hear my cry nor see my plight, for whoever hears our cry or sees our plight and does not help us, God can throw him headlong into Hellfire.'

It seems that these two men also lacked the good fortune to join Hussein's caravan, just like Ubaydullah b. Hurr.

The fort of the *Banū Maqātil* was, perhaps, the last stopping point on Hussein's journey before he reached Karbala. This is why at the end of the night, he again ordered the young men to store up a lot of water, quench themselves and their mounts, and then gave the order to move out. Barely an hour had passed when Hussein, who was upon his steed, received a vision and said: 'To God we belong and to Him we return, praise belongs to God, the Lord of the Worlds.'

He repeated these words two or three times, then his son Ali the Elder came and asked: 'O father! May I be your ransom! Why did you praise God and utter these words?'

Hussein said: 'My son! I had a vision of a rider calling out: 'People are coming and death is coming to them!' And I realized that he was speaking about us.'

Ali the Elder said: 'Father, may God never show you evil, are we not in the right?'

'Of course, by He who is the return of the servants.'

'Then why should it matter if we die righteous?'

'May God grant you the best that He gives a son from a father!'

After encountering Hurr b. Yazid, Hussein was restricted in his movements, insofar as he and his force of horsemen were shadowing the caravan. Whenever they wanted to head into the desert, they were prevented. And sometimes they would try and drive Hussein towards Kufa, but he would not let them. So they continued on in the same direction.

While this was going on, a rider approached on a fast horse. He was armed and kept his identity hidden, coming from Kufa. Both Hussein's caravan and Hurr's horsemen stood waiting for him, but when he arrived he greeted Hurr rather than Hussein, then gave Hurr a letter from Ubaydullah b. Ziyad, which read:

'When this letter reaches you, detain Hussein in an empty stretch of land, without shelter or access to water. I have bid my messenger to remain with you until my command be done.'

When Hurr read the letter of Ubaydullah, he told Hussein: 'This is the letter of Ubaydullah b. Ziyad, telling me to detain you where I stand. This is his messenger, who will remain with me until I have fulfilled this order.

Then he asked that Hussein and his companions stop in this place, which was devoid of water and habitations. Hussein and his companions responded: 'Let us set down in this village over there...' and pointed to *Nīnawā* '...or that one...' and pointed to *Ghāḍiriyya* '...or that other one' and pointed to Shafiyya.'

Hurr replied: 'No, by God I cannot.' Then he pointed to the man who had brought the letter: 'This man has been sent to watch me.'

While Hussein and Hurr argued, Zuhayr b. al-Qayn demanded that they fight, telling Hussein: 'May my mother and father be your sacrifice! O son of God's Messenger, by God if we only had to face these men it would have been enough for us. So how will we face further reinforcements? Why don't we attack now, for it will be easier to fight them than to fight the ones who will come!'

Hussein said: 'I will not be the one to initiate hostilities.'

Zuhayr: 'Then there is a village right over there on the banks of the Euphrates, protected by a moat. If we take refuge in there and fight them, it will be easier than fighting those who will come.'

'What is the name of that village?'

'ÝAqar'

'O God, I seek refuge in you from ÝAqar!' And he refused to go.

The situation between Hussein and Hurr was very tense, but Hurr had not been ordered to fight. Perhaps if he had been, he would have. For his part, Hussein refused to open the bloodshed, and so no confrontation took place between them.

Hussein turned to Hurr and said: 'Come with us a little further, then we will set down.'

So they travelled until they reached a spot on Thursday the second of Muharram; a piece of land close to a small river. Whereat Hurr and his forces prevented Hussein from going any further.

Hussein asked: 'What is this place called?'

He was told: 'This land is called Óaff.'

'Has it any other name?'

'It is also known as Karbala.'

Hussein wept and said: 'O God! I seek refuge in your from misery (*karb*) and tribulation (*balā'*).

Then he took a handful of its dust and smelled it. Then he took out a piece of clay from his cloak and told them: 'This is the clay Gabriel brought to my grandfather when he said: This is the earth of Hussein.' They have the same scent.'

Hussein said: 'God and His messenger have spoken the truth, this is the place of misery and tribulation. My father passed this place when he was going to Siffin while I was with him. He stopped and asked its name. When he was told 'Karbala,' he said: 'Here is where their caravan will halt, here is where their blood will be spilled.' He was asked what he meant, to which he answered: 'It is hard for the Household of the Prophet to stay here."

Then Hussein turned to his companions and said: 'Set down, for here is where our caravan stops, where our men stand and where our blood spills.'

So the people dismounted and set down their burdens in sight of the Euphrates, Hussein's tent was struck up for his family in one spot and the tents of his brothers and cousins surrounded it, while the tents of his companions were set up on the other side. Hurr and his companions also dismounted and set up their tents facing those of Hussein.

This is how the site of the battle was chosen; it was clear that Hussein's caravan would never leave this place.

Rahman turned to his comrade, Abdullah, and said: 'What did Hussein mean when he said that God and His messenger had spoken the truth?'

Abdullah: I think he was referring to the tradition of Umm Salama, in which she said: 'God's Messenger was sitting in my house one day, when he said: 'Let no one disturb me.' So I waited, then Hussein came in and I heard God's Messenger sobbing loudly, so I went to see what was happening and Hussein as in the room and the Prophet was stroking his head and crying. I said: 'By God, I didn't realize he had disturbed you.'

God's Messenger said: 'Gabriel was in the house and when Hussein came into the room, he asked me: 'Do you love him?"

I said: 'In this world, yes.'

'Your nation will kill this one in a place called Karbala...'

Then he gave me some of its dirt.'

It seems that Hussein knew of this story and that is why he said that God and His messenger had spoken the truth.

In twenty-four days, Hussein's caravan had travelled from Mecca to Karbala, making sixteen stops at points along the way, spending a day or two in each.

Rahman: Why do they call this place "Karbala" – is it from 'misery' (*karb*) and 'tribulation' (*balā'*).

Abdullah: It could mean that, but it could also be made up of karb – meaning 'sanctuary' – and *balā* - meaning 'God' – in other words, God's sanctuary in the language of ancient Babylon.

When Hussein arrived at Karbala, he had forty five horsemen – including nineteen of his own household – and a hundred footsoldiers.

Since he arrived at Karbala, Hussein had behaved as though he knew himself to be a martyr, even though he was determined not to yield an inch to his enemies. He was on the side of righteousness, and it was his enemies who had aggressed against him. It was they who had prevented him from entering Kufa or returning to Medina. One of the things he did in this state was to inquire from the Bedouins in the area who owned the land, and having been directed to its owners, he purchased the land from them for sixty thousand dirhams – much more than what it was worth. He did so on the condition that they would direct whoever came this way to his grave once he had been slain, and to host them as guests for three days. The amount of land he bought was four miles by four miles.

The Prophet's Household rested their mounts in that barren place; a completely flat stretch of land devoid of hills and habitations. They were completely exposed to their enemies.

The following morning, Hussein took a pen and ink and wrote a letter to his brother:

'In the name of God, the Compassionate, the Merciful. From Hussein b. Ali to his brother, Muhammad b. Ali, Ibn Hanafiyya and the Hashemites with him. It is though as the world never was, and as though the Hereafter never was not. Peace.'

Then he gave one of his companions the letter and sent him to his brother, who was still in Medina.

As for Hurr b. Yazid, he had sent a letter to Ibn Ziyad informing him that Hussein was detained at Karbala and asking for further instructions.

When Ibn Ziyad received this letter, he wrote a threatening message to Hussein. In it, he said: 'O Hussein, word has reached me that you are detained in Kerbala; the Commander of the Faithful, Yazid b. Muawiya has written that I should not rest until I have sent you to meet your maker, or until you return to the fold of my government and the government of Yazid.'

When Hussein read this letter, he threw it to the ground and said: 'A people who buy creatures' satisfaction at the price of the Creator's will never succeed.'

The one who brought him the message said: 'O Abu Abdullah, what is your reply to the governor's letter?'

Hussein said: 'I have no answer for him, for he has earned the punishment of Hell.'

So the messenger returned to Ibn Ziyad and told him what had happened and Ibn Ziyad was furious.

Ubaydullah was sending thousands of soldiers to Karbala. In his search for a field commander for this army, he settled upon *Umar b. Sa'd b. Abu Waqqāṣ*, whom he had dispatched to Dastbay with four thousand Kufans to put down a Daylamite uprising there. He had promised Umar b. Sa'd the governorship of Rayy if he succeeded in this mission, but this was before he had heard of Hussein's presence in Karbala.

At this point in time, Umar b. Sa'd had gathered his men in the region of *Humām A'yan*, where they were making preparations to march on Dastbay, but Ubaydullah b. Ziyad recalled him and when he returned he told him: 'First deal with Hussein, then proceed with your original mission.'

Umar b. Sa'd told him: 'If you could excuse me from this, then do so.'

'Alright. If you give up your governship in Rayy.'

'In that case, give me a day to think about this matter.'

Ibn Ziyad granted this request, and so Umar b. Sa'd went to ask the advice of his most trusted friends. All of them warned him against fighting Hussein, even Hamza b. Mugheira b. ShuÝba, his nephew, told him: 'By God, Uncle, do not sin against your Lord and violate your ties of family by going against Hussein! By God, it would be better for you to lose everything in the world than to meet God with Hussein's blood on your hands!'

Umar b. Sa'd told him, 'I shall do that, God willing.'

The next day he went to Ibn Ziyad and said: 'May God make you prosper, you gave me charge of this matter and wrote a letter publicly appointing me as governor of Rayy. If you want me to proceed with my mission to Dastbay, then I will. And you can send some Kufan nobleman who will suffice you better in battle in my stead.'

He began to give Ibn Ziyad the names of some men who might lead the army against Hussein, but Ibn Ziyad interrupted: 'Do not presume to teach me the names of the Kufan nobility, I did not ask for your advice on who to send. Either go with the army, or resign your post.'

When Umar b. Sa'd saw that Ibn Ziyad was determined to press on with his plan, he yielded and said: 'I will go to Hussein.'

He spent the night restless, fearful of what he was going to do, caught between the reproach of his conscience and his worldly ambition. He recited the poem:

Ubaydullah has called me above his own people
to take a path on which I have embarked for my here and now
By God, I neither know nor understand
I see myself between a rock and a hard place,
Do I give up the wealth of Rayy while it is my ambition
or do I go sinfully to slay Husayn,
Hussein is my cousin and the dangers are many
but in Rayy lies my consolation,
They say that God created Paradise
and Hell and punishment and burning chains,
If they are right in what they say
then I shall repent to the All-Compassionate in a year or two,
And the Lord of the Throne will forgive me my error
even it is the greatest sin known to Man and Jinn
And if they lie, then the world's beauty is great
and its wealth will last forever
Lo! Verily this world is better in the here and now
a reasonable man does not give up the whole world for religion.

This is how Umar b. Sa'd made his decision. Now, instead of going to Daylam, he took his four thousand horsemen to Karbala, giving *Khālid b. 'Arfaṭa* charge of his vanguard and *Habib b. Jummāz* the battle standard. They reached Karbala on the third of Muharram, a day after Hussein had arrived there.

When Hussein and his companions saw the army of Umar b. Sa'd approaching with *Khālid b. 'Arfaṭa* and *Habib b. Jummāz* at its head, Abdullah b. Muslim told his friend: 'Glory to God! I heard Suwayda b. Ghafla say: 'I was with the Commander of the Faithful, Ali, when a man came to him and said: 'I have come to you from the valley of *Qurā. Khālid b. 'Afraṭa* is dead.'

Ali replied: 'He has not died.'

The man insisted that he was dead, but still *Ali* responded: 'He is not dead.' Then he turned his face away from him. The man became exasperated and said: 'Glory to God! I tell you he is dead and you insist he is not!?'

'By He in whose hand is my soul, *Khālid b. 'Afrata* will not die until he has lead the army of perfidy, whose banner is borne by *Habib b. Jummāz*.

When word of this reached *Habib b. Jummāz*, he came to the Commander of the Faithful and said: 'I adjure you by God concerning me, for I am your follower and you have said such a thing about me! No by God, I am not capable of doing it!'

Ali said to him: 'And who are you?'

'I am *Habib b. Jummāz*.'

Ali said: 'If you are *Habib b. Jummāz*, it will be none other than you that carries it.'

So Habib turned away from him, but the Commander of the Faithful said again: 'If you are he, then you will carry it.' And he really did!'

When Umar b. Sa'd's entire force had reached Karbala, he called *'Urwa b. Qays al-Aḥmasī* and said: 'Go to Hussein and ask him what he plans on doing and what caused him to leave Mecca when he had been settled there?'

'Urwa b. Qays excused himself and said: 'Commander, I was one of those who wrote to Hussein; I am too ashamed to face him. Send someone else, if you will.'

So Umar b. Sa'd called a man called *Kathīr b. Abdullah al-Sha'bī*, a vicious and profligate sinner. He told him: 'Go to Hussein and ask him why he has come here!'

He said, 'I will go to him, and by God if you like I will kill him too.'

'I did not ask you to kill him, I asked you to enquire as to his purpose here!'

So *Kathīr* went to Hussein's tent, but when *Abu Thumāma al-Ṣā'idī* saw him, he told Hussein: 'God protect you, O Abu Abdullah! The most evil, treacherous and violent of men has come to you.'

Abu *Thumāma* barred his way and said: 'Throw down your sword.'

'No, by God, I will not set down my sword or my honor. I am Umar b. Sa'd's messenger. Hear me and my message, or I will go.'

'Then I will hold your sword's hilt until you say what you have come to say.'

'No, by God, no one touches my sword!'

'Then speak and keep your distance from Hussein, for you are a treacherous man.'

Kathīr became angry and returned to Umar b. Sa'd, saying: 'They will not let me near Hussein to deliver your message.'

Umar b. Sa'd assigned another man of his entourage, *Qurra b. Qays al-Hanẓalī* and asked him to inquire after Hussein's intentions.

When he approached and Hussein caught sight of him, he asked his companions: 'Do you know this one?'

Habib b. Muẓāhir said: 'Yes, he is a member of the TamĐm tribe. I always knew him to be a man of sound opinion, I never expected to see him here.'

He stood in front of Hussein, greeted him and delivered the message of Ibn Sa'd.

Hussein replied: 'O man! Inform your master that I only came here because the people of your city wrote to me asking me to come. If they have changed their minds, then I will go back to whence I came.'

The man listened and then made to leave. *Habib b. Muẓāhir* turned to him and said: 'Woe to you, Qurra! I thought you knew better than to wrong the Household of the Prophet, what on earth made you the sort of man to bring this message. Stay with us and help this man!' And he pointed to Hussein.

'You have spoken the truth, but I will go back to my master with your response, then I will think on what you have said.'

When *al-Hanẓalī* informed Umar b. Sa'd of what Hussein had said, Umar said: 'May God spare me from having to fight and kill Hussein.'

Then he wrote a letter to Ibn Ziyad, saying: 'When I encountered Hussein, I sent a messenger to ascertain his intentions. He says that the people of this region wrote to him and sent messengers asking him to come to them, and he has done so, but that if they have changed their minds and no longer want him here, he will depart.'

When Ibn Ziyad read Umar b. Sa'd's letter, he recited the verses:

Now that our claws have seized him
he hopes to escape, but now it is too late!

He wrote to Umar b. Sa'd, saying: 'Give Hussein and all of his companions the chance to pledge allegiance to Yazid b. Muawiya. If they do that, we see what our judgment will be.'

When Umar b. Sa'd read this letter, he said: 'I did not think Ibn Ziyad intended mercy.' And he forwarded the letter to Hussein.

Hussein told the messenger: 'I will never accede to Ibn Ziyad's demand. And if that means nothing but death, then I welcome it.'

When Ibn Ziyad heard of Hussein's response, he grew angry, took all of his entourage to the outskirts of Kufa and announced a full-scale mobilization of the Kufan garrison.

Then he wrote to Umar b. Sa'd: 'Deny Hussein and his companions access to water, do not allow them a single drop, just as they did to the righteous martyr, Uthman b. Affan.'

Umar b. Sa'd did as he was bid, sending *Amr b. Hajjāj* with five-hundred horsemen to hold the road leading to the river and prevent them from taking water from it. This was on the seventh day of Muharram.

When Hussein's companions attempted to reach the water, Abdullah b. Hasseen called out: 'O Hussein! Think of this water as though it were beyond the sky itself, you shall not taste a single drop of it until you die.'

Hussein said: 'O God, let him die thirsty and never forgive him!'

Amr b. Hajjāj called: 'O Hussein! The dogs drink the water, the farmers' pigs drink the water, and donkeys and wolves too. But you shall not have a drop until you drink the boiling waters of Hell!'

Hearing these words spoken to Hussein was harder for his companions than their being denied water.

When Abdullah b. Muslim saw that Hussein was being denied water, he turned to his friend and said: 'Glory to God! Hussein is one of those who brought water to Uthman b. Affan when he had been besieged in his palace; he and his brother Hasan brought water to him and his people. And even if Uthman died thirsty, what crime has Hussein's baby and womenfolk committed, when they are the ornaments of God's Messenger?'

Rahman: It seems that we are witnessing crimes never before seen, not even during the Age of Ignorance.

In Kufa, after the general mobilization was announced, Ibn Ziyad gathered the people and told them: 'O people! You have tried the

House of Abu Sufiyan and found them as you like, and you know that this Commander of the Faithful, Yazid b. Muawiya, has good conduct, praiseworthy governance and genuine concern for his flock; he gives generously and keeps our roads safe, just as his father, Muawiya, did before him. Yazid treats God's servants generously and enriches them; through him, God has increased your sustenance a hundred fold. He has ordered me to equip you and send you to battle against his enemy, Hussein, so heard him and obey.'

With this speech, Ibn Ziyad revealed that fighting Hussein was the direct order of Yazid. Then he placed Kufa under the command of Amr b. al-HarÐth and told people to gather in the palm groves, and secure the bridge so that no one could cross it.

Then he called *Shihāb al-Harithī, Muhammad b. Ash'ath b. Qays, Qa-'qā' b. Suwayd and Asmaa b. Khārija*, and told them: 'Walk amongst the people, enjoin them to obedience and propriety, warn them of the consequences of sedition and encourage them to join the army.'

So they went out, walking around Kufa and reprimanding people. They were joined by *Kathīr b. Shihāb*, a crier who was making his rounds of Kufa, bidding people to remain united and avoid division, and encouraging them to abandon Hussein's cause.

Thereafter, from dawn until dusk, Ibn Ziyad was dispatching groups of soldiers to fight Hussein, swelling the ranks of Umar b. Sa'd. At the same time, he had placed watchmen around Kufa to ensure that no one left, lest they join Hussein or take him drinking water; these armed guards he placed under the command of *Zaḥr b. Qays al-Ju'fī*. He also set up a line of communication between himself and Umar b. Sa'd's force, with dispatch riders bringing him regular updates of the situation.

But there were still those who were able to evade Ubaydullah and escape his grasp because they could not bring themselves to fight Hussein; they tried to stay back from his summons.

In response, Ibn Ziyad sent *Suwayd b. Rahman al-Munqarī* to Kufa by horse and ordered him to ride around the outskirts of the city in search of deserters.

As for the large contingents that Ibn Ziyad had sent to Karbala, amongst them were men like *Yazid b. Rakāb al-Kalbī*, who had two thousand men with him, *Hasseen b. Numayr al-Suklūnī*, with four thousand, Amr b. Qays, also with four thousand, and *Sinān b. Anas*, with a further four thousand.

When *Shabbath b. Rab'ey al-Riyāḥī*, one of those who had written to Hussein 'Come to us, for we have no Imam' and widely considered the most knowledgeable jurist in Kufa, avoided Ubaydullah's summons, the latter sent someone after him to ask: 'Are you ill? If you are obedient to us, then go forth to fight out enemy!'

So Shabbath went forth and Ubaydullah put him in charge of a thousand horsemen, after he had bestowed some gifts upon him and won his affection.

This is how men and horses gradually arrived in Karbala, until Umar b. Sa'd had thirty thousand men at his disposal, both mounted and on foot.

Ibn Ziyad issued strict orders that anyone capable of bearing a sword or spear, or even a stick or a rock, must join the army going to Karbala to fight Hussein, until there was no one who had not gone to fight the Leader of the Youth of Paradise.

Such was the extent of this that when *Qa'qā'* b. Suwayd found a stranger from Syria who had come to Kufa to collect some inheritance, he took him to Ibn Ziyad, who asked him: 'Why are you not going to fight Hussein?'

'I am a stranger who has come from Syria, I came to collect a debt owed to me by a man from Iraq.'

'Kill him so that other deserters learn their lesson.' And when the people saw this, they all joined the army without exception, save those who had either fled or been imprisoned.

Meanwhile, in Karbala, Hussein was sitting with his companions in his tent, when a man called *Harmatha b. Salīm* came in. He greeted Hussein and said: 'O Abu Abdullah! We fought beside your father in Siffin, and when we stopped in Karbala, he led us in prayers. When he finished his prayer, he took a handful of the earth and smelled it, saying: 'Woe to you, O earth! Upon you will be slain a people who will enter Paradise without any accounting!'

And when I returned from campaigning to my wife, *Jurdā' b. Samīr* – a follower of Ali - I said to her: 'Isn't your comrade, Abu al-Hasan, strange? When we stopped in Karbala he picked up a peace of its earth and smelled it, then said: 'Woe to you, O earth! Upon you will be slain a people who will enter Paradise without any accounting!' From where did he obtain this knowledge of the Unseen?'

My wife answered: 'Away with you! The Commander of the Faithful only speaks the truth.'

Then your father, Ali, was slain and I forgot about this until you came here and Ubaydullah b. Ziyad sent me to fight you. Then I recognized that this was the place where your father set down, from where he took the earth all those years ago, and I remembered his words. Whereat I detested what I had done and I came to you to tell you what I heard your father said... O Abu Abdullah, you will soon be slain!'

Hussein asked him: 'So are you with us, or against you?'

'O son of God's Messenger, I am neither with you not against you. I have left behind my family and children and I am afraid what Ibn Ziyad will do to them.'

'Then leave this place so that you will not see us being slain, for by God anyone who sees us being slain and does not help us, he will only enter Hellfire.'

So the man fled as fast as he could so that he would neither see nor hear what would happen.

But in spite of the great multitude of people who were now arrayed against Hussein, there were still those believers here and there who were able to reach him to defend him.

One such person was Abdullah b. Umayr from the Alim tribe. He had settled in Kufa and made his home near the well of *Ju'd al-Hamadānī* with his wife, who was from the tribe of *Nimr b. Qāsiṭ*. When he saw the people assembling in the date groves to go and fight Hussein he said: 'By God, I have been eager to fight the polytheists, but I am sure that God's reward for fighting those who wish to harm the son of the daughter of their prophet is greater still!'

So he went to his wife and told her what he wanted to do. She told him: 'You are right! May God reward you and set right your affairs, go and take me with you!'

So they went until they came to Hussein and stayed with him.

Another person who came to Huayn was *Amr b. Abu Salāma al-Dāllānī*. He tried to leave Kufa in secret to join up with Hussein, but he was intercepted by *Zajr b. Qays al-Ju'fī*, to whom Ubaydullah b. Ziyad had given command of five hundred horsemen to intercept those joining Hussein. Yet he managed to elude Ibn Qays and reach Hudayn in Karbala.

Also able to escape Ubaydullah's men and reach Hussein in Karbala was *Habib b. Muẓāhir al-Asadi*, who had been ecstatic at the coming of the Prophet's Household; he was an elderly Companion but a ferocious fighter who terrified his enemies. He had played a key role in bringing Hussein to Kufa, so when he saw how many men had assembled to fight the Prophet's Household, he turned to Hussein and said: 'O son of God's Messenger, there is a tribe of the Asad nearby, will you let me go to them by night and call them to help you? Perhaps God will protect you through them!

Hussein agreed and Habib set out in the middle of the night in disguise until he reached their tribe, whereat he introduced himself and they recognized him. They said: 'What is your need, cousin?'

'I bring you the best that anyone could ever bring his people; I am here to summon you to help the son of the daughter of God's Messenger. He is with a band of the faithful, one of whom is better than a thousand lesser men. They will never abandon him nor surrender him to their enemies so long as they draw breath. This Umar b. Sa'd has surrounded him with more than twenty two thousand soldiers. You are my people and my tribe, so I have come to you with this advice: Come with me this day and you shall have renown in this life and the best reward in the next! I swear by God that none of you shall be slain standing beside the son of the daughter of God's Messenger, save that he will be in the company of Muhammad in the highest levels of Paradise!'

A man called Abdullah b. Bishr stood up and said: 'Let me be the first to answer your call!' Then he recited the verses:

When they resist, people know
and horsemen, when they stand firm
That I am a brave and intrepid warrior
who fights like a ferocious lion

Then all the men of the tribe rushed to Habib and pledged their support; ninety men joined him and set out with him for Hussein. But there was one of them, called Jabla b. Umar, who was weak in his faith and hastened under cover of darkness to Umar b. Sa'd to warn him that men from his tribe were coming to help Hussein. Ibn Sa'd called on *Azraq b. Harith al-Ṣaydāwī* and put him at the head of four hundred horsemen to accompany Jabla back to the tribe. The two forces, who were heading in opposite directions, met on the banks of the Euphrates, almost in sight of Hussein's camp. They clashed and Habib called out to Azraq: 'Look at what you have and what we have! Begone and leave us to be troubled by someone else!' Azraq refused and the Asad tribesmen were demoralized when one of them said: 'We don't stand a chance against Ibn Sa'd's cavalry!' So they withdrew to their tribe and Habib came back to Hussein and informed him of what had happened. When Hussein heard what had happened, said: 'There is no strength save in God, the High, the Exalted.'

Once Ibn Sa'd's army in Karbala had reached full strength and the desert had been filled with soldiers, Ubaydullah wrote to him: 'I leave no excuse for you not to fight Hussein. You have the advantage in men and horses. So see to it you do not start anything until you have consulted me morning and evening about everything which he does.' And Ibn Sa'd would obey Ibn Ziyad's orders completely.

On the seventh day of Muharram, the siege on the Prophet's Household had intensified; Umayyad soldiers now barred their access to water entirely and they had used up their supplies. Each of them suffered burning thirst; men, women and children all suffered in the heat, but between them and water there were only points of spears and blades of swords. Hussein asked his brother, Abbas to fight his way to the river for water, giving him twenty footsoldiers carrying waterskins and another thirty on horseback. They advanced down the road, with *Nāfi' b. Hilāl al-Bajalī* carrying their banner. Amr b. HajjÁj, who had been tasked with holding the road by Ibn Sa'd called out: 'Who goes there!'

Nāfi' said: 'We have come to drink from the water which you have denied us!'

Amr replied: 'Drink up, but take none to Hussein!'

Nāfi' said: 'No by God, I will not taste a drop of it while Hussein and his companions and family remain thirsty!' Then he called to his companions: 'Fill up your water-skins!'

Amr b. Hajjāj's men attacked them and the two sides fought; some of Hussein's men filled water skins while others fought. Abbas led them and they were able to bring some water back to the tent of Hussein.

But such a small quantity of water was not sufficient for more than one hundred and fifty men, women and children.

With the Prophet's Household cut off from water and suffering from dire thirst, Hussein got up, resting on the hilt of his sword, and called out to the army of Umar b. Sa'd at the top of his voice: 'I adjure you by God, do you know me?'

They said, 'Yes, you are the son of the daughter of God's Messenger, and his grandson.'

'By God, do you know that God's Messenger is my grandfather?'

'Oh God, yes!'

'By God, do you know that my father is Ali b. Abu Talib?'

'Oh God, yes!'

'By God, do you know that my mother is Fatima al-Zahra, the daughter of Muhammad, God's Chosen?'

'Oh God, yes!'

'By God, do you know that my grandmother is KhadĐja b. Khuwalid, the first believing woman?'

'Oh God, yes!'

'By God, do you know that my great uncle is Hamza, the Master of Martyrs?'

'Oh God, yes!'

'By God, do you know that Ja'far who soars through Paradise is my uncle?'

'Oh God, yes!

'By God, do you know that this turban that I wear is the turban of God's Messenger?'

'Oh God, yes!'

'By God, do you know that Ali was the first person to believe in Islam, the most knowledgeable of them, the wisest of them and the walÐ of every believing man and woman?'

'Oh God, yes!'

'Then on what basis do you permit the shedding of my blood, while my father protects the Pool (*ḥawḍ*) which men protect as they would a wellspring, and the banner of God's praise will be in his hand on the Day of Resurrection?'

'We know that, but we will not leave you until you die of thirst!'

When Hussein's women and daughters heard this exchange, they began to cry aloud, so Hussein sent his brother Abbas and his son Ali, saying: 'Silence them, for they will have much to weep about soon!'

Hussein sent word to Ibn Sa'd: 'I wish to speak to you, meet me between our camps tonight.'

Ibn Sa'd reluctantly agreed and came with twenty horsemen, and Hussein did likewise. When they met, Hussein bid his Companions to remain at a distance, leaving him with just his brother, Abbas, and his eldest son, Ali. Ibn Sa'd gave similar instructions to his men, leaving him with his son, *Hafṣ* and a retainer. Hussein addressed Umar: 'Woe to you! Do you not fear God to whom is your return? Will you fight me while you know who I am? O wretch! Leave them and join me, for I will bring you closer to God.'

Umar b. Sa'd responded: 'I fear you will destroy my abode.'

'Rather I will build it for you.'

'I fear I will lose my holdings.'

'I will leave something better for you from my property in Hejaz.'

'I fear for my family.'

'I will guarantee their safety.'

But Ibn Sa'd would not accept Hussein's summons, so Hussein left him, saying: 'What is wrong with you, may God slaughter you as you sleep! He will not forgive you when you are resurrected. And by God, I hope you will eat but a little of Iraq's prosperity.'

He answered derisively: 'O Abu Abdullah! There's plenty of barley to go around!'

Then each of them returned to his respective camp.

Even though Umar b. Sa'd had refused Hussein's offer to join him, he did write to Ibn Ziyad, saying: 'God has put out the fire, united the opinions and set right the Nation. This Hussein has agreed to return to whence he came, or for us to convey him to a border post where he will live as an ordinary Muslim, with the same rights and responsibilities, or to sit down with the Commander of the Faithful, Yazid, and discuss things as they stand. This will satisfy you and set right the Nation.'

Umar b. Sa'd had diluted facts with lies in his letter; Hussein had indeed offered to go somewhere else. But Ibn Sa'd added that Hussein was willing to go and speak to Yazid – a brazen lie which he attributes to Hussein, because the fundamental dispute was about Yazid's caliphate, and Hussein had already said before: 'May Islam rest in peace if the Nation must suffer a shepherd like Yazid!' So how could he agree to go and discuss things with him?

In any case, when this letter reached Ubaydullah b. Ziyad, he read it to a group of his companions, amongst whom was Shimr b. Dhil al-Jawshan, who advised Ibn Ziyad: 'Do not accept anything less than him pledging allegiance to you personally, for so long as he does not do that, he has strength and dignity and you have weakness and impotence. Accept nothing short of his submission to your judgement, and his companions too. Then if you punish him, you have the right, and if you forgive, you have the right to do so... word has reached me that Hussein and Umar b. Sa'd are meeting one another in between the camps for discussions by night.'

Ibn Ziyad said: 'Your opinion is the best. Go with this letter to Umar b. Sa'd and tell him to offer Hussein and his companions the chance to submit to my judgment. If they do that, then give them safe passage to me. If not, kill them all.'

He then wrote to Umar b. Sa'd: 'I did not send you to Hussein to discuss matters, offer him safety, or give him an intercessor! Look, if Hussein and his companions will submit to my judgement, then give them safe passage to me, but if they refuse, then advance on them until you have killed them and made an example of them. This is what they deserve. If you kill Hussein, give his body to the horses hooves, for he is in open rebellion, and if you do that you shall have the reward of an obedient servant. But if you refuse, resign and give control of the army to Shimr b. Dhil al-Jawshan. You now report to him. Peace.'

Karbala: Prelude to Battle

It was clear to all that the land on which Hussein and his companions had pitched their tents on one side, and the Umayyad army under the leadership of Umar b. Sa'd had pitched theirs on the other, would be the site of the coming battle.

On his side, Hussein had been clear about his position from the outset, believing that he was charged by God with the responsibility of defending the truth and standing up to falsehood, and responding to the call of those who wanted him to be their Imam and their leader.

Meanwhile, his enemies had also made their position clear; they desired power and revenge; they were resolved to kill him and his companions in the most brutal manner imaginable. Ubaydullah had been clear about that in his letters to his field commander.

The battle, in truth, began when Shimr b. Dhil al-Jawshan arrived on the scene on the night of Thursday, the ninth of Muharram. Shimr, as we said, brought orders to advance on Hussein's forces and specified the time for the attack, once necessary preparations had been completed.

Umar b. Sa'd had, at the end of his last letter to Ibn Ziyad, tried to forestall bloodshed, presenting Hussein's offer to return to Medina or to depart for some distant land. This was a genuine offer; Hussein had no interest in fighting, he only sought what was right; like any divine leader, his only interest was making his enemies fully responsible for whatever they did, and that is why he offered to return to the place from he had come. In this way, he resembled God's Messenger and his companions when they made the treaty of Hudaybiyya. The Prophet and his companions had set out to perform the pilgrimage in Mecca, not intending to fight the polytheists, although they carried swords, as was customary at that time.

And when they faced the Quraysh's men, who prevented them from visiting God's House, they did not insist on going. They were content to return to Medina. The crucial difference between these two events was that the polytheists did not try to force the Prophet to pledge allegiance to Abu Sufiyan with the threat of violence, while in Karbala, Hussein was not given the choice between going to Kufa, on the basis of the people's intivation to him, or returning to Medina. He was only given two options: surrender or die.

Shimr brought two letters with him to Karbala, first was one to Umar b. Sa'd forbidding him from letting Hussein leave, and the second was to Abbas and his brothers, promising to give them safety if they abandoned Hussein.

When he conveyed Ibn Ziyad's letter to Umar b. Sa'd, the latter told him: 'Woe to you, leper! May God curse you and what you have brought me! By God, I think it is you who persuaded Ibn Ziyad to reject my offer; you have ruined everything I have worked for here. But then you are a devil; you cannot help your nature.'

He added, 'By God, Hussein will never surrender. He is his father's son.'

Shimir ignored him and said: 'Tell me, Umar, what are you doing here? Are you obeying your orders and fighting the enemy, or should I take control of the army?'

Umar b. Sa'd, in whom ambition for the governorship of Rayy burned, said: 'No, villain, but I will take care of it myself. You go and lead the infantry.'

Umar b. Sa'd sent word to Hussein of Ubaydullah's rejection of his offer to return to Hejaz or to go somewhere else, and his offer to surrender to him in return for safe conduct.'

Hussein said: 'By God I will never place my hand in that of *Ibn Marjāna*.' Then he recited the verses of poetry:

'The grazing cattle fear no aggressor in the dark of night
nor do I call Yazid
On the day when he gives injury out of scorn
and death lies in wait for me to swerve.'

As for the second letter which Shimr brought, it was for Abbas and his uterine brothers, Abdullah, Ja'far and Uthman, the sons of Ali. The story was that Shimr, who was one of the main people encouraging Ibn Ziyad to shed Hussein's blood, was from the same tribe as their mother, *Umm al-Banīn – the Banū Kilāb* – and he knew that the outcome of the battle between Hussein and the Umayyad army would be the massacre of Hussein and all of his companions. So before leaving Kufa, accompanied by *Abdullah b. Abu al-Maḥall*, the nephew of Umm al-BanĐn, Shimr went to see Ubaydullah b. Ziyad. Abdullah told him: 'May God make the governor prosper,

Ali b. Abu Tālib used to live in Kufa and he approached our tribe for a bride, so we married him to a girl called *Umm al-Banīn bt. Ḥāzim*, who gave him Abdullah, Ja'far and Uthman. This makes them our cousins. They are with Hussein as we speak, so would you see fit to write a letter to them promising safe conduct?'

Ubaydullah said: 'Yes, you are most noble.' Then he bid his scribe write a letter promising them safety, which Shimr then brought to the battlefield.

He approached Hussein's camp and called out: 'Where are our cousins? Where is Abbas and his brothers?'

They came to him and said: 'Who are you and what do you want?'

Shimr said: 'Cousins, you are granted safety. There is no need to get yourselves killed with Hussein; you can remain the loyal subjects of the Commander of the Faithful, Yazid.'

Abbas grew angry at these words and shouted in Shimr's face: 'God damn you and your safety. Will you promise us safety but not the son of God's Messenger? You tell us to obey men who are cursed and the sons of cursed men, while abandoning the son of Fatima al-Zahra?'

With this brazen reply, Shimr returned to his camp crestfallen, having realized that all of Ali's children shared their father's spirit, just as Umar b. Sa'd had learnt of Hussein.

Having witnessed these events, *Rahman Ṣāliḥ* turned to his companion, Abdullah and said: 'What are they waiting for? Why don't they attack?'

Abdullah: Hussein's companions are distinguished from all other men by their insight; they believe in what they do and are firmly convinced of the righteousness of their cause; you will not find any hesitation in them, nor in Hussein, their leader. As for their enemies, they know that they are upon falsehood; they take one step forward and another step back.

Rahman: You mean Ibn Sa'd?

Abdullah: Yes, Umar b. Sa'd, and everyone in his camp. I do not mean Shimir, of course. He is unlike anyone else there; a man without conscience, wicked to the core, who cannot wait so much as another hour for the battle to begin. Umar b. Sa'd, on the other hand, is trying to stall; he hopes God will make something happen to avert the battle. He knows Hussein well and is related to him; they both used to sit beneath Ali when he was on the pulpit in Kufa and listen to his lectures. But Umar has been blinded by the promise of a governorship in Rayy and his ambition for worldly wealth; this is what brought him to Karbala.

Hussein is a man of the Hereafter, while Umar is a man of this world. He does not fear shedding Hussein's blood out of fear for his afterlife, but rather out of fear for the life he is living right now! He fears that the balance might shift and then it won't be easy being the man with the blood of the Prophet's grandson on his hands, when there are still people alive who heard the Prophet on many occasions say things about him like: 'Hussein is of me and I am of Hussein.' And: 'Hasan and Hussein are the leaders of the youth of Paradise.'

Rahman: What about Ubaydullah b. Ziyad? Does he not fear the same thing?

Abdullah: Ubaydullah is known to be a coward, why else do you think he is sending anyone capable of holding a sword, a spear or even a stick against Hussein? It's so that they'll all share in the guilt of killing the grandson of the Prophet and no one will be able to come after him!

Rahman: Do you think he has any hesitations about killing Hussein?

Abdullah: Never! He is a man after Shimir's own heart; wicked and cruel. He is, after all, the son of Ziyad, the son of his father – we don't know where he came from in truth. But this man does fear Yazid b. Muawiya, who appointed him to face Hussein in return for the governorship of Kufa and Basra; he fears being removed from his post. So he has a double motivation: He desires power and he fears Yazid. As for Umar b. Sa'd, he is delaying in the hope that either Yazid or Ubaydullah will change their minds; that is why he delays the attack.

When the army of Umar b. Sa'd had denied water to the Prophet's Household despite the severe heat, they themselves did not only enjoy drinking the water, but swimming in it also. Umar b. Sa'd himself went to the banks of the Euphrates with Sa'd b. Ubayda to make use of the waters. While they were in the water, a man approached Umar b. Sa'd and said: 'Ibn Ziyad has sent Juwayra b. Badr al-TamĐmĐ with orders to cut off your head unless you fight Hussein and his companions.'

Between his political ambition for Rayy and his fear of death, Umar b. Sa'd hastily emerged from the waters, mounted his horse and called for his weapons.

Then he gave the orders for his companions to attack Hussein.

It was at Sunset on the ninth of Muharram that the army began to advance.

At that time, Hussein was seated before his tent, with his legs drawn up around his sword. His head was slumped against his knees. Suddenly he heard his sister, Zaynab calling out: 'Brother! Do you not hear the sounds?'

Hussein lifted his head without taking heed, with a pleasant expression on his face. He said: 'I saw God's Messenger in a dream just now. He told me: 'You are coming to me.''

Whereat Zaynab struck her face and said: 'O woe to us!'

'There is no woe for you, sister. Be still, may God have mercy upon you.'

While they spoke, Abbas came rushing over and said: 'Brother! Do you see them coming?'

Hussein got up and said: 'Go to them and ask what their intentions are?'

Abbas went with twenty horsemen, including *Zuhayr b. al-Qayn and Habib b. Muẓāhir*, and said: 'What are you doing? What has happened?'

'The governor has sent orders that you will either submit to his judgment or face execution.'

'Do not be hasty, let me go back to Abu Abdullah and tell him what you have said.'

They stopped and said: 'Go to him and bring us his response.'

So Abbas returned to Hussein to tell him what had happened, while the others who had come with him stayed behind to address the army. *Habib b. Muẓāhir* told *Zuhayr b. Qayn*: 'Why don't you or I talk to these people?'

Zuhayr said: 'Since you had the idea, you speak to them.'

So Habib raised his voice and said: 'By God, the worst of people tomorrow will be those who go to God have killed the descendants of His prophet, his offspring and his household, the righteous people of this city who strive by morning and remember God abundantly day and night, and their pious followers.'

'Azra b. Qays derided him: 'Absolve your soul as much as you like, O Habib!'

Zuhayr responded: 'O *'Azra*! It is God who absolves the soul and guides it, so beware of God and take my advice; I warn you by God not to be amongst those who aid those who have gone astray in killing innocent souls!'

ÝAzra said: 'O Zuhayr! We did not think you were followers of this household; you were a supporter of Uthman!'

'Does the fact I am standing here not show you that I am of them? By God it was not me who wrote to Hussein, sent him messengers, or promised him my support. Rather, it was the road that brought us together, and when I saw him I was reminded of God's Messenger and his position with regards to him. I knew what enemies from your party he would have to face, so I knew I had to help him and join his party, and place myself before him lest you violate God's rights and the rights of His messenger!'

As for Abbas, he went back to Hussein and told him what had happened. Hussein told him: 'Go to them and see if you can delay them until tomorrow, keep them of us this night so that we can spend it worshipping our Lord, supplicating to Him and seeking His forgiveness, for He knows that I love worshipping Him, reciting His book and supplicating and seeking forgiveness much!'

So Abbas went back with Hussein's request and asked them to delay the battle until the next day. Umar b. Sa'd turned to Shimr and said: 'What do you think, Shimr?'

Shimr replied: 'What do you think? You are the commander and it is your decision. If it were up to me, I would have done as I was told and not delayed the battle.'

Umar b. Sa'd said: 'I did not want to be.'

Then he turned to his army and asked: 'What do you think?'

Amr b. Hajjāj b. Salama al-Zubaydī spoke up and said: 'Glory to God! By God, if they were from Daylam and they had asked for this, you should have granted it to them!'

Qays b. Ash'ath spoke next: 'If you grant them their request, they will launch a surprise attack in the morning.'

Umar b. Sa'd said: 'By God, had I known they would do that I would not have granted them this night.'

He turned to Abbas and said: 'We have set a tryst for tomorrow; if you surrender, we will take you to Ubaydullah b. Ziyad. If not, then you will not escape us.'

Once Umar b. Sa'd had returned to his encampment and *'Abbas* and his companions to their tents, *Rahman al-Ṣāliḥ* turns to his friend, Abdullah: So that's it, then. There is definitely going to be a battle. But why did Hussein postpone it?

Abdullah: He explained why; he wants to worship God on the last night of his life; he loves to worship, to recite the Qur'an and to seek God's forgiveness, and perhaps there is something else he intends.

THE COMPANIONS

After *'Ishā'* prayers on the tenth night of Muharram, Hussein gathered his companions and addressed them:

'In the name of God, the Compassionate, the Merciful. Praise be to God, Lord of the Worlds. Blessings be upon God's Messenger and his Household. I magnify God, Blessed and Exalted, and praise Him in ease and in hardship. O God! Verily I praise you for ennobling us with prophethood, teaching us the Qur'an, giving us understanding of the religion and bestowing upon us hearing, sight and sense, and that you did not make us idolaters!

Surely I know no companions better or more loyal than mine, nor any household more righteous and more united than mine. May God grant you all abundant good. I think that tomorrow shall be the last day they give us, so I release you all from your oaths. Go and be free; you have no responsibility towards me. This night will cover you, so escape under cover of darkness, and let each man take one member of my household with him to safety. May God bless you all; disperse amongst the fertile lands and cities, for these people are only after me and when they have me they will seek no one else.'

When Rahman heard Hussein's words, he turned to Abdullah and said: 'I think Hussein only delayed the battle to say what he said now, to give those who wanted to live a chance to escape the battle!'

Abdullah: 'This is in addition to what he said before about spending the night in worship, reciting God's Book, seeking God's clemency and spending the last night of his life in this world in prayer and contemplation. This is the way of the *people*, they see this world as a place of gathering provisions and not a place of enjoyment.

After Hussein had spoken, his companions raised their voices, each one clamouring to speak. Muslim b. ÝAwsaja al-Asadi stood up and said: 'Shall we abandon you? And what excuse will we give to God if we did that!? By God, I will fight them; I will plunge my spear into their chests and strike at them with my sword so long as its hilt remains in my hand! No, I will never abandon you! Even if I had no weapons to fight with, I would throw rocks at them until I die with you!'

Then *Sa'eed b. Abdullah al-Hanafī* stood up and said: 'By God we will not leave you until God knows that we have protected you in the absence of God's Messenger!'

He added: 'By God, if I knew I would be slain and brought back to life, then burnt alive and scattered like dust, and this would be done to me seventy times, I would still not leave you until I meet my fate before you. How can I not do this, for it is only a single death, but after it there is nobility without end!'

Then Zuhayr b. Qayn stood and spoke: 'By God, I would rather be slain and brought back to life, then slain again a thousand times, if that meant God would repel harm from you and the youths of your household!'

Other companions made similar statements: 'By God, we shall never abandon you, may we be your sacrifice! We will protect you with every part of our bodies, and if we are slain then we have done our duty!'

As for Hussein's family, they spoke with the voice of Abbas b. Ali: 'Our refuge is with God and the sacred month! O son of the daughter of God's Messenger, what would we say to people when we go back to them? Would we say: We abandoned our master, the son of our master and the pillar of our faith? We left him as a target for arrows, exposed to spears and food for scavengers while we saved our own skins? That we did not protect him from arrows, nor shield him from spears, nor strike out with our swords to protect him!? God forbid!

No, by God, O son of the daughter of God's Messenger! We will never abandon you; we will lay down our lives for you. We live with you, we die with you, we go where you go. For God has made life after you unbearable!'

Then the Imam turned to the sons of Aqeel and said: 'Your family has already suffered its share of killing with your brother, Muslim. You do not need to stay here.'

They said: 'No, by God, we will not leave; may our lives, our property and our family be your ransom!'

When Hussein heard their pledges, he invoked God's blessings upon them and went to his tent.

It appears as though Zaynab heard Hussein's words and how his companions responded. When she saw him going back to his tent, she put on her robes and went to him, saying: 'O bereavement! Would that I had not lived to see this day; today is the day my father, Ali, was slain; today is the day my mother, Fatima, passed away; today is the day my brother, Hasan, died! O successor of those who have gone ahead, O forefather of those who shall survive!'

Then she struck her face in grief and Hussein came and consoled her.

There was much distress in the camp of Hussein on that night; the desire to resist injustice was mixed with tension, tempered by the firm resolve that they would not give up, no matter the cost. The ladies of the Prophet's Household looked at their menfolk, knowing that they would lose them on the morrow. Their fear of the battle to come and the fact that it was not at all clear what would happen thereafter only served to heighten the tension that enveloped them, especially when there were but a few fighting men in the camp compared to their enemies who filled the desert in all directions. For each of Hussein's companions, there were five hundred soldiers, bearing all manner of arms – swords, spears, bows, slings and more – and whose hearts were filled with spite and rancour.

This is in addition to the fact that those who had accompanied Husayn for worldly ambitions did not share the determination or faith of his true companions; one by one they deserted him, to the extent that Sukayna bt. Hussein would recount: 'I sat in the middle of the tent, when I heard a whimper behind me. So I went out quietly, lest any of the other ladies notice, and saw my father, Husayn sitting with his companions around him, with tears streaming down his cheeks. He said: 'O people, you came with me because you thought I was going to a people who had pledged allegiance to me with their tongues and hearts. But Satan has now taken hold of them and made them forget God's remembrance; their only purpose is to kill me and whoever defends me, then take my family prisoner. I fear that you might not know this, or you know this but are ashamed to say anything. We, the Prophet's Household, do not engage in guile or betrayal; so whoever amongst you does not wish to help us may leave, for night is a cover and the way is not generous. But whoever stands with us now shall be with us tomorrow in Paradise, safe from the wrath of the All-Merciful. God's Messenger has said: 'My grandson, Hussein, will be slain isolated, alone and thirsty in the land of Karbala. Whoever helps him has helped me and has helped his descendent, the *Qā'im*.'

Sukayna added: 'By God, he had not finished speaking before people began to leave in groups of ten and twenty, until only some seventy or eighty remained. I saw my father lower his head in sadness. It took all my strength to choke back my sobs and stay silent.'

Then Sukayna returned to the tent where the ladies were, her eyes overflowing with tears. Umm Kulthum saw her and said: 'What's the matter?'

She told her all that had transpired, and when Umm Kulthum heard Hussein's words, she cried out: 'O woe, grandfather! O woe, 'Ali! O woe, Hasan! O woe, Husayn! O woe, how few are our helpers!' Then she said, 'If only our enemies would kill us instead of my brother.'

Then women huddled together, weeping. And when Hussein heard their cries, he came in and Umm Kulthum told him: 'O brother, remind [our enemies] of who your father and grandfather were, and your grandmother and your brother!'

Hussein replied: 'I told them but they would not listen, I admonished them but they paid no heed. They do not care what I say – their only goal is to kill me. I enjoin you all to fear God, the Lord of all creation, and to endure this tribulation. I leave you in the care of God, the Unique, the Everlasting, who has neither taken any consort nor any offspring. Then he said: 'And they did not wrong Us, rather they used to wrong only themselves.'

Husayn wanted his uprising to remain pure, so he did not want anyone to remain with him for worldly ambitions. He did not even want those to remain with him who were indebted to others. One of his companions told him on the eve of '*Ashūrā*: 'I am indebted to someone.'

Hussein said: 'No one who is indebted to someone else should fight beside me.'

Husayn's concern for human affairs sprang from his absolute conviction in his principles and values, and in his uprising, whose only goal was to revive the true religion from every angle, including the angle of personal morality.

There is another man amongst Hussein's companions called Muhammad b. Bashir al-HaÃramĐ, who was told that his son had been arrested in Rayy. He said: 'I sacrifice him and myself for God.' Then he added: 'I did not desire that he should be arrested, nor that I should outlive him.'

When Hussein heard this, he said: 'May God have mercy upon you, you are freed from your pledge to me; go and see to your son's release!'

The man replied: 'May I be torn apart by wild beasts if I leave you, O Abu 'Abdullah! I will never leave you, only to ask caravans about your fate, and to betray you when your followers are so few! No, by God it will never be. I will not leave you!'

On the eve of the Tenth of *Muḥarram*, Hussein divided his time between three activities:

First, Supplication, seeking forgiveness, prayer and reciting the Quran. These occupied most of his time, because he had asked for a delay in fighting the day before for this purpose.

Second, preaching to and advising his companions.

Third, going to the womenfolk, enjoining them to patience and speaking to them of the Hereafter; how they should look at this world as a temporary abode, and not a permanent one; an abode of trials and testing.

It was on that final night the Imam informed his companions that they would all be slain: 'None of you shall remain save my son, Ali *Zayn al-'Abidīn*, for God will not cut off my descendants through him; he shall be the father of eight Imams.'

All of his companions responded: 'Praise be to God who ennobled us with the chance to help you, and honoured us with being slain beside you – shall we not be pleased to be with you forever?'

Husayn told them: 'May God grant you all abundant good.'

Then he told them that once they are slain, the enemies will reach the tents and that his infant child will also be slain.

Qasim b. al-Hasan, who was then only thirteen years old, asked: 'O uncle! Will these enemies reach our tents such that they kill an infant in his mothers arms!?'

Hussein replied: 'May your uncle be your ransom, Abdullah will be slain when my soul is consumed by thirst and I return to the tents to ask for water, but I do not find any. So I will say: 'Give me my son.' And they will bring me him and I will carry him in my arms and hold him close to my mouth. Then a sinner will strike him with an arrow and slaughter him while he is babbling. The blood will overflow in my hands, and I will look up to the heavens and say: 'O God, I endure and sacrifice for You!"

So Qasim began to think how Abdullah shall be slain even though he is still an infant, and will that happen while Qasim himself is still alive? Then, he asked his uncle: 'Will I be slain too, O Uncle?'

Hussein took him in his arms and said: 'How does death taste to you, nephew?'

Qasim answered: 'O uncle, for you it is sweeter than honey!'

Hussein then told him: 'Then you shall be one of those slain with me, after enduring great suffering.'

Also on that night, once Hussein knew that his companions were sincere in their intentions and that only those destined for martyrdom on the morrow now remained, he opened their eyes such that they could see what blessings awaited for them with God in Paradise, and he informed them of their stations. They saw all of this and they began to see houses and palaces therein. The Imam would tell them: 'That is your abode, that is your palace, these are your levels.'

This was not something strange that Hussein did, for those *people* who had gone before also revealed such things to their companions in times of difficulty. For example, Moses revealed this to the magicians of Pharaoh when they believed in God and showed them their places in Paradise.

The water situation in the camp of Husayn on the Ninth of *Muḥarram* was truly tragic.

Sukayna b. Hussein later recounted: 'Our water was so scarce by the Ninth of *Muḥarram* that thirst overcome us; the water was completely exhausted, the skins were empty and the pots which had contained water dried out completely in the heat.

By evening, some of the other girls and I were extremely thirsty, so I went to my aunt, Zaynab, to tell her how thirsty we were in the hope that she had kept some water for us. I found her in her tent with my infant brother, Abdullah, who was forever sitting and standing, flailing about like a fish out of water. My aunt was telling him: 'Patience, nephew, patience. How can you have patience in this terrible state? It is so hard for your aunt to hear your cries and not be able to do anything for you!'

When I heard my aunt, I began to cry, and she asked me: 'What has made you cry?'

I said: 'My little brother's state.' I did not tell her of my thirst because I did not want to cause her any more distress.

Then I said to her: 'O aunty, if you asked some of the other ladies in the camp, perhaps they would have some water.' So she got up and took the infant in her hand and when to the tents of my uncles, but they did not have any water either, and some of the children in the camp were following her in the hope that she might have water for them.

My aunt sat in the tent of my uncle, Hasan's sons, and asked if any of the tents of the other companions had any water, but there was none. When she was sure that there was no water, she returned to her tent, with almost twenty little children running behind her, all thirsty and asking for water! So I began to weep.

As we were crying with my aunt, one of my father's companions passed by, *Bureir b. Khuḍayr al-Hamadānī*, the head of the Qur'an reciters in Kufa. When he heard our crying, he threw himself to the ground and called out to his companions: 'What do you all think!? Does it make you happy that the daughters of Fatima will die thirsty while there are swords still in our hands? No by God, there is no good in life after them. Rather we shall die before them!'

Then he said to them: 'My friends, let each of us take one of this young ladies and fight our way to the greenery before they die of thirst, and if we are attacked, we will fight back.'

Yaḥyā al-Māzanī said: 'The soldiers are determined to fight us, without a doubt. And if we take these young ladies with us, perhaps one of them will be felled by an arrow or a spear and we will be the cause of that. It makes more sense for each of us to take a container and fill it with water for them. If anyone attacks us, we will defend ourselves and if any of us is slain, it will be for the sake of Fatima's daughters.'

Bureir replied: 'You are right.'

Then they took containers and headed for the river. There were four of them. The guards sensed their approach and challenged them: 'Who goes there?'

Bureir said: 'I am Bureir and these are my companions. We are overcome with thirst and want to go down to the Euphrates.'

The guards said: 'Stay where you are until we inform our commander.' Bureir and the commander were relatives, so when the guards told him of the former's approach, he gave orders that they be allowed to drink.

When Bureir and his companions went down to the banks of the river and felt its coolness, they began to weep and called out: 'May God curse Ibn Sa'd! This water flows freely, while the lips of the Prophet's Household taste not a drop of it!' Then Bureir said: 'My friends! Remember why we came; fill your containers and make haste, for the hearts of Hussein's children burn with thirst. We should not drink until the daughters of Fatima have been quenched!'

They said: 'Yes, by God, Bureir. We will not drink before Hussein's children!'

When one of the guards heard this, he said: 'You were not allowed to approach to river to take water to this rebel! By God, I will inform my commander. And if he takes no notice, I will fight you with my sword until word reaches Ibn Sa'd himself!'

Bureir replied: 'O man! Keep quiet!' Then he approached the guard, intending to seize him and take him prisoner, so the guard turned and fled to his commander, who told them: 'Don't let them escape; bring them to me. If they refuse, fight them.'

When the guards blocked the path, they told Bureir: 'Our commander will not let you take water to your master.'

Bureir said: 'Then what?'

'Your blood will spill.'

'Woe to you! I'd rather you spill my blood before I spill a drop of this water; not one of us has drank from the river, our only concern is the children. By God you will have to spill our blood before we let you take this water from us.'

One of the enemies said: 'Leave them be. These men are willing to die for a little water which will be of no use to them anyway!'

Another said: 'Do not contravene the orders of Ibn Sa'd!'

The enemies encircled them, so *Bureir* and his companions placed the containers of water on the ground and stood over them. Then one of his companions carried them on his shoulders. The enemies focused their attacks on him from every side, trying to hit the containers with arrows. One arrow hit the rope of the container and pierced the man's shoulder. But though the blood flowed over his robe and feet, when he saw that the water container was safe, he said: 'Praise God who made my shoulder a guard for my container!'

When *Bureir* saw that the enemies would not give up, he called out: 'Woe to you! O supporters of the sons of Sufiyan, do not stir up trouble and let the swords of the sons of *Hamadān* stay in their scabbards!'

At this point, *Bureir* had almost reached Hussein's camp. One of the companions heard Bureir's call and said: 'I hear *Bureir* calling out!'

Hussein told his companions to go to him. So a group of them rode out to where *Bureir* and his companions were encircled. When the soldiers saw Hussein's companions approach, they fled. *Bureir* brought the water to the camp and set the container on the ground. He told the children: 'Drink up, O children of God's Messenger!'

At the sight of the water, the little girls became excited and called out all at once: '*Bureir* has brought us water!' And they threw themselves upon the container, embracing it, putting their cheeks on it and kissing it. But when they crowded around the water container, its stopper slipped off and the water gushed out. Then the little girls cried out: 'The water has spilled out, O *Bureir*!'

Bureir struck his forehead and said: 'O what calamity this rushing has caused for the thirst of the daughters of God's Messenger!'

On one of the occasions that Hussein visited the tents of his companions on the eve of *'Āshurā* to advise them, he said: 'Whoever has brought a woman with him, let him take her to the BanÙ Asad.'

Ali b. *Muẓāhir* stood up and asked: 'Why, O master?'

Hussein said: 'My womenfolk will be taken prisoner once I am slain, and I fear the same fate will befall your womenfolk as well.'

Ali b. *Muẓāhir* went into his tent, and his wife stood up out of respect for him, greeting him with a smile. He said to her: 'Please do not smile at me.'

She said, 'O Son of *Muẓāhir*! I heard the Son of Fatima speaking to you, but at the end there was some commotion and I did not know what he said.'

Ali replied: 'O wife, Hussein told us that whoever had brought a woman with him should take her to the tribe of her uncle, because tomorrow he will be slain and his own womenfolk taken prisoner!'

His wife asked: 'So what will you do?'

'Get ready so that I can take you to your uncle's tribe, the *Banū Asad*.'

She got up and struck her head against the tent-pole: 'By God you are unfair to me, Son of *Muẓāhir*! Are you happy that the daughters of God's Messenger should be taken prisoner while I am free? Are you happy that Zaynab should have the cover torn from her head, while I keep mine? Are you happy that the daughters of Fatima will have their jewellery seized, while I adorn myself with mine? Are you happy that your face should be bright in the presence of God's Messenger, while mine will be blackened with shame in the presence of Fatima? By God, just as you help the men, we will help the women.'

At this, *Ali b. Muẓāhir* went back to Hussein, weeping. Hussein asked: 'Why do you weep?'

'Master, the lady of Asad refuses to do anything except stay and help you.'

Hussein's eyes watered and he said: 'May you be granted abundant good on our account.'

THE NIGHT BEFORE

That night, Hussein moved between his personal tent – in which he would supplicate, pray and recite the Qur'an – and between the tents of his womenfolk and those of his companions.

Ali b. Hussein would later recount: 'While I was sitting on the eve of the Tenth of *Muḥarram*, my aunt was looking after me in my illness. My father withdrew to his tent with a servant of *Abu Dharr al-Ghiffārī* and began to polish and sharpen his sword, reciting the poetry:

'O time! You are an unworthy friend,

For at the day's beginning and its end,

How many a good man you have unjustly slain,

Time no substitution accepts, nor change,

But the decision rests with the Lord of Majesty,

And everyone alive must, one day, take this journey.'

He repeated this poem two or three times before I understood it and what he meant by it; I was choked with grief, but I fought back my tears and stayed silent. It was then I knew that the tribulation had come.

As for my aunt, Zaynab, she also heard what I had heard – and she is a woman, and women have some fragility in them – and she could not control herself. She rushed out clutching her robe and went to Hussein, crying: 'O calamity! Would that I had died before this day! This is the day on which my mother, Fatima died, and my father, Ali, and my brother, Hasan! O successor of those who came before, and predecessor of those who will come after!'

Hussein consoled her and said: 'O sister, do not let Satan deprive you of your good sense.'

'By my mother and father, O Abu Abdullah, can I not be killed in your place?'

Hussein could barely hold back his tears. Zaynab said to him: 'Take us back to the grave of our grandfather.'

Hussein said: 'Would that I could; if the sand grouse was left alone at night it would dose and sleep.'

'O woe! Will you let the sanctity of your person be violated? That is more than my heart can bear!'

She tore the front of her robe in grief and fell down to the ground, sobbing. When she composed herself, Husayn said: 'O sister, be wary of God and console yourself as God would want you to; know that all the inhabitants of the earth shall one day die and even the inhabitants of the heavens will not remain forever. Everything shall perish save the countenance of God who created the earth with his power and shall bring back the Creation again, He is the One, the Unique.'

Then he said: 'My father was better than me, and he has died. My mother was better than me, and she has died, my brother was better than me and he has died. And for me and them, and for every Muslim, God's Messenger is an exemplar.'

'Zaynab, you must promise me that you will not tear your clothes, nor strike your face, nor call out with woe and distress when I perish.'

Hussein spent the eve of the Tenth of *Muḥarram* preparing his companions for the coming battle, morally, spiritually and militarily; polishing and sharpening their swords, inspecting their weapons and surveying the site of battle. Whatever preparations were required for the morrow, Hussein made them his concern.

He had instructed his companions to bring the tents close together and to fix them firmly in place, arrayed in such a way that they would only have to face the enemy from a single direction; the tents would protect their flanks and rear.

Once the preparations for battle had been made, Hussein spent that last night with his companions, praying, seeking God's forgiveness and supplicating until the dawn.

And just as was the case for the men, so too was it for the women. Zaynab spent that entire night praying to her Lord, worshipping Him and pleading for His assistance, as did the rest of the women from the Prophet's Household. Their tents hummed with their prayers until the dawn.

Hussein tried several times to make his enemies see reason by any means possible, so that battle might be avoided and they might be spared the sin of violating the sanctity of the Prophet's Household and their companions. When *Bureir b. Khuḍayr* – a man known for his piety and devotion – came to Hussein and said: 'O son of God's Messenger! Will you permit me to go to this sinner, Umar b. Sa'd and admonish him, that he might take admonition and desist from this course of action?'

Hussein: 'You may do that, O *Bureir*.'

So *Bureir* went to Umar b. Sa'd, entered his tent and sat down without giving a greeting of peace. Umar became angry and said: 'O brother of *Hamadān*, why do you not give me the greeting of peace? Am I not a Muslim who knows God and His messenger, and testify to the truth?'

Bureir replied: 'If you knew God and His messenger as you claim, then you would not have brought an army to kill the grandson of God's Messenger. And if that wasn't enough, this is the river Euphrates, which shimmers as though it were life itself, the dogs and pigs of the desert can drink from it, but Hussein b. Ali, his brothers, womenfolk and household will die thirsty because you have prevented them from going to take water from the river. And you mean to tell me that you know God and His messenger!?'

Umar b. Sa'd lowered his head for a moment, then looked up and said: 'By God, O *Bureir*, I know with certainty that whoever fights them or violates their rights will surely be in Hellfire. But would you have me give up governorship of Rayy for someone else? For I cannot let myself do that!'

Then he recited to *Bureir* the verses of poetry that he had composed in Kufa when Ubaydullah b. Ziyad had ordered him to go and fight Hussein. He said:

Bureir came back to Hussein and said: 'Umar b. Sa'd will kill you for the sake of his governorship over Rayy; Satan has taken control of these people.'

Hussein: 'He will not enjoy it for long, for he shall be slaughtered in his bed.'

As the dawn approached, Hussein went out to survey the area surrounding his camp and take in the lay of the land. *Nāfi' b. Hilāl al-Jamalī* saw him go, so he took his sword and went to protect him.

Hussein asked what had brought him out at such an early hour.

Nāfi' told him: 'O son of God's Messenger! I was worried when I saw you head out towards the tyrant's army at this hour!'

'I came out to inspect the field of battle in case there was a chance for them to rush in with a cavalry charge. Today we will attack and they will attack.'

Once he had inspected the place, he took *Nāfi'* by the arm and returned to the camp, saying: 'This is it. God's promise always comes to pass.'

Then he turned to *Nāfi'* and said: 'Will you not take the path between those two mountains while it is still dark and save yourself?'

Nāfi' threw himself upon Hussein's feet and began to kiss them, saying: 'Then may *Hilāl's* mother be deprived of him! My master, my sword is worth a thousand and my horse the same, so by God who has blessed me with you, I will not leave you until I have worn them both out.

Then Hussein went to the women's tents and met Zaynab, while *Nāfi' b. Hilāl* remained behind the tent, waiting for him. He heard Zaynab ask Hussein: 'Have you probed the intentions of your companions? For I fear that they will desert you when battle begins.'

Hussein said: 'By God, I have tested them and found each and every one of them to be courageous and bold; they long to die defending me as a babe longs for its mother's breast!'

When *Nāfi'* heard these words, tears began to stream over his cheeks. He went to *Habib b. Muẓāhir* and told him what Hussein and his sister had said. Habib told him: 'By God, were I not awaiting his command, I would rushed at the enemy with my sword on this very night!'

'I left Hussein with his sister, and I think the rest of the women share her worries. Can you gather your comrades and address the women in such a way as to calm their hearts and allay their fears. For I cannot abide to see her grieved so.'

Habib got up and called his companions: 'O protectors of the Prophet's Household! O lions in the face of adversity!' And all the men gathered in his presence. He told them Hashemites: 'Return to your positions and remain vigilant.'

Then he turned to his companions and told them what *Nāfi'* had seen and heard. They said: 'She should not worry so, for if we were not waiting for Hussein's command, we would hasten to battle this moment!'

Habib said: 'Come with me so that we can show the womenfolk that they have nothing to fear.'

So they went and stood outside the women's tent and Habib called out: 'O jewels of God's Messenger! These are your protector's blades, which shall not be sheathed save in the necks of those who would do you harm, these are the teeth of your servants, who swear that they shall sink them into the hearts of those who would aggress against you!;

Some of them women came out crying and said: 'O you good men, protect the daughters of God's Messenger and the Commander of the Faithful!'

Then the men began to cry too, until the ground was soaked with their tears.

As for Umar b. Sa'd's side, he had sent Shimr b. Dhil al-Jawshan in the middle of the night to spy on Hussein's camp with a group of his companions. When they approached the camp, they heard Hussein reciting the following verses of the Quran: 'Do not grieve for those who are active in unfaith; they will not hurt God in the least: God desires to give them no share in the Hereafter, and there is a great punishment for them. Those who have bought unfaith for faith will not hurt God in the least, and there is a painful punishment for them. Let the faithless not suppose that the respite that We grant them is good for their souls: We give them respite only that they may increase in sin, and there is a humiliating punishment for them. God will not leave the faithful in your present state, until He has separated the bad ones from the good. God will not acquaint you with the Unseen, but God chooses from His Messengers whomever He wishes. So have faith in God and His Messengers; and if you are faithful and Godwary, there shall be a great reward for you.'

So Shimr's companions called out: 'By the Lord of the Ka'ba, it is we who are good and you who are bad, and God has separated us from you!'

Bureir heard these words, came out of his tent and interrupted them: 'The likes of you are good, while Hussein b. Ali is bad? By God, you are nothing but cattle who do not know what they are doing. So, O enemies of God, I give you glad tidings of humiliation on the Day of Resurrection and a painful punishment!'

'Allah shall fight you and fight your master soon enough!' Shimr Retorted.

'Are you trying to scare me with death? By God, death besides the grandson of God's Messenger is dearer to me than life with you. By God, Muhammad's intercession will not reach a people who have shed the blood of his descendants and his Household!'

One of Hussein's companions came to *Bureir* and said: 'May God have mercy on you, O Bureir. Abu Abdullah says that you should return to your post and not talk to them.'

In addition to this, the night of *Ashura* had other surprises in store. One was that Umar b. Sa'd had thirty members of the Quraysh tribe from Kufa amongst his men. They came to him and said: 'The son of the daughter of God's Messenger gives you three options and you do not accept a single one of them? Verily your works are ruined and wretched are the ones who follow you.'

Then they fled from Umar's camp and joined Hussein's forces.

At Dawn, Hussein's head drooped for a moment. He awoke suddenly and said to his companions: 'Do you know what I saw in my dream just now?'

They said, 'What, O grandson of God's Messenger!?'

'I saw myself surrounded by vicious dogs wanting to tear me to pieces. One of them was a spotted dog and he was the most vicious towards me. I think that whosoever is going to take my life will be afflicted by leprosy. But I also saw God's Messenger and a group of his companions. He said to me: 'My son! You are the martyr of Muhammad's household! And the inhabitants of the heavens are rejoicing at your coming. So let your breakfast be with me this evening. Hurry, my son and do not delay! This angel descends from the heavens to collect your blood in a green vessel.'

Then he said: 'The matter is decided. Soon it will be time to leave this world.

Even though the night of *Ashura* was a night of anxiety for Hussein's companions, especially the women and children, in that they were surrounded by thousands of vicious enemies, they still saw that night as the final night of their lives in this world. This meant that they felt close to God's mercy and satisfaction, and close to Paradise whose breadth is like the breadth of the heavens and the earth of this world, prepared for the Godwary. They even went so far as to gladden each other with this prospect.

Rahman b. Abd Rabbihi al-Anṣārī and *Bureir al-Hamadānī* met at the entrance to the camp, and *Bureir* began to joke with Rahman and make him laugh.

Rahman told *Bureir*: 'Leave off, Bureir! Now is not the time for frivolity!'

Bureir said: 'By God, my people know that I have never had any time for frivolity. Rather, by God, I am gladdened by our situation and what we will encounter on the morrow.'

He added: 'By God, there is nothing between us and the embrace of the maidens of paradise save the swords of our enemies! How I wish they would bring them down upon us!'

As the night drew to a close and all the enemies had fallen asleep. Hussein told his companions: Go and dig a trench around our camp like the one at the Battle of the Trench! Then tomorrow we will set it alight, forcing the enemy to come at us from a single direction. Because if they attack us and keep us occupied, there will be no one to protect the women and children.'

So they dug a trench around the rear and flanks of their camp, filling it with kindling and wood. Then they said: 'If they attack tomorrow, we will set it alight so that they cannot attack us from the rear.'

That was the last thing they did that night. After that they occupied themselves with prayer and worship, with some going to rest for a short while before the break of day.

As for *Rahman al-Ṣāliḥ* and *Abdullah b. Muslim*, they had sat in the corner of the tent speaking quietly. Rahman said to his companion: 'What has happened and what do you think will happen tomorrow?'

Abdullah: After all you have seen, how can you ask about the past?

Rahman: I saw everything, yes, but I confess I am perplexed. I do not understand how it came to this! Isn't this Hussein b. Ali, Hussein the son of Fatima, the daughter of God's Messenger? So how can he now be surrounded by those who claim to follow his grandfather, and pray, and fast and make pilgrimage on the basis of his religion?

How have the Prophet's Household come under attack like this? How do those men dare to do this? Is a man not preserved in his offspring?

Abdullah: Many of those who are with Umar b. Sa'd remember the words uttered by God's Messenger concerning the status of his household, like: 'Allah has made my Household in my Nation like the ark of Noah; whoever boarded it was saved and whoever turned away from it drowned.' And like: 'I am leaving amongst you two weighty things which if you hold fast to them you will not go astray; the Book of God and my progeny, my Household; they shall not separate until they return to me at the Pool.'

Rahman: Does that mean that the Nation has abandoned God's Book as surely as they have abandoned their prophet's progeny?

Abdullah: Of course.

Rahman: Is that not strange when it has been less than fifty years since God's Messenger passed away? Did our Lord not say: 'Indeed We have sent down the Reminder, and indeed We will preserve it'? So when the Nation abandons the Prophet's Household who will not be parted from the Book, does that not indicate that the Reminder has been lost, and it has not been preserved, just as the Prophet's Household have not been preserved?

Abdullah: Don't let yourself be led astray; the Reminder is – as we speak – exemplified by Hussein and his companions; they are preserving the Reminder.

Rahman: And when this band has been slain, how will the Reminder be preserved?

Abdullah: Hussein only came here to preserve it.

Rahman: But you say that the Reminder is exemplified by them; so when they perish at the hands of these enemies, will the Reminder still remain?

Abdullah: See here, my brother. When the Prophet emigrated from Mecca to Medina, did his emigration preserve God's sacred House, or did he lose it?

Hussein has come to this place and God will preserve the Reminder through him.

Rahman: I don't understand. How can God protect the Reminder through Hussein if he is slain?

Abdullah: The Book, as words, letters, phrases and meanings, is already preserved between two covers in the hands of the people; there is no house save that it has a copy of the Qur'an in it! But what is at stake here is not its text, but its interpretation. The hypocrites are those who have usurped the position of the Caliphate and claimed that they exemplify God's religion, while at the same time committing oppression and violating every precept, great or small, of this religion. And when these usurpers murder Hussein, everyone will know that the religion was exemplified by Hussein and that the true religion is the religion of Hussein, while the religion of the Umayyad clan is pure hypocrisy.

At this very moment, Hussein is telling people through his position and his deeds that God desires truth, not falsehood; genuine faith, not pious lip-service; that it is possible for people to claim that they represent the religion while disobeying it utterly; and that the Nation must open its eyes and follow the people of truth. Do you not hear God's words: 'O you who have faith! Be wary of God, and be with the Truthful'?

As you can see, these words are addressed to the faithful, and they mean that someone can be part of the Muslim community and known as a believer, but not counted amongst the truthful. Truthfulness means nothing less than what Hussein is doing right now, in that we see he is ready to have his blood shed for its sake. As for his enemies, they are after worldly gains. Hussein has made this world a means to obtaining the Hereafter, while his enemies have made the Hereafter a means for obtaining this world. Do you not see how they make a show of religiosity to deceive the common man?

Do you not see how they neglect one of the most important aspects of the religion, namely justice, and take God's property as a monopoly amongst themselves, and see His servants as cattle?

Hussein is God's authority over His creation; and through him, Our Lord will conclusively establish His authority over all of those who fight against him tomorrow, and those who follow them, and those who do the like of what they do or are pleased with such an act!

Rahman: But I don't think Hussein is going to defeat them, so how will he establish justice amongst the people?

Abdullah: No, in worldly terms he will not win, but he will receive divine assistance nevertheless, because Hussein – as I told you already – is fundamentally disinterested in this world. He is not after power, authority or government. Hussein wants to show the Nation today, as well as everyone who will come afterwards, that there are two religions with the name "Islam": the first is the religion of the Umayyad clan, whose name is "Islam" but whose essence is pre-Islamic ignorance; the second is the religion of the Prophet's Household, the essence of which is the same as the essence of the pure message brought by all the prophets sent to mankind.

These people fear Hussein for worldly reasons, while Hussein fears them for the sake of the Hereafter, so Hussein holds fast to the Hereafter, while they sin and oppress for the sake of this world.

Rahman: But Hussein will not win in any case.

Abdullah: If Hussein's goal was to win with his companions against that army, you are right, but the prophets in this sense did not win either; many of the righteous were oppressed and defeated in this world. Did Cain not slay Abel? Did Nimrod not try to burn Abraham? Did Pharaoh not try to kill Moses and thousands of the Israelites?

No, most of the prophets did not defeat their enemies in the material sense, but they delivered their message and through their guidance the people were guided. Hussein is doing the same now, and each person is responsible for his or her own deeds, as our Lord says: 'Indeed We have guided him to the way, be he grateful or ungrateful.'

SUNRISE

Dawn had not yet broken on the morning of the tenth of Muharram, sixty-one years after the hijra, but Hussein's companions were already up and making tayammum for prayer, for they had no water for ritual ablutions. Then they stood for prayer behind the Leader of the Youth of Paradise. And after prayer, Hussein began to ready his men for battle; he had thirty-two horsemen and forty footsoldiers, eight of whom were descendants of Ali and sixteen were from the Hashemite clan. He divided his forces into left and right flanks and the centre.

On the right flank, he placed *Zuhayr b. al-Qayn*, with *Habib b. Muẓāhir* on the left. The battle standard, he gave to his brother, Abbas b. Ali, and placed him at the centre of his forces. Meanwhile, the tents were arrayed behind them to ensure that the enemy could only attack from a single direction.

As for Umar b. Sa'd, he divided his army into five parts; he placed his right flank under the command of *Amr b. al-Hajjāj al-Zubaydī*, his left under Shimr b. Dhil al-Jawshan, his cavalry under *'Adhra b. Qays al-Aḥmasī*, his footsoldiers under *Shibith b. Rab'ey al-Riyāḥī*, while the centre remained under his command; he gave the battle standard to his servant, Durayd.

Umar b. Sa'd's forces numbered at least thirty thousand, while Hussein's men – even by the most generous of estimates – numbered less than a hundred.

When the two sides prepared for battle, Hussein and his companions ignited the kindling and fuel in the trench they had prepared the night before; this surprised their enemies, who had expected to be able to surround the encampment, attack from all directions and swiftly massacre Hussein and his followers. But when they advanced and saw the fire burning in the trench, they realized that things were not going to be so easy and that their plan had failed.

Shimr bayed at the top of his voice: 'O Hussein! Are you so eager to burn that you could not wait for the Resurrection Day?'

Hussein replied: 'Who speaks? It sounds like Shimr b. Dhil Jawshan?'

His companions said, 'It is he.'

Hussein said: 'Son of a shepherdess! It is better that you should be engulfed by flames!'

Muslim b. 'Awsaja, who had seen Shimr while shooting arrows, turned to Hussein and said: 'O Abu Abdullah! Let me shoot him, for this sinner is a grievous enemy to God and a terrible oppressor, and God has given us an opportunity to rid the world of him!'

But Hussein refused: 'Do not shoot, for I will not be the one who open hostilities.'

Then a companion of Umar b. Sa'd, named *Mālik b. Abu Juwayra al-Mazanī*, approached, and when he saw the roaring flames, he clapped his hands together and called out: 'O Hussein! O companions of Hussein! You are given glad tidings of Hellfire, for you have brought it forth in this world!'

Hussein asked who said these words and was told that it was Ibn Abu Juwayra. He replied: 'O God, throw him into the fire and let him taste its heat in this world!'

When the man heard this, he became angry and wanted to make a show of his bravery, so he spurred his horse and turned it as though he wanted to attack Hussein. But no sooner had he spurred it, than the horse threw him onto his back, his foot still caught in one of its stirrups. The horse galloped with him until it brought him close to the Hellfire and dragged him into it, setting him aflame. Hussein fell down in prostration, then raised his head and said: 'What a supplication, and how quick a response!'

This happened in full view of both sides. When a soldier in the army of Umar b. Sa'd, *Masrūq b. Wā'il* saw what happened to Ibn Abu Juwayra, he knew this was because of Hussein's supplication and began to distance himself from the ranks of the army. When Umar saw this, he asked: 'Why do you shrink from battle?'

'By God, I have seen that which you do not from the people of this household. By God, I will not fight Hussein!' And he withdrew.

A similar fate as that of Ibn Abu Juwayra befell Muhammad b. AshŶath. On the morning of the Tenth, Hussein raised his voice in supplication, saying: 'O God! We are the household of your prophet, his descendants and his nearest and dearest, so break those who have oppressed us and usurped that which is rightfully ours; You are All-hearing, All-responsive.'

When *Muhammad b. Ash'ath* heard this, he called out: 'O Hussein! What nearness do you have to God's Messenger that is for no one else?'

Hussein recited the verses: 'Indeed God chose Adam and Noah, and the progeny of Abraham and the progeny of Imran above all the nations; some of them are descendants of the others, and God is all-hearing, all-knowing.' Then he said: 'By God, my grandfather, Muhammad, is from the progeny of Abraham, and the guiding progeny are from Muhammad's Household!'

Hussein asked his companions: 'Who is that man?'

They told him: '*Muhammad b. Ash'ath b. Qays al-Kindi*.'

Hussein raised his hands to the sky and said: 'O God! *Muhammad b. Ash'ath* claims that there is no nearness between me and Your messenger! O God! Humiliate him this day so that he will never be honoured after it!'

It was not long before *Muhammad b. Ash'ath* was exposed to danger. He had dismounted in order to empty his bowels, when suddenly a black scorpion came and stung him. He fell down while defecating and ended up rolling around in his own excrement. Soldiers looked on while he rolled around, half-naked, because of the scorpion's sting.

While his men were lining up for battle on the morning of *Ashura*, Hussein would switch from supplication to addressing his men, and from addressing his men to supplication. His heart was ever occupied with the remembrance of God and his tongue with the act of thanksgiving; there was not a single moment in which he was not mindful of his Lord, for God was his only goal. Something people heard him say when the horses awoke and he raised his hands in supplication was: 'O God! You are my assurance in every distress and my hope in every difficulty. In all that befalls me, You are my reliance. How many an affliction which cases the heart to weaken, the mind to dull, friends to forsake you and enemies to revile you, have I set down before You and complained about, seeking solace in You rather than anyone else, and You relieved me of it. You are the keeper of every blessing, the master of every good thing, the object of every desire!'

Then he turned to his companions and said: 'Praise God who has made the Hereafter for the godwary, and Hellfire for the faithless. By God, we have surely not sought worldly gain through our actions, such that we would complain. God has decreed that you and I shall be slain this day, so you must be steadfast and fight bravely.

Hussein brought his horse near, mounted it and advanced towards the enemy with a group of his compaions. To *Bureir b. Khuḍayr*, who rode in front of him, he said: 'Speak to them, O Bureir and advise them.' Bureir advanced until he was very close to them; they were ready to attack the camp, sitting on the backs of their horses with their hands resting on the hilts of their words. Bureir called out: 'O you people, beware of God, for indeed the weighty-thing of Muhammad rests upon your backs. Those are his descendants, his family, his daughters and his female relatives. So let us have it! What do you wish to do with them?'

They responded: 'We wish to deliver them to the governor, Ubaydullah b. Ziyad, to do with them as he sees fit.'

'Will you not, then, allow them to return to whence they came?! Woe to you, O people of Kufa! You have forgotten the letters you wrote to him, the promises you gave him from your own selves, which you invoked God to witness, and God suffices as a witness!

Woe to you! You invited the Household of your prophet, claiming that you would give your own lives to protect theirs. But when they came, you surrendered them to Ubaydullah b. Ziyad and barred them from the waters of the Euphrates, which the Jews, Christians and Zoroastrians are free to partake of, and even pigs and dogs can drink! What a terrible thing it is you have done to the descendants of Muhammad!

What is wrong with you? May God not quench your thirst on the Day of Resurrection! You are the worst of people!'

Some of them retorted: 'O man! We don't know what you are talking about!'

'Praise God who has increased my insight with regards to you. O God! I disassociate myself from the actions of these people! O God! Cast their violence amongst themselves, until they meet you while you are wrathful of them!'

Whereat the enemy army began to shoot arrows in his direction, and he returned to Hussein.

Umar b. Sa'd and his soldiers tightened the noose around Hussein and moved closer to the camp. Hussein came out to them on his horse and addressed them loudly so that the whole army could hear his words:

'O people! Listen to my words and do not be hasty, until I have admonished you as is your right over me, and until I have explained myself to you. If you accept my explanation, believe my words and treat me fairly, that will be more felicitous for you, and you will have no excuse for doing violence to me. But if you do not accept my explanation, and will not treat me fairly, 'So conspire together, along with your partners, leaving nothing vague in your plan, then carry it out against me without giving me any respite.' 'My guardian is indeed God who sent down the Book, and He takes care of the righteous."

While Hussein was speaking, his sisters came out of the tents, for they had heard his words. They cried out and wept aloud and his daughters wept aloud, so he sent Abbas and Ali Akbar to them with the instructions: 'Quiet them, for by my life, they will have plenty of time to cry!' And when they had fallen silent, Hussein praised God and magnified Him, then invoked His blessings upon Muhammad, His angels and His prophets.

He spoke in an unparalleled manner, such that amongst the enemy, one man would turn to another and say: 'I have never heard anyone more eloquent in speech than Hussein before him or after him!'

Then he said: 'Inspect my lineage and look at who I am, then refer to your own selves and reproach them; do you think you have the right to kill me and violate my sanctity? Am I not the son of your prophet's daughter? Am I not the son of his legatee, his cousin and the first person to believe in God and accept what God's Messenger brought from his Lord?

Is Hamza, the Master of Martyrs, not my father's uncle?

Is Ja'far, who soars through Paradise upon two wings, not my uncle?

Have you not heard the words of God's Messenger about me and my brother: 'These two are the leaders of the youth of Paradise?' Or his words: 'I am leaving amongst you two weighty things, the Book of God and my descendants of my household, and you will never go astray after me so long as you hold fast to them?

So if you believe what I say, and it is the truth, for by God I have not lied so long as I knew that God hates lying and those who lie, and whoever contrives a lie shall be harmed by it. And if you do not believe me, then amongst you are those who can ask and they will tell you it is true. Ask *Jābir b. Abdullah al-Anṣārī*, *Abu Sa'eed al-Khudrī*, *Sahl b. Sa'd al-Sā'idi*, *Zayd b. Arqam* and *Anas b. Mālik*; they will tell you that they have heard these words from God's Messenger about my brother and me.

Will this not prevent you from shedding my blood?'

At this point Shimr b. Dhil Jawshan interrupted Hussein's, addressing his own men, saying: 'He worships God on a precipice, if I understood what he was saying!'

Habib b. Muẓāhir retorted: 'By God, I think you worship God on seventy precipices! And I bear witness that truly you did not understand what he said, for God has placed a seal upon your heart!'

Hussein continued his address, saying: 'If you are in doubt about this, do you doubt that I am the son of your prophet's daughter? For by God there is no other son of the daughter of the prophet in the East or the West, whether amongst you or anyone else, except me.

Woe to you! Do you seek me because I have killed one of your people, destroyed some of your property, or done some injury to you?'

Everyone remained utterly silent, as if they had birds perched upon their heads. No one spoke up.

So Hussein called out: 'O *Shabath b. Rab'ey*! O *Hajjār b. Abjar*! O *Qays b. al-Ash'ath*, O *Yazid b. al-Harith*! Did you not write to me, telling me to come, saying that the fruit was ripe and the leaves were green? Did you not tell me to come to an army that was ready?'

They said: 'We did not.'

'Glory to God!' Exclaimed Hussein, 'By God, yes you did!'

After a few moments of silence, Hussein continued his address: 'If you dislike me, then let me depart for my place of safety.'

Qays b. al-AshŶath called out: 'Will you not submit to the judgement of your cousins? They will only treat you well and no harm will come to you!'

Hussein replied: 'You are your brother's brother, do you desire that the Hashemites seek you for more than just the blood of Muslim b. Aqeel?

No, by God, I will not give you my hand in submission, nor will I flee like a slave!

Servants of God, I have sought refuge in my Lord and yours lest you make conjectures, and I seek refuge in my Lord and yours from every arrogant wrongdoer who does not believe in the Judgement Day!'

Then he dismounted his horse and ordered *Uqba b. Sam'ān* to tie it.

After Hussein's address, *Rahman Ṣāliḥ* turned to Abdullah b. Muslim and asked: 'I think Hussein still holds out hope that these people will return to their senses, don't you agree?'

Abdullah b. Muslim: Hussein has a message. Just like the prophets, his goal is to guide the people. And I think Hussein will keep trying to guide them for as long as he is able. He does not want them to fight him and enter Hellfire; he wants them to be guided to the right path. Do you not hear Hussein weeping each morning, and Zaynab asking him: 'What has made you weep, O Abu Abdullah?' And he replies: 'I weep for these people who will enter Hellfire on my account.'

Hussein's heart is filled with love for God and His servants; if only one of those soldiers will repent of this deed and go from the side of Ubaydullah b. Ziyad to that of Hussein, he would welcome him with kindness, even if it was Umar b. Sa'd himself, or even Shimr. Just as God keeps open the door of repentance for His servants until their spirit reaches their neck at their time of death, so too does Hussein leave open the door of repentance for his enemies until the last moment.

Hussein has come here only to defend God's *tawhīd* and all of the values, principles and morals that the prophets brought. That is why Hussein advises these people as the prophets advised their own. One of the most important things that he wanted to stress in his sermon was that this universe has a Lord, and that people are servants of their Lord; if they obey Him, this is a grace and a blessing from Him, and if they disobey Him, it is only of their own selves and deeds; and all people are responsible for their own actions. No one can blame his Lord for his own disobedience, nor can he think of his obedience as some favour he is doing for his Lord, because before obedience there is divine assistance, but disobedience's only cause is people's low desires.

Rahman: And what do the Umayyad clan say?

Abdullah: If any of them believe in God and His messenger, they attribute their own acts of disobedience to his Lord, and thinks that all the evil and oppression he commits is God's will. Did you not heard of Hasan and Hussein's letter to *Hasan al-Baṣrī*?

Rahman: No.

Abdullah: 'Hasan al-*Baṣrī* wrote to Hussein asking him about Divine Determination (qadr). Hussein replied to him: 'Whoever does not believe in Divine Determination, both its good and its evil, has disbelieved. But whoever burdens God with human sins, has indeed contrived a grave lie against God. Verily God is not obeyed by force, nor is He sinned against by compulsion, nor does He abandon His servants to destruction. Rather, He is the possessor of all He has endowed them with, the source of their ability to do whatever He allows them to do; if they choose to obey Him, God will not dissuade or detain them from it, and if they choose to disobey Him and He wishes to be kind to them, then He will prevent them from what they have chosen to do. But if He does not do that, then He has not forced them to do it, nor has He burdened them with predestination; He has only made them able to choose, after giving them fair warning and establishing His manifest authority over them, and empowered them to do as He bids them while leaving them able to disobey His commands. Praise God who has empowered His servants to obey Him, but who – through that power – obtain that which He has prohibited, and who excuses those who expose themselves to His punishment. May He accept this praise which I offer, for it is upon that that I go and by that I speak, and His is the praise.'

Rahman: I don't understand some of what you said.

Abdullah: Hussein is saying that the Divine Decree and Determination (*al-qaḍā' wa al-qadr*) are something real, and believing them is a necessary part of the religion. This is because God has not abandoned His creation; rather to Him belong Creation and Command. No one can do as they please if this goes against God's will; matters have not been delegated to mankind in their entirety, for God has power over His servants. And yet this power does not deprive them of free-will, for this is what He wants for them; to be able to do as they please. At the same time, this does not mean that their sins are God's doing, and anyone who claims such a thing is inventing a terrible lie against his Lord. Hussein says: 'But whoever burdens God with human sins, has indeed contrived a grave lie against God... rather, He is the possessor of all He has endowed them with, the source of their ability to do whatever He allows them to do.' So it is God who has given freedom and choice to His servants; He has made them free to do or not do. So human deeds emanate according to the will of God's servants, but the power to act is a gift from God to His servants, which is granted to them in each new moment. So Man's power to choose is not detached or independent from God's will; it is our Lord who grants this power to His servants, and they can do whatever they desire, whether good or evil, or they can choose to not do. Insofar as they are able to do either, the action is attributed to them, whether in obedience or disobedience. But sometimes God restrains His servants from disobedience and this is an act of Divine Grace towards the one whom He restrains. But sometimes God allows His servant to choose as He pleases. So God is free from any association with the deeds of His servants; these deeds are not attributed to Him. But as for the Umayyad clan, they believe in determinism (jabr) rather than free-will (*ikhtiyār*); they do not take a single step except that they attribute it to God.

Hussein wants his enemies to know that they will be held accountable for what they are doing to him, his companions and the people of his Household; they will be questioned about it, and they cannot escape from its consequences tomorrow. He says in one of his poems:

'O worst of people! You have exceeded yourselves in aggression,

And disobeyed the Prophet Muhammad in our regard,

Were you not admonished about us by the Best of all Creation?

Was not my grandfather singled out by God for praise?

Is my mother not Fatima, possessed of illumination?

And my father, Ali, the brother of the best of the human race?

Cursed and abased you are for your acts of abomination

A raging fire shall be your final destination.'

Rahman: What is the duty of the Nation right now towards Hussein?

Abdullah: To protect him! For whoever betrays the grandson of God's Messenger today shall not have the Prophet as his intercessor on the Day of Resurrection. That is the least we can say!

Rahman: Then let us go to the villages nearby and see if we can bring some of the faithful to protect Hussein!

Abdullah: And how many do you think will come?

Rahman: Does it matter? We cannot just sit here waiting for those criminals to attack us and Hussein, so that we can be overwhelmed by sheer numbers...

Abdullah: However men we bring, it will not change the reality on the ground. There are more than thirty thousand soldiers over there!

Rahman: Did you not say that the duty of the Nation is to protect Hussein?

Abdullah: I did.

Rahman: Then let us make them aware of their duty and try to do something, so that we will have at least done our duty... perhaps God will do something after that.

Abdullah: So what do you think we should do? And how will we escape the noose of our enemies?

Rahman: They are occupied by their discussions with Hussein.

Abdullah: And what if they spot us, will they not kill us?

Rahman: I do not think so. They have not been given any orders to attack those who abandon Hussein's army; they only want the head of Hussein, as he himself said not long ago. As for us, they have no interest in us.

Abdullah: Then let us place our trust in God.

So each of them took a sword and snuck out from Hussein's camp. They slipped past the soldiers of Umar b. Sa'd with relative ease, for they had taken a path through the palm trees. They entered the first village they found, about a mile from Karbala, and entered its mosque to perform their prayers. But those praying there recognized them outsiders, for their appearance differed completely from those in the village. The villagers asked what had brought them there, so they told them quite openly why they had come. But the villagers suspected them of being spies sent by Ibn Ziyad, trying to find out their position with regards to Hussein, so they detained them and took them to the head of Ibn Ziyad's police force, Hasseen b. Numayr, who in turn sent them to Kufa, where they were imprisoned and their story comes to an end.

Hussein mounted his horse again and approached the enemy lines. Having opened the Qur'an and placed it above his head; he asked them to heed his words, but they refused. He said to them: 'Woe to you! You do not have to heed my advice, but at least hear my words, for I only call you to the path of right-guidance, so whoever obeys me shall be guided, and whoever disobeys me shall perish.

All of you have disobeyed my command and refused to listen to my words, you have been bribed with abundant gifts and your stomachs have been filled by illicit gains, so a seal has been set on your hearts. Woe to you! Will you not heed? Will you not listen?'

So the soldiers of Umar b. Sa'd began to reproach one another and said: 'Let him speak!' Then they fell silent and listened.

Hussein stood before them, praised and magnified God, then invoked His blessings upon Muhammad, upon the angels and the prophets and messengers altogether. Then he said: 'O people, between me and you is the Book of God and the Sunna of my grandfather, God's Messenger.'

Then he asked them to bear witness to who he was, and his parents, his grandfather and grandmother and told them that he was carrying the sword of the Prophet, and wearing his armour and turban. Then he asked them: 'So what is it that has brought you forth to kill me and shed my blood?'

They said: 'We know all this already, but we will not leave you until you die thirsty.'

'Wretched and accursed be you! Were you out of your minds when you called for our help, so that when we rushed to your aid in earnest you brought down the swords you hand promised us on our necks, and set us ablaze with a fire we had kindled for our enemies and yours? Did you do that so to become an asset for your enemies against your friends, and a means against them for your enemies, without the latter treating you justly, but merely granting you illicit worldly gains? Would you harm us in return for a miserable life, while we have done nothing to you, nor expressed any displeasure with you?

May you have woe upon woe! You brought us here and abandoned us! The sword was set aside and the heart was at rest, but without consideration you formed an opinion and swarmed upon it like locusts until you covered it like a carpet. Then you broke your word, so may you be wiped out, O slaves of the Nation, O dividers into parties, O renouncers of letters written, O twisters of words, O confederacy of sinners, O spittle of Satan, O extinguishers of good practice, O murderers of the children of prophets, O destroyers of the progeny of legatees, O slanderers of noble lineage, O persecutors of the faithful, O you who call on the Imams in jest, O you who have divided the Qur'an into pieces! Foul is that which they have sent ahead for themselves, and in punishment they shall dwell forever.

Will you then follow the son of Harb and betray us?

Yes, by God, you are a people well known for treachery; your roots have been nourished by it and your branches have been wrapped in it; your hearts have grown accustomed to it and your breasts have been enveloped by it; you are the foulest fruit in appearance to the onlooker, and in taste to the one who takes it. Lo! God's curse is upon the recalcitrant, who break their oaths after affirming them, and you have made God a burden upon yourselves, so by God you are they!'

Then he said: 'Lo! The bastard son of a bastard has given us the choice between death and humiliation, and we will never accept humiliation! God rejects, as does His messenger and the faithful, and stone-lands good and purified, protected mountain spurs, and lofty souls, that we should prefer obedience to tyrants over a noble and bloody death.

Lo! I have given you fair warning! Lo! I shall not desist, though my men are few, my enemies are many, and my helpers have betrayed me.'

He continued: 'I swear by God, you will not remain more than a horses gallop until it turns on you like the turning of a quern, and spins you like the spinning of its axle. A promise given to me by my father from my grandfather. So prepare yourselves and your partners, and do not let your affair distress you, then do your worst to me without granting any respite, for I have placed my trust in God, my Lord and yours. There is no beast save that He will seize it by its forelock, verily my Lord is upon the Right Path.'

Then he raised his hands to the heavens and said: 'O God deny them the rain of the heavens, give them years like the years of Joseph, and place the slave of Thaqif in authority over them that he might quench them with a bitter draught. For they have lied to us and betrayed us, and You are our Lord; we have placed our trust in You and turned to You, and to You is the return.'

Hussein left no moment on the day of *Ashura* save that he made some use of it; he addressed his own companions and his enemies time and again, in which he mentioned the values and principles contained in the messages of the prophets and legatees from before him. One such address was a short sermon in which he mentioned everything connecting to this world and the Hereafter, which he directed to the army of Umar b. Sa'd. So after praising and magnifying God, he said:

'O servants of God! Beware of God and be on guard in this world, for verily if this world remained constant for anyone, or if anyone would have remained in it, then the prophets would have been more deserving of its constancy, more entitled to satisfaction therein, and more satisfied with the Divine Decree in its regard. But God has made this world as a trial, and made its inhabitants to pass away; whatever is new will wear out, whatever is pleasant will fade, whatever is joyous will darken; this world is but a mountainside at whose summit rests the citadel of the Hereafter. So gather provisions and the best provision is godwariness (*taqwā*), and be wary of God, that you might prosper.'

When Hussein finished his speech and wanted to return to the tents, some of Umar b. Sa'd's men began to shoot arrows and javelins in his direction. One of them, called *Umar al-Tahawī*, of the *Tamīm* tribe, struck Hussein with an arrow between his soldiers, which stuck in his robes.

This was their response to a sermon which contained prophetic illuminations and admonitions, such as advising them to godwariness and calling them to God and goodness, and being aware of the consequences of their actions in this life, especially when these were connected to justice and oppression.

And just as Hussein gave many sermons admonishing his enemies, his companions also went forth to admonish the army of the Umayyad clan.

Zuhayr b. al-Qayn rode out on an armoured horse, bristling with weapons, and faced the army of Umar b. Sa'd. He raised his voice: 'O people of Kufa! Beware of God's punishment! Beware!

Each Muslim is obliged to advise his believing brothers, and we are still brothers, following one religion and belonging to a single community, so long as no blood has been shed. You deserve our advice, but if we fight, then there is no protection for either of us; you are one people and we are another.

Allah has tested us and you through the progeny of His prophet, Muhammad, to see what we will do and what you will do. We call upon you to assist them and forsake the tyrants, Ubaydullah b. Ziyad and Yazid b. Muawiya, for you have known nothing from them except evil throughout their reign. They gouge out your eyes, cut off your hands and feet, make exemplary punishments of you and crucify you on the trunks of palm trees. They kill your best and brightest, like *Hujr b. 'Adī* and his companions, *Hani b. 'Urwa* and others like them.'

The army of Umar b. Sa'd began to revile him and praise Ubaydullah b. Ziyad. They began to call out: 'By God, we will not rest until we slay your master and everyone with him, or deliver him and his companions to the governor!'

Zuhayr told them: 'Servants of God! The son of Fatima is more deserving of your affection and assistance than the son of Sumayya! If you do not help him, then I seek refuge for you in God lest you slay him, so let him do as he wishes!'

Shimr b. Dhil Jawshan shot an arrow at him, shouting: 'Shut up! May God shut you up! We are sick of your prattle!'

Zuhayr retorted: 'O son of a man who urinates on his own heels, I was not addressing you, for you are a beast. By God I doubt you know more than two verses of God's Book, so have glad tidings of humiliation on the Day of Resurrection and a painful punishment!'

Shimr said: 'Allah shall see you and your master dead shortly!'

Zuhayr replied: 'Is it with death you think to frighten me? By God, death with Hussein is dearer to me than eternal life with the likes of you!'

Then Zuhayr turned to the people and said: 'O servants of God! Do not let this vile man or the like of him tempt you away from your religion! By God, those who shed the blood of Muhammad's household and his descendants, slay those who help them and assail his womenfolk will not receive his intercession!'

Then a man called from behind him: 'Abu Abdullah sends for you, for by my life if there was a believer like that of Pharaoh's family amongst them, he would have advised his people and done everything he could to guide them. You have advised them as much as you can.'

Hussein came out of his tent, approached the enemy lines and called out: 'Where is Umar b. Sa'd? Call him here for me.'

Umar b. Sa'd did not want to come out to meet him, nor did he want Hussein to come to him, but he had no choice at the insistence of his men. When he came out, Hussein addressed him: 'O Umar, if you kill me, do you claim that the bastard son of a bastard will make you governor of Rayy and Jurjan?

By God, you will never get the chance to enjoy it – a divine promise. So do whatever you will, for you shall neither be pleased with this world after me, nor the Hereafter. It is as though I see your head on a spike in *Kufā*, the children pelting it with stones.'

Whereat Umar b. Sa'd became angry, turned away and returned to his tent.

As the thirst of Hussein and his companions increased, they tried to dig wells, but they could not reach water. It is narrated that when his thirst became intense, Hussein said to his brother, Abbas: 'Gather your household and dig a well.' They do as they were asked and found rocks, then they dug another and found more of the same.

Umar b. Sa'd's soldiers continued to tighten their lines around Hussein's camp hour after hour. When *Hurr b. Yazid al-Riyāḥī* saw that the army were determined to kill the Prophet's Household, his own conscience reproached him for his role in this; how he had prevented them from returning to Medina or going to Kufa. He came to Umar b. Sa'd and said: 'O Umar, will you really fight him?'

Umar b. Sa'd replied: 'Yes, and a bloody battle it will be too; the least of it will be cutting off heads and hands.'

'Why wouldn't you accept any of the options he gave you?'

'If it was up to me, I would. But your governor has refused.'

Hurr went quiet and left Umar b. Sa'd, withdrawing a little way from his own companions. One of his men, Qurra b. Qays stood beside him. He said: 'Qurra, have you watered your horse today?'

Qurra said: 'No.'

'Don't you think you should give it some water?'

Qurra thought Hurr was only planning to leave the army so as to avoid the battle, and that perhaps he did not anyone to see him. So he told Hurr: 'I haven't watered him, but I think I will go and water him now.'

Then Qurra withdrew from his position, and Hurr began to approach Hussein slowly, whereat *Muhājir b. Aws* saw him and called out: 'What are you planning to do, Hurr? Are you going to attack?'

But Hurr did not answer him, he only began to tremble and shake. *Muhājir* asked him: 'What's the matter with you? By God I have never seen you like this! If anyone asked me who the bravest man in Kufa was, I would have thought it was you. So what is this I now see?'

'By God, I see myself given the choice between Heaven and Hell.' Then he fell silent for a minute and said: 'And, by God, I will not choose anything above Heaven, even if it means I will be cut into pieces and burned.'

Then he struck his horse and began to ride towards the camp of Hussein. And as he approached the camp of Hussein he placed his hand on his head and said: 'O God, to you I turn penitently, so turn to me with forgiveness! For I have put fear in the hearts of Your friends and the children of Your prophet's daughter!'

He approached, with his head lowered, ashamed before his Lord. He stood quietly before Hussein, who asked him: 'Who are you?'

Hurr said: 'May I be your sacrifice, O son of God's Messenger, I am the one who prevented you from going back, diverted you from the main road, and detained you in this place! I did not think that they would refuse the offers you made to them, or that matters would come to this. By God, if I knew that they would do to you what I think they are about to do, I would have done things differently. I repent to God for what I have done – do you think there is any repentance for it?'

Hussein replied: 'Yes, God will forgive you. So get off your horse.'

Hurr said: 'I promise you will have no horsemen or foot soldier better than I. I will fight them for you from my horse until I meet my end!

O son of God's Messenger! I was the first to come out against you, so let me be the first to be slain for your sake, for I must be one of those who greet your grandfather, Muhammad, tomorrow on the Judgement Day.'

Hussein told him: 'May God have mercy on you, do whatever seems appropriate to you.'

Then Hurr told Hussein of his story from when he left Kufa. He said: 'When Ubaydullah dispatched me to intercept you, I left the governor's palace and someone called out behind me: 'Good tidings await you, Hurr!' I turned, but no one was there.

I asked myself: 'What are these good tidings when I am going to Hussein, and I did not plan on following you!"

Hussein told him: 'You have attained goodness and a reward!'

It appears that Hurr was not alone when he came to Hussein; his son had accompanied him too, and he had told him before he rode to Hussein's side: 'Hussein is calling for help, but no one will help him. Do you not think we should fight for him and give our lives for his cause? For we cannot endure Hellfire and I do not want our accuser on the Judgement Day to be Muhammad, God's chosen prophet!'

His son told him: 'By God, I will follow you.'

And after he had joined Hussein's side, Hurr felt his faith renewed and he wanted to save his people from their error and guide them to the truth as he was guided. So he asked Hussein for permission to address them. So he approached them and raised his voice:

'O people of Kufa! Your mothers shall suffer loss and tears!

I call you to follow this righteous servant of God, who you promised to protect with your lives but when he came to you, you abandoned him and turned against him, detained him, oppressed him, surrounded him from every side, prevented him from travelling in God's broad earth and made him like a prisoner in your grip, unable to avail or protect himself, and you denied him, his womenfolk, his children and his household access to the waters of the Euphrates, which are drunk by the Jews, Christians and Zoroastrians, and in which wallow the pigs and dogs of the fertile lands. And you will keep them in this state until you kill them or they die of thirst! Wicked is your treatment of Muhammad's descendants after him, may God not quench your thirst on the Hot Day.'

Then he fell silent for a moment, before saying: 'If you will not help him and fulfill your oaths to him, then let him go wherever he wishes in God's land. Do you not have faith in God and affirm the prophethood of Hussein's grandfather, Muhammad? Do you not believe in the Resurrection?'

But these admonitions were of no avail, for his people had ears with which they could not hear, eyes with which they could not see and hearts with which they could not comprehend. They were like cattle, or even more astray.

THE BATTLE

Battle began on the morning of *Ashura* when Umar b. Sa'd approached Hussein's camp and told his servant, Durayd: 'Lower your banner.' Durayd did so and he notched an arrow in his bow, shooting it towards Hussein. He said: 'Bear witness to the governor that I was the first to shoot.'

The arrow landed in front of Hussein. He stepped aside and withdrew.

One of Hussein's companions retorted: 'I bear witness that you shall be the first of this Nation to enter Hell!'

With Umar b. Sa'd's shot, the entire Umayyad army began to shoot arrows at the camp. They came like rain, and every single one of Hussein's men was struck.

Hussein told his companions: 'May God have mercy on you, go forth to a death from which there is no escape, for these arrows are the messengers of those people to you.'

When Hussein saw so many of his men cut down, he struck his hand upon his beard and said: 'Allah's anger was severe with the Jews when they ascribed a son to Him; His anger was severe with the Christians when they made Him a trinity of three; His anger was severe with the Magians when they worshipped the Sun and the Moon instead of Him; and His anger is severe with a people who have resolved to murder the son of their prophet's daughter. But by God I shall not grant them anything they want, even if I have to meet God drenched in my own blood.'

Then he called out: 'Is there anyone who will come to our aid? Is there anyone who will protect the dignity of God's Messenger?'

Whereat the women wept and raised their voices in lamentation.

Amongst the companions of Umar b. Sa'd were two members of the *Anṣār*; Sa'd b. al-Harith and his brother Abu al-Hutoof. When they heard Hussein's call for assistance and the weeping of his women and children, they drew their swords and turned them on their comrades, fighting to protect Hussein, killing three men before they themselves were slain.

After both sides had withdrawn to their camps, lesser confrontations began between individuals and small groups. *Yassār*, the servant of Ziyad b. Abeeh came out with *Sālim*, the servant of Ubaydullah b. Ziyad, from Umar b. Sa'd's tents looking for a fight. They made for *Habib b. Muẓāhir al-Asadi* and *Bureir b. Khuḍayr*.

But Hussein told them: 'Hold back.' And did not permit them to go and fight.

Abdullah b. Umayr of the *Banū 'Ulaym*, a man who lived in the hinterland of Kufa came out. When he had seen people getting read to go out and kill Hussein, he said: 'By God I used to fight the idol-worshippers enthusiastically!' So he joined Hussein's caravan, and when Hussein looked at him and saw that he was of tall stature, with powerful forearms and broad shoulders, he permitted him to go and face the two of them, saying: 'I think he may slay entire generations of men!' So he went out and Yassar asked him: 'Who are you?'

When *Abdullah b. Umayr* told him, *Yassār* replied: 'We don't know you. We want *Zuhayr b. Qayn and Habib b. Muzāhir*!'

'You think you have a choice? No one will come out from our side save that he is better than you!'

Then he attacked *Yassār*, striking him with his sword until he was dead. But while he was occupied, *Sālim* attacked him, calling out: 'The slave has surpassed you!' But Abdullah paid no attention to him until he was upon him. *Sālim* struck out with his sword, but Abdullah parried with his left hand, losing some fingers. Then he turned on him and struck him dead.

Abdullah went forth, having slain both men, reciting the poetry:

'If you don't know who I am, I am a son of Kalb
enough for me is my house in *'Ulaym*, enough!
I am a man of power and muscle!
I do not tire in distress!'

He did not return to the camp, but stayed behind to taunt the enemy and fight anyone who would come out to meet him. While this was going on, his wife, who had come out to see the battlefield, took up a tent pole and shouted: 'May my mother and father be your sacrifice! Fight to protect these good people, the descendants of Muhammad!'

Abdullah tried to send her back to the camp, but she refused, saying: 'I will not leave you until I die with you!'

Hussein called out to her: 'May the Prophet's Household grant you good, come back to the tents, may God have mercy on you! *Jihād* is not a duty upon women!'

Her husband kept fighting until he was slain.

When he was slain, *Hurr b. Yazid al-Riyāḥī* turned to his son who had come to Hussein's camp with him and said: 'Attack these wrongdoers, my son!' So the boy went out to the battle field and kept fighting until he was slain.

And when his father saw him cut down, he said: 'Praise be to God who blessed you with martyrdom protecting the son of the prophet's daughter!'

Then *Abul-Sha'thā', Yazid b. Ziyad b. al-Muhāṣir al-Kindi* sought Hussein's permission to shoot his arrows, which the latter granted.

Previously, *Abul-Sha'thā'* had been a soldier in Umar b. Sa'd's army, but when they had rejected Hussein's offers to avoid bloodshed, he came over to Hussein's side.

Now he stood in front of Hussein and shot arrows towards the enemy. With every shot, Hussein said: 'O God! Make his arrows strike true, and let his reward be Paradise!' And when he had exhausted his arrows, he charged into the fray, reciting the poetry:

'I am Yazid and *Abul-Muhāṣir*
braver than a lion ready to pounce
O Lord! I am a helper of Hussein
and of Ibn Sa'd a deserter and forsaker.'

And he kept fighting until he was slain.

The battle continued between the two sides in fits and starts. Groups of Umar b. Sa'd's soldiers would sometimes attack from the flanks, only to be repelled by those of Hussein, and sometimes the fighting took the form of single combats.

Amr b. al-Hajjāj al-Zubaydī, who had Umar b. Sa'd's right flank had launched an attack against Hussein's men. But when he and his men approached, Hussein's companions went down on their knees and thrust their spears upwards, so the horses would not charge and shied away, then Hussein's companions rained arrows upon them, killing some and wounding others.

Shimr b. Dhil al-Jawshan also attacked the Imam's left flank, only to be greeted by the spears of Hussein's companions. As had happened on the right flank, their horses also shied away and many of them were killed and wounded by arrows.

Bureir b. Khuḍayr, one of Hussein's companions, came out to fight, reciting the poetry:

'I am Bureir and the youth of *Khuḍayr*
I shall strike at you and see no harm
That our goodness be known to the righteous
such is the good deed of one who is pious (*barīr*)'

Bureir was one of God's righteous servants; he fought fiercely, calling out: 'Come here, O you who would murder the faithful! Come here, O you who would murder the sons of Badr's veterans! Come here, O you who would murder the family of the best of messengers!'

A man called *Yazid b. Mu'qal* came out to meet him and said: 'O Bureir! What do you think God has done with you?'

Bureir replied: 'He has done good to me, and evil to you!'

'Liar! You were once an honest man! Do you not remember when we travelled together through the lands of the *Banū Lūdhān* and you told me: 'Uthman b. Affan was immoderate towards himself, Muawiya b. Abu Sufiyan is astray and leads others astray, but the Imam of guidance and truth is Ali b. Abu Talib?'

'I bear witness that those are my views and my words.'

'And I bear witness that you are astray!'

'Then let us perform *mubāhila* and ask God to curse the liar and slay the one who follows falsehood!'

The man accepted, and they invoked God to curse the liar and let the one who follows truth slay the one who follows falsehood. Then they fought and exchanged blows; *Yazid b. Mu'qal* struck Bureir with his sword but it did no harm, but Bureir's strike split Yazid's head in two, and Yazid fell down with the blade still lodged in his skull.

But while Bureir was occupied with Yazid, *Raḍī b. Munqad al-Abdī* leapt upon him and the two grappled. Bureir was able to throw him to the ground and sit upon his chest. But one of *Raḍī's* comrades, *Ka'b b. Jābir al-Azadī* came to his aid with a spear and buried its point in Bureir's back. When Bureir felt this, he got off RaÃĐ's chest, having wounded him severely. But he was weakened and fell to the ground, then Ka'b came to him and struck him with his sword until he killed him.

Later, when Bureir's killer returned home, his wife told him: 'You went against the son of Fatima and killed Bureir, the foremost of the Quran reciters. I shall never speak to you again!'

And when Bureir's killer met his cousin, the latter told him: 'Woe to you, Ka'b! Did you kill *Bureir b. Khuḍayr*? In what condition do you expect to meet your Lord on the next day!?'

Whereat Ka'b felt ashamed, but like all wrongdoers he placed the blame upon his Lord, saying:

'Had my Lord wished, I would not have been there to fight
nor would He have blessed the son of a tyrant
That was truly a shameful and ignoble day
reviled by people in their gatherings
O if only I had been a handful of dust
and on the day of Hussein in the grave buried
O woe, what shall I tell my Maker?
What is my excuse on the Day of Accounting?'

And this is the meaning of God's words: 'The polytheists will say,

'Had God wished we would not have ascribed any partner [to Him], nor our fathers, nor would we have forbidden anything."

After Bureir, *Hurr b. Yazid al-Riyāḥī* went out to do battle after seeking Hussein's permission.

Hurr was a man renowned for his bravery; he could face entire armies without fear, never mind individuals. It is hardly surprising, then, that he cut down every challenger, even while he bled from every limb and his horse had been struck on all sides. Hasseen b. Numayr told Yazid b. Sufiyan: 'This is Hurr, who you were hoping to kill!'

Yazid b. Sufiyan said: 'Yes!' And he went out to face him. He told Hurr: 'Do you agree to duel?'

Hurr replied in the affirmative, so the two fought and in no time at all, Hurr had dispatched him, as though his life was but a thing in Hurr's hand.

Thereafter the Kufans were wary of him; no one else would challenge him. So he raised his voice: 'O enemies of God and enemies of His messenger! You wrote to Hussein and promised to help him, but when he came to you pounced to kill him and deceived him? God will not grant you the intercession of His grandfather on the Day of Resurrection!'

Then he charged at them, reciting the poetry:

'I would be a treacherous leader and a traitor's son
had I fought Hussein, son of Fatima
With my heart set on betraying and abandoning him
while holding to the allegiance of this damned oathbreaker
So woe to me should I not come to his aid
against every heart that does not feel regret

Then he threw himself into the midst of the enemy and laid into them with his sword, slaying more than forty men.

Then he returned to Hussein's encampment, reciting the poetry:

'It is death, so do and let whatever you do be
You are no doubt sipping at death's cup
Whilst defending the son of *Muṣṭafā* and his household
Perhaps you shall attain the harvest of what you have sown
Ruined are a people who disobey God, their Lord
Seeking to ruin the religion, and the religion is a path
Intentionally seeking to murder Muhammad's household
While their grandfather on the Resurrection Day shall intercede.'

Hurr remained in the camp, tending to his wounds.

While the battle between Hussein's followers and their enemies continued, the mother of *Wahab b. Abdullah b. Junāb al-Kalbī*, who was a Christian who had converted to Islam at Hussein's hand only seventeen days before *Ashura*, came to her son and said: 'Get up, my son, and help the son of the daughter of God's Messenger!'

He replied: 'I shall do my utmost, God willing.'

Then he went out, reciting:

'If you not know me, then I am a son of Kalb
you shall see me and see my striking
And my charge and gallantry in battle
you shall know my rage after the rage of my comrades
And resist grief on a day of grief
and my fighting in battle is no game.'

He kept on fighting them, seeking death while protecting the truth until he had slain a multitude of the enemy. Then he returned to his mother, with whom was his wife, and stood in front of them, saying: 'O mother, are you proud of me?'

She said, 'No, by God, I am not proud. Not until you are slain protecting the son of the daughter of God's Messenger!'

So when he made to return to the battle, his wife clung to him, saying: 'By God, I ask you not to torment me with yourself!'

They had been married only ten days prior.

His mother told him: 'Pay her no mind, go and fight in front of the son of the daughter of God's Messenger that you may obtain the intercession of His grandfather on the Day of Resurrection!'

So he went forth, reciting:

'I guarantee you, O mother of Wahab
with the thrust of my spear and the strike of my sword
A faithful lad strikes with the Lord's power
that a wicked people may taste the bitterness of war!'

He fought on until his right hand was cut off, but he paid it no mind. He kept fighting until his left was severed too. And while he was like that, he heard his wife calling out behind him – having taken up a tent pole – : 'O Wahb! May my mother and father be your sacrifice! Keep fighting for the good people, the family of God's Messenger!'

He turned to her and said: 'One minute you tell me not to fight, the next minute you cheer me on!'

She said, 'O Wahb! I have put aside this life and given up this world since I heard the call of Hussein: 'O woe! We are alone! O woe! How few helpers we have! Is there no one to protect us? Is there no one who will shelter us?'

Wahb returned her to the camp, then went back to fight until he was slain.

When his wife saw him struck down, she ran to him and sat by his body, wiping the blood and dust from his face. Shimr b. Dhil al-Jawshan saw this and sent a slave called Rustam after her, he struck her with a tent pole and beat her to death on the body of her husband.

She was the first female companion of Hussein to be slain.

But as if this was not bad enough, the soldiers of Ibn Sa'd cut off Wahb's head and threw it to his mother, who was standing at the entrance to the encampment. She picked up the head, kissed it and wiped the blood from it. She told it: 'Paradise is yours!'

Then she took up a tent pole and attacked the enemies, killing two men. Hussein came to her and said: 'O Umm Wahb, come back, for women are excused from *Jihād*!'

She came back, saying: 'My God, do not cut off my hope!'

Hussein said: 'Allah will never cut off your hope, Umm Wahb! You and your son will be with God's Messenger and his descendants in Paradise!'

This is how Imam Hussein's companions went out one after another to defend truth, justice and faith; each one of them displayed his full awareness of this in the verses of poetry he would recite while fighting. These same verses also displayed their nobility, loyalty and determination to fight unto death.

Amr b. Qaḍa al-Anṣārī came out fighting in front of Hussein, reciting the verses:

'The *Anṣār* battalion surely knew
that I will protect the sacred ground
With the striking of a righteous youth
before Hussein; my lifeblood, my abode'

This man was one of those who at some points stood in front of Hussein to protect him from arrows and attacks with his hand and his very life.

As he fought, he was able to fell a number of men and wound others before he was slain.

One of his brothers, *Ali b. Qarḍa*, was in the army of Umar b. Sa'd. He called out: 'O Hussein! You led my brother astray and deceived him until you killed him!'

Hussein responded: 'Allah did not lead your brother astray. Rather he guided him and misguided you!'

'May God kill me if I do not kill you or die trying!' So he made for Hussein, but *Nāfi' b. Hilāl* blocked his path, before stabbing him and bringing him down. But he was not slain; his comrades fought off *Nāfi'* and saved *Ali b. Qarḍa*.

Another one of these men endowed with insight, who fought with such rare bravery at Hussein's side until they were slain, was *Nāfi' b. Hilāl al-Jamalī*. He had gone into battle reciting:

'I am *Hilāl al-Jamalī*
I follow the religion of *Ali*
I shall strike you with my blade
He was slain after a fierce fight with the enemy.

It is truly amazing that Hussein and his companions became more radiant and more at peace as their situation became more dire, until even their enemies were saying: 'Look! These people don't care about death!'

Hussein had told them: 'Patience, noble sons, for death is but a bridge that will take you from difficulties and hardships to gardens broad, beautiful and everlasting! Which of you would dislike moving from a prison to a palace? For your enemies, it will be just like one who moves from a palace to a prison where they will be punished!'

He added: 'My father related to me from God's Messenger that this world is the believer's prison and the disbeliever's paradise, and that paradise is a bridge for the former – the believers – to their paradises, and a bridge for the latter – the disbelievers – to Hellfire. I do not lie, nor have I been lied to.'

The truth is that Hussein's companions were some of the bravest individuals that mankind has ever known, as one poet says:

'A people, if they are called to repel a calamity
and horsemen between a rock and a hard place
Wear their hearts as armour as though
they are protecting treasures most precious.'

One of Umar b. Sa'd's soldiers described their bravery of Hussein's companions as follows: 'A band of men fell upon us with hands upon their swords like ferocious lions. They scattered our horsemen left and right; threw themselves towards death, rejected all offers of safety, with no desire for wealth. Nothing could stand between them and death. Had we only continued fighting single combat with them, they would have wiped us out entirely!'

That Hussein's tiny band of companions were able to inflict such heavy losses on the Kufans, to the extent that, had single combat continued, they would have certainly defeated them, is due to their high morale and the fact that they were people seeking martyrdom, in that there was nothing that could stand before their swords.

Muslim b. 'Awsaja came out, reciting the poetry:

'If you ask about me, I am a lion
from a branch of the tribe of Asad
Whoever aggresses against us has no sense
and has disbelieved in the religion of the Almighty'

He slew whoever came out to face him, and when the enemy commanders saw that no one could bring him down, *Amr b. al-Hajjāj* called out to his troops: 'Don't you know who you are fighting? These are the elite warriors of the city, men of insight, people seeking death! Anyone who goes out to fight them will be slain, despite their small numbers. But, by God, if you would only throw stones at them, you would have already killed them!'

Umar b. Sa'd said: 'True. Yours is the sound opinion. Send word that no one should engage in single combat from now on.'

Amr b. al-Hajjāj launched an attack on Hussein's right flank, but the men there held firm and met his cavalry with spears raised, driving them back. The cavalry retreated, pursued by Hussein's men. But this caused a break in their ranks, so *Amr b. al-Hajjāj* called out: 'Kill those who have renounced the religion and divided the communited!'

Hussein called back: 'Woe to you, O *Ibn al-Hajjāj*! Do you incite people against me? Have we renounced the religion while you remain upon it! When our souls leave our bodies you shall know that you will be the first to reach Hellfire!'

Amr b. al-Hajjāj came again, this time from the direction of the Euphrates, to attack the camp. One of those they encountered was *Muslim b. 'Awsaja. Muslim b. Abdullah al-Ḍubābī* attacked him, assisted by *Abdullah b. Khashkāra al-Bajalī*. The fierce fighting kicked up a great cloud of dust. And as it cleared, *Muslim b. 'Awsaja* could be seen fallen, drawing his last breaths. Hussein and *Habib b. Muẓāhir* went to him and Hussein said: 'Allah have mercy on you, O Muslim! Among the faithful are men who fulfil what they have pledged to God. Of them are some who have fulfilled their pledge, and of them are some who still wait, and they have not changed in the least.'

Habib b. Muẓāhir knelt close to Muslim as he lay on the ground, and said: 'Your death is difficult for me to bear, O Muslim! Be gladdened with news of Paradise.'

Muslim replied weakly: 'May God give you glad tidings of good.'

'If I did not know that I will soon be following you, I would have liked you to make your final bequest to me.'

Muslim said, pointing to Hussein with his finger: 'I bequeath to you this one. Make sure you die protecting him.'

'I will, by the Lord of the Ka'ba!'

Then *Muslim b. 'Awsaja* breathed his last.

And when one of Muslims servant girls heard that her master had died, she called out: 'Woe, Muslim! Woe, my master! Woe, sons of Awsaja!'

But the companions of Umar b. Sa'd called out, cheerfully: 'We have slain Muslim!'

Shibath b. Rab'ey, one of the leaders of Ibn Ziyad's army, said to them: 'May your mothers be deprived of you! Do you take pleasure in killing the likes of *Muslim b. 'Awsaja*?! By my Lord, he has a noble position amongst the Muslims. I was with him at the battle for Azerbaijan and he killed six of the enemy before the Muslim cavalry had closed in!'

Once most of Hussein's companions had been slain, Umar b. Sa'd ordered his left and right flanks to attack Hussein's camp. As for Hussein's companions, they came out one or two at a time, fought and were slain. This eventually took its toll on their numbers because they were so few. While the soldiers of Ibn Sa'd numbered in their thousands, so their casualties were not as noticeable.

Then Umar b. Sa'd gave the orders to set fire to Hussein's tents and destroy the encampment so that his soldiers could attack from every direction. Shimr b. Dhil al-Jawshan attacked with a group of his men from one side, and *Amr b. al-Hajjāj al-Zubaydī* attacked from the other. Hussein's remaining companions were forced to divide themselves into groups of three and four to protect the tents. Whenever one of enemies approached, Hussein's men would attack them while they were trying to pull down the tents, so they would kill him or drive him off.

Shimr was one of the first to reach the tents and was able to pierce Hussein's tent with his spear and call out: 'Give me some fire so I can burn this down on top of their heads!' The daughters of God's Messenger cried out and fled the tent.

Hussein called out: 'Woe to you! Do you call for fire to burn down my house upon its people?'

Shibath b. Rab'ey said to Shimr: 'Are you a terrorizer of women now? Glory to God! I have never heard anything more foul than what you just said, nor seen any stance more evil than yours!'

Whereat Shimr felt ashamed in front of his comrade. Zuhayr b. al-Qayn and a group of Hussein's men came after him, driving him and his companions away from the tents.

Hussein's prayer

As the time for prayer approached, *Abu Thumāma al-Ṣaydāwī* saw the Sun pass its zenith. He said to Hussein: 'O Abu Abdullah, my life for you, I see the enemy closing in, but I will not let them reach you without killing me first! But I would like to meet God having offered one final prayer with you since its time approaches.'

Hussein looked to the sky and said: 'You remembered the prayer, may God count you amongst those who pray and remember. Yes, its time has just commenced.'

He said to his companions: 'Ask them to give us time for prayer!'

But when they did so, Hasseen b. Numayr called out to Hussein: 'Your prayer will not be accepted, even if we do!'

Habib b. Muẓāhir retorted: 'What!? You think God will not accept the prayer of the family of God's Messenger, but he will accept that of a donkey like you!?'

Hasseen flew into a rage and attacked *Habib b. Muẓāhir*, but Habib struck his horses face with his sword, so the horse reared up and threw Hasseen to the ground. But his companions came rushing to his aid and rescued him.

Then Umar b. Sa'd's men attacked Habib, who launched himself into battle, reciting:

'I am Habib, my father is *Muẓāhir*
a gallant warrior and fierce fighter
You have amassed a multitude and more
but righteousness is plainly ours
Yours is treachery when you need be loyal
but we are more worthy than you and more steadfast

Closer to the truth and absolved from guilt too!'

He fought a group of Umar b. Sa'd's soldiers; one of them from the tribe of TamÐm attacked him and pierced him with his spear. As Habib was getting up, Hasseen b. Numayr struck him on his head with a sword, and he fell down. The man from TamÐm came and cut off his head. His death grieved Hussein greatly, who said: 'To God I give myself and my loyal companions.'

Then Hussein pointed to him, saying: 'May God have mercy upon you, O Habib! You would recite the entire Quran in a night; you are certainly virtuous!'

Habib was the first to give his life for the performance of prayer on the day of *Ashura*.

After *Habib b. Muẓāhir* had been slain, Hussein stood for prayer. In front of him stood *Zuhayr b. al-Qayn* and *Sa'eed b. Abdullah al-Hanafī*. Most of Hussein's companions had, by this point, been slain, and only a few now remained. Hussein led them in congregation in the manner of the fear-prayer (*ṣalāt al-khawf*).

While Hussein stood in prayer, the enemies made to attack him. They began to shoot arrows at him. But whenever an arrow came in his direction, *Sa'eed b. Abdullah al-Hanafī* blocked it with his own body to prevent it striking Hussein. They kept shooting until Hussein had finished his prayers, by which time Sa'eed had been pierced by many arrows. He fell to the ground and said: 'O God! Curse them as you cursed *'Ād* and *Thamūd*! O God give your prophet my salutations, and tell him of the pain and wounds I have received, for I endured these in order to help the descendants of your prophet!'

He turned to Hussein and said: 'Have I fulfilled my pledge, O son of God's Messenger?'

Hussein replied: 'Yes, you will stand before me in Paradise.'

Sa'eed died with thirteen arrows sticking in him, not to mention the wounds he had sustained from sword and lance.

With his prayers complete, Hussein turned to his companions and said: 'O noble men, Paradise, with its open doors, flowing rivers, ripe fruit, is surely near at hand, and the messenger of God and those martyrs slain in the way of God are surely expecting you and waiting to greet you. So defend God's religion and the religion of His prophet, and protect the family of God's Messenger and that of his descendants. God has tested you through us, so you will be our neighbours and the people of our affection. So go forth that God might bless you from us.'

Then Hurr and Zuhayr b. al-Qayn attacked the enemy together, fighting fiercely side-by-side. If one came under attack and was cut off, the other would come to his aid. They continued like this for some time.

Hurr kept fighting until they hamstrung his horse, but he got up and kept fighting on foot even after that, reciting:

'You may hamstring me, but I am the son of the free
and braver than a ferocious lion,
I am not one who becomes weak in adversity
I stand firm where others flee!'

After he had been worn down with wounds, the enemy surrounded him and struck him down. Hussein's remaining companions rushed to his aid and brought him back to Abu Abdullah while he still drew breath. Hussein wiped the dust from his face and told him: 'You are free (*ḥurr*) as your mother named you; free in this world and free in the Hereafter!'

When Hurr passed away, Ali Akbar recited the following eulogy:

'Surely the best freeman (*ḥurr*) is *Hurr* of the *Riyāḥ*
steadfast in a melee of spears
The best freeman, for Hussein called
and he did what was right for himself on the morn.'

Hurr had a brother called *Muṣʿab* on the side of Umar b. Sa'd. He was enraged by his brother's death and turned on the soldiers of Ibn Sa'd as a result. He fought them until he himself was slain.

This is how three members of Hurr's family were slain alongside Hussein; Hurr, his brother and his son.

After Hurr had been slain, Zuhayr b. al-Qayn came to Hussein, asking permission to go and be martyred. He struck his hand to his shoulder and said:

'I will go forth, you are surely guided aright
and today meet your grandfather, the prophet
Hasan, and Ali who was agreed upon
and the young man who soars with two wings
And God's lion, the living martyr.'

Hussein allowed him to go, and he attacked the enemy reciting:

'I am Zuhayr, the son of al-Qayn
I shall drive you back with my sword from Hussein
Hussein is one of the grandsons
from the progeny of the righteous, pious and good
That is God's Messenger, truly
I will strike you down, I see no shame in it!'

As was the case with Hussein's other companions, Zuhayr was not facing a single opponent, but was surrounded by a multitude of them. In Zuhayr's case, some attacked him with arrows, others with spears and others still with swords. Those who slew him were *Muhājir b. Aws al-Tamīmī* and *Kathīr b. Abdullah al-Sha'bī*.

When Zuhayr fell, Hussein called out to him: 'May God not make you distant; may He curse your killer with the curse of those who turned into apes and swine!'

Then *Amr b. Khālid al-Azadī* went forth, reciting:

'Today, my soul, you go to the All-Merciful
walking with the spirit and with the scent of basil
Today you shall be recompensed for all the goodness
you have done with the passage of time
Whatever has been written on the tablet for the righteous
today shall be erased with forgiveness
Do not fear, my soul, for every living thing must die
patience is your best guarantee of safety.'

Then he fought until he was slain.

After him came his son, *Khālid b. Amr*, who recited:

'Patience in the face of death, sons of *Qaḥṭān*
so that you will enjoy the satisfaction of the All-Merciful
Possessed of majesty, might and the proof
exalted, lofty and generous
O father! You have gone to the heavens
in a beautiful palace of marble!'

Then he too fought until he was slain.

Sa'd b. Hanẓala al-Tamīmī was the next to go forth. He recited:

'Endure the blades and fangs
endure them to enter Paradise
And enjoy the beautiful damsels, a trifle
for those who desire victory without doubt
O my soul, struggle for it that you might rest
and in pursuit of goodness do your best!'

And he too fought until death.

Then came *Umayr b. Abdullah al-Mudhḥajī*, reciting:

'Sa'd and the *Mudhḥaj* surely know / that I am fierce and decisive

I shall rise up with my sword at the head of this host / and leave behind a people who veer from side to side

And are the prey of the most vile and lame of beasts.'

He was set upon by a multitude of the enemy and *Muslim al-Ḍubābī* and *Abdullah al-Bajalī* killed him together before cutting off his head.

Then *Amr b. Khālid al-Ṣaydāwī* turned to Hussein and said: 'Peace be with you, O Abu Abdullah. I wish to join my comrades now, for I cannot bear to stay behind and see you killed alone.'

Hussein said: 'You go ahead. We will catch up with you soon.'

Then he went out, fought and was slain.

Hussein's companions fought with full knowledge of what they stood for and complete faith in it. This meant that they would keep fighting until their very last drop of blood. Not a single one of them surrendered at Karbala and there was only one prisoner taken alive

– *Sawwār b. Hamīr al-Jābirī al-Hamadānī*. He ended up a prisoner because he was so badly wounded in the fighting that he collapsed from exhaustion and was seized. Ibn Sa'd wanted to kill him, but his own tribe interceded for him and he survived another six months before dying from his wounds.

Hussein's companions were from many different places and many different tribes; some were from Hejaz, others from Kufa, others still from Basra or Yemen. With Hussein were men who fought and died. *Rahman b. Abdullah al-Yazanī*, from Yemen, came out to do battle, reciting:

'I am the son of Abdullah of the family of Yazan
my religion is that of Husayn and Hasan
I shall strike you like a youth from Yemen
expecting thereby success in the eyes of the All-Trustworthy.'

And he fought to the end.

Just as there were men from all tribes and lands with Hussein, so too were there men of all ages. In addition to *Habib b. Muẓāhir*, who was almost ninety years old at this point, Hussein was also accompanied by *Jābir b. 'Urwa al-Ghaffārī*, an elderly man who had fought beside the Prophet at Badr and Hunayn. At Karbala, he went out to fight the enemies of Hussein with his turban wrapped around his waist to support his back, and his eyebrows bound up with a headband so that he could see clearly. Hussein looked at him and said: 'Thank you for your efforts, O shaykh!'

Then he went out to face the enemy, saying:

'Truly it is known of the tribe of *Ghaffār*
and Jundub, then the tribe of *Nizār*
That we gave aid to Ahmad the chosen messenger
and his household, the righteous leaders
Upon whom sends blessings the Creator of trees

the Lord of all beasts and the Maker of birds!'

Then he fought and was slain.

Then *Nāfiʿ b. Hilāl* began to shoot at the enemy with what few arrows he had remaining, striking down some of them. He recited the poetry:

'I launch them, their heads marked
it does the heart no good to worry about them

And once his arrows were spent, he drew his sword and charged at them:

'I am of *Hilāl* and I am the son of Bajal
my religion is that of Hussein and Ali
I will strike you until I meet my end
and complete my life with my finest deed.'

He killed twelve soldiers of Umar b. Sa'd, whether by arrow or by blade, not to mention those who were wounded by him. They struck him with their swords until they had broken both his arms, then took him prisoner and dragged him before Shimr who took him in front of Ibn Sa'd. Blood was running from his head, his face and his arms. Umar b. Sa'd said: 'Woe to you, *Nāfiʿ*! What made you do this to yourself!?'

Nāfiʿ replied disdainfully: 'My Lord knows what I intended. By God, I killed twelve of you, not to mention all those that I wounded. I do not blame myself for trying, and had I still been able to use my arms, you would have never taken me alive.'

Shimr said to Umar b. Sa'd: 'Kill him, for God's sake!'

Umar replied: You brought him. If you want him dead, you do it.'

Shimr drew his sword to kill him and *Nāfiʿ* said: 'By God, if you were a Muslim you would be afraid to meet God with our blood on your hands. Praise God who let us die at the hands of the most evil of His creation!'

Then Shimr killed him.

Then both *Abdullah al-Ghiffārī* and *Rahman al-Ghiffārī* went to Hussein and said: 'Peace be with you, O Abu Abdullah! We long to give our lives defending you!'

'Of course, come closer to me.'

They approached him, weeping. Hussein said: 'Sons of my brother, what gives you cause to cry? For by God I expect that you shall soon both be content!'

They replied: 'May we be your sacrifice! No by God, we do not cry for ourselves, rather we cry for you. We see that you are surrounded on all sides and there is nothing we can do to protect you!'

Hussein told them: 'May God reward you with the best reward of the pious for your concern and for lending me your support.'

Then Hussein bid them farewell as they said: 'Peace be with you, O son of God's Messenger!'

'And peace be with you both, and God's mercy and blessings!'

Then they fought bravely until they were slain.

The martyrdom of Hussein's companions proceeded quickly; in ones and twos they bid farewell to Hussein before going to fight to the death.

Two of these individuals were *Sayf b. al-Harith b. Sarī' al-Hamadānī* and *Mālik b. Abdullah b. Sari'*, his cousin. They too fought until they were slain.

Amr b. Muṭā' al-Ju'fī went forth, reciting:

'I am *Umayr*, my father is *Muṭā'*
in my right hand is a slicing blade
Brown with glistening teeth
it shimmers radiantly
This day I like to be struck down
beside Hussein fighting valiantly!'

He fought until he was slain.

Then *Yaḥyā b. Salīm al-Māzanī* went out:

'I shall strike them asunder
with a blow as fierce as thunder
Without weakness or languor
Today I do not fear death as it comes closer'

And he fought until he was slain.

After he was slain, *Qurra b. Abu Qurra al-Ghiffārī* stepped forth:

'*Banū Ghiffār* surely know
and the Khandaf and the *Nizār*
That I am a ferocious lion
and I will surely pounce on these sinners!

And deal a grievous blow on behalf of the noble sons!'

He killed eight men before he was finally brought down.

After Qurra came a man called *Mālik b. Anas al-Kāhilī*, reciting:

'*Kāhila* know and so does *Dūdān*
and *Khandaf and Qays of 'Aylān*
That my people mean woe for generations
and I am the foremost of those warriors!'

He fought to the death.

And even while Hussein's companions were being cut down left, right and centre, those who were still alive spared no opportunity to try and guide their enemies and warn them against carrying out any further injustice. They warned them of the punishment of Hellfire on the Day of Resurrection; unlike Umar b. Sa'd's supporters, whose goal and language were completely of this world. The slogan of Ibn Sa'd's men was submission to the worldly authority of Yazid and holding fast to his allegiance and obedience. All they spoke about was of this world and worldly wealth, while the companions of Hussein spoke of truth, justice, and everlasting reward or punishment on the Day of Resurrection – exactly as the prophets themselves had spoken.

One of those who tried to admonish the soldiers of Ibn Sa'd was *Hanẓala b. As'ad al-Shubbānī*, one of the last companions still alive. He stood in front of Hussein protecting him from arrows, spears and swords with his own body. He began to call out to the people: 'O people! I fear that a day will come for you like the Day of the Confederates! The fate that befell the people of Noah, *'Ād* and *Thamūd* and those who came after them! God does not desire any injustice for his servants!

O people! I fear for you a day on which you shall turn and flee, on which you shall have no protector from God!

O people! Do not murder Hussein lest God pronounce His punishment upon you! And whoever invents a lie has surely failed.'

Hanẓala had already admonished the enemy before the battle began, but they rejected his words harshly, reviling and cursing him and his companions. Hussein said: 'O son of *As'ad*, may God have mercy upon you. They have brought down God's punishment on themselves by rejecting the truth that you summoned them to and by hurling abuse at you and your companions. So what about now, now that they have murdered your righteous brethren?'

HaÛala said: 'You are right, may I be your sacrifice. Shall we not then go to our Lord and meet our brothers?'

Hussein said: 'Of course. Go to what is better for you than this world and all that is in it, to a kingdom that never fades.'

HanÛala said – taking this as a permission to go and fight from Hussein – 'Peace be with you, O Abu Abdullah, and on your household. May God bring us together in Paradise!'

Hussein said: 'Amen. Amen.'

Then *Hanẓala* approached the enemy and fought fiercely. He was slain by a group of them.

Hussein's companions competed with one another to attain martyrdom while defending the truth, the leader of truth and the path of truth, with the clear knowledge that they would be cut down by swords and spears, and have their heads severed. This is what distinguishes them from all other soldiers throughout history; they had not the slightest hope of surviving, but they felt and believed that, through their sacrifice, they were nurturing the sacred tree that God had sent all of his prophets and messengers to plant upon this earth, while their enemies were trying to tear it out from its roots. This tree was, of course, the tree of faith, piety, good and righteousness; and Hussein's companions believed that God was with them and their final destination was Paradise, just as that of their enemies was Hellfire.

'Ābis b. Shubayb al-Shākirī, one of the most devoted supporters of the Prophet's Household, went to *Shūdhab*, his bondsman, and said: 'O *Shūdhab*, what do you intend to do?'

'What shall I do? I shall fight with you to protect the son of the daughter of God's Messenger until I am slain!'

'I thought as much. Go now to Abu Abdullah so that he may offer you up as he did for the rest of his companions, and so that I might offer you up too. If there was anyone else with me who I had more authority to send forth, I would have liked that he come before me so that I could offer him as a sacrifice. This is a day on which it behoves us to seek whatever divine reward we can in it, for there will be no deeds for us after this day – only judgement.'

So ShÙdhab went and wished peace upon Hussein as he bid him farewell, then he went out, fought and was slain.

After he had been killed, *'Ābis* turned to Hussein and said: 'O Abu Abdullah, by God I swear that there is no one upon this earth, whether near or far, who is dearer or more beloved to me than you. And if I had anything dearer to me than my own life and blood that I could give to protect you from harm, I would have given it.

Peace be with you, O Abu Abdullah! I ask God to bear witness that I am upon your guidance and the guidance of your father!'

Then he advanced, drawing his sword and striking it upon his helmet. When the enemy saw him, one of them called out: 'O people! This is the lion of lions! This is the mighty son of Abu Shubayb! Don't let anyone go out to fight him, because he is one of the bravest of men!'

'Ābis called out: 'Is there no one who will face me?'

But no one would agree to come out to fight him.

Umar b. Sa'd said: 'Strike him with stones!' So the soldiers began throwing stones at him from every direction, and when he saw that no one was going to come and fight him, he threw down his armour and helmet and rushed at them without any protection. One of Hussein's companions called out: 'Have you gone mad, *'Ābis*!?'

He said: 'Yes, by God, mad with the love of Hussein!'

He fell upon the enemy and they scattered in all directions from in front of him; there was not one of them that fell within his reach save that he cut them down.

But once he had suffered many wounds, they surrounded him

from all directions and struck him with whatever they had; swords, spears, arrows, even stones, until he was felled and killed.

Then they pounced upon him and cut off his head. A struggle broke out as each of them claimed to be his killer. Umar b. Sa'd came and said: 'Do not argue. No one man slew him. Rather you killed him together.' With these words he broke up the scuffle.

Another man who fought bravely for his beliefs was *Yazid b. Mu'qal* from the tribe of *Mudhḥaj*. His father had been a Companion of the Prophet. He came out, reciting:

'If you do not know me, I am the son of *Mu'qal*
Sharp and ferocious, not unarmed
In my right hand a polished sword blade
by which I shall overcome any fighter I meet in battle
Protecting Hussein, the noble and good
son of God's Messenger, the best prophet ever sent'

Then he fought fiercely until he was slain.

In addition to men from every land and tribe, Hussein's camp also included slaves, whom Hussein treated in the same way as everyone else. John, the bondsman of Abu Dharr and an African slave, came to Hussein to ask to fight. But Hussein told him: 'You are under no obligation to me John, you came with us for food and shelter, but you do not need to share our fate!'

John replied: 'O son of God's Messenger! Shall I stay with you while things are easy only to abandon you when they are hard? By God, my smell is unpleasant, my lineage is ignoble and my skin is black. So give me the comfort of Paradise, that my smell become pleasant, my lineage noble and my face luminous!'

He added, with tears streaming down his face: 'No, by God, I shall never leave you until my blood has mingled with that of the Prophet's Household!'

So Hussein permitted him to fight, and he went forth saying:

'What do the disbelievers think of an African's striking
with a sword, striking for the Household of Muhammad
I shall protect them with my tongue and hand
hoping for Paradise on the Day I am brought forth!'

Then he fought until he was slain.

Hussein came and stood beside his body and said: 'O God, make his face luminous, his scent pleasant and raise him up with the righteous, and make him one of the followers of Muhamad [the Prophet] and his Household!'

THE SACRIFICE

It was indeed a day of sacrifice, as Hussein's companions, whether one by one or in groups, went forth to receive the honour of martyrdom before Hussein. One of the most wonderful examples of this on that day was when a group of companions, including *Amr b. Khālid al-Ṣaydāwī*, his bondsman *Sa'd*, *Jābir b. Harith al-Salmānī* and *Mujammiʿ b. Abdullah al-ʿĀidī* went forth and attacked the Kufan forces together as if they were seeking out their own death rather than the death of their enemies. They penetrated the enemy ranks, fighting every step of the way, until Umar b. Sa'd had to order his entire army to surround them and cut them off from what remained of Hussein's forces. When this happened, Hussein sent his brother Abbas to save them. When the latter attacked, the enemy scattered before him and he opened up the way to the group of companions, all of whom had been wounded by this time. While they made their way back to Hussein's camp, the enemy again approached and surrounded them. But they did not falter, instead they launched themselves at the enemy with their swords slashing, in spite of their wounds, and kept fighting until every last one of them had been slain.

While Hussein sat and death swirled all around him as his companions were cut down one by one, he saw a young man not yet eleven years old, whose name was *Amr b. Janāda al-Ansārī*, approach him. And when he stood before him asking permission to go and fight. Hussein told those with him: 'This young man's father was slain in the battle. I do not think his mother would be pleased for the same to befall him.'

The young man said: 'O Abu Abdullah, it is my mother who bid me go and fight, and my mother who dressed me for battle!'

So Hussein permitted him to go forth, and he went reciting:

'Hussein is my leader, and the best of leaders
who gladdens the heart of the messenger and warner
Ali and Fatima are his parents
do you know anyone to be his peer?
He has the appearance like the morning sun
dazzling like the luminous moon!'

No one knew if this was his poetry or something that his mother had taught him to say. But he stepped out onto the battlefield with grief and longing. He fought until his was slain, whereat the enemy threw his head into Hussein's camp. His mother took the head and wiped the blood from it, then she took it and struck one of the enemies nearby with it before returning to the tents. There, she picked up a tent pole and charged at the enemy, saying:

'I am an old and frail woman
devastated, grieved and weak
But I will strike you harshly
to protect the children of Fatima the noble!'

But Hussein came and brought her back to the camp after she had struck a couple of the enemy with the pole.

Sometimes, a few of Hussein's companions would fight for a while and then, after sustaining some injuries, would return to Hussein to restore their vigour by looking at his face or hearing a few of his words. Then they would go back out to fight until they had won the honour of martyrdom. One person who did this was *Hajjāj b. Masrūq al-Juʿfī*. He was Hussein's muÞadhdhin. His face had chest were soaked in blood, and he began to say:

'Today I shall meet your grandfather, the prophet
then your father, the generous Ali
That is the one who we know to be the legatee'

Hussein told him: 'I shall send them after you.' Then *Hajjāj* went out, fought and was slain.

Another who fought and was slain was *Yaḥyā b. Kathīr al-Anṣārī*, who went forth reciting the poetry:

'I shall crush the life from the son of Hind
and cast him down with the warriors of the *Anṣār*
And emigrants whose spears are blood-soaked
beneath a cloud of the faithless' blood
Soaked during the time of the Prophet Muhammad
and today soaked in the blood of the tyrants
They betrayed Hussein and tragedies abound
satisfied with Yazid and satisfied with Hellfire
By God, my Lord, I will keep on striking out
at these sinners with a violent blade
This is a sure duty for a member of the Azad
every day a clash and a charge.'

Then he fought until he was slain.

Hussein's companions displayed bravery, courage and endurance to the level of their faith and insight, something which amazed their enemies and friends alike. Umar b. Sa'd's soldiers saw, even when they had killed the majority of Hussein's companions, a man fighting so fiercely that he put to flight anyone who crossed his path before returning to Hussein, reciting:

'I am gladdened to have been guided to meet with Ahmad / in the gardens of Paradise, raised up high!'

Then he would return to battle again and fight the enemy once more, until a band of Umar b. Sa'd's soldiers surrounded him, and when he had been worn down through wounds and exertion, they killed him and took his head. Then, when they asked after his name they were told it was *Abu Amr al-Nahshalī*, a pious man who had spent his days in prayer.

Hussein's companions were truly unusual in their bravery and conviction; their conviction was demonstrated by the battle poetry that they would recite, just as their bravery was shown by how each and every one of them was prepared to face an entire army by himself.

Mālik b. Dāwūd was one of Hussein's companions. He went out, reciting the poetry:

'For you comes *Mālik* the lion
a valiant youth defending the noble people
Seeking God's reward in Paradise
glory to Him, the Sovereign, the Knower'

He plunged into the army of the enemy and fought them hard, killing a number of them before they all attacked him together and cut him down.

It was not only the freemen in Hussein's camp who displayed such conviction and bravery, even the slaves who were with them shared these qualities. Hussein had a Turkish bondman by the name of Aslam, a reciter of the Quran who was well-versed in Arabic. He went out to fight, reciting:

'The sea burns from my thrust and cut
and the sky flees from my arrows and javelins
My sword shines in my right hand
it splits the hearts of the arrogant and envious.'

He also said:

'Today I shall quench you with a bitter cup
with a slicing blade that never blunts
In the fray of battle with my shield
I shall drive you back from Hussein son of Ali!'

He slew a multitude of enemies before he was surrounded from all sides and cut down. Hussein came to him and wept, cradling him and holding his cheek to his own, while he still had the breath of life. The young man opened his eyes and embraced Hussein, smiling and saying: 'Who is luckier than I, when the son of God's messenger has placed his cheek against mine?'

Then he died in Hussein's arms.

One by one, the men came to Hussein, saying: 'Peace be with you, O Abu Abdullah!' And Hussein would respond: 'And with you be peace! We are right behind you.' Then he would recite God's saying: 'Of them are some who have fulfilled their pledge, and of them are some who still wait, and they have not changed in the least.' Then the men would attack the enemy and fight unto death.

In their faith in the Prophet's Household they found the sustenance they needed in such hardships, especially when they would repeat to one another the words of God's Messenger: 'There are four people for whom I will intercede on the Resurrection Day; the one who strikes with his sword in defence of my progeny, the one who looks after their needs, the one who rushes to them when they are in need, and the one who loves them with his heart and tongue.'

The last of Hussein's companions to be slain was *Suwayd b. Amr al-Khath'amī*. He fought valiantly until he fell to the ground covered from head-to-toe in wounds, surrounded by other casualties. He did not know what was going on around him. Then he heard some people shouting: 'Husayn has been killed!' Whereat Suwayd desperately searched for some weapon and found his dagger, for they had taken his sword, so he got up and began to fight with his dagger. Two of Umar b. Sa'd's men rushed at him and killed him with their spears.

Now that all the companions had been slain, all that remained with Hussein were his Household; his brothers, sons and the sons of Abu Talib and Aqeel.

Martyrdom of the Prophet's Household

On the night of *Ashura*, when Hussein's companions were discussing the forthcoming battle. The companions insisted that they go and fight before any members of the Prophet's Household and they absolutely refused to allow any of them to be slain before themselves. This was because they understood the status of the Prophet's Household in the eyes of God and His messenger, and because the reason they had joined the caravan of Hussein in the first place was to protect him and his household. But when the last of the companions were slain, only Hussein's household remained with him; the sons of Ali, of Ja'far, Aqeel, Hasan and Hussein; they gathered together and began to bid each other farewell, with their hearts firmly resolved to fight on to the very end.

These men bore the traits of their fathers and forefathers; beginning with the spirit of chivalry, bravery, determination, nobility and heroism, ending with the love of martyrdom in the way of God, and encompassing every Hashemite virtue in between.

The first to go out and face the enemy was the dearest of Hussein's sons, Ali Akbar, who was the great-grandson of the Prophet from his father's side and the great-grandson of Abu Sufiyan from his mother's. His mother was *Laylā bt. Abu Marra b. 'Urwa b. Mas'ūd*, and *Laylā's* mother was the daughter of Abu Sufiyan. In this way, Ali Akbar was a relative of Yazid b. Muawiya, and also a relative of Umar b. Sa'd, who was of the Quraysh.

So when Ali Akbar came to his father, seeking permission to go and fight, desiring to go to God's Paradise, even though Hussein was fully committed to sending his sons forth as martyrs in the way of his Lord, he could not hold back his emotions. He told Ali Akbar: 'Be considerate of our state and do not hurry off to battle, for we cannot bear to be separated from you!' But Ali Akbar would not desist, and so his father eventually acceded to his request.

And while he made preparations to go into battle, Hussein looked at him sorrowfully and his eyes welled up with tears. Then he looked to the heavens as if complaining to God about what the enemy would do to them. Then he held up his grey hear in his hand and said:

'O God! Bear witness against those people, for there goes out to them a young man who most resembles your prophet Muhammad in his appearance, behaviour and speech, and whenever we missed our grandfather, we would look at him!'

'O God! Deny them the blessings of the earth, divide them into groups, factions and sects, and let their rulers never be pleased with them, for they called us with the promise of assistance, only to betray us and fight against us!'

Then he called out to Umar b. Sa'd: 'What is the matter with you, O Ibn Sa'd! May God cut off your family, withhold His blessings from you and empower someone over you who will murder you upon your own bed, just as you have cut off my family and ignored my relation to God's Messenger!' Then he recited the verse: 'Indeed God chose Adam and Noah, and the progeny of Abraham and the progeny of Imran above all the nations; some of them are descendants of the others, and God is all-hearing, all-knowing.'

Despite all of the affection he had for his son, Hussein was still ready to send him forth to martyrdom in the way of God for the sake of those principles and values which righteous people throughout history had given their lives for. It was Hussein himself who dressed his son for battle, strapping on his armour and helmet, wrapping his waist with a girth that he had received from his father, the Commander of the Faithful, and helping him to mount his horse.

Ali Akbar almost could not bring himself to bid farewell to the women and children who had gathered around him and embraced him, or his father and the rest of the Hashemites who had assembled. How striking he must have appeared when he rode out to face the army of Ibn Sa'd and the enemy soldiers caught sight of him for the first time. One of the Syrians called out: 'You are related by blood to Yazid, so if you wish we will grant you safe passage and you may go wherever you please.'

Ali Akbar responded: 'By God, blood relation to God's Messenger is more worthy of your consideration than blood relation to Abu Sufiyan.'

In this way he rejected their poisonous offers of safety, just as Abbas and his brothers had refused similar offers.

Ali Akbar launched his attack, reciting:

'I am Ali, son of Hussein, son of Ali
We – by God's House – are nearest to the Prophet
By God, a whoreson will not rule over us
and I will strike you with my sword to protect my father
The striking of a youth of *Hashem* and *Ali*!

He attacked the right flank of Umar b. Sa'd's army and drove them back after killing some of them. Then he attacked the left flank and plunged into their midst. He faced no group of men save that he routed them, nor did any brave soldier stand his ground save that he cut him down. Ali Akbar made twelve such forays against the enemy, and killed so many that the enemy began to cry out from the numbers slain by his hand.

Ali Akbar, overcome by thirst, exhaustion and wounds, returned to his father, saying: 'O father; thirst is killing me and steel is weighing me down. Is there any water left to renew my vigour against the enemy?'

Hussein began to weep, and said: 'Go back, my son – may God bless you – and fight a little longer, because soon your grandfather, God's Messenger, will come and quench your thirst with a such a draught that you will never be thirsty again!'

'My son! It is hard for your grandfather, the chosen messenger, and Ali, the agreed-upon successor, and upon your father, to hear you call them but not be able to answer you, to hear you shout for their help but not be able to assist you!'

Then Hussein gave his son his ring and said: 'My son, put it in your mouth and go back to fight your enemy.'

So Ali went back to battle to face certain death defending the religion of his grandfather and his family, with no hope of surviving, determined to fight to the end:

'In war there are truths raised up
and from it come some lessons
By God, the Lord of the Throne we will not
stop fighting you or lay down our swords.'

He attacked them again and again, felling group after group. One of the enemy, whose name was *Marra b. Munqadh al-Abdī*, saw him and said to those around him: 'May all the sins of the Arabs be upon me if this youth comes within my reach and I do not deprive his mother of him!'

This man lay in wait amongst the ranks, waiting for an enemy to take Ali Akbar unawares.

While Ali Akbar was launching one of his attacks, Marra b. Munqadh ambushed him and shot him with an arrow through the neck. Then, while he was wounded, struck him on his head with a sword and pierced his back with a spear. Ali Akbar slumped forward in the saddle and held onto his horse, but the blood gushing from his wound meant the horse could not see where it was going. So instead of taking him back to Hussein's camp, it carried him further into the enemy lines, and they fell upon him en masse, cutting him with their swords.

And as he felt his life slipping away, he called out: 'O father! Peace be with you! My grandfather, God's Messenger, has come with an overflowing cup and quenched my thirst so that I will never be thirsty again! He tells you to come quickly, for he has a cup ready for you as well.'

And then he died, his spirit leaving this world. Hussein called out at the top of his voice: 'O woe, my son!' And the women began to wail loudly, but Hussein quietened them, saying: 'There will be ample time for tears.'

Hussein attacked the enemy like a hawk attacks its prey; scattering them in all directions as he made for his son's body, saying to himself: 'My son, Ali! My son, Ali!' When he reached him, he leapt down from his horse and threw himself upon his son's body, taking his head and putting it on his lap and wiping the dust and the blood from his face. Then he put his cheek against his son's and said: 'My son! May God destroy the people who murdered you, how insolent they are towards the All-Merciful, and in violating the sanctity of the Prophet's blood!'

His eyes welled up with tears and he said: 'Life is not worth living without you, my son. But now you are at rest from the worries of this world; you have gone to a pleasant place of rest, to Paradise and God's pleasure. No, your father has been left with this world's worries, but he will be soon with you again.'

His aunt, Zaynab came out calling: 'O, woe! My son! O woe! We are alone! O woe! Our beloved! Would that I could take your place!'

Hussein went to her and returned her to the tent, repeating the words: 'To God we belong and to Him we return.'

Then Hussein turned to the young Hashemite men who were with him and told them: Take your brother to the tents; they took him from the place where he was slain to the camp which they had been fighting in front of. Ali Akbar was the first of Abu Talib's descendants to be slain on that day.

After Ali Akbar had been slain, the men of the Hashemite clan competed with one another to attain martyrdom in the way of God; the first to go out after him was Abdullah b. Muslim b. Aqeel. He entered the battlefield, while his mother Ruqayya, the daughter of Imam Ali, stood at the flap of her tent watching him. He charged at full speed towards the enemy, reciting the poetry:

'Today I shall meet Muslim, and he is my father
and a band who gave their lives for the religion of the Prophet
They are not a people known to lie
but the best and noble of lineages
From *Hāshim*, the foremost people of consequence.'

In three charges, he was able to fell a number of the enemy. So they began to shoot at him from a distance. A man called *Amr b. SAbuḥ* launched an arrow which Abdullah b. Musim blocked with his hand, but the arrow pierced his hand and stuck into his forehead. He could not pull the arrow out, so he called out: 'O God! They disregarded us and sought to abase us, so kill them as they have killed us, and abase them as they tried to us.'

While he was in this condition, another man attacked him with a spear and impaled him through his chest. He fell to the ground, a martyr. His spirit departed. Then *Amr b. Sabuḥ*, whose arrow had struck him, came and tried to pull the arrow from his head. But he could not do it, so the arrow stayed where it struck.

Then Hussein turned to the rest of his household and said: 'Attack them, may God bless you, and hasten to Paradise, the abode of faith.'

After Abdullah went his brother, Muhammad b. Muslim b. Aqeel, who fought no less valiantly before he was finally surrounded by the enemy and cut down.

Then a group of Abu Talib's descendants attacked the enemy all at once. Hussein told them: 'Endure death, my nephews, for by God you will not be lowly after this day!'

Many of them fell in battle, including *Hasan b. al-Hasan al-Muthannā*, who was wounded eighteen times and lost his right hand but still did not die. Instead he was taken prisoner. *Asmaa b. Khārija*, his maternal uncle, intervened on his behalf with Ibn Sa'd, who accepted his pleas for his nephew and said: 'Leave *Abu Hussān* with his nephew.' He died shortly thereafter.

After that, Rahman b. Aqeel went out to fight:

'My father is Aqeel, so know my station
from *Hāshim* and the *Hāshim* of my brethren
Amongst us is Hussein, the foremost of the generations
Leader of the youths in Paradise's gardens.'

And he fought them to the death.

Then came Ja'far b. Aqeel, who charged the enemy, reciting:

'I am the *Abṭaḥī* and *Tālibī* lad
from the clan of *Hāshim* and *Ghālib*
We are truly the masters of the wolves
amongst us is Hussein the best of the best.'

The enemy shot him with an arrow and killed him.

Then Abdullah b. Aqeel the elder came out, and he was married to *Maymūna bt. Ali*. He went forth, reciting:

'Leave the desert without vegetation
eave the noble son of Aqeel
Who responds to the call of the Prophet
with his polished sword of Indian steel!'

He fought bravely until he was covered in wounds, then a group of enemies attacked him all at once and killed him.

Whenever one of the sons of Aqeel were slain, his brother would come out to fight, until nine of them had given their lives in defence of the truth, the leader of truth and the path of truth. Then came *'Awn b. Abdullah b. Ja'far al-Ṭayyār*, whose mother was Zaynab. He recited:

'If you know me not, I am the son of Ja'far
the truthful martyr in the gardens of paradise
In which he flies with verdant wings
this is honour enough for me in the sight of men!'

He fought and died while his mother, Zaynab, watched from the flap of the tent.

Then the descendants of Abu Talib continued competing with one another to attain martyrdom, going into battle alone or in groups, with complete conviction in their cause, until the turn came of *Qasim b. al-Hasan*, who was still a young boy who was yet to reach maturity. His mother was Umm Walad, or Ramla, and she was also the mother of his brothers Abdullah the elder and Ubaydullah the younger. After his father's martyrdom, it was Hussein who had brought him up as if he was his own beloved son, and the latter loved him a great deal. It is said that Hussein planned to marry him to his daughter Sukayna.

Qasim came to his uncle to ask permission to go and fight. Hussein got up and embraced him with eyes full of tears, and Qasim began to weep with him, before kissing his uncle's hands, begging him to let him go and fight. When Hussein finally acceded to his request, he went out to fight and began to recite:

'If you do not know me, I am the scion of al-Hasan
the grandson of the chosen and trusted Prophet
Here stands Hussein, a prisoner held to ransom
between people, may they never be quenched by rain!'

At that moment, Qasim's face was luminous like the moon. He was dressed in a shirt and mail and had a pair of sandals on his feet. While he was fighting, a strap on his left sandal was cut. He stopped to fasten it without thinking of the enemy – because clearly he attached less importance to them than his shoe! – then *Amr b. Sa'd b. Nafīd al-Azadī* said: 'By God, I'm going to get him!'

His companion, *Hamīd b. Muslim* turned to him and said: '*Subḥānallah*! What do you mean by that? Even if that child came and struck me I would not raise my hand against him! Leave it, can't you see all those who have surrounded him?'

But he would not be dissuaded: 'No, by God, I'm going to get him!'

So while Qasim was distracted with his sandal, *Amr b. Sa'd al-Azadī* came and struck him on the head with his sword, splitting it. Qasim fell to the ground, calling out to his uncle.

Hussein rushed to him like a hawk rushes after its prayer, breaking through the ranks of the enemy until he reached his nephew's killer. He struck him with his sword, but Amr blocked with his forearm, and it was severed at the elbow by Hussein's strike. He cried out with such a scream that the entire army heard it. Kufan horsemen charged in to save him from Hussein, but in the process he was knocked to the ground and trampled to death beneath their hooves.

The cavalry charge kicked up a great cloud of dust, and as it settled, there stood Hussein above the head of his nephew, scratching the ground with his feet. Hussein said: 'By God, it breaks your uncle's heart that you called him but he could not come to you, or he came to you but could not help you, or that he helped you but could not save you... away with the people who murdered you on a day in which victims were many, but helpers were few.'

Then he carried him on his chest, with his feet dragging along the floor. He brought him to the tent and laid his body down beside the body of his son, Ali Akbar, and the other martyrs of his household.

Hussein raised his hands to the sky and said: 'O God! Number their days, slaughter them left and right, let none of them escape, let none be forgiven!'

He turned to what was left of his household and said: 'Patience, my cousins! Patience, my household! You shall never see lowliness from this day onwards!'

After Qasim was slain, his brother, Abdullah b. Hasan went forth, and he was known for his handsomeness. He began to recite:

'If you don't know me, I am the son of Haydar
a ferocious and fearsome lion in battle
My enemies are like a swarm of locusts
they shall be fed the sword to its full measure!'

One of the Kufans saw him and said: 'I will kill this youth.' Someone said to him: 'Woe to you! What do you want to achieve by killing him?'

'I will do it!' Then he attacked him and cut off each of his hands in turn, before striking him down dead.

After Qasim and Abdullah came their brothers, Umar, Bishr and Ahmad, all of them children of the grandson of the Prophet, Imam al-Hasan. Every last one of them fought to the death.

With the martyrdom of Hasan's children, Hussein was left alone with his brothers. They were all determined to die defending him. The first to go forth was Abu Bakr b. Ali, whose name was Abdullah. Her mother was *Laylā bt. Mas'ūd b. Khālid al-Tamīmī*. He went forth, reciting:

'My elder is Ali, full of glory
from *Hāshim*, the honest, generous and virtuous
This is Hussein, the son of the Prophet heaven-sent
whom we protect with our cleaving blades
I give my life for him, as an honoured brother
O my Lord! So give me abundant reward!'

The enemy attacked him, gathering around him in a group; some shot him with arrows, other attacked with swords, others still with spears, until he too was slain.

Then came his brother, Muhammad b. Ali, who recited the poem:

'I shall endure that God might judge between us
and between Yazid, that vile tyrant
Astray is he that follows Yazid and his offspring
and opposes Ali while he is virtuous and preeminent
To God we disassociate from people who have come out
to fight us unjustly, they are a people gone astray!'

Then he fought until he was slain.

Then came Umar b. Ali, seeking to avenge his brother's death. He struck down the latter's killer before the enemy surrounded him completely; he struck out at them blindly, saying:

'Leave, O enemies of God! Leave Umar!
Leave the snarling, sullen lion
Who strikes you with his sword and will not flee
he will not run like some craven coward.'

He kept fighting until they overwhelmed him and killed him.

Then Ali's sons came out one after another; *Ibrahīm*, who fought until death, and Ubaydullah, who did the same.

The Martyrdom of Abbas

When Abbas saw how many of his family had been slain, he gathered his full brothers, Abdullah, Ja'far and Uthman, the sons of *Umm al-Banīn bt. Khālid b. Hazzām al-Kilābiyya*, whose name was Fatima. He told them: 'Come with me and protect your master to the death, so that I might offer you to God and I see that you have fulfilled your pledge to God and His messenger.'

It was not easy for Abbas to ask his brothers to go to fight and die before him, but he only did that so that he could offer them as a sacrifice to God and thereby earn the reward of one who is steadfast.

Abbas' brothers disagreed about who should go first. Abbas said to Abdullah: 'You go, brother, that I might see you slain and offer you up.'

So Abdullah, who was twenty-five years old, went forth reciting the poetry:

'I am the son of the dauntless and virtuous
that is Ali, the best and most righteous
The severe sword of God's Messenger
who terrified the enemy every day.'

He fought bravely before being overwhelmed and cut down.

The man who dealt him a fatal blow was *Hani b. Thubayt al-Haḍramī.*

Ja'far b. Ali was the next to go forth and he was nineteen years of age. He attacked, saying:

'Surely I am Ja'far, of noble deeds
the son of Ali the righteous
My two uncles are sufficient honor for me
I shall defend Hussein and his eminent cause.'

And while he was fighting, *Khawallī al-Aṣbahī* shot an arrow at him and it lodged in the side of his head. He fell forward on his horse, then the enemy swarmed upon him and killed him.

Uthman b. Ali, twenty-one years of age, came next, reciting:

'I am Uthman of glorious deeds
my elder is Ali the purest in action
This is *'Husayn*, the best of the best
the master of all, great or small.'

He fought fiercely before he was struck by an arrow and fell from his horse; the enemy fell upon him and cut off his head.

After these men had been slain, only Abbas was left with Hussein. With his brothers gone, he knew the time had come to sacrifice himself for Hussein.

Abbas was thirty-four years old at the time, and he was extremely handsome. He rode a tall horse, but his feet would still touch the ground. They called him, 'The moon of the Hashemites' because of his appearance. He came to Hussein and asked permission to go and fight. It was difficult for the two of them to part at that moment;

for Abbas, because he knew there was no one else left to protect Hussein and the womenfolk of the Prophet – who were reassured by his presence with them. As for Hussein, it has hard for him to see his brother slain in battle. He told him: 'O my brother, you are my standard-bearer!' (By which he meant if he fell in battle and the flag fell, it would signify the end of the battle.)

Abbas replied: 'I cannot endure these hypocrites any longer. I wish to avenge myself upon them!'

'Then go and get a little water for those children.'

Abbas came forth to face the enemy and admonished them and warned them of God's wrath: 'This is Hussein, the son of the daughter of God's Messenger. You have killed his companions and his household, and those are his women and children who are dying of thirst! So give them some water, for the heat is torturous for them.' Then he said: 'Let me go to Rome or India and never return to Hejaz or Iraq.'

Shimr called out: 'O son of *Abu Turāb*! Even if the entire face of the earth was made of water, and it was in our hands, we would not give you one drop of it until you pledge allegiance to Yazid.'

Abbas returned to Hussein and dismounted his horse to inform him of what had happened, when he heard the child crying from thirst, and he could bear it no longer. So he leapt on his horse again and faced the enemy with his sword in hand, reciting the poetry:

'I swore by God, the Might and Exalted
that today my body shall surely be stained with my blood
Standing before a man of nobility and integrity
that is Hussein, the pinnacle of glory!'

Four thousand men surrounded him. He lashed out, killing foot soldiers and unhorsing riders, and they scattered as prey scatter before a lion. They climbed hills and mounds, and began shooting at him with their bows. But he still stood firm as a mountain, unmoved by the storm of arrows.

In the army of Umar b. Sa'd was a man called *Mārid b. Ṣudayf al-Taghlabu*. When he saw what Abbas had done to his comrades, he called out: 'Damn you all! If each of you just took a handful of dirt and threw it, you would have buried him by now! Is now a time to act with good sense!?'

He called at the top of his voice: 'I adjure whomsoever has the allegiance of the [true] ruler, Yazid, upon his neck, that he shall stand aside. This one is mine!'

Then he took a spear and a sword in his hand and went to fight Abbas. Abbas stood still and did not move until, when *Mārid* approached and tried to stab him with his spear, Abbas seized the spear and turned it against him. *Mārid* almost fell from his saddle.

Abbas called out: 'O enemy of God! I shall slay you with your own spear!' So *Mārid* circled Abbas and then rushed at him, but Abbas was able to spear him in his waist. His horsed bucked and he fell to the ground, but he could fight on foot because of his bulk, so he began to panic. Shimr called to his companions: 'Woe to you! Save your comrade before he is slain!'

But Abbas was too quick for them. He struck *Mārid* with his spear and threw him to the ground. *Mārid* called out: 'O people! Shall I be thrown from my horse and killed with my own spear!?'

And when he saw that he was going to die, he began to plead for his life: 'O son of Ali, mercy for your prisoner!'

Abbas said: 'You think you can deceive me?'

Then he plunged the spear into his neck and he fell to the ground, writhing in his own blood.

When the enemy saw *Mārid*'s fate, they feared Abbas even more. No one stood in his way, so his way to the river became clear and he hurried there and plunged into the river with his horse, without any concern for who war nearby. He plunged his hand in the water to drink, but when he felt its coolness he remembered Hussein and his household and he threw the water away, saying angrily:

O soul! After Hussain nobody does count!
After him, you should to nothing amount,
Here is Hussain nearing his end
While you drink of cool water?!
By God! Such is not a deed
At all enjoined by my creed!

Then he filled his waterskin without drinking a single drop, mounted his horse again and headed for the camp. A large number of enemies ambushed him and encircled him. He began to strike out left and right, knocking down horsemen with the waterskin still on his back. He cleared them from his path, reciting:

I do not fear death when it calls upon me,
Till among the swords you bury me.
My soul protects the one
Who is the Prophet's grandson,
Abbas am I, the water bag do I bear
When I meet evil, I know no fear!

He road through the palm trees until he was able to make for the camp without losing the waterskin. *Zayd b. Raqqād al-Jahnī* lay in wait for him behind a palm, accompanied by *Hakīm b. Ṭufayl al-Sandasī*. He leapt out and struck Abbas' right arm, slicing off his hand. Abbas said:

'By God, even if you take my right hand
I shall defend my faith to the very end
And an Imam true to his conviction do I defend,
A son of the trustworthy Prophet whom God did send'

He gave no heed to his severed right hand, because his only concern was bringing the water to Hussein's women and children. The attackers struck a second time and this time were able to sever his left hand. Then a multitude of enemies rushed at him. Abbas began to recite:

'O heart, do not fear the faithless
I give you tidings of God's mercy
With the prophet, leader of the righteous
In their aggression they have taken my left hand
But I shall send them, O Lord, to the heat of Hellfire.'

He kept making his way to the camp. When Ibn Sa'd saw him with the waterskin on his back, he called out to his men: 'Woe to you! Shoot that waterskin with arrows! By God, if Hussein drinks that water, you will all be finished!'

Arrows fell on Abbas like rain; one struck the skin and its water began to pour out. It was then that Abbas knew that he would not be bringing water to Hussein's camp. He stopped where he was, going no further towards the camp. And the enemy began to pepper him with arrows; one struck his chest, another his eye. He reached to pull the arrows out, but his hands were cut off. The helmet fell from his head as he shook violently to dislodge the arrows. One of the enemy took this opportunity to strike him over the head with a stave and he fell to the ground, calling out: 'O Abu Abdullah! Peace be with you!'

Hussein was standing by the flap of his tent, watching from affar. When he heard his brother's call, he launched himself into battle like a ferocious lion and the enemy fled in all directions. And when he reached his brother and saw his severed hands, his bloodied face, his body covered with wounds, the battle standard still by his side and the waterskin torn open, Hussein wept aloud: 'Now my back is broken, my means are few and my enemy rejoice at my misfortune!'

Then he left his brother where he lay and attacked the enemy, striking out at them, saying:

'Whence do you flee, when you have slain my support? Whence do you flee, when you have murdered my brother?'

Then he returned to the tents, broken and distressed, wiping away his tears so that the women would not see them, mumbling to himself:

'O bright moon, you were my helper
in every distress and affliction
Life is most bitter after you
but we shall meet again on the morrow upon truth
Lo! To God I complain and for Him I endure
whatever hardship may come my way.'

When his daughter, *Sakīna*, saw him returning to the tents alone, she went to him and said: 'O father! Where is my uncle *'Abbāṣ*.'

'Your uncle has been slain.;

She began to weep, crying: 'O woe, my uncle!' And when Zaynab heard this she came out of the tent weeping: 'O woe, our loss!'

Hussein said: 'Yes, by God, woe for our loss after you, O Abu al-*Faḍl*.'

After Abbas had fallen in battle, there was no one left with Hussein. He looked left and right, but saw nothing save the broad expanse of dust before him. Death was all that remained. He called out: 'O *Musim b. Aqeel, O Hani b. 'Urwa, O Habib b. Muẓāhir, O Zuhayr b. al-Qayn*, O pure heroes and valiant warriors! How is it I summon you but you do not answer me? How is it I call your names and you do not hear me? You are asleep. How I wish you would awaken. Has death prevented you from coming to the aid of your Imam?'

'These are the womenfolk of the Prophet, consumed by grief because they have lost you! So get up, O noble men and protect the honour of the Prophet from the wrongdoers! By God, surely death has taken you and this false world has betrayed you, else you would surely have come to my aid and heard my call. Here we are, distressed, but we will meet you soon. For we belong to God and to Him we shall return.'

Then he raised his voice and called out:

'Is there no one to defend the honour of God's Messenger?'

'Is there no believer who fears God in our regard?'

'Is there none who will help us seeking God's pleasure?'

'Is there none who will support us seeking His reward?'

And the women began to cry loudly.

He turned to the tents of his brothers and saw them empty, then he turned to the tents of Aqeel's sons and saw them empty too, and the tents of his companions too. He repeated to himself: 'There is no power or strength besides with God, the Exalted and High.'

Then he went to the tents of the women, going first to the tent in which his son, *Zayn al-'Ābidīn* lay on a skin, sick. He came to him and found Zaynab looking after him. When Ali saw his father, he wanted to get up, but he could not because of the severity of his condition. He told his aunt: 'Sit me up, for the son of God's Messenger has come.'

So Zaynab sat with him and supported him. Hussein asked about his illness and he praised God. Then Ali said: 'O father, what did you do this day with those hypocrites?'

Hussein replied: 'My son, Satan has taken hold of them and caused them to forget God's remembrance, and opened fighting between us and them, until the ground was awash with our blood and theirs.

'Father, where is my uncle, *'Abbāṣ*'

But when Zaynab heard the name Abbas, she choked back her tears and looked to Hussein, how was he going to respond.

Hussein said: 'My son, your uncle has been slain.'

Ali b. Hussein began to weep, then he asked about each of his uncles and brothers in turn, and Hussein would tell him their fates.

He kept asking until his father said: 'My son, know that there is no man alive in these tents except me and you. Whoever you ask about has fallen in battle.'

Ali said to his aunt, Zaynab: 'O aunty, bring me my sword and a stick!'

Hussein said: 'What do you intend to do with them?'

'I shall lean on the stick and protect you with the sword! There is no good in life after you!'

Hussein embraced his son and held him to his chest: 'My son, you are my successor over those women and children; they are alone and afraid, surrounded by danger on all sides. You must quiet them if they cry, and comfort them if they are afraid, for they have no one else.'

Then, just as Hussein commended the women and children to the care of Ali b. Hussein, he commended his son to the care of the women: 'This son of mine is my successor over you.'

Then he turned to Umm Kulthum and said: 'Take him, lest the earth be without any descendants of Muhammad's household.'

Then they returned *Zayn al-'Ābidīn* to his bed.

CHILD MARTYRS

The last persons to be slain before Hussein himself were three children from his family. They were:

First: *Ali Aṣghar*, who was six years old at the time

Second: Abdullah the infant, who was six months old

Third: Abdullah b. Hasan, Hussein nephew and the last martyr whose death was witnessed by Hussein.

As for *Ali Aṣghar*, the *Imām* had come to the tent and sat beside it, wearing a dark green cloak, and said: 'Bring me my son Ali, so that I can say goodbye to him.' They brought *Ali Aṣghar* (whose mother was *Umm Isḥāq bt. Ṭalḥa b. Ubaydullah al-Tamīmi*) and Hussein took him into his arms and kissed him, then said: 'My son, woe to those people when tomorrow [they will face] your grandfather, Muhammad.'

But while he was speaking, *Abdullah b. Uqba al-Ghanawī* shot an arrow and pierced *Ali Aṣghar*'s neck while he sat in his father's arms.

The enemy had decided in those moments to shoot arrows at any man, woman or child who came out of the tents, and after they killed *Ali Aṣghar*, Hussein caught his blood in the palm of his hand and when it filled up he cast it onto the ground, then he bore his son's body until he placed it was the rest of the martyrs of his household.

As for Abdullah the infant, the second child to be killed in Hussein's arms, Umm Kulthum had come to him and said: 'O brother, your son Abdullah has not been able to drink for three days, so ask the enemy for some water to give him!'

Hussein took his son and carried him towards the people, saying: 'O people! You have slain my companions, my cousins, my brothers and my sons; all that remains is this child of six months who cries due to thirst – give him a drink of water.'

He paused for a moment, then said: 'An adult may be blamed, a child cannot be. So take him and give him water, for his mother's milk has dried up.'

Hussein addressed the people while the child's mother, *Rubāb*, stood at the flap of the tent, watching to see what would happen, hoping that Hussein would obtain a few drops of water to moisten his lips and save him from death by thirst.

The people facing Hussein had three options to choose between: They could either give him a small quantity of water to quench his child, they could take the child from him and quench it themselves, or they could refuse his request in their own way. They chose the latter, in that *Harmala b. Kāhil al-Asadi* strung an arrow in his bow; an arrow made specially to kill large men, as they did not make arrows specially to kill small children. He shot it into the neck of the infant, severing it completely, and the blood began to flow into Hussein's hands.

Hussein took the blood in his hands and threw it towards the heavens, saying: 'Away with these people, for your grandfather, the chosen prophet, will be their accuser on the Resurrection Day.'

Then he looked to the heavens and said:

'My tribulations are a trifle when I know that God sees all. O God, the infant of *Ṣāliḥ's* camel was not something You took lightly. My god! If you have withheld assistance from us, then give us something better than it, and take revenge upon the wrongdoers for us. Let whatever has befallen us in this life be a provision for us in the life to come. O God, you are a witness against those who slew the people most resembling your messenger, Muhammad, and intend to wipe out the descendants of your prophet.'

Hussein heard a voice tell him: 'Do not worry, O Hussein, for he shall have a wetnurse in Paradise.'

Then Hussein climbed down from his horse and prayed over the body of his son before digging a small grave for him with his sword, and buried him covered in his own blood. It has been said that not a single drop of the blood Hussein cast upwards towards the heavens returned to the earth.

SORTIES BEFORE THE END

Even after his brothers, sons and companions had fallen in battle, Hussein's resolution did not flag. If anything, as more and more martyrs were cut down, he became ever more determined to defend the truth until his last breath. His bravery was most visible when he was left facing the enemy alone; they had only killed his companions to reach him, and now only he remained.

Hussein was awaiting the final, most important moment of his life, the moment of martyrdom when his soul would ascend, contented to its Creator.

Had he not, after all, said: 'I long to see my forebears as Jacob longed to see Joseph'?

These moment when he would go to meet his Lord, his grandfather and his forbears had drawn near.

As for his enemies, they had become even more cruel and determined to murder Hussein, driven by their base desires.

After they had killed his two small children, Hussein mounted his horse and stood before the enemy, his sword in hand with no hope of surviving, determined to die. He was saying:

'I am the son of Ali, the best of *Hāshim's* clan
that is enough of an honour for me to boast
My grandfather is the most noble messenger God sent
and we are God's radiant lamp upon the earth
Fatima is my mother, the daughter of Ahmad the pure
my Uncle is Ja'far who soars with two wings
Amongst us, God's Book came down openly
amongst us are mentioned guidance, revelation and good
We are God's trust to all mankind
we are gladdened by this amongst the beasts and announce it
We are the keepers of the Pool, we will quench our ally
with the cup of God's messenger, it cannot be denied
In Resurrection our lovers will arise
while those who hate us on the Resurrection Day shall lose.'

Then he challenged the enemy to face him in single combat, and he slew each and every warrior who came out to face him, until a great number had fallen by his hand.

Abdullah b. Ammar b. Abd Yaghūth, one of Umar b. Sa'd's soldiers, said: 'I have never seen one so afflicted, whose sons and household have been slain, more composed than [Hussein]! Men attacked him but he fought them with his sword and drove them off as a predator terrifies a flock. They were thirty thousand, but they would flee whenever he attacked them, as if they were locusts! Then he would return to his place and wait for them to attack the enemy again, or fight some individuals of them.

And when they saw that whoever went forth to face him was cut down, the enemy held back from meeting him in single combat. So Hussein began to charge at them and attack the right flank of the enemy, saying:

'To be killed is more fitting than to endure disgrace / and disgrace is more fitting to enter Hellfire

By God, what is this, and this is my refuge'

Then he attacked the left flank, saying:

'I am Hussein, son of Ali
I shall not allow myself to be abased
I defend the women and children of my father
I follow the religion of the Prophet.'

He kept charging into the fray, unhorsing some men and wounding others. Umar b. Sa'd said to his troops: 'Woe to you! Do you know who you are fighting? This is the son of the stout, balding one [i.e. Ali]! This is the son of the killer of Arabs! Attack him from all sides!'

But Hussein paid no heed to them and continued fighting.

The number of archers firing arrows at him numbered four thousand.

Hussein had struck terror into the hearts of the enemy, such that he turned the right flank to the left and the left flank to the right, and the centre of the enemy force upon itself. He would plunge into their midst and burst from them again, covering the ground with their blood.

And whenever he charged in and killed some of them, he would return to the flap of his tent saying: 'There is no power or strength except with God, the Exalted and High!'

Then one brazen soldier in Umar b. Sa'd's army, who had come from Syria, called *Tamīm b. Quḥṭaba*, approached Hussein and called out at the top of his voice: 'O son of Ali! How much longer do you plan on fighting? Your sons, relatives and followers have all been slain and you are still fighting thousands with just your sword!'

Hussein retorted: 'Did I come to fight you, or did you come to fight me? Did I bar your way or did you bar mine? You have killed my brothers and my sons; nothing remains between us except the sword. There is no more time for talk!'

Then Hussein challenged him to fight, saying: 'Come and let me see what you have!' So he approached Hussein, and the latter gave a shout, drew his sword and struck his neck, throwing him several cubits away.

Then another man called *Yazid al-Abṭaḥī*, who was renowned for his bravery, came out to fight Hussein. He drew his sword and attacked, but Hussein struck him first and cleaved him in two.

When Hussein saw the apprehensiveness of the enemy and heard the crying of the children because of thirst, he made for the path leading to the river, which was guarded by four thousand troops under the command of *Amre b. al-Hajjaj al-Zubaydī*. He was able to drive off the enemy and plunge into the river with his horse. When he entered the water, his horse lowered its head to drink, but Hussein said: 'You are thirsty, as am I. But I shall not taste water until you drink.' And when the horse heard Hussein's voice, it lifted its head and refused to drink, as though it understood his words.

Hussein said: 'Drink and I will drink.' Then he dipped his hand into the water and brought out some water and brought it to his mouth, when an enemy archer from the tribe of *Dāram* shot him with an arrow that lodged in his neck. He pulled it out and held his hands beneath his neck, and when they filled with blood he cast it up to the heavens and said: 'O God, I complain to You about how they are treating the son of Your prophet's daughter. O God, number their days and kill them left and right, and leave not one of them upon the earth!'

And so that Hussein would not try to drink water again, one of the enemy called out: 'O Abu Abdullah! Are you enjoying drinking water while your women and children are under attack?'

So Hussein threw the water from his hand and came up the path, driving off the enemy. But his tents were still untouched.

He kept attacking the enemy along the path despite his thirst, and they counter-attacked too. Whenever he made for the water, they attacked him and blocked his path. While he was doing this an enemy soldier called Abu al-Hutoof shot him with an arrow in his forehead. He pulled it out and the blood flowed over his face and beard. He said: 'O God, verily You see how these disobedient servants of Yours are treating me!'

He did not try to make for the river again as the fighting raged back and forth between him and the enemy. In one attack, Shimr came with a large number of men and cut Hussein off from his camp. Some of them approached the tents, but Hussein called out: 'Woe to you, O followers of the house of Abu Sufiyan! If you have no religion and do not fear the Resurrection, then at least be as free men in this world of yours! Go back to your tribes if you are Arabs as you claim!'

Shimr said: 'What are you saying, O son of Fatima?'

'I said this fight is between you and me, it has nothing to do with the womenfolk, so stop your thugs from attacking my family while I still live.'

Shimr replied: 'You may have that, son of Fatima.'

He called out: 'Leave the man's family alone and focus on the man himself, for by my life he is a worthy opponent!'

They came at him from every side, so he began to attack them and they him. Under the command of Shimr b. Dhil Jawshan, they surrounded him from all directions. A man called *Mālik b. Nasr al-Kindi* rushed at Hussein, cursed him and struck him on his head with a sword. The blade split the helmet and wounded him; the helmet filled with blood. Hussein cursed him: 'May you never eat or drink with your right hand, and may God raise you with the oppressors!' The enemy withdrew and he was able to return to the tent, remove his helmet and call for a bandage. He wrapped it around his head and took a new helm, which he wrapped a turban around. Then Shimr and his soldiers returned to their positions.

Now certain that death was near at hand, Hussein told his sister: 'Bring me an old robe that no one will want, so I can wear it under my clothes so that I will not be stripped bare when I am slain.'

So she brought him a pair of coarse trousers that were worn by folk of humble means. But he said: 'No, for these are clothes of abasement. So he took one of his good robes and tore it before putting it under his clothes.'

Despite the dire situation in which he found himself, Hussein had the presence of mind to entrust a book to his daughter, Fatima, to give to Ali b. al-Hussein when he recovered from his illness. Hussein, by virtue of his status as God's trustee upon His earth, and His authority over His servants, had to ensure that the legacy of the prophets was given to the Imam after him. He had also left some items with Umm Salama in Medina, with instructions to deliver them to his eldest son.

After that, he called his family, saying:

'O Sukayna, O Fatima, O Umm Kulthum! Peace be with you, for this is our final meeting, and your grief has drawn near.'

They raised their voices in crying and lamentation, calling out: 'We cannot bid you farewell!'

Sukayna asked: 'If you have surrendered yourself to death, then on whom shall we depend?'

Hussein replied: 'O light of my eyes, how can one without helper or supporter do anything but surrender to death? Be patient upon God's decree and do not complain, for verily this world will pass away but the Hereafter will endure!'

Sukayna said: 'So take us back to the sanctuary of your grandfather, God's Messenger!'

'Would that I could.;

She cried bitterly and Hussein took her into his arms, wiping the tears from her eyes and reciting the poetry:

'There is time for that after me, O Sukayna
You shall cry when fate overtakes me
Do not break your father's heart with tears of grief
while he still lives and breathes
When I am slain, then you may
bring these tears, O best of womenfolk!'

Then he enjoined his household to patience and to wear their veils. He told them:

'You must be ready for tribulation. Know that God will protect you, defend you and save you from the evil of our enemies. He will make sure that everything turns out well for you and punishes your enemies with all manner of afflictions. God will recompense you for your suffering with all manners of blessings and honours. Do not complain [of God's will] and do not say anything that does not befit your station.'

While Hussein was bidding his family farewell, Umar b. Sa'd called out to his companions: 'Attack, while he is preoccupied with himself and his family. For by God, if he is focused on you, your right hand will be no better than your left!'

So they attacked and shot arrows at him. Arrows were falling in the midst of the tents, some of tore the women's clothes, scaring them back into the tents.

Then the women watched Hussein to see what he would do. He attacked the enemy like a ferocious lion. Everyone who stood in his way was cut down by his sword. Arrows were hurtling at him from every direction, but he took them in his chest and torso.

Something strange that happened during those moments was that some elders of Kufa were standing on a hill watching events unfold, weeping for Hussein and praying: 'O God! Send your assistance to him!' Sa'd b. Ubayda, who was one of them, said: 'O enemies of God! Will you not go and help him?' None reponded.

Hussein's attacks against the enemy were most aggressive, because he knew he was heading for certain death, while the enemy fled from him, seeking to live.

When he killed a large number of them, Shimr looked at Umar b. Sa'd and said to him: 'O commander! By God if Hussein fought all the people in the world, he would wipe them out to a man. I suggest that we form to groups; one to attack him with swords and spears, and another with arrows.'

Hussein heard him say that and retorted: 'Do you incite people to kill me?'

Then he attacked, calling out: 'O evil nation, vilely have you Muhammad with regards to his family after him! You shall never fear killing a righteous man again after you have slain me, rather it shall seem trifling to you! I swear by God, I hope that my Lord shall ennoble me through your abasement and take revenge on you from whence you cannot imagine!'

Then *Hasseen b. Mālik al-Sukuni* retorted mockingly: 'O son of Fatima! With what shall he avenge you against us?'

'By turning your violence against yourself, by shedding your blood and then pouring out a painful punishment upon you!'

After enduring seventy-two wounds, Hussein withdrew to rest, repeating to himself: 'There is no power or strength except with God the Exalted and High.' While he stood, weakened from fighting, someone threw a rock at him and struck his forehead. Blood flowed from the wound and he took his robe to wipe the blood from his eyes, then he was struck by a three-pronged arrow in his chest. And as he fell from his horse, he called out: 'In God's name and with God, and upon the religion of God's Messenger.'

Then he raised his head to the sky and said: 'My god, you know that they are killing a man save for whom there is no other grandson of a prophet on the face of the Earth.'

Then he took the arrow out by pushing it through his back, and blood gushed from the wound like a fountain. He placed his hand on the wound and when it filled with blood, he threw it to the heavens and placed his hand on it again. When it filled with blood a second time, he wiped it over his head and face, then said: 'By God, this is how I will be when I meet my grandfather, Muhammad. I shall be bathed in my own blood when I say: 'O Messenger of God, so-and-so and so-and-so murdered me.'

After Hussein fell from his horse, he remained sprawled across the ground, unable to get up. But the people were afraid to kill him and stood all around him. When he was in this state, Abdullah b. al-Hasan, a young boy who had not yet reached maturity, saw his uncle on the ground and surrounded by enemies and ran to his aid. He escaped his mother's hand and Zaynab tried to catch him, but he got away from her. He approached Hussein and threw himself upon his uncle. *Baḥr b. Ka'b* brought readied his sword to kill Hussein, and the young boy called out: 'O son of an unclean woman, do not hit my uncle!'

Baḥr was enraged by these words and, instead of striking Hussein, turned his blow against the boy, who parried it with his hand, which was cut off save for a flap of skin. And so it hung there. Abdullah called out: 'O uncle! They have cut off my right hand!' Hussein held him to his chest and said: 'O nephew, be patient with your injury and think of it as something good, for God will be reuniting you with your righteous forefathers!'

Then Hussein raised his hands in supplication, saying: 'O God, you have given them provision for a while, so divide them into groups, factions and sects, and let their rulers never be pleased with them, for they called us with the promise of assistance, only to betray us and fight against us!'

Harmala b. Kāhil al-Asadi was stood at Hussein's head. He shot the boy with an arrow and killed him; Abdullah b. al-Hasan became the third child to be slain on the Day of *Ashura* in Hussein's arms.

AND THE HEAVENS WEPT BLOOD

While Hussein lay on the ground, the women of the Prophet's Household tried to come out of the tents and come to him on the battlefield, but Shimr b. Dhil al-Jawshan attacked their tent in full view of Hussein. He pierced it with a spear and then called out: 'Give me some fire so I can burn it down over the heads of everyone in it!'

Hussein called out: 'O son of Dhil al-Jawshan! You call for fire to burn my family, may God burn you with fire!'

Shabath b. Rab'ey came and reproached Shimr for what he had done, so Shimr desisted. Then he called out: 'What are you waiting for? Can't you see he's covered in wounds from spears and arrows? Kill him!'

Zar'a b. Sharīk struck the Imam on his left shoulder, while Hasseen b. Numayr shot him through his neck, while another struck his back and knocked him face-down onto the ground. He cried out in pain. *Sinān b. Anas* stabbed him with a spear in his collarbone, then in his sternum. An arrow shot through his neck and *Ṣāliḥ b. Wahab* stabbed him in his flank.

Hilāl b. Nāfiʿ said: 'I was stood near Hussein as he died. By God I have never seen one being murdered in his own blood with a more content or brighter expression on his face. The light of his face distracted me from the fact he was being killed. He asked for some water in this state, but they refused to give him any.

One of the soldiers there said: 'O Hussein! You shall not taste water until you drink it from the boiling pus of Hellfire!'

Hussein retorted with a weak voice: 'I shall drink from the boiling pus of Hell? No, I will return to my grandfather, God's Messenger and live with him in his house; a goodly place beside a mighty king, and I shall complain to him of what you did to me!'

Whereat they became enraged, such that God did not put in a single one of their hearts a shred of mercy.

And when his suffering became dire, he raised his eyes to the heavens and said: 'O God, lofty is Your position, exalted is Your power, severe is Your might; You have no need of Your creatures, Your glory is magnificent, You do whatever You will; Your mercy is close; Your promise is true, Your blessings are abundant, Your tests are good; You are near at hand when called, You encompass all You create, You accept the repentance of the one who repents to you; You can do whatever You want; You attain whatever You seek; You are grateful when thanked and mindful when remembered; I call upon You in my hour of need, I need you in my time of poverty; I flee to you in fear, weep to you in affliction and seek your assistance in weekness. It is sufficient for me to rely upon you!

O God judge between us and between our people, for they deceived us, betrayed us, acted treacherously towards us and murdered us. We are the offspring of Your prophet, the children of Your beloved Muhammad who You chose for Your message and to whom You entrusted Your revelation. So give us relief and an escape from our affair, O Most-merciful of the mercifiers!'

Then he said: 'I shall be patient with your decree, O Lord! There is no god save You, O Granter of relief to those who seek relief, I have no lord except You, nor object of worship besides You. I shall be patient with your judgement, O helper of those who have no helper, O Eternal-One who shall never fade! O He who gives life to the dead! O He who sits in judgement over every soul with what it has earned! Judge between us and them, and you are the best of judges!'

Hussein's horse came and circled around him, staining its forelock with his blood. Umar b. Sa'd called out to his companions: 'Seize that horse! For it is the most excellent of horses!'

Horsemen circled around Hussein's horse, but it began to kick out with its hooves, until it had killed a number of them and wounded others.

Then Umar b. Sa'd said: 'Leave it alone, let us see what it will do.'

So once the horse felt safe from being seized, it approached Hussein again and began to wipe his blood upon its forelock and to sniff him, then it whinnied loudly before turning towards the tents.

When the women saw the blood-stained horse and saw its saddle hanging from it, they came out of their tents, striking their faces and weeping, for they knew they were completely alone. They rushed to the place where Hussein had fallen and Zaynab called out: 'O woe, Muhammad! O woe, Ali! This is Hussein cut down dead at Karbala! Would that the heavens crash down upon the earth! Would that the mountains crumble to dust!'

She approached Hussein, and Umar b. Sa'd and a group of his men had assembled nearby. Hussein was dying. She called out: 'O Umar, will you just stand there and watch while they murder Hussein!?'

Umar b. Sa'd turned his face away from her, with tears soaking his beard.

Then she turned to the people and said: 'Woe to you! Is there a single Muslim amongst you!?'

But no one answered her.

Then Umar b. Sa'd called out to the people: 'Go and finish the job!' So *Khawlī b. Yazid al-Aṣbahī* rushed to take his head, but he started to tremble and could not bring himself to do it.

Then *Amr b. al-Hajjāj* stepped forward, but when he looked into Hussein's eyes he felt as though he was looking at the eyes of God's Messenger himself, so he stepped back again.

Finally, Shimr came forward and kicked Hussein onto his back with his foot. Then he sat down on his chest and took firm hold of his beard. He had to strike his neck twelve times before he was able to take Hussein's noble head.

After Hussein was so brutally killed, the skies darkened and glowed red. There was no stone except that blood was inexplicably found beneath it. Blood rained down from the sky, and its stain could not be washed from clothes.

Having committed the most heinous of crimes, the homicidal savages would not be deterred from anything else. Those beasts now took to marauding the Imam. One man took his shirt. Another took his turban. A third took his sandals. One took his sword. Then a man named Bajdal came. He saw the Imam wearing a ring covered with his blood. Instead of taking the ring off, he cut his finger off and took the ring! Qays ibn al-Ash'ath took his velvet. The Imam's worn out garment was taken by Ibn Hawiyyah al-Hadrami. Ibn Khaythamah al-Jufi and few others fought over his bow and outer garments. A man from among them wanted to take his underpants, since all his other clothes had been taken. This man said, "I wanted to take it off, but he had put his right hand on it which I could not lift; therefore, I severed his right hand. I noticed his left hand was also protecting it, so I cut his left hand also.

Umar b. Sa'd then ordered his horsemen to trample upon the bodies of martyrs while the women and children watched in horror. The heads of the martyrs were severed - including the children's - and were raised on pikes. The families of the Prophet were taken prisoner and sent to Yazid. They were paraded through a long and arduous route and given a humiliating display as they were being whipped and tortured.

In the midst of the chaos and savagery, the martyrdom of Hussein and his companions turned them into quintessential heroes, epitomizing virtues of faith, nobility and purity, generosity, bravery. As for their enemies, they became symbolic of every evil, falsehood, and vice. Hussein is seen as a man who faced death, so that an entire nation gets to know the true meaning of life.. A man who was killed once, but continues to come back to life a million times over.. One who was slain in solitary, without supporters or helpers, but who has billions marching every year to answer his call.. He was thirsty, only to have the world remember him every time they drink.. A man who was shown utter hatred, only to turn into the focal point of compassion.. One whose light they tried to extinguish, only to become a flame that inspires those seeking a revolution forever. A man who died whilst hungry, yet hundreds of millions are fed in his name.. A man whose tents were ransacked and burnt down, but has millions of homes named "*Husseiniyah*" after him, in every corner of the globe..

Hussein became a singular figure who fills history with his grace and grandeur, becoming a meta-historical legend, epitomizing the perennial struggle between good and evil.

www.ingramcontent.com/pod-product-compliance
Lightning Source LLC
Chambersburg PA
CBHW031040110426
42740CB00047B/753
9780994240927